Thomas O`Gorman

The American Church History

Thomas O`Gorman

The American Church History

ISBN/EAN: 9783743329799

Manufactured in Europe, USA, Canada, Australia, Japa

Cover: Foto ©ninafisch / pixelio.de

Manufactured and distributed by brebook publishing software
(www.brebook.com)

Thomas O`Gorman

The American Church History

The American Church History Series

CONSISTING OF A SERIES OF DENOMINATIONAL HISTORIES PUBLISHED UNDER THE AUSPICES OF THE AMERICAN SOCIETY OF CHURCH HISTORY

General Editors

VOLUME IX

American Church History

A HISTORY

OF THE

ROMAN CATHOLIC CHURCH IN THE UNITED STATES

BY

THOMAS O'GORMAN

PROFESSOR OF CHURCH HISTORY IN THE CATHOLIC UNIVERSITY OF AMERICA, WASHINGTON, D. C.

New York
The Christian Literature Co.

MDCCCXCV

CONTENTS.

BOOK II. THE ORGANIZED CHURCH.

PART I. THE GROWTH OF THE CHURCH FROM THE BEGINNING OF THE HIERARCHY TO THE FIRST PROVINCIAL COUNCIL OF BALTIMORE (1790–1829).

PART II. THE GROWTH OF THE CHURCH FROM THE FIRST PROVINCIAL COUNCIL OF BALTIMORE TO THE FIRST PLENARY COUNCIL (1829–52).

HISTORY OF THE ROMAN CATHOLIC CHURCH.

BY

REV. T. O'GORMAN,

PROFESSOR OF CHURCH HISTORY, CATHOLIC UNIVERSITY, WASHINGTON, D. C.

BIBLIOGRAPHY.

The Vinland Episode.

American Quarterly Review. April, 1890. "The Norse Hierarchy in America."

Baring-Gould, *Iceland: Its Scenes and Sagas.* London, 1863.

Beamish, *Discovery of America by Northmen.* London, 1841.

Beauvois, *Origine et Fondation du Plus Ancien Évêché du Nouveau Monde.* Paris, 1878.

Congrès International des Américanistes. 1875–90.

Crantz, *History of Greenland.* London, 1820.

De Costa, *The Pre-Columbian Discovery of America by the Northmen.* Albany, 1890.

Fiske, *The Discovery of America.* Vol. i., chap. ii. Boston, 1892.

Flatey Jar-Bok (The Flatey Book). Published by the Royal Danish, General Staff, Topographical Department, Copenhagen, 1893.

Gaffarel, *Études sur les Rapports de l'Amérique et de l'Ancien Continent avant Colomb.* Paris, 1869.

Gravier, *Découverte de l'Amérique par les Normands au X. Siècle.* Paris, 1874.

Heywood, *Documenta Selecta e Tabulario Secreto Vaticano quæ Romanorum Pontificum Erga Americæ populos curam ac studia tum ante tum paulo post insulas a Christophoro Columbo repertas testantur Prototypia descripta.* Romæ, 1893.

Historical Memorials of Greenland. Copenhagen, 1838–45.

Jelic, *L'Évangélisation de l'Amérique avant Colomb.* Paris, 1891.

Meriwale, *Conversion of the Northern Nations.* London, 1866.

Rafn, *Antiquitates Americanæ.*

Reeves, *The Finding of Wineland the Good.* London, 1890.

Smith, Toulmin, *The Discovery by the Northmen in the Tenth Century.* London, 1842.

Wheaton, *The Northmen.*

The Spanish Missions.

Arlegui, *Cronica de Zacatecas.*

Bancroft, G., *History of the United States.*

Barcia, *Ensayo Cronologico.*

Beaumont, *Cronica de Michoacan.*

Betancurt, *Teatro Mexicano.*

Bullarium Ord. F. F. Minor. S. P. Francisci.
Collecion de Documentos para la storia de Mexico.
Cronica Serafica.
Duran, *Storia de los Indios.*
Gillow, Eulogio G., *Apuntes Historicos.* Mexico, 1889.
Menologio Franciscano.
Sazagun, *Storia de las Casas de Nueva España.*
Shea, *History of the Catholic Missions.* New York, 1855.
— —, *The Catholic Church in the Colonial Days.* New York, 1886.
Vera, Fortino Hipolito, *Apuntamientos Historicos.* Mexico, 1893.

FLORIDA.

Brewer, *Alabama.* Montgomery, 1872.
Charlevoix, P. de, *Histoire la Nouvelle France.* Vol. i. Paris, 1744.
De Orc, Luis, *Historia de los Martires de Florida.* 1604.
Fairbanks, *History of Florida.*
Fiske, John, *The Discovery of America.* Vol. ii., chap. xi. Boston and New York, Houghton, Mifflin & Co.
Parkman, *The Pioneers of France in the New World.*
Roberts, *An Account of the First Discovery and Natural History of Florida.* London, 1763.
Roman, *A Concise Natural History of East and West Florida.*
Ruidiaz, Eugenio, *La Florida, su Conquista y Colonizacion.* Madrid, 1843.
Thwaites, Reuben Gold, *The Colonies.* Chaps. iv. and xiii. Longmans, Green & Co., 1892.
Williams, *Territory of Florida.* New York, 1837.
Winsor, *Narrative and Critical History of America.* Vol. ii., chap. xi. Edited by Justin Winsor. New York and Boston, Houghton, Mifflin & Co.

NEW MEXICO, ARIZONA, AND TEXAS.

Bancroft, H. H., *History of New Mexico and Arizona.* Vol. xvii. San Francisco, 1889.
Bandelier, A. F., *An Historical Introduction to Studies among the Sedentary Indians of New Mexico.* Boston, A. Williams & Co., 1881.
— —, *Indians of the Southwest.* Cambridge, 1890.
— —, *The Gilded Man.* New York, D. Appleton & Co., 1893.
Blackmar, Frank W., *Spanish Institutions of the Southwest.* Baltimore, Johns Hopkins Press, 1891.
Defouri, *Historical Sketch of New Mexico.*
— —, *The Martyrs of New Mexico.*
Ladd, Horatio O., *The Story of New Mexico.* Boston, D. Lothrop & Co., 1891.
Lummis, Charles F., *The Land of Poco Tiempo.* New York, 1893.
Morfi, *Memorias para la Historia de la Provincia de Texas.*
Prince, L. Bradford, *Historical Sketches of New Mexico.* New York, Leggat Brothers, 1883.
Shea, *Penalosa's Quivira Expedition.* New York, 1882.
Yoakum, *History of Texas.* 1856.

California.

Adam, *Life of Ven. Padre Junipero Serra.* San Francisco, 1884.
Bancroft, H. H., *California.* Vols. xviii.–xx. In vol. xviii., chap. ii., is given a very complete bibliography on the history of California.
Blackmar, *Spanish Institutions of the Southwest.*
Dwinelle, *Colonial History of San Francisco.*
Gleason, *History of California.*
Tuthill, *History of California.*
Winsor, *Narrative and Critical History of America.* Vol. viii., chap. iv.

The French Missions.

Allen, *The History of Norridgewock.* 1849.
Archives of the Archbishopric of Quebec.
Bancroft, G., *History of the United States.* Vols. i.–iv. Boston, 1862.
Biard, *Relation de la Nouvelle France.* Lyon, 1616.
Bigot, V., *Relation de la Mission des Abnaquis.*
Bressani, *Relation de la Nouvelle France.*
Brown, *The History of Illinois.* New York, 1844.
Carayon, *Première Mission des Jésuites au Canada.*
Carr, Lucien, *Missouri.*
Cavelier, M., *Relation du Voyage entrepris par feu M. Robert Cavelier, Sieur de la Salle.* À Manate, De la Presse Cramoisy de Jean Marie Shea, 1858.
Champlain, *Voyages.* Paris, 1690; New York, 1881.
Charlevoix, *Histoire de la Nouvelle France.* 3 vols. Paris, 1744.
Chauchetière, *Vie de la B. Catherine Tega Kouita.*
Chaumonot, *Sa Vie écrite par lui-même.*
Claiborne, *Mississippi as a Province, Territory, and State.* Jackson, 1880.
Cooley, Thomas McIntyre, *Michigan.*
Copway, *The Ojibway Nation.* Boston, 1851.
Dillon, *The History of Indiana.* Indianapolis, 1843.
Documents relating to the Colonial History of the State of New York. Albany, 1855.
Doyle, H. A., *The English in America.* London, 1882.
Drake, *Indians of North America.*
Dreuillettes, *Epistola Rev. P. Gabrielis Dreuillettes, Societatis Jesu Presbyteri ad Dominum Illustrissimum, Dominum Joannem Wintrop, Scutarium.* Neo-Eboraci in insula Manhattan, Typis Cramoisianis Joannis Mariæ Shea, 1864.
Dumont, *Mémoires Historiques sur la Louisiane.*
Dunn, J. D., *Indiana.*
Du Pratz, Le Page, *Histoire de la Louisiane.*
Faillon, *Histoire de la Colonie Canadienne.*
Farmer, *History of Detroit and Michigan.* Detroit, 1884.
Fisher, George Park, *The Colonial Era.* New York, 1892.
Francis, Convers, *The Life of Father Rale* (in *Library of American Biography*, conducted by Jared Sparks). Boston, 1845.
Gravier, Le R. P. Jacques, *Relation de ce qui s'est passé dans la Mission de l'Immaculée Conception au pays des Illinois depuis le mois de Mars 1693 jusqu'en Fevrier 1694.* De la Presse Cramoisy, 1857.

Gravier, Le R. P. Jacques, *Relation ou Journal de Voyage en 1700.* De la Presse Cramoisy, 1859.

Greswell, William Parr, *The History of the Dominion of Canada.* Oxford, Clarendon Press, 1890.

Hennepin, Louis, *Nouvelle Découverte.* Amsterdam, 1698.

Histoire de la Colonie Française. Montreal, 1868.

Histoire de la Colonie Française en Canada. Villemarie, 1865.

Jogues, Le R. P. Isaac, *Novum Belgium, Description de Nieuw Netherland et Notice sur René Goupil.* À New York dans l'ancien Nieuw Netherland, Presse Cramoisy de J. M. Shea, 1862.

Ketchum, *Buffalo and the Senecas.*

King, Rufus, *Ohio.*

Kip, *Jesuit Missions.* New York, 1847.

Law, *The Colonial History of Vincennes.* Vincennes, 1858.

Le Clercq, *Établissement de la Foi.* Paris, 1691; New York, 1881.

Lescarbot, *Histoire de la Nouvelle France.*

Lettres Édifiantes et Curieuses. Paris, 1781.

Louisiana Historical Collections.

Margry, *Origines Françaises des Pays de l'Amérique du Nord.* Paris, 1888.

Marquette, *Voyage et Découverte de quelques pays et nations de l'Amérique Septentrionale.* Paris, chez Estienne Michallet, Rue S. Jaques à l'image S. Paul, 1681.

Marshall, *Christian Missions.*

Martin, Felix, S.J., *The Life of Jogues.* New York, Benziger Brothers.

——, *Vie du P. de Brébeuf.*

Maurault, *Histoire des Abenakis.*

Millet, Le R. P. Pierre, *Relation de sa Captivité parmi les Onneiouts en 1690.* Nouvelle York, Presse Cramoisy de Jean Marie Shea, 1864.

Montigny, De, *Relation de la Mission du Mississippi en 1700.* A la Presse Cramoisy de Jean Marie Shea, 1861.

New York Coll. Documents. Vol. iii.

O'Callaghan, *History of New Netherland.*

Parkman, Francis, *A Half-century of Conflict.* Vol. i. Boston, 1892.

——, *Count Frontenac.* 1887.

——, *La Salle and the Discovery of the Great West.*

——, *Pioneers of France in the New World.* Boston, 1890.

——, *The Jesuits in North America.* 1890.

——, *The Old Régime in Canada.* 1887.

Pilling, James Constantine, *Bibliography of the Algonquian Languages.* Washington, 1891.

Registres des Baptesmes et Sépultures qui se sont faits au Fort Du Quesne pendant les années 1753-1756. Nouvelle York, Isle de Manate, De la Presse Cramoisy de Jean Marie Shea, 1859.

Relation de la Louisiane ou Mississippi. Amsterdam, 1734.

Relation des Aventures et Voyage de Mathieu Sagean. A la Presse Cramoisy de J. M. Shea, 1863.

Relation des Jésuites (1611-72). Quebec, 1858.

Roberts, Ellis H., *New York* (in *American Commonwealths Series*). Houghton, Mifflin & Co., 1892.

Shea, John Gilmary, *A Description of Louisiana by Father Louis Hennepin.* New York, John G. Shea, 1880.

——, *Discovery and Exploration of the Mississippi Valley.* New York,

1852. Also the complete series entitled *De la Presse Cramoisy de Jean Marie Shea.*
Shea, John Gilmary, *Discovery and Exploration of the Mississippi Valley.* Redfield, Clinton Hall, New York, 1852.
——, *History of the Catholic Missions among the Indian Tribes of the United States.*
——, *The Catholic Church in Colonial Days.* New York, 1886.
Smith, *History of Wisconsin.*
Strickland, *Old Mackinaw.* Philadelphia, 1860.
Tassé, *Les Canadiens de l'Ouest.* Montreal, 1873.
Têtu, *Les Évêques de Québec.* Quebec, 1889.
Thwaites, Reuben Gold, *The Colonies.* New York, 1892.
Tranchepain, La Rev. Mère St. Augustin de, *Relation du Voyage des premières Ursulines à la Nouvelle Orléans.* De la Presse Cramoisy, 1859.
Van Fleet, *Old and New Mackinac.*
Wallace, Joseph, *The History of Illinois and Louisiana.* Cincinnati, 1893.
Williamson, *History of Maine.*
Winsor, Justin, *Cartier to Frontenac.* Houghton, Mifflin & Co., 1894.
——, *The Mississippi Basin.* New York, 1895.
——, *Narrative and Critical History of America.* Vols. iv. and v. New York, 1889.
Wisconsin Historical Collections.

The English Missions and the Hierarchy.

General Sources.

Acta et Decreta Concilii Plenarii Baltimorensis. Vol. iii. Baltimore, 1886.
Acta et Decreta Sacrorum Conciliorum Recentiorum Collectio Lacensis. Freiburg im Breisgau, 1870.
Annales de la Propagation de la Foi.
Archives of the Archdiocese of Baltimore.
Archives of the Congregation de Propaganda Fide. MSS., Rome.
Archives of the Diocesan Chanceries.
Berichte der Leopoldinen Stiftung.
Bullarium de Propaganda Fide.
Catholic Historical Researches.
Concilia Provincialia Baltimori habita ab anno 1829 usque ad annum 1840. Baltimore, 1842.
Concilii Plenarii Baltimorensis II. Acta et Decreta. Baltimore, 1868.
Concilium Plenarium totius Americæ Septentrionalis Fœderatæ habitum anno 1852. Baltimore, 1853.
Finotti, *Bibliographia Catholica Americana.* New York, 1872.
Proceedings of the United States Catholic Historical Society.
Shea, *Life and Times of Archbishop Carroll.* New York, 1888.
——, *The Catholic Church in Colonial Days.* New York, 1886.
The complete series of the following journals: the *Catholic Miscellany,* the Boston *Pilot,* the New York *Freeman's Journal.*
The complete set of the Catholic directories.
United States Catholic Historical Magazine.

Special References.

Abbelen, *Sketch of Life and Character of Mother Caroline Friess.*
Alerding, *History of the Catholic Church in the Diocese of Vincennes.*
Baunard, *The Life of Mother Duchesne.*
Bayley, *A Brief Sketch of the Early History of the Catholic Church.*
——, *Memoirs of Rt. Rev. G. S. Bruté.*
Berger, *Life of Rt. Rev. John N. Neumann.*
Blanchet, *Historical Sketches of Catholicity in Oregon.*
Bozman, *History of Maryland.* Baltimore, 1837.
Brann, *The Most Rev. John Hughes.*
Brent, *Biographical Sketch of the Most Rev. John Carroll.* Baltimore. 1843.
Brownson, *Life of Demetrius Augustine Gallitzin.*
Brüner, *Katholische Kirchengeschichte* (in Quincy's *Illinois*).
Burgler, *Geschichte der Kathol. Kirche Chicago's.*
Campbell, *Life and Times of Archbishop Carroll.*
Catholic Educational Exhibit in Chicago.
Clarke, *Lives of the Deceased Bishops.* New York, 1872.
Corby, *Memoirs of Chaplain Life.*
Cornelison, *The Relation of Religion to Civil Government in the United States.*
Cornell, *The Beginnings of Catholicity in Yonkers, N. Y.*
Currier, *Carmel in America.*
——, *History of the Religious Orders.*
De Barbery, *Elizabeth Seton.* Paris, 1868.
De Goesbriand, *Catholic Memories of Vermont and New Hampshire.*
De Smet, *New Indian Sketches.*
——, *Oregon Missions and Travels over the Rocky Mountains.*
——, *Western Missions and Missionaries.*
De T'Serclaes, *Le Pape Léon XIII.* Chap. xxii.
Desgeorges, *Monseigneur Flaget.*
Deuther, *Life and Times of Bishop Timon.*
Dilhet, *État de l'Église ou Diocèse des États-Unis.*
Doherty, *Address on the Centenary of the Cathedral of St. Louis.* St. Louis, 1876.
Domenech, *Journal d'un Missionaire au Texas et au Mexique.*
Eckels, St. John, *Maria Monk's Daughter.*
Elliott, *The Life of Father Hecker.*
England, *Bishop England's Works.* 5 vols.
Fitton, *Sketches of the Establishment of the Church in New England.*
Foley, *Records of the English Province.*
Gambrall, *Church Life in Colonial Maryland.* Baltimore, 1885.
Hammer, *Der Apostel von Ohio.*
Hamon, *Vie du Cardinal de Cheverus.*
Hassard, *Life of Archbishop Hughes.*
Hawk, *Contributions to the Ecclesiastical History of the United States.*
Heitman, *Historical Register of the Officers of the Continental Army.* Washington, 1893.
Hewit, *The Life of Father Baker.*
Hill, *History of the Church in Burlington, N. J.* Trenton, 1876.
Historical Sketch of the College of the Holy Cross, Worcester, Mass.
Historical Sketch of Villa Nova College.

History of Georgetown College.
History of Mount St. Mary's of the West. Cincinnati.
Houck, *The Church in Northern Ohio.*
Hughes, *The Works of Rt. Rev. John Hughes.*
Hyland, *The World's Columbian Catholic Congresses.*
Janssens, *Sketch of the Catholic Church in the City of Natchez.*
Johnson, *Foundations of Maryland.*
Johnston, *History of Cecil County, Maryland.*
Keily, *Memoranda of the History of the Catholic Church in Richmond, Va.*
Kempker, *History of Catholicity in Iowa.*
Lambing, *History of the Catholic Church in the Diocese of Pittsburg.*
Lathrop, *A Story of Courage.*
Lyons, *Silver Jubilee of the University of Notre Dame, Indiana.*
Maes, *Notes on the Church in Monroe, Mich.*
———, *The Life of Rev. Charles Nerinckx.*
Marty, *Dr. Johann Martin Henni.*
Mazzuchelli, *Memorie istoriche ed edificante.* Milan, 1844.
McGirr, *The Life of the Rt. Rev. W. Quarter.*
McGovern, *The Life and Writings of Rt. Rev. John McMullen.*
McMahon, *Historical View of the Government of Maryland.* Baltimore, 1831.
McSherry, *History of Maryland.* Baltimore, 1852.
Mitchell, *Golden Jubilee of Bishop Loughlin.*
Moosmuller, *S. Vincenz in Pennsylvanien.*
Moreau, *Les Prêtres Français Émigrés aux États-Unis.*
O'Connell, *Catholicity in the Carolinas and Virginia.*
O'Connor, *Archbishop Kenrick and his Work.*
Palladino, *Indian and White in the Northwest.*
Pennsylvania Magazine of History.
Plessis, *Relation d'un Voyage aux États-Unis en 1815.*
Ravoux, *Reminiscences, Memoirs, Lectures.*
Read, *Sketch of Bishop England.*
Reilly, *Conewago: A Collection of Catholic Local History.* Martinsburg, 1885.
Roman, *Historical Sketch of the Flathead Indian Nation.*
Rozier, *One Hundred and Fiftieth Celebration of the Founding of Ste. Geneviève, Mo.*
Satolli, *Loyalty to Church and State.* Baltimore, John Murphy & Co., 1895.
Scharf, *History of Maryland.* 3 vols. Baltimore, 1879.
———, *The Chronicles of Baltimore.* Baltimore, 1874.
Shea, *The Hierarchy of the Catholic Church in the United States.* New York, 1886.
Shepard, *The Early History of St. Louis and Missouri.*
Shriner, *History of the Catholic Church in Paterson, N. J.*
Spalding, J. L., *Life of Archbishop Spalding.*
———, *Sketches of the Early Catholic Missions of Kentucky.*
———, *Sketches of the Life, Time, and Character of the Rt. Rev. Benedict Joseph Flaget.*
St. Mary's Seminary of St. Sulpice, Baltimore.
Taaffe, *History of St. John's College, Fordham, N. Y.*
The Maryland Archives.

The Woodstock Letters.
Timon, *Missions in Western New York.*
Treacy, *Catalogue of our Missionary Fathers.*
Verrwyst, *Missionary Labors.*
Walsh, *Origin of the Catholic Church in Salem, Mass.*
Webb, *The Centenary of Catholicity in Kentucky.* Louisville, 1884.
White, *Appendix to Darras's History of the Church.*
——, *Life of Mrs. Eliza A. Seton.* New York, 1853.
White, Father Andrew, S.J., *Relatio Itineris ad Marylandiam.* Baltimore, 1874.

THE ROMAN CATHOLIC CHURCH.

INTRODUCTION.

Origins—The Vinland Episode.

THE Catholic Church is conspicuous in the United States. The number of her adherents, the wealth of her churches, the activity of her religious orders of men and women, her parochial schools, colleges, academies, and universities, her compact and widespread hierarchical organization, attract universal attention. Whether the observers be friends or foes, she cannot be and is not ignored. She is a huge fact in the life of the republic. Her present homogeneity is remarkable if we consider the various sources whence she sprang and the various elements of which she is composed. The Southern States were originally evangelized from Spain. Florida, Alabama, Texas, New Mexico, Arizona, and California received the gospel from Cuba and Mexico at the hand of missionaries who came from Spain, working under the jurisdiction of Spanish bishops residing in Spanish colonies. Their work began early in the sixteenth century. The Northern States were evangelized by missionaries who came from France and were under the jurisdiction of French bishops. Their work began in the first years of the seventeenth century. The

Central States on the Atlantic coast were evangelized by missionaries who came from England in the "Ark" and "Dove" in the seventeenth century; they were under the jurisdiction of the Vicar Apostolic of London until Baltimore was erected into an episcopal see. Spain, France, and England, and back of them Rome, Jerusalem, Bethlehem, and Nazareth, are the sources of our Catholicity. The independence of the American church from any intermediate authority, and its direct dependence on the center of Catholicity, was contemporaneous with our national independence. Since then, as the various Territories that had been French and Spanish colonies were annexed to the United States, their missions also were absorbed into our independent American church organization. By this process of extension and evolution was formed the church of the United States—the compact, homogeneous body that is the admiration of the Catholic world, and which received but the other day its crowning in the appointment of a resident apostolic delegate in the capital of the nation.

The history of the Catholic Church naturally divides itself into two epochs: the mission epoch and the organized epoch. The former extends from the earliest arrival of the Catholic missionary in the beginning of the sixteenth century to the appointment of Bishop Carroll in 1789, as to the regions under English control at the time of the Revolutionary War; from the beginning of the sixteenth century to the dates of their annexation to the Union, as to the regions that were French or Spanish in 1789. This period again subdivides itself into three parts: the Spanish, French, and English missions. The latter epoch is that of the organized American church extending from 1789 to our own day. During this century the church has grown by accretions from Spain, by accretions from France, by the natural increase of her first Catholic colonists, by conversions to her fold, and above all, by the vast emigration to her shores from Catholic lands.

But before entering upon this study, a word about an episode which has the enchantment that comes from distance of time, and would look like some fanciful myth did not history give it a certainty that cannot be denied. It is the passage of Catholicity on our shores four hundred years before Columbus gave to the Old World the lasting possession of America. The church came and went with the Norsemen, without, however, leaving on our land any durable trace, so far as our present knowledge goes. But the coming and going are recorded in Norse literature and Roman archives.

The tenth and eleventh centuries were the period of greatest activity for the Northmen of Scandinavia. On the shores of England, Ireland, France, Italy, and Greece their viking boats poured out hordes of warriors who spread desolation far and wide and planted colonies that have entered into the make-up of Europe. Westward, too, they pushed their way. The islands of the North Atlantic, the Orkneys, Shetlands, and Faroes, became Norse outposts. But it was in Iceland that grew up their most vigorous and renowned offshoot. It was reached by them in 784. Very soon there was settled in that mid-Atlantic island a population of fifty thousand Norsemen, who set up a republic bound to the mother country by a very slender allegiance. A rich Icelandic literature sprang up before England, France, Italy, and Spain had come into possession of their present languages. The historical records of Iceland especially are unequaled by anything contemporaneous elsewhere, and hardly surpassed by anything done in modern times.

These are our authorities for the history of the Norse occupation of Greenland, which was discovered at the end of the ninth century, colonized at the end of the tenth century, and Christianized at the beginning of the eleventh century. About one hundred years thereafter a bishop was assigned to the Greenland church. His see was at Gardar. From the first bishop appointed, in 1112, to the last one appointed by Innocent VIII. and confirmed by Alexander VI. in 1492, the year of the discovery by Columbus, a period elapsed of three hundred and eighty years of a hierarchy—consequently of organized church life—regular and continuous down to the year 1409; fitful and interrupted from 1409 to 1492. Between the two extreme dates, in the palmiest period of Greenland Christianity, there were on its inhospitable shores one bishop, a cathedral, fifteen churches, four or five monasteries, and a Catholic population of ten thousand souls. This information rests on historical evidence that is irresistible.

Likewise it is absolutely certain that southwest of Greenland a country was discovered, and for hundreds of years was visited frequently, and inhabited for periods of two or three years at a time by traders and missionaries from Greenland and Iceland—a country known in Icelandic and other annals as Vinland the Good. This is not the place to vindicate the authenticity and veracity of the sagas, especially those contained in the "Hauksbók" and the "Flateyjarbók." We hold it as absolutely certain that Vinland was on the American mainland, and as all but absolutely demonstrated that it was on the New England coast. We believe that Boston has made no mistake in raising a statue to Leif Ericsson, the discoverer of Vinland.

One proof, and only one, is wanting. Greenland is still covered with the ruins of churches, of monasteries, and of the homes of the Scandinavian settlers. But in Vinland, so far, no trace of buildings has been found. The archæological proof is wanting. The old mill at Newport, the

Dighton Rock on the Taunton River, the remains of Norumbega on the Charles River, are not allowed by serious historians to be vestiges of the Norse discoverers of America.

Now the truth is, the narratives of the sagas do not call for any such corroboration. Nowhere do they state that the Northmen made permanent settlements in Vinland, but only temporary visits for timber and peltries, or missionary voyages to evangelize for a season the natives. Solid buildings were not necessary for such sojourns; it is no wonder, then, that ruins are not to be found, though we fancy smaller remains, such as pottery, tools, and various implements, marking their passage, may yet be unearthed. And, moreover, the Skraellings—such was the name given by the discoverers to the savages of Vinland—hindered the permanent settling of the newcomers. Very true, centuries later a handful of Europeans landed on the very same shores touched by the Scandinavians and drove the natives before them into the interior; but the Europeans had firearms, whereas the Scandinavians were almost matched in weapons of war by the bow and arrow and the stone hatchet of the Indian. We need not wonder then that no permanent Scandinavian settlements were made, and it is useless to demand that we produce vestiges of them.

In a word, Vinland was civilly a trading-post and ecclesiastically a missionary station of the mother colony and church of Greenland. We must therefore expect to find in ecclesiastical history only incidental allusions to Vinland as an out-station. But such allusions, scant as they may be, are precious to the historian, and tell much to the imagination. We confess at once that we have in the records only such incidental allusions to the work of the church in Vinland.

The first Bishop of Greenland was Eric Gnupson or Upsi. He was appointed in 1112, but was not consecrated until 1120. The "Annales Regii Islandorum," which gives the history of Iceland down to 1307, informs us that this bishop never went to his duties in Greenland, but did missionary work in Vinland, where he died, probably for the faith. This statement hints that the Greenland voyagers had entered into continuous intercourse with the natives, and that the work of evangelizing them was attempted. Cranz goes so far as to say that from 1110 to the time of Bishop Upsi (1120), Scandinavian colonists lived in Vinland, and that they had become merged by intermarriage in the surrounding tribes.

In 1246, under Bishop Olaf, the seventh incumbent of Gardar, the holy see asked the Peter pence from Greenland. And from this time forward we find Greenland mentioned by name and Vinland by implication only in various documents regarding the Peter pence of the diocese of Gardar, as well as in the accounts of the collectors contained in the financial records of the Vatican. The Archbishop of Drontheim, appointed in 1276 to make the collection, applied to Pope John XXI. for permission to send collectors in his stead, giving as reasons the distance and the length of time that he would have to be absent from his see in Norway. In consequence Nicholas III. in 1279 granted extraordinary faculties to the collectors appointed by the Archbishop of Drontheim.

We gather from a bull of Martin IV. in 1282 that the tithes of the diocese of Gardar were paid in produce of the country—teeth of walrus, hides, and furs; that they were shipped to Norway, and there converted by sale into current money. But what interests us most is that in the bull of 1279, dispensing the Archbishop of Drontheim from a personal visit to Greenland, and delegating his appointees thereto, we read the following words: "To collect the tithes and the products of the communes, as well in the diocese of Gardar as in the islands and neighboring territories." From this we conclude that lands outside Greenland were known and were under the jurisdiction of the Bishop of Gardar, and were inhabited by the faithful, or at least were exploited by them. In this passage we see an implicit reference to Vinland.

What products gathered in these various collections, or what share of them, came from Vinland we can only conjecture. The statements in the financial records of Rome (the "Liber Censuum") give but the totals for the diocese of Gardar, and only name the products as walrus teeth, hides, and furs. Now we know from the sagas that furs were an article of barter between the Scandinavians and the natives of Vinland. This is not to say that all the furs were from that colony, for seals were abundant in Greenland. We do find in the report by the nuncios of Sweden and Norway of the collections made between 1326 and 1330 one article that could have come only from Vinland—"a cup of transatlantic wood valued at ten golden florins": "*Unus ciphus de nuce ultramarina, existimatus* 11 *florenos auri.*" The cup may have been worked in Greenland, but the wood must have come from Vinland, for two reasons: first, there was no wood in Greenland; secondly, there was wood in Vinland, and wood used precisely for ornamental and domestic purposes. The sagas tell us that the main staple of commerce between Vinland, Norway, and Greenland was wood. This was what made the voyages to Vinland so profitable, and kept the crews there for years at a time getting out their cargoes. Moreover, the saga of Thorfinn Karlsefne narrates how the wood of Vinland was worked to domestic purposes, and how it was valued at high prices, a Bremen merchant having paid Karlsefne a large sum for his scale-pans, or, as others will have it, for the bar with which he closed his door.

During the administration of Bishop Alfus (consecrated in 1376) came to the Catholic inhabitants of Greenland the first notice of the danger that was to exterminate them a few years later. The savages they had met in Vinland in the beginning of the eleventh century—the Skraellings—made a raid into Greenland. These tribes are supposed to have been the descendants of the American glacial man, and to be represented now by the Eskimos of Greenland. They were no doubt driven northward by more numerous and more cultured bands of Indians coming from the south—the present American red man, to whom, in the course of time, they shall have to yield, and by whom they shall be driven to seek a home in northern climes. It must be remembered that the early Norse colonists found no aborigines in Greenland.

Meanwhile the intercourse between Greenland and Norway was declining and becoming more and more infrequent. A curious entry in Icelandic annals (1386) states: "A ship came from Greenland to Norway which had lain in the former country two whole years. The men who returned by this ship brought the news of Bishop Alf's death from Greenland, which had taken place there six years before." According to this entry not for six years at least had there been any communication between the two countries. The black death which swept over Europe in the middle of the fourteenth century may have had something to do with this neglect of its colony by Norway. But there was a political measure that had much more to do with it. As discovery and first colonization are always the result of individual enterprise, so also the prosperity of the colony and its communication with the mother country, and especially its commerce, depend on individual activity and love of gain. In 1380–87 Queen Margaret of Norway, on whose head were united the crowns of Denmark and Norway, made the trade of Greenland a royal monopoly, to be carried on in ships belonging to or licensed by the sovereign. In consequence the colony gradually fell into oblivion, and being thus abandoned, grew too weak to resist the invading Skraellings. The gradual closing in of ice-parks may also have made communication more and more difficult.

The following letter of Nicholas V. (1448), commissioning two bishops in Iceland to see to the spiritual wants of the desolate Greenlanders, tells the sad story:

"Whereas my beloved children who are natives of and dwell in the great island of Greenland, which is said to lie on the extremest boundaries of the ocean, northward of the kingdom of Norway and in the district of Throndjem, have by their pitiful complaints greatly moved our ear and awakened our sympathy; and whereas the inhabitants, for almost six hundred years, have held the Christian faith, which by the teaching of their first instructor, King Olaf, was established amongst them, firm and immovable under the Roman see and the apostolic forms; and whereas in after years, from the constant and ardent zeal of the inhabitants of the said island, many sacred buildings and a handsome cathedral have been erected on this island, in which the service of God was diligently performed until heathen foreigners from the *neighboring coast*, thirty years since, came with a fleet against them, and fell with fury upon all the people who dwelt there, and laid waste the land itself and the holy buildings with fire and sword, without leaving upon the island of Greenland other than the few people who are said to be far off, and which they, by reason of high mountains, could not reach, and took off the much-to-be-commiserated inhabitants of both sexes, particularly those whom they looked upon as convenient and strong enough for the constant burden of slavery, and took home with them those against whom they could best direct their barbarity. Whereas moreover the same complaint further saith that many, in the course of time, have *come back from said captivity*, and after having here and there rebuilt the devastated places, now wish to have the worship of their God again established, and set upon the former footing; and since they, in consequence of the before-named pressing calamity, are wanting the necessary means themselves, to support their priesthood and superiors, and therefore, during all that period of thirty years, have been in want of the consolations of the bishops and the services of the priests, except when some one, through desire of the service of God, has been willing to undertake tedious and toilsome journeys to the people whom the fury of the barbarians has spared; whereas we have a complete knowledge of all these things, therefore, we now charge and direct you, brethren, who, we are informed, are the nearest bishops to the said island, that ye, after first conferring with the chief bishop of the diocese, do nominate and send them a fit and proper man as bishop."

However, for reasons that we know not, this decree remained without effect. Fifty years later the Greenlanders renewed their petition to Innocent VIII. Their situation was pitiful. Left to themselves for a century without bishop and priests, they had fallen into ignorance and complete forgetfulness of the religion of their ancestors. The only memorial of it that remained among them was a corporal on which the last priest a hundred years before had consecrated the holy eucharist. Around this they congregated occasionally for such worship as tradition had handed down. Moved by their pitiful petition, Alexander

VI., successor of Innocent VIII., confirmed for the see of Gardar a Benedictine monk, Mathias, whom Innocent VIII., before dying, had named to that see. The document from which we gather these details is a letter of Alexander VI. (1492–93) to the Roman congregations, ordering that the necessary briefs and papers of appointment be delivered to the appointed bishop without the ordinary expenses of chancery. From it we learn also that one of the causes of the interruption of communication between Europe and Greenland was the intense cold and the abundance of ice-packs.

It is strange that we have this last historical mention of the Catholic colonization of Greenland in the very year that Columbus set out from Spain and landed on the island of San Salvador. Thus did the church of Greenland pass out of sight and memory, though in 1520 the last Catholic Archbishop of Drontheim, Eric Walkendorf, sought to gather information of the long-unheard-of see of Gardar, with the intention of renewing communication with the lost suffragan. But the Reformation swept over Norway, ended the hierarchy there, and then silence and oblivion fell upon Catholic Greenland. What became of the descendants of Scandinavia we know not. But they have left behind them ruins of churches and Catholic inscriptions on stray fragments that perpetual snows enshroud. Thus with Greenland, and, indeed, long before the disappearance of Greenland, ended the Vinland episode in the history of the Catholic Church in the United States.

It can hardly be doubted that the long and frequent intercourse of the Scandinavians with the natives of the American mainland during centuries of commerce and years of captivity, that the missionary expeditions of bishops and priests to our shores, left behind some vague knowledge of our religion, some Catholic practices and customs which, in the course of time, became more or less overgrown with superstitions. This may explain, to some extent, the traces of Christianity found by early French explorers and missionaries among the tribes along the St. Lawrence. It might also explain the Christian practices and emblems found among the more southern tribes, and spare us the theories, not yet historically established, that the Apostle St. Thomas, or the Irish monks St. Columba and St. Brendan, penetrated as far as Mexico and evangelized the natives of the south. There is no impossibility or improbability of intercourse between all the tribes of America from Mexico and even Peru to the colder regions of Canada. There are in different sagas and in the relation of the Zeni brothers strong indications of such an intercourse. The legends of St. Thomas and the Irish monks are fascinating but conjectural. They are a field in which the imagination loves to roam, but in which the historical sense finds small satisfaction.

BOOK I. THE MISSION PERIOD.

PART I. THE SPANISH MISSIONS.

CHAPTER I.

SPAIN IN NORTH AMERICA.

THE results of the discovery of Columbus may be studied in the religious or in the secular sphere. In either case, they were profitable and glorious for the crown of Spain and the Catholic Church. In the secular sphere the dominions of Charles V. were widened to an empire such as the world had never seen. Love of glory and gain fired the hearts of the scions of Spanish nobility. Mexico and Peru, Florida and New Mexico, were startled by the guns and horses, the flashing swords and moving plumes of the irresistible Castilian invaders. Gold flowed in a steady stream into the coffers of Madrid, at what cost to the poor natives Las Casas has made known to the world. The greed and rapacity of the first adventurers must be held mainly responsible for the enslavement and the cruel treatment of the red men, who had appeared to Columbus, when he landed on San Salvador, so guileless, docile, and inoffensive.

Nevertheless the Spanish government cannot be held blameless. To be sure, it was constantly giving orders, not only while Isabella reigned, but throughout the lives of Ferdinand and Charles V., against overworking, oppressing, and especially enslaving the natives. But America was far away, and the crown was kept in ignorance of the excesses to which the white man went in his conduct toward his red brother, until Las Casas found his way to the royal ear. Yet, after making all allowances, we must say that the government that approved repartimiento and encomienda of Indians is not blameless; it should have known, if it knew anything of human nature, that such a system, dangerous at any time and in any place, must inevitably issue in the enslavement and extermination of the Indian in the presence of men who were maddened by thirst for gold as man never was before. It is to the glory of the church that Las Casas and his brother Dominicans resisted the evil passions of their countrymen with vigor and perseverance until the accursed system was broken down.

However, it would be false to suppose that the Indian has been exterminated by the Spaniard. Not only he has not been exterminated, but he is to-day the South American fashioned to Christian and civil life; for undoubtedly the population of South America is mainly of Indian blood. There the Indian is not a ward, but a free man, a member of the national life and the national church; and is working his way, through revolutions and disorders of various sorts, to a higher civilization; and will yet take a front rank, if you but give him time, in the grand march of humanity to the goal of progress.

In the glory of this result Spain may well claim a share; yet it has been mainly the work of the church. Not less than the state, she awoke at once after Columbus's discovery to the work she had to do in the new field. When all others abandoned the Genoese sailor, did she not take him up, shelter, encourage, push him at court, bless him as he sailed away from Palos, and more than queen or king rejoice at his return? She saw in the New World a widening of the kingdom of God on earth. Rome lost no time in taking advantage of the wonderful event. A pope secured to Spain by all the weight of his authority the newly found world. Twelve priests commissioned by him accompanied Columbus on his second voyage and began the conversion of the natives. From that time (1494) until 1512 the priests serving the Spanish colonists and the missionaries working among the natives depended for jurisdiction on the see of Seville. The church in the Spanish colonies became detached from Seville when the see of San Domingo was erected in 1512, and assumed control of religion in the Americas. A few years later (1522) a see was erected in Santiago de Cuba. The erection of Mexico followed in 1530. These two dioceses are the centers whence sprang the missions in Florida, New Mexico, Arizona, Texas, and California. The southeastern portion of the United States was ecclesiastically dependent on Santiago de Cuba, and at a later date on Havana. The southwestern portion was ecclesiastically dependent on Mexico, and at a later date on Guadalajara, and later still on Durango.

Of the nations of Europe that competed for supremacy in the New World none has left a more interesting record than Spain. She failed; but her passage through North America is tinged with romance and borders on the marvelous. Spain owned at one time the territory stretching from the Mississippi westward to the Pacific and northward to the present State of Oregon, and also the territory stretching eastward from the Mississippi to the Atlantic coast, and northward up into the Carolinas. How much remains to mark her passage?

Florida preserves no traces of Spain beyond geographical names. In Louisiana, Spanish laws, or their influence, are on the statute-books, and Spanish blood flows in the veins of many of the older families. Texas shows less of the passage of the Spaniard; a few laws, mostly obsolete, are in the statute-books, a few towns retain traits of old Spanish life, a few families trace their lineage to the earliest colonists, and some noble ruins of mission churches dot the land. New Mexico is the most Spanish corner in the United States; the language of Castile is spoken there to a considerable extent; the general appearance of many towns tells of old Spanish life; the work of the Spanish missionaries is still visible, not only in the churches they built, but in the lives of the Indians they converted; old grants, laws of settlement, and municipal life among the descendants of the colonists and the civilized Indians tell of Spanish domination during two centuries. In Arizona only geographical names and a few ruined churches are witnesses to the presence in past time of the proud hidalgo. In California the evidences of Spanish occupation are disappearing rapidly before the onward march of American civilization. The nomenclature of the country, the few remaining Spanish families, the many missions, ruined or repaired, the laws relating to land, the numerous archives, civil and religious, are the silent though eloquent reminders of the passage of Spain.

It now becomes my task to review briefly the history of those Spanish missions. I must speak successively of the southeastern mission (Florida) and of the southwestern missions (New Mexico, Arizona, Texas, and California).

CHAPTER II.

THE PRELIMINARY EXPLORATIONS IN FLORIDA (1513-65).

IT is probable that Americus Vespucius, returning home from his first voyage (1498), sailed along the eastern coast of Florida as far north as the Chesapeake. However this may be, a map still extant, known as the Cantino map, bearing date 1502, shows north of Cuba a mainland terminating in a peninsula very like in shape to Florida. The conclusion is obvious that some navigator must have visited and surveyed, more or less accurately, the shores of the Gulf of Mexico and the eastern shore of Florida a certain distance northward.

Among the Lucayan Indians of the Bahamas there was a legend of a "fountain of youth" to be found in the island of Bimini, to the north. This legend struck the imagination of a young hidalgo, Juan Ponce de Leon, who had been a companion of Columbus in his second voyage. In 1512 he obtained a royal patent empowering him to discover this wonderful fountain. Early the following year he set sail with three caravels, and on March 27th he made land, which he coasted as high as 30° 8′, about the position of St. Mary's River, Cumberland Sound. March 27th that year was Easter Sunday, and from the feast he named the land Pascua Florida. He hurried back to Spain to report his discovery and receive wider powers and privileges than the royal patent of 1512 had given him.

By a new patent he was empowered "to settle the island Bimini and the island Florida." It was also provided that the natives must be summoned to submit to the Catholic faith and the authority of the king of Spain; they were not to be attacked or captured if they submitted. It was only in February, 1521, that he was able to realize the project. Letters that he wrote to Charles V. and to the Cardinal of Tortosa, afterward Pope Adrian VI., before starting, show that not love of glory merely, or greed of conquest and wealth, actuated him, but that he had the higher and nobler motive of bringing the boon of Christianity to lands sunk in heathenism. He sailed with two vessels, carrying everything needed for a permanent settlement, and was accompanied by secular priests to minister to the colonists, and religious—of the order of St. Dominic, most likely—to evangelize the natives. The precise place or time of his landing we know not. Whether the holy sacrifice of the mass was offered up, or any of the ministrations of religion were performed on the soil of Florida in this expedition, we can only conjecture. What is certain is that the natives opposed their settling, fiercely attacked them while they were engaged in putting up temporary homes for shelter, and that Ponce de Leon was dangerously wounded by an arrow. He gave up the hope of making good his footing in the face of the warlike disposition of the Indians, and sailed back to Cuba, to die almost immediately of his wound.

It was proved very early that Florida was not an island, as it was called in the cedula granted to Ponce de Leon in 1512. In 1519 Alvarez de Pineda coasted the northern shore of the Gulf of Mexico as far as Tampico in Mexico, meeting on his way the mouth of a vast river he named Rio de Santo Espiritu—our Mississippi—on whose waters he spent six weeks trading with the natives. Likewise explorations along the western coast of Florida showed that it was the southeastern spur of a continent stretching northward. At this time, too, the expedition of Magellan's crew around the world by way of the straits that now bear his name opened the eyes of Europe to the fact that west of the New World there lay an immense ocean between it and Asia. Now, as the old notion still possessed the mind of Europe that the main purpose of the western voyages was to find a route to the spices and wealth of the Asiatic regions, and as the Straits of Magellan were a roundabout way, inconvenient because of distance and stormy seas, it became a matter of the first importance to discover a waterway through the American mainland to the Pacific Ocean, and thence to Asia, in the latitude of Spain and Europe. Then began that pathetic and thrilling story of a persistent search for a northwest passage that has evolved in our days into a search for the open Arctic Sea. The first who tried our coasts for the western passage was Ayllon. The Chesapeake, he thought, might be the sought-for break through the barrier of land.

The year before Ponce de Leon had started on his unfortunate attempt of colonization, Vasquez de Ayllon, one of the judges of San Domingo, a man of wealth and ambition, had dispatched a caravel to explore the coast north of the limits assigned by patent to Ponce de Leon. The caravel met in 30° 30′ a river, which was called from the feast of the day (June 24th) the St. John's River, a name it retains to this day. After further cruising, the caravel returned to report to Ayllon. He proceeded immediately to Spain to obtain the royal permission to settle the discovered territory. This was granted to him in June, 1523. It is to be remarked that he was ordered by the terms of the cedula (the Spanish name for the grant) to run up the coast eight hundred leagues; this order shows that Spain, by right of the discovery of Columbus and the Partition Bull of Alexander VI., claimed as her own all the mainland north of the Gulf of Mexico, and called it Florida—a claim that brought her, a few years later, into conflict with France, and, still later, with England, both of whom set up counter-claims based on discoveries in North America prior to any explorations and settlements of Spain above the Gulf of Mexico.

But what interests us most are the religious provisions of the cedula. Ayllon was bidden "to attract the natives to receive preachers who would inform and instruct them in the affairs of our holy Catholic faith, that they might become Christians." The document goes on to state: "And whereas our principal intent in the discovery of new lands is that the inhabitants and natives thereof who are without the light of the knowledge of faith may be brought to understand the truths of our holy Catholic faith, and that they may come to the knowledge thereof and become Christians and be saved, and this is the chief motive you are to bear and hold in this affair, and to this end it is proper that religious persons should accompany you, by these presents I empower you to carry to the said land the religious whom you may judge necessary, and the vestments and the other things needful for the observance of divine worship; and I command that whatever you shall thus expend in transporting the said religious, as well as in maintaining them and giving them what is needful, and for the vestments and other articles required for the divine worship, shall be paid entirely from the rents and profits which in any manner shall belong to us in the said land." These noble and emphatic words of the great emperor, Charles V., his disinterested generosity in providing for religion means and ways out of the crown's revenues, prove that Spain, while extending her empire throughout the

New World, was actuated by regard for Christianity, and by the desire to spread it, no less, if not more, than by lust of conquest and the desire to garner wealth.

In the month of June, 1526, Ayllon set out with three large vessels carrying six hundred persons and all the requisites for a permanent colony. With him went two Dominican fathers and a lay brother. One of the two fathers, Antonio Montesinos, was a man who deserves to stand in history by the side of Las Casas, for he preceded Las Casas in protest against the enslavement of the Indians. It was in San Domingo, on a Sunday, in 1511, that he preached a sermon "very piercing and terrible," telling his hearers that they were living in mortal sin, and that their greed and cruelty were such that for any chance they had of going to heaven they might as well be Moors or Turks. The infuriated Spaniards demanded an apology and retractation from the rash preacher. On the next Sunday the sermon was still more pointed, for he declared that the monks of his order would refuse the sacraments to any man who should maltreat Indians or engage in the slave-trade. Brave and undaunted abolition preachers are not the monopoly of our country and century. We feel like thanking God that the feet of Antonio Montesinos, the first of American abolitionists, trod the soil desecrated by the slavery of the black man during two hundred years, purified by the atoning blood of the slave-holder, redeemed and glorified by hecatombs of liberty's soldiers.

Ayllon and his colony reached the Chesapeake, and formed a settlement they named San Miguel, not far from the spot where almost a century later the English founded Jamestown in Virginia. A temporary chapel was erected, and the holy sacrifice of the mass was celebrated as long as the settlement lasted. It did not last long. Ayllon died in the month of October, 1526. A severe winter set in, with disease in its train. The settlers quarreled among themselves; the Indians attacked them. When spring returned, the colonists, disgusted and despairing, reëmbarked on the two vessels anchored in the river. One foundered, the other made its way to Hispaniola. Of the six hundred that had started out the year before in high hopes, only one hundred and fifty returned.

Many expeditions without practical results were yet to be undertaken before Spain gained firm possession of Florida. Among these were the attempts of Pamfilo de Narvaez in 1527, and of Hernando de Soto in 1538. They concern our history only because missionary priests went with them. Pamfilo de Narvaez had in his five ships six hundred persons, among them some secular priests and five Franciscans, whose superior was Juan Xuarez. The fleet was driven by storm into a bay of the Florida coast, named by him Bahia de la Cruz, and supposed to be Appalachee Bay. Narvaez disembarked, and ordered the ships to sail along the coast and stand ready to meet him, while he proceeded on shore. Ignorance of the country or mismanagement separated the land and water forces. The ships failed to make the junction. Want of provisions and attacks of Indians forced the unfortunate Spaniards to trust themselves to some small boats they had hurriedly constructed. No trace of them was ever found afterward. Out of the whole expedition only four men escaped—Cabeza de Vaca, the treasurer, Dorantes, Castillo, and a negro named Stephen. They wandered among the Indians of the Southwest, and ten years after the start of the expedition reached Petatlan, in the province of Sinaloa, Mexico. This journey of Cabeza de Vaca, and the report he made of it, entered into the romance of the day, and led to important results, as we shall see when we come to treat of the church in New Mexico.

In April, 1538, from San Lucar, Spain, six hundred as well-born and brave men as ever marched beneath the banner of Castile sailed for Florida under command of Hernando de Soto. Among them were eight secular priests and four religious; their names have not been preserved. The royal cedula issued to De Soto specifically mentioned that he was to carry ecclesiastics and religious on his expedition, at his own cost, to instruct the natives in Christianity. We can safely conjecture that the holy sacrifice of the mass was offered on American soil during the wanderings of De Soto until the battle of the Mauvila, a bloody conflict on the Alabama River in which hundreds of Indians fell. During that battle the stores of the expedition were fired and all things requisite for the holy sacrifice were consumed. Most of the priests perished in the long, weary marches from the Gulf of Mexico up to Virginia and from the Atlantic to the Mississippi, in whose turbid waters the ill-fated leader was buried. De Soto was a conqueror of the school of Pizarro, under whom he had served; ambitious of glory, greedy for gold, harsh to his men, cruel to the natives. He made no permanent conquest, though no leader of former Floridian expeditions visited such a vast extent of territory; nor can he be called the discoverer of the Mississippi, if to discover is to be the first to find and see; for Alvarez de Pineda (1520) had noticed the mouth of the great river, had ascended it some distance, and named it the River of the Holy Ghost. And yet there is a certain glamour about this expedition that makes it one of the most thrilling in history, and the name of De Soto one of the most romantic in the record of explorers.

Five attempts in which the military and religious powers of Spain were combined for the same end had been made to effect a foothold in Florida, and had failed. It was evident that the Indians of the mainland were not the childlike and mild race that Columbus had met in the islands of the semitropical gulf. Moreover, the expeditions had proved that no golden realms, no semibarbaric civilization, existed in the north such as Cortez had found in Mexico and Pizarro in Peru. Was it worth while sacrificing more lives for barren regions where roamed half-naked savages? Yet it was becoming more and more evident that the holding of Florida was of the first importance to Spain—was a political and commercial necessity.

The two great nations of Europe—England and France—were casting coveting glances toward the Western hemisphere, and only absorbing interests and cares at home delayed them from bringing about the partition of America. Already England at a very early day had sent her Cabots (1497–98) and John Rut (1527); France her Denis of Honfleur (1506), Aubert of Dieppe (1508), Baron de Léry (1518), Verrazano (1523), and Jacques Cartier (1534). It was imperatively necessary that Spain should not allow these two rivals to come too near her splendid possessions on the Gulf of Mexico, and that she should hold for their protection the southern half of the northern mainland. This was the political necessity. The reefs of Florida were, of all the Gulf region, the most dangerous to caravels flying before the strong winds of the Atlantic. Many a ship bringing to the colonies men and stores, many a one sailing back to Spain with rich freights of the precious metals, was wrecked and shattered on the treacherous keys, and became the prey of the waves or the Indians. It was imperatively necessary to have there life-stations, so to speak—communities who could bring aid to crafts in distress, or at least secure the salvage. This was the commercial necessity. But the vexing question was, how to make good a foothold on a coast swept by such wild savages, whose descendants even in this century held at bay the army of the United States.

While Las Casas, in 1536, was resting amid his labors for the freedom of the Indians in a Dominican monastery in Guatemala, he wrote a work ("De Unico Vocationis Modo") on the only true mode of conversion, maintaining that to make war on heathen or infidels, because they were heathen or infidels, was wrong, and that the only lawful method of bringing men to Christ was that of reason and persuasion. He was preaching the ways of peace to an audience that believed in the ways of conquest, violence, and force. The audience sneeringly challenged him to put his beautiful theory to practice in some wild Indian tribe. He took them at their word, and chose for his experiment the wildest tribe known, living in an inaccessible country, desperate fighters, whom the Spaniards had tried three times to reduce, and had failed. The country was called the "Land of War," and was situated north of Guatemala. Las Casas exacted from the authorities that, if he succeeded in bringing the natives of that land to Christianity and to the recognition of the supremacy of the Spanish monarch, the province should be placed under the immediate protection of the crown and the system of repartimiento and encomienda should never be allowed to take root there. The promise was made.

Some Dominican monks, companions of Las Casas in the monastery, had been mastering the native dialects of the country while he was writing the book that called forth this challenge. They now set to work putting the Christian truths to meter, the meter to music; and found some Indian traders who consented to carry with their wares the hymns and music into the dreaded land. The warlike tribe was interested, and invited the monks themselves to come. Father Luis Cancer de Barbastro was the first to go; Las Casas and another monk soon followed. Before a year the tribe was converted, and the cacique came to the governor of Guatemala—the stern Alvarado—to acknowledge before him in person the supremacy of Spain. It is but justice to add that the promise made to Las Casas by the governor was kept and ratified by Charles V. The "Land of War" was named the "Land of Peace"; the name Vera Paz, which the province still retains on our maps, is a lasting testimony to the noblest conquest ever made by Spaniards in the New World.

Now, ten years later, the same Father Luis Cancer de Barbastro resolved to repeat the conquest on the northern mainland. Ponce de Leon, Ayllon, Narvaez, and De Soto had gone forth in the panoply of war, and had fallen back before warlike savages. He would go with no companions but his brother monks, with no weapon but the cross and the rosary; and what he had accomplished in the "Land of War" he would do in Florida, drenched without avail with the blood of many of the best missionaries and soldiers of Spain. To Spain he went (1547) to lay his project before the court. It was approved, and he received a patent to carry it out. The preceding expeditions had kidnapped many natives from Florida who were scattered throughout the various Spanish colonies. Father Luis knew that they could be of service to him as interpreters, and that their return in his company would be the strongest proof to the Floridians of the peaceful and beneficent character of his mission. With the patent he carried back a royal command that all Floridian natives, wherever found in the colonies, should be given up to him. Unfortunately the command was not obeyed, and he sailed for Florida (1549) without this powerful support, trusting in God to make a way for him.

With him went a band of his Dominican brethren. History has preserved the names of some of them: Gregory de Beteta, Diego de Tolosa, Juan Garcia. On Ascension day they anchored not far from Tampa Bay, on the western shore. Father Luis had prudence as well as zeal. His plan was to cruise until he found a friendly tribe that would allow him to land. But the captain of the ship had no such patient design, and gave him the choice to land where the ship lay or at once sail back. The companions of the heroic Dominican were for abandoning the enterprise under the circumstances, but he resolved to go on; he had neglected no means of ordinary prudence, he was not responsible for the obstinacy of the captain, he would trust in God. Some Indians were in sight. A small boat carried Father Diego de Tolosa and three lay companions to the shore, and they followed the natives beyond a thicket. A few hours later a Spaniard who had been captured some years before and was a prisoner among the Indians reached the ship at anchor in the bay, and gave information that the father and his companions had been murdered. But just then one of those companions, a Floridian Christian woman whom Father Luis had found in Mexico and had taken as interpreter of the expedition, came to the water's edge and assured him that they were alive. Uncertain, anxious to know the truth, to save his brethren or with them die the martyr's death, Father Luis, in spite of remonstrances from his companions aboard, entered a small boat, and as the terror-stricken sailors refused to touch land, leaped into the water and waded ashore. No sooner had he reached the dry beach and knelt in prayer than he was surrounded by the Indians in wait and butchered in view of the Spaniards. Thus died on the soil of the United States, truly a martyr to a grand cause and a noble idea, the fellow-crusader of

Las Casas, one of the most remarkable men Spain has sent to the New World.

The failure of this peaceful expedition was enough to discourage any further efforts. Yet in 1555 the Archbishop of Mexico, and the Bishop of Santiago de Cuba, who had jurisdiction over Florida, urged upon the court of Spain the importance and necessity of colonizing that territory. The political and commercial reasons for so doing were growing stronger year by year. It was decided to make another effort; and while the humanitarian policy of Luis Cancer de Barbastro was not set aside as far as the treatment of the Indians was concerned, it was felt that nothing but a military occupation of the dreaded coast would answer the national purposes. Fifteen hundred soldiers, many settlers, with all things requisite for the colonization and cultivation of the land, gathered in thirteen vessels, were confided to the command of Tristan de Luna. Four Dominican fathers, with a lay brother under a provincial vicar, Peter de Feria, accompanied the expedition. They reached Santa Rosa Bay August 1, 1559. A partial disembarkment was made to explore the country round about before making a permanent settlement. On September 19th a cyclone struck the fleet, destroying eight vessels, and driving the others to sea. Many of the crew and passengers were lost and the stores destroyed. Those that escaped remained on land for two years. Temporary houses and a chapel were erected, and provisions came to them from Mexico. But discouragement and mutiny set in; the inexcusable severity of the unfortunate commander, Tristan de Luna, exasperated his followers. In this sad condition they were found by Villafane (1561), who was on his way to north Florida. This arrival broke up the settlement. Some went back with De Luna to Havana; the larger number took passage with

Villafane, who sailed up to Santa Elena, Port Royal Sound, doubled Cape Hatteras, reached the Chesapeake, but returned without making any settlement.

In the autumn of that same year Philip II., king of Spain, announced that he would allow no further attempts to colonize Florida, which had already cost too much money and blood. The only imperative reason for occupying Florida would be to keep France from getting a foothold there, and there seemed to be no danger of that. But in this presumption Philip was deceived. Just at the time that Villafane was sailing back to Havana with the remnants of De Luna's splendid expedition, John Ribault, a Huguenot sent by Coligny, prime minister of France and the acknowledged head of the Huguenot faction, was founding a Huguenot colony in Port Royal Sound, and named the fort erected there Charlesfort, in honor of the king of France. This settlement proved a failure, it is true, and was soon abandoned; but in 1564 Laudonniére, another Huguenot, entered the St. John's River, took possession in the name of France, and built a fort which he named Fort Caroline, in honor of the king. And now France—and not only France, but Protestantism—was in the very heart of the territory claimed by Spain and often explored by her since the days of Columbus, and dearly purchased by her wrecked gold and the bleaching bones of her soldiers and missionaries. It behooved Spain to make a supreme effort, or see her supremacy in the New World threatened by a political and religious foe. The effort was made, and succeeded in assuring the possession of Florida to Spain for over two centuries.

At that time the admiral of the Spanish fleet—the same who later led the Armada against England—was Pedro Menendez de Aviles. To him was intrusted the task of driving off the French and planting in Florida a permanent Spanish colony. A royal grant was issued to him March, 1565, with full powers to occupy and settle colonies in Florida. Among other conditions he was obligated to bring with him and maintain at his expense twelve religious, and four members of the Society of Jesus. The news of the occupation by the French Huguenots at the mouth of the St. John's River, and the further announcement that reinforcements were about to be sent to that settlement, hastened the departure of Menendez. Without waiting for the whole fleet, part of which was to follow when ready, he set sail from Cadiz June, 1565, with nineteen vessels carrying over fifteen hundred persons. On the 28th of August he made the Florida coast in a harbor that he named St. Augustine, from the saint of the day. Ten days later he crept up the coast to Fort Caroline and found there the French fleet just arrived under command of John Ribault. Menendez then and there challenged the intruders to a naval engagement, but the challenge was not accepted; the Frenchmen, cutting their cables, slipped past the enemy into the open sea, and outsailed the Spaniards, who after a short chase returned to St. Augustine.

Thinking himself safe from further attack, Menendez proceeded to debark his men and stores. A hurried fort was constructed, and the foundations of the oldest city of the United States were laid. The solemn taking possession—the dedication, so to speak, of the town—was performed on the feast of the Nativity of the Blessed Virgin (September 8, 1565), with due religious ceremonies. Menendez was mistaken if he thought he was safe from Ribault. The French ships soon appeared before the harbor, and it might have gone hard with the new town and its inhabitants if a hurricane, followed by a violent rainstorm that lasted some days, had not arisen to scatter the French fleet and furnish cover to one of the most daring feats that Spanish conqueror ever performed in the New World. Leaving wind and rain to wreak their fury on the vessels of the rash Frenchmen, the Spanish commander, with five hundred men, pushed through the rain, the everglades, and the swamps by day and night to the French fort on the St. John's River, found it unsentineled—for what foe could be abroad in such weather?—stormed it, and put to the sword one hundred and forty-one inmates—men, women, and children. Only a few escaped through the woods and made their way to a small craft at anchor in the offing, and thence to France to tell the news. It was St. Matthew's day. Menendez rechristened the fort San Mateo, left in it a garrison of three hundred men, and returned with the rest of his force to St. Augustine. Father Mendoza, the parish priest of the new city, came forth in surplice, crucifix in hand, to meet the hero of the massacre. He, kneeling with his men, kissed the cross; then, arising, they entered the town amid the chant of the Te Deum.

Some days after Menendez was advised that a number of Frenchmen, evidently the remnants of the wrecked fleet of Ribault, were stranded on the outer sand island of Matanzas Inlet. They were one hundred and forty, only a portion of the crew that had escaped from the foundered ships. They begged either means of going back to France or permission to make their way overland to Fort Caroline. Menendez refused the first, and as to the second, explained how there was no longer a Fort Caroline. He demanded an unconditional surrender, to which the wretches, seeing no way out of their present condition, consented. No sooner had they been disarmed and ferried over to the mainland in batches of ten, than they were put to the sword, none being spared but a few Catholics among them. A few days later another party of wrecked Frenchmen, three hundred and fifty in number, made their appearance on the coast. Seventy of those—among them Ribault—consented to surrender in the same manner, and in the same manner were dispatched. The rest, trusting to the Indians and Providence, preferring any hardships to unconditional surrender, wandered inland and set up a temporary fort. They were not left long in peace. Menendez pursued and attacked them behind their palisades. This time they surrendered, but on condition that their lives should be spared. Menendez promised, and kept his word.

This latter fact is the strongest argument to refute an accusation brought by French historians against the inhuman Spaniard. A sailor, who somehow escaped from the former butcheries and eventually turned up in France, is the only authority for the assertion that Menendez had promised life to the wrecked men in the two first cases just mentioned as condition of their surrender. Menendez himself, in his official report, does not mention any such promise. Considering that he kept his promise when he did make one, we are inclined to believe him rather than the escaped Frenchman as to the point of the unconditional surrender of the two stranded companies of sailors. This is not saying that we justify his conduct. We think it inhuman and to be reprobated; while we allow that there may be found some justification for him in the age, which was one of fierce religious warfare, and in his own circumstances, which were not such as to enable him to feed such a large number of men in addition to his own. We regret that the first city of the United States was given such a baptism of blood.

CHAPTER III.

THE PERMANENT SETTLEMENT OF FLORIDA (1565–1762).

THUS were the Spaniards left in possession of Florida; and the possession lasted for abóut two hundred years, when the English colonies of South Carolina and Georgia grew strong enough to oust them. We can give but the briefest synopsis of this long occupation. In order to understand the church's work and situation it must not be forgotten that two classes of ecclesiastics were side by side on Floridian soil. There were secular priests, directly under the jurisdiction of the Bishop of Santiago de Cuba, and later on of the Bishop of Havana. Those secular priests were stationed in St. Augustine and at the other posts held by the Spanish soldiers and settlers. There was constantly, with exceptions of vacancies between the incumbents, a parish priest with a certain number of assistants in St. Augustine, which was a regularly constituted parish; in the other posts there were chaplains. When a vacancy occurred, generally the religious in the province acted during the interim in the stead of the secular priests, as the records abundantly show. As for the Indian missions, only regulars were employed—at first Dominicans, then Jesuits, and after the two former had abandoned the field, then Franciscans, who from the year 1577 occupied the field exclusively. I shall make but occasional and brief reference to the secular clergy and their work; for as the purely Spanish population did not take on any great expansion, neither did the secular clergy and its work. The glory of the Floridian church is in its martyrs, its missionaries, and they were the regulars.

In 1566 came some Dominicans, two of whom, with thirty soldiers, were sent to the Chesapeake. The intention of Menendez was to occupy the bay as a northern advance post and as a possible strait to the western ocean. The plan was baffled. The vessel that carried the missionaries and the garrison failed to reach its destination, and sailed back to Spain.

Philip II. had asked of St. Francis Borgia, general of the Jesuits, to detail some of his subjects to go with Menendez. Two of them sailed in 1566. They were Peter Martinez and John Rogel, with a lay brother. The vessel reached the coast of Florida at a point unknown to the captain. Father Martinez volunteered to join a reconnoitering party in a small boat. No sooner had they pushed off when a storm came up that drove the vessel out to sea; it reached Havana some time after. Martinez and the reconnoitering party were left to the mercy of the Indians, who, sparing the sailors, massacred the missionary on Cumberland Island.

In 1568 four Jesuit fathers and six brothers arrived. They dispersed throughout Florida to various points. One of them, Father Sedeno, took up his abode on Amelia Island; he is the pioneer priest of Georgia. With him was the lay brother Baez, who wrote a grammar of the aboriginal language and prepared a catechism. Father Rogel, who had gone to Cuba to found a school for Floridian boys, returned and set up a mission on Santa Elena Island, Port Royal Sound; he is the pioneer priest of South Carolina. It is well to remember that the statement that catechisms and other religious books were translated into the native idioms means a great deal. It means not only that such translations serve for the fresh missionaries who have to learn the language, but also that they are for the use of the natives; and this implies that the aborigines are taught to read, and consequently that the missionaries are school-masters—that the school is set up by the side of the church. It is a well-ascertained fact that in time the native Floridians learned writing, for we have the signatures of some of them still extant. There is nothing astonishing in this when we remember that the church had been constantly at work in Florida from 1565 to 1763, almost two hundred years. Contact with Christianity and civilization during so long a period must naturally have had an effect on the Indians, among whom at one time Christians were reckoned by the twenty and thirty thousand.

Once more did Menendez attempt to settle a military and missionary post on Chesapeake Bay, and this time he sent Jesuits instead of Dominicans. Fathers Segura and Louis de Quiros, with six lay brothers, left St. Augustine in August, 1570, sailed up the Potomac some distance, and landed at a place not ascertained. But soon after the vessel that brought them had left they were put to death by the Indians. Menendez, discouraged, gave up the project which, if realized, might have changed the course of history on our shores, or at least have delayed the disappearance of Spain from Florida.

St. Francis Borgia, when he heard of this last disaster to his American subjects, recalled the surviving Jesuits from Florida and ordered them to Mexico. Menendez died in 1574, leaving the ecclesiastical status of the province in a deplorable condition. Fortunately, two years afterward the Franciscans took up the field abandoned by the Dominicans and Jesuits, and retained it until it passed out of Spanish hands.

Their labors began in 1577. Fifteen years later four fathers and two lay brothers were at work, and two years later four more fathers with one lay brother increased the band of heroic missionaries. As their numbers increased, so also the number of Christian Indians; by degrees they extended the line of their missions from the coast northward and southward and into the interior a distance of one hundred and fifty or two hundred miles. The progress of mission work and conversions was arrested for a while by a persecution excited (1597) by a young chief who tired of the restraints of Christianity on his passions, and enlisted on his side the unconverted Indians and those as bad as himself. There was a widespread looting of the mission chapels; five fathers and one lay brother fell victims to the fury of the persecutors.

Not only did the Franciscans labor as preachers of the gospel and die as martyrs to their duty, but they also reduced to grammar and put into print some of the many dialects of Florida. Father Francis Pareja published in Mexico (1612–27) two catechisms in the Timuquan language, a *confessionario*, and a grammar, and is said to have written treatises on purgatory, heaven, and hell, and a book of prayers. An item such as this tells volumes as to the progress of the church.

Florida was in the diocese of Santiago de Cuba. It was visited (1607) by Bishop Juan Cabezas de Altamirano, who inspected most of the missions and administered the sacrament of confirmation. In 1616 a delegate was sent by the bishop to make the visitation. By the year 1634 there were in Florida thirty-five Franciscans, maintaining forty-four missions, and the number of Christian Indians was between twenty-five and thirty thousand. St. Augustine had three hundred inhabitants, mostly Spaniards, a parish church, a convent of Franciscans, two hospitals, and a number of religious confraternities. The greatest need of the province was a resident bishop, and though the holy see had been petitioned (1655) to erect St. Augustine into a bishopric, or at least a vicariate, nothing was done at the time.

This was the palmy period of Catholicity in Spanish Florida. It extends from 1625 to 1700. Prosperity and peace begat here on a small scale the result often met with on a larger scale in the church of other lands: I mean neglect of duty, disobedience, and disunion. No doubt the absence of a bishop made the evil worse. When Gabriel Diaz Vara Calderon, Bishop of Santiago, came in 1674 to make the canonical visitation of this part of his diocese, he found such ignorance among the Indians that he had to order the teaching of catechism on Sundays and holidays, and to command under severe penalties all masters to send their Indian servants to the catechetical instructions. One cheering item of this visitation, and a proof that the Floridian church was on the highway to self-support, is that he gave minor orders to seven young men. Evidently a native clergy was growing up. His visitation lasted eight months, and he must have come very close to the English settlements in South Carolina. His confirmations amounted to 13,152, proof of a large Catholic population. He toned up the clergy, enlarged and beautified the churches, and increased the number of missionaries. In the year 1684 a diocesan synod was held in Cuba. Its decrees were law in Florida, and special regulations were made for the Indian missions of that province.

Abroad in the north was looming up a danger that was destined to destroy the church in Florida, as we shall see presently; but within there was at this time an evil no less pernicious. A premonition of this evil was given in 1674, during the administration of Bishop Calderon. Before coming in person for the visitation, he had delegated from Cuba a secular priest to make a report on the condition of the province. The Franciscans refused to acknowledge the delegate, and demanded that one of their order should hold that office. In 1688 Don Diego Evelino de Compostella, newly appointed Bishop of Cuba, sent to Florida a learned Cuban priest to examine the condition of the church and report to him. Again the Franciscans refused to recognize his right to visit canonically their convents and missions, for the reason that he was not the bishop nor a religious of their institute, and quoted in their favor a former royal order, as if the king were the authority in such matters. They went further, as they were logically bound to do; one of them wrote a work in which he denied that Florida was part of the diocese of Cuba, and asserted that its bishop had no right to send a delegate to examine the Franciscan missions. Truly success had made them overbold and closed their eyes to the truth that force comes from obedience and union, especially in the presence of the foe.

A foe was hovering on their northern frontier. The palmy period of the Floridian church was about to come to an end. The territory now covered by Georgia, the two Carolinas, and Virginia had been claimed originally by Spain as a part of Florida. We have seen how various attempts had been made by her to occupy and hold the Chesapeake, but without success. In 1584 Raleigh landed on the coast of Carolina, at Roanoke, a colony that was short-lived and disappeared mysteriously forever. The territory from the St. Lawrence to the St. John's River was ceded by the English crown in the grant of 1606 under the name of Virginia. The grant of 1620 cut off the portion above the present Virginia's northern line, leaving as Virginia the country south of that line. A further dismemberment took place in 1663, erecting under the name of Carolina a province comprising the present States of North and South

Carolina and Georgia. In 1669–70 William Sayle planted a colony near the site of Charleston, and this was the beginning of South Carolina. In 1679 some Scotch Presbyterians settled at Port Royal, two days' sail from St. Augustine. The Spaniards attacked this settlement in 1680 and destroyed it. Then began the struggle that was to end in the destruction of their power and their missions in Florida.

Anticipating the coming danger, the governor of St. Augustine, in 1684, tried to persuade the Christian Indians living near the border line of the English possessions to move southward, that they might be out of harm's way and nearer to the protecting troops of the capital. The unsuspecting Indians refused to abandon their homes. Soon after, at the instigation of Moore, governor of South Carolina, the Appalachicolas attacked the mission of Santa Catalina, on the island of that name off the coast of Georgia, and the mission of Santa Fé, in the province of Timaqua, destroyed the chapels and houses of the missionaries, burned the villages, massacred many, and carried off not a few to be sold as slaves in the Carolinas. In 1701 began in Europe the war of the Spanish Succession, between Germany, Holland, and England on the one hand, and France and Spain on the other. This war overleaped the Atlantic, and had its counterpart on American soil between the English of the Carolinas and Georgia and the Spaniards of Florida.

A land expedition under Colonel Daniel, composed of Carolinian militiamen and an Indian contingent, and a naval expedition under Governor Moore of South Carolina, after spreading destruction on their paths, effected a junction before St. Augustine, October, 1702, and laid siege to the city. It lasted fifty days. The inhabitants fled into the interior, leaving the garrison under brave Zuniga to hold the fort. The appearance of a Spanish fleet with reinforcements caused Moore to burn his ships and retreat overland with Daniel; not, however, until they had set fire to the town. The news of the destruction of St. Augustine produced a deep sensation in Spain. The king ordered that the revenues of the vacant bishoprics of the kingdom should go to the rebuilding of the church, the convent, and the public buildings of the ill-fated city. It is to the dishonor of the English that they intentionally gave to the flames a valuable library, the collection of many years.

Another attack from Carolina under the same Governor Moore was made two years later (1704), with the intention of breaking up the missions and carrying off slaves. It cannot be denied that there was religious as well as national hatred in the enterprise. A sudden dash was made into the territory of the Appalachees, where missions were numerous and flourishing. A bold stand against the raiders was maintained by Lieutenant Mexia, with thirty Spaniards and four hundred Indians, as long as the ammunition lasted. Many were killed and many made prisoners, among them Lieutenant Mexia, Fathers Parga, Miranda, and Delgado. Some of the prisoners were handed over to the Indian allies of the English, and were tortured and burned at the stake. Father Parga was thus treated in spite of Father Miranda's protestations and prayers and Father Delgado's attempt to rescue him, for which brotherly service Delgado was slain on the spot. Ten towns of the province were looted, their churches destroyed, and the sacred contents carried off. Proceeding on their way, the invaders came to Fort San Luis, which they found too formidable to attack; they offered Mexia, four Spanish soldiers, and Father Miranda for a ransom so considerable that the commander was unable to give it. In barbarous revenge the prisoners were tortured and put to death with all the ingenious cruelty of the Indians. The scenes of the martyrdom of the northern Jesuits, so graphically described by Parkman, were enacted beneath the balmy skies of Florida, with the connivance, if not under the eyes and by the command, of the governor of a Christian colony. Moore went back from this raid with a thousand Christian Indians for the slave-markets of Carolina.

These repeated attacks completely ruined the missions north and west of St. Augustine. The few remaining Christians in the Appalachee country fled for protection to Mobile, under cover of the French guns. From that quarter, too, danger threatened the Spaniards, now inclosed between the English possessions in the north and the French possessions in the Mississippi Valley. Pensacola was taken and destroyed by the French in 1719. The time was nearing when North America was to be cleared for the great struggle between the two great rivals, France and England. Between them, and before they came into deadly contact, Spain was doomed to be crushed and brushed out of the way.

It was in the midst of those misfortunes and forebodings that was realized a long and earnest wish of the Christians of Florida—the appointment of a resident bishop. The first was Dionisio Rezino, preconized as Bishop of Adramitum, *in partibus infidelium*, and auxiliary to the Bishop of Santiago de Cuba; he was consecrated in Merida, Yucatan, in 1709. No record shows how long he resided in St. Augustine, though there is evidence that he gave confirmation in that city on June 29, 1709. It is known that he died in Havana on September 14, 1711. A vacancy of twenty years followed, during which interval the province was visited twice by delegates of the Bishop of Santiago. Nothing can give a better idea of the deplorable state of the missions about this time than the Visitor's report of

1727; Florida, that had contained a hundred years before almost thirty thousand Christian Indians, could show in that year only one thousand.

The second Bishop of Florida, Martinez de Tejada, preconized Bishop of Tricali, *i. p. i.*, and auxiliary to the Bishop of Santiago, came to St. Augustine in 1735. The city at that time had a population of fifteen hundred souls—Spaniards and negro slaves—under the spiritual care of one parish priest and two assistants. The residence of Bishop Tejada in Florida extended over ten years, during which time he made three visitations of the entire province. Evidently the orders of the king of Spain, already alluded to, in regard to the rebuilding of the church of the city had not been carried out; for the cathedral in 1735 was but a small chapel, fifty by thirty-six feet, so inadequate that most of the congregation had to remain out on the square during divine service. Among many good works which the bishop either renewed or inaugurated, special mention should be made of a classical school which he opened for the training of young clerics. The English invasions had put an end to the many flourishing Indian schools of the province; this was the only one left.

An incident recorded during the bishopric of Tejada gives an insight into the composition of the Floridian clergy, the larger portion of which were Franciscans. They formed an independent province known as Santa Elena de Florida. The election of the provincial in 1745 was the occasion of grave controversy, and was declared later on to be null by the higher authorities. The difficulty came from national rivalries, and the rivalries were between the religious imported from Spain and the religious born in America. Here we have evidence that the native clergy was strong, and that the movement so well known among us now as Americanism was a factor in the church of America one hundred and fifty years ago. Is it any wonder, when it is remembered that previous to this incident the church had existed in Florida for one hundred and eighty years? The Spaniards of the province had been native Americans for generations, and it was but natural that they should prefer a native to an imported priesthood.

During the administration of Bishop Tejada, St. Augustine was attacked once more from the north. The attack was led by Governor Oglethorpe of Georgia. The country between the Savannah and the St. John's rivers was a part of the old Carolina claim; but when the Carolinas became royal provinces the king reserved this unsettled district as crown lands (1717). In 1732 James Oglethorpe formed a company for the settlement of this tract, which was to be named Georgia in honor of George II. The city of Savannah was founded by English settlers under the lead of Oglethorpe in 1733; a year later the town of Ebenezer was founded by exiled Germans from Salzburg; Augusta was planted in the same year as an outpost in the Indian country. Two years later Frederica was founded at the mouth of the Altamaha, on the Spanish frontier. In 1739 war broke out in Europe between Spain and England. Fearing an attack from the Spaniards of Florida, Oglethorpe decided to take the offensive, marched into Florida with two thousand troops supported by a fleet of seven ships, and laid siege to St. Augustine. Though troops from Carolina came down to reinforce the Georgians, Oglethorpe was compelled to abandon the siege; for sickness had set in among his men, and there were many desertions. Two years later (1742) the Spaniards in their turn attacked Frederica by land and sea; but Oglethorpe held the place gallantly until the arrival of English vessels frightened off the besiegers.

These wars and constant dangers of war ended the ruin of Catholicity in Florida. When the third bishop, Ponce y

Carasco, came in 1751, there were in the immediate vicinity of St. Augustine only four Indian missions, with one hundred and thirty-six souls; in other words, there was no Catholicity in Florida outside of the Spanish population of the city. Very little is known of the administration of this third bishop, preconized Bishop of Adramitum, *i. p. i.*, and auxiliary to the Bishop of Santiago, for he left Florida in 1755. And now we are nearing the end.

Havana fell into the hands of the English in 1762. The bishop of the city, Peter Augustine Morrell de Santa Cruz, was summoned by the Earl of Albemarle, the British commander, to give him aid in extorting forced levies from the clergy of his diocese. Because of his refusal he was accused of conspiracy, taken by force to an English vessel, and carried off to Charleston. Thence, after a stay of some weeks, he was allowed to go to St. Augustine. The bishop put his forced sojourn in Florida to good use: he made the canonical visitation of St. Augustine and the surrounding missions, confirmed six hundred and thirty-nine persons, and consoled and encouraged the clergy and people. He was conveyed back to his see after peace had been made between Spain and England. The peace cost a great price. In order to recover Havana, Spain had to cede Florida. This cession was indeed advantageous to the English, for it rounded out their possessions (the seaboard from the St. Lawrence to the Gulf of Mexico was now under the British flag), but it put an end, for a time, to Catholicity in Florida. A general emigration of Spaniards soon followed the disappearance of the Spanish flag. They left behind them the witnesses of their passage in churches, which in better and later days became once more the homes of a flourishing Catholicity.

The further history of Catholicity in Florida belongs to the second part of this work.

CHAPTER IV.

THE PRELIMINARY EXPLORATIONS OF NEW MEXICO (1539–82).

NEW MEXICO is a century older in European civilization, and several centuries older in a semicivilization of its own, than any other part of the United States. It had its walled cities of stone long before the time of Columbus, and has some of them yet. Romantic as it is in itself, with its vast adobe buildings, its abrupt mountains, its rock-walled cañons, its sunburned mesas, its gaunt, treeless plains, its intense blue sky, and over all its oriental sunlight, it is no less romantic in its history of the Spanish conquest, recording superhuman marches, awful privations, devoted heroism, and sudden and overwhelming rebellions.

The American is to be found there to-day, and what changes in the strange people he may bring about in the future we can only conjecture. But up to the present time New Mexico has remained what it was three hundred years ago, in spite of the stars and stripes, the Yankee trader, the wild cowboy, and the tireless prospector. There are the nine thousand Pueblo Indians, peaceful, sedentary, tillers of a soil snatched from barrenness by a system of irrigation as old as themselves, Catholics since the days the Franciscans came to them, and, though Catholics, wedded still to some of their ancestral superstitions, and, like their ancestors, frequenting the mysterious estufas, to which no stranger is admitted. There are the ten thousand Navajo Indians, sullen, nomad, horse-stealing, dwellers in the saddle, attached to the old paganism; in a word, such as they were when the Spaniards encountered them. There are the Mexicans, descendants more or less pure of the Castilian invaders, poor but hospitable, shiftless but courteous, as Catholic as their forefathers. The Pueblos have nineteen compact little cities, the wonder of the traveler; the Navajos roam the prairies with their tents; the Mexicans live in some hundreds of villages.

In 1581–83 Espejo visited seventy-five pueblos during his progress through the Southwest, and estimated the population at two hundred and fifty thousand—a mere guess, and an extravagant one. There never were in the Southwest in historic times more than thirty or thirty-five thousand Indians. The ruined pueblos scattered up and down the land are evidences not, as so many think, of vast populations that have disappeared, but of frequent migrations, when the old home was abandoned and a new one was set up. The Apache, a drought, an epidemic, a volcanic disturbance, a hundred unknown superstitious omens, caused the tribes to bid farewell to the walls of a former dwelling, to seek a better site and rebuild their terraced cities elsewhere.

Some of the pueblos were of great size, containing from two hundred to one thousand inhabitants. Wegegi, in the Chaco Cañon, was 700 feet in circumference; Pueblo Bonito was 544 feet by 314; Chipillo, 320 by 300. At Taos and the western pueblos the Indians are living to-day where the Spaniards found them. Taos is 250 by 130 feet, and five stories high. Most of the ruined pueblos were built on the top of hills or mesas. The most remarkable is Acoma; it is almost inaccessible, except by a narrow trail and steps cut in the mountain side.

The pueblo is thus described by Mr. John Fiske: "The

typical form of the pueblo is that of a solid block of buildings making three sides of an extensive rectangular inclosure or courtyard. On the inside, facing upon the courtyard, the structure is but one story in height; on the outside, looking out upon the surrounding country, it rises to three or even five and six stories. From inside to outside the flat roofs rise in a series of terraces, so that the floor of the second row is continuous with the roof of the first, the floor of the third row is continuous with the roof of the second, and so on. The fourth side of the rectangle is formed by a solid block of one-story apartments, usually with one or two gateways, overlooked by higher structures within the inclosure. Except these gateways there is no entrance from without. The only windows are frowning loop-holes, and access to the several apartments is gained through skylights reached by portable ladders." It is a joint tenement affair, so to speak. The Pueblo Indians were organized in clans. They were governed by a council of sachems, the principal sachem being called by the Spaniards a *gobernador*. They had an organized priesthood and an elaborate ceremonial. In every pueblo there was at least one estufa or council house for governmental and religious meetings. The pueblo of Zuni seems to have had at one time five thousand inhabitants. The ruined pueblo of Hungo Pavie, in the valley of Rio Chaco, could have accommodated one thousand. Pueblo Bonito, in the same valley, had room for three thousand.

The use of adobe brick or stone in building and the gathering of large numbers in vast communal houses, or pueblos, as the Spaniards called them, are the most distinctive marks of the grade of culture attained by the Indians in this province; and the culture goes on increasing from New Mexico, through Mexico and Yucatan, down to Peru, where it reaches its highest development. North of

New Mexico are the wandering, roving tribes, who get their subsistence by the chase. In New Mexico and south are the Sedentary Indians, whose subsistence comes mainly from agriculture. The staple of agriculture is maize or Indian corn, a grain that deserves a written history, for it has had much to do with the making of America. The region in which lived the New Mexican Indians is by nature arid; it was only by irrigation that it was rendered fertile. It was the maize that suggested the irrigation. For this reason the pueblos are always found situated near a river, and their gardens, outside the walls, are easily accessible to the water by canals and sluices.

It may therefore be said that the Indians of New Mexico had raised themselves out of savagery into barbarism, but not yet into civilization. A word in explanation. Where society rests on a natural basis of subsistence—the chase, fishing—you have savagery; such was the condition of the Indian tribes north of New Mexico. Where an artificial basis of subsistence, such as agriculture, has been established, and the substitution has not been wrought out to its ultimate results for want of time or other unfavorable circumstances, you have barbarism. Where the substitution has been wrought out to its ultimate results of machinery, trade, buildings, transportation, etc., you have civilization. The Indians of New Mexico, being agriculturists, were in the middle stage between savagery and civilization. Agriculture furnished them not only food, but clothing also. When the chase ceases to be the main occupation of man, he must look to some other source than skins of animals wherewith to clothe himself; and if no domestic animals whose wool may be done into texture are at hand, then must he search for material in his agriculture. Such was the case with the Indians of New Mexico. Cotton supplied them clothing as maize supplied them food.

Thus it will be seen that the Spanish missionaries of New Mexico had to deal with a people not altogether barbarous, who knew something of building, and were capable of raising to the uses of religion churches not unworthy to stand on European soil. If the ruins of their pueblos are still the wonder of the traveler, so also their churches, ruined or preserved, are evidences of the zeal of the friars and of the skill and faith of the Indians under their charge. The conquerors gave the natives what they lacked for a more perfected agricultural existence: better implements, iron, improved and quicker modes of building and weaving, plants, vegetables, and fruits unknown, and above all, domestic animals—the cow, the sheep, the horse. Missionaries gave them schools in which not only letters, but trades and industry, were taught. A fairer field by far was this for religion to work in—because there was a basis of natural advance on which to build up religion—than the northern territory, where roamed and warred constantly the Huron, the Iroquois, the Dakota; or than the southeastern seaboard of Florida, where dwelt savages only less nomadic than the tribes just named; or even than California, where the missionary found the least warlike and most degraded of all the aborigines. The field being so favorable, it is no wonder the success was great.

The home of the Pueblos lay within the territory now comprised in Arizona, New Mexico, southwestern Colorado, and southeastern Utah. About these people a double tradition, one European, the other American, had gathered and commingled, encompassing them with a romantic interest, which was not the least motive that drew the Spaniards from Mexico to the exploration and occupation of their country. The European tradition, current among the Spaniards, related that a certain bishop of Lisbon, after the conquest of Spain by the Mohammedans in the eighth century, emigrated with a large following to an island or a group of islands out in the Atlantic Ocean, and founded seven cities there. The Island of the Seven Cities was known in the middle ages as Antilia. The name "Antilles," given the West Indies, preserves to this day the legend of the Seven Cities. As these fabulous towns were not found on any islands in the Gulf of Mexico, they were transferred by the imagination of the Spaniards to some remote and hidden quarter in the continent.

The Indian tradition, current among the Nahuatl tribes of Mexico and Central America, related that in the distant past their ancestors had issued from Seven Caves, situated in the north. The Seven Cities and the Seven Caves became mixed up into one and the same legend in the thoughts of the Spaniards. When Cabeza de Vaca (1536) suddenly appeared in Culiacan with the story of his wonderful journey through the interior of the continent from Florida to northern Mexico, the popular conclusion was that in that direction the Seven Cities should be sought. It is astonishing what a part in discovery was played by legends and fables of this kind. The empire of the Grand Khan lured on Columbus, the fountain of youth drew Ponce de Leon, the Seven Cities were the dream of Father Mark of Nizza and of Coronado, Gran Quivira attracted Coronado and Oñate far to the north. After the Spaniards had become convinced that the Seven Cities were not to be found in New Mexico, the Gilded Man, El Dorado, was hunted through all South America. The fabled city of Norumbega was sought for by French and English along our northern Atlantic seacoast.

Mendoza was viceroy of New Spain in the City of Mexico when Cabeza de Vaca arrived from the north in the province. There was at that time in Mexico a Franciscan friar who had seen much service in the New World. He had been with Pizarro in Peru and with Alvarado in Guatemala. He was a native of Nice, and was called Father Mark of Nizza. Mendoza chose him to go and find the Seven Cities in the country whence Cabeza de Vaca had returned. His guide was to be the negro Stephen, companion of Cabeza de Vaca in his wanderings, and some Mexican Indians were to be his fellow-travelers. Mr. A. F. Bandelier, in a late work, "The Gilded Man," gives a most minute and interesting description of the long journey, accurately maps the route, and identifies the spots named in Father Mark's report. Suffice it to say here that the Seven Cities of Cibola which he reached, or rather saw from a hilltop, were the Zuni pueblos of New Mexico.

The good monk has been accused of exaggeration, if not of downright falsehood, when in his report he compared the cities of Cibola to the City of Mexico, and when he stated that the houses of Cibola were adorned with turquoises and precious stones. Now, as to the first point, we will do well to remember that the City of Mexico of the year 1539—the only one Father Mark had seen and known—had not more than one thousand inhabitants, and consisted of a group of houses within a very small space. As to the second point, it has been ascertained in our days that a custom formerly prevailed among the Zunis of decorating the thresholds of their houses with green stones. The friar was correct in his main statements; the exaggeration was the result of subjectivism; it was in the excited imagination of the Spaniards, who dreamed of finding in the north the Mexico and Peru of the south, and in the light of their dreams read the friar's narrative. He had not found gold or silver, it is true; but he had found a fertile land and settled tribes living in large buildings. So the Seven Cities of romance were at last discovered. Images of vast palaces and great wealth floated before the eyes of his hearers. There was no difficulty in finding men and means for the occupation and conquest of the new country.

An expeditionary corps of three hundred Spaniards and eight hundred Indians was easily raised. The command was given by the viceroy Mendoza to Coronado. For a full account of this remarkable expedition and a minute identification of the route we refer the reader to Bandelier's "Gilded Man" or to H. H. Bancroft's "Arizona and New Mexico," the eighteenth volume of his work. The Zuni pueblos were reached in due time, and the sight of them brought to the leader and his followers bitterest disappointment, so far below their expectation was the reality; and brought to poor Father Mark bitterest reproaches from his fellow-explorers; for he was one of Coronado's followers. They did not stop to consider how far above his relation were their expectations, or how little their expectations were warranted by his relation. Coronado pushed his researches as far northwest as the Grand Cañon of the Colorado in Arizona, and as far northeast as the center of Kansas, according to Bandelier; as the boundary-line between Kansas and Nebraska, according to Bancroft. Finding the Seven Cities to be only Indian pueblos, he allowed himself to be lured by another fable on the authority of one or a few Indians. It was the fable of Gran Quivira, a large and wealthy city, that drew him to the northeast and brought him out on our great American plains. Quivira turned out to be only a group of Indian tepees inhabited by natives on the lookout for buffaloes. In the spring of 1542 Coronado returned to Mexico sick in body and disappointed in hopes. He had found no precious metals, no great cities, no wealthy kingdoms.

All returned with him save a few, and these had found what they came for. They came not for gold, cities, and kingdoms, but for souls to save, and, God willing, for the crown of martyrdom. They found the souls; why go back? And they found the martyrdom too. Three priests, Fathers Mark, John of Padilla, and John of the Cross, and one lay brother, Louis, were the ecclesiastical portion of Coronado's expedition. After Coronado had arrived at Cibola he sent back a small guard to Mexico to bring to Mendoza the report of his journey. Father Mark joined the returning guard, Bandelier says for reason of ill health, others say to escape from the taunts of his companions and from their attempts to wreak their vengeance on him for his exaggerated account of his previous journey. When Coronado took up his homeward march, Fathers John of the Cross and John of Padilla and lay brother Louis remained behind to preach the gospel to the natives. Father John of the Cross fixed his residence among the Indians near the present Bernalillo, and lay brother Louis near by. Nothing more was ever heard of them. We do not know for certain, but we may well conjecture that they fell victims to their zeal.

With Father John of Padilla remained as companions and volunteers for the mission a Portuguese, Andres del Campo, a mestizo or half-breed, and two Indians, Luke and Sebastian, who had been adopted by the monks in Mexico, perhaps had become members of the third Order of St. Francis, but at any rate were called "donados," the word meaning that they had devoted their lives to the service of the missionaries. In addition to these were two other free Indians and a negro. These men chose to remain with the friar and share his fate. The field of labor that John of Padilla selected was Quivira, whither he had accompanied Coronado. They reached the wigwams that bore that name in the summer months of the year 1542. The Quiviras received him gladly and listened to his teachings. His zeal thirsted for wider fields. In spite of the warnings of those among whom he dwelt in safety, he determined to visit other tribes. The determination cost him his life. He had not journeyed far when a band hostile to the Quiviras met him. Conscious now of the danger, and knowing that resistance was useless, that flight was out of the question, trusting that one victim might divert the attention and cruelty of the enemy from the rest, Padilla ordered his companions to flee and leave him alone. They complied regretfully and sorrowfully with the order; but before losing sight of him they saw him kneel to await the coming of the savages and receive the death-blow. They made their way back to the Quiviras and thence to Mexico, and thus the story of the death of Padilla has come down to us. Fifty years after the landing of Columbus the protomartyr of the church of the United States fell in Kansas, about six hundred miles west of the Mississippi. At this early date the cross had been carried by Catholic missionaries throughout the whole extent of our Southern States, from the Chesapeake, whither Ayllon went in 1526, to the Mississippi, reached by De Soto in the spring of 1542, the very year of Padilla's death; and from the Mississippi to the Colorado in northwestern Arizona, visited by one of Coronado's captains in 1540; and the cross had had its martyr.

The story of Coronado's expedition and Padilla's death seems to have faded from the memory of the Spaniards in Mexico, for no attempt was made in the direction of Cibola until the year 1581, almost forty years afterward. Their energies were spent in extending settlements in the northern provinces of Mexico, discovering and exploiting mines, and building cities. The most northern outpost in 1581 was San Bartolomeo. There lived a pious Franciscan lay brother, Augustine Rodriguez. He was seized with the desire to carry the gospel to the tribes of the north, of whom he heard much from the surrounding Indians, went to Mexico to plead the cause of those heathen savages still sitting in the shadow of unbelief, was heard favorably, received as companions two young fathers, Francis Lopez and John of St. Mary, and with them made his way to the country of the Pueblo Indians. They gave it the name it has borne since, and now bears—New Mexico. The mission prospered, and as the work was becoming too great for the small band, Father John was sent back to Mexico for more helpers. On the way he was surprised while asleep by roving Indians, and was killed. Of the two missionaries who were awaiting in New Mexico his return with recruits, Father Lopez was massacred by the savages and buried by his remaining companion, Brother Rodriguez. What became of the latter was for a long time unknown. It was only in 1626 that light was thrown on his fate. According to Father Salmeron, who was a missionary in New Mexico at that date and has left his "Relaciones," Rodriguez was killed soon after the death of Father Lopez. The field of their labors was in the neighborhood of Albuquerque.

The Franciscans of Mexico were naturally very anxious about the fate of their brethren who had departed for the north, and the viceroy deemed it proper that something should be done to ascertain what had become of them and to help them if still alive. A rich citizen of Mexico, Don Antonio Espejo, was willing to undertake the hazardous venture at his own expense. Gathering together a body of fourteen volunteer soldiers, a few native servants, horses and mules to carry provisions and arms, and taking as companion the Franciscan father Bernardino Beltran, he started, in 1582, on an expedition which, according to H. H. Bancroft, was productive of geographical results as substantial as the larger and more pompous journey of Coronado. But they did not find the three Franciscan missionaries alive; nor is it known that Father Beltran did any mission work on this expedition.

CHAPTER V.

THE SPANISH OCCUPATION OF NEW MEXICO—THE RISE AND DECLINE OF THE MISSIONS (1598–1848).

DON JUAN DE OÑATE, in whose veins ran the commingled blood of Cortez and Montezuma, obtained in 1588 a royal patent to occupy and settle New Mexico. However, it was ten years later (1598) that he finally overcame all the vexatious delays opposed to his project by the Mexican authorities, and was allowed to start by the viceroy. The expeditionary corps was made up of four hundred settlers and their families, a body of Spanish soldiers and Indian auxiliaries, and horses and cattle of various kinds. The missionary corps was composed of seven Franciscan fathers and two lay brothers under the superiorship of Father Martinez. On the frontier of the new province, the banks of the Rio del Norte, solemn possession of the country was taken in the name of Christ and of the king of Spain, and the first Spanish town of New Mexico, Real de San Juan, was founded and dedicated with fitting religious and civil ceremonies, thirty-three years after the foundation of St. Augustine in Florida.

From this center Father Martinez distributed his priests in the country round about, and the work of the New Mexican missions began. Naturally the beginnings were difficult, and the success was slow. In the spring Oñate sent back to Mexico a captain with his report of the occupation. Fathers Salazar and Martinez accompanied him to make their report to their superiors and ask for an increase of missionaries. Salazar died on the way, and Martinez, enfeebled by age and the hardships of a long life of labor in America, was retained in Mexico and replaced in the superiorship of the New Mexican missions by Father John de Escalona, who departed from the capital with six or eight additional fathers. With them went two hundred soldiers as reinforcement for the commander, Oñate.

Meanwhile he had moved his headquarters to a point west of the Rio Grande, near Ojo Caliente, where he founded the town of San Gabriel. The recruits reached this point in October, 1599. After their arrival Oñate selected an escort of eighty men to explore the country in the direction formerly followed by Coronado. During his absence disorder and discouragement fell upon those he left behind in San Gabriel. The unfriendly attitude of the natives, caused by ill treatment and outrages on their women at the hands of the idle Spaniards, the scantiness of food, brought about by prodigal waste and failure of the crops, disregard of authority, and mutiny, determined the colonists to break up the settlement and retreat to Mexico. Even some of the missionaries, under pretext that Oñate, so long absent, must be lost and should never return, joined the ranks of the discontented and departed with the larger number. The superior, Escalona, with a few of the braver Spaniards, remained at the post. It was well they did so; for shortly after the desertion Oñate rode in with his troop, sent in pursuit of the cowards, and what with threats and what with conciliation, persuaded them to return.

The settlement being restored, the work of the missions was resumed with new ardor. Already large numbers of Indians had embraced Christianity and had been baptized. By the year 1608 the baptisms amounted to eight thousand, and eight additional priests had come from Mexico with a new superior, Alonso Peinado. Santa Fé was founded in the year 1605, and became henceforth the center of Spanish dominion and missions in New Mexico. Among the missionaries who labored here at this early period one deserves special mention, Father Salmeron, who in 1618 took up his abode among the Jemes tribe, composed a catechism and other works in their language, and baptized sixty-five hundred of them during the eight years of his ministry.

In 1621 the missions of New Mexico, counting at that time sixteen thousand converts, were erected by the Franciscan chapter of Mexico into a custodia or guardianship under the title of the "Conversion of St. Paul." The first custodio or guardian was Alonso Benavides, who arrived from the south the following year (1622) with twenty-seven friars. In a short time the number of conversions grew rapidly, so abundant was the harvest from the blood of the early martyrs, so fervent the zeal of the living. The arduous and constant labors of the missions thinned the ranks of the laborers quickly. But by order of the king of Spain, to whom the lack of workmen and the promise of the harvest had been made known, thirty new friars and a number of lay brothers arrived in 1628–29. At this time Santa Fé had a population of two hundred and fifty Spaniards, seven hundred half-breeds, and some Indians. The church that Benavides found in the capital was but a small and unworthy hut. One of his first cares was to erect a convent and a church, which he describes as creditable anywhere.

About this time the commissary-general of the Franciscans residing in Mexico moved the question of naming a bishop for the province, which up to this date had been within the jurisdiction of the see of Guadalajara. The superior of the missions was vicar-general of the bishop, commissary of the holy office, and had from Leo X. and Adrian VI. the power of administering confirmation. Pius

V. in 1567 had decided that the missions and the settlements of whites were full canonical parishes in the sense of the Council of Trent. Here, unlike the missions of Florida, there were no seculars in charge of the whites, but all, Indians and whites, were in charge of the Franciscans. In 1620 the see of Durango was erected by Paul V., and henceforth New Mexico passed under the jurisdiction of the latter bishopric. In order to corroborate his request for a local bishop, the commissary-general, who, it must be remembered, was not and never had been on the ground, advanced exaggerated statistics of the Christianity of the province that the real facts do not bear out. A safer authority to follow is Benavides, who went in person to Spain and made to the king a report on the New Mexican missions, dated Madrid, 1630. Eighty thousand natives had been baptized since the beginning of evangelization; of these about thirty-five thousand were living, at the time of the report, in ninety pueblos, grouped about twenty-five missions or *conventos*, each pueblo having its church or chapel.[1] The missions or *conventos* must be understood as the residences of missionaries. Each residence had in charge one or more pueblos in its neighborhood.

During all these years new Spanish settlements were

[1] The number given here is an average of my own. Accounts vary. According to H. H. Bancroft, vol. xvii., p. 162, the report of Benavides shows that there were fifty friars serving sixty thousand Christianized natives in ninety pueblos, grouped around twenty-five conventos. Shea, "The Catholic Church in Colonial Days," p. 201, states: "In these missions Father Benavides assures us that eighty thousand had been baptized, and that in the territory of New Mexico there were forty-three churches." Again Bancroft, p. 172, says: "I close this chapter with a note from Vetancour's standard chronicle of the Franciscans, written about 1691, but showing the missions as they existed just before the revolt of 1680." There was at that time a total Christian population of twenty-four thousand, of whom twenty-four hundred were Spaniards. According to Bandelier, the population of New Mexico at the time of the Spanish occupation was no more than forty thousand, and in the year of the rebellion, 1680, no more than thirty thousand. Amid all these variations I feel safe enough in adopting the number thirty-five thousand; that is to say, the whole population was reckoned by the missionaries as being within the church.

being founded in the province. Spaniards, half-breeds, and Catholic Indians from the mother colony of Mexico were in constant intercourse with the New Mexican tribes; took lands among them, formed centers of trade, and married into them; not a little Castilian and Aztec blood commingled with that of the Pueblo Indians. For instance, a number of Tlascalan Indians came to Santa Fé, established a quarter there and built a church for their special use—San Miguel de los Tlascaltecos. With those colonists came into the New Mexican legends and traditions traces of Tenoctitlan's vanished fame, of Aztec story, of Montezuma and his glory. This gave rise to the theory adopted by some students of ethnology that the Aztecs had originally emigrated from the parent Pueblo tribes of New Mexico, and had carried away with them from the frowning cliffs and mesas and fortresses of the north the traditions they immortalized in the valley of Mexico. In reality the connection was the other way. Not a few historical conclusions rest on just such a wrong method of induction.

From 1650 to 1680 is the palmy period of the New Mexican missions. As many as sixty members of the Order of St. Francis at one time were in the field, and it seemed as if no storm could uproot from the soil the great tree of Catholicity which they had planted, watered with their blood, and tended with their labors. Yet grievous dangers, even in that period of prosperity, were on the horizon, threatening to overwhelm the glorious work with ruin. Of those dangers some lay within the New Mexican church and some without.

No church has lasted long that remained in the mission state, deprived of the church's normal apostolic organization, bishop, and diocesan clergy. Regulars are the providential initiators and creators of the church in pagan lands from the days of St. Benedict down to our own time; but they are not the divinely appointed maintainers and preservers of the church. They blaze the way and make the road for the hierarchy and the diocesan army. The history of missions proves this truth abundantly. Now New Mexico not only had no resident bishop, but was only nominally under the jurisdiction of one far distant. We do not read that he had attempted to make his nominal jurisdiction real, and we shall see a little later on that when he did make the attempt, he met with violent opposition from the Franciscans. This condition of things was a source of weakness and a danger.

The king of Spain, and the viceroy of Mexico, acting under orders of the king, deserve unstinted praise for the protection they always gave to the work of the church among the American natives conquered by Spanish arms. More than protection did Spain give—money and means in abundance for the glory of God and the furtherance of his kingdom among the benighted pagans of the New World. Her flag was in the breeze wherever the cross was raised, her helmeted soldier was to be found at the side of her missionary. The Spanish nation ever believed that it had a duty to God and man to perform in the dominions given it by Providence; and nobly, generously, with such means and in such way it knew and thought proper, did it fulfill the duty. But such a close union of church and state, more than any other relation we can imagine, demands to be carried out with prudence, loyalty, and mutual respect, in order that the agents of both be inspired and guided by the true spirit of the church and the true spirit of a Christian nation.

Precisely in the intermediate agencies is the fatal rock on which that ideal relation finds its wrecking. Perfect churchmen and perfect statesmen are rare; so rare that a Leo and a Charlemagne are as an oasis in history. There were dissensions, frequent and bitter, in Santa Fé, between the civil power, the governor, and the ecclesiastical power, the father guardian, superior of the missions. For instance, in 1664 Governor Penalosa arrested and imprisoned the superior, was summoned to Mexico before the Inquisition for his act, and was condemned to make reparation. Such dissensions were a danger, for they brought contempt on both powers in the eyes of the Indians, with whom medicine-man and cacique were sacred. I need scarcely add that the Spanish settlers were not always models of the Christian morality they professed. Indians, as other men more civilized, choose to forget the frailty of man, and, in matters of religion, judge the tree by its fruit. These dangers were internal to the New Mexican church.

Without the church one danger was to be found in the neighboring tribes of savages; the other lurked amid the Pueblo Indians themselves. The savage tribes from whose attacks the great communal houses of the semicivilized Pueblo Indians, with their strong high walls, were fortresses and places of refuge are classed under the general name of Apaches. H. H. Bancroft [1] enumerates the many divisions of this people. Prominent among them are tribes that until late times were the terror of the southwestern territories—the Comanches, the Yutes, the Navajos, the Mojaves, the Yumas. Their occupation was to pounce upon the quiet pueblos and *conventos*, carry off what they could, and retreat into the impregnable gorges and cañons, or the still more impregnable cliffs of the mountainous districts. These wild thieves were the dread of the Christian missions. Many the church and convent they burned to the ground, many the Christian Indian they carried into captivity. The missionaries lived in constant fear of those Bedouins of the West.

[1] "The Native Races," vol. i., chap. v.

But the greatest danger to the missions lay in the New Mexican converts themselves. Though the greater number were Christians, and the majority of the Christians were baptized members of the church, yet not all realized in their lives the teachings of the gospel. Many were in reality pagans, who clung to their old superstitions and religious rites with the greater tenacity that so many of their fellow-tribesmen had renounced them, and that they were driven to secrecy to keep up the fierce religion of their forefathers. The paganism and its rites were kept alive and escaped the watchfulness of the authorities by two means: secret societies under the lead of medicine-men, and secret places of meeting. This very secrecy and impunity were strong temptations which even the better Christians could not resist. And so, even among the members of the church, beneath the outward appearances of Christian living and conduct the old leaven was not dead, but was at work ready to break forth in favorable circumstances.

The place in which the Indians met for their heathen ceremonies was the estufa, or the sweat-house. Every village had from one to six of these places. It was a large subterranean room, at once bath-house, town-house, council chamber, club-room, and temple. It was situated either in the great building or underground in the courtyard between the buildings. At Jemez the estufa is one story, twenty-five feet wide and thirty feet high. The ruins of Chettro Kettle contain six estufas, each two or three stories in height. At Bonito are estufas one hundred and seventy-five feet in circumference. Here the chiefs met for secret council and worship of the gods.

It is from this cryptopaganism that came the ruin of the missions in 1680. No doubt the love of liberty, the desire to shake off the hated yoke of the Spanish master, had much to do with the rebellion; but it was founded more largely still on religious grounds. The Pueblo Indians, more than the other American tribes, were attached to their aboriginal religion, and had secretly continued its practice. Friars and governors had done their best to stamp out every vestige of it, using to some extent physical punishment for alleged sorcery and communion with the devil, as also for plotting with the Apaches; for it is not to be denied that the haters of Christianity were willing to ally themselves with their inveterate foes to encompass its destruction. In 1680, and for a few years preceding, the whole province was covered with a network of hidden conspiracy.

Some faithful Indians gave repeated warnings to the missionaries, and they in turn warned the governor. He was slow to believe, and, at the first evidences that he was taking precautions, the insurrection broke out at once on all sides. It was the plan of the New Mexicans to exterminate the Spaniards, and none was spared save the most beautiful of the women and girls, reserved for a worse fate than death. Twenty-one missionaries and four hundred Spaniards fell in the first onslaught. Those who could escape sought refuge in Santa Fé, where they were besieged during five days by thousands of infuriated Indians. The brave governor, Otermin, seeing no way to salvation but a sortie and a retreat to the Mexican frontier, gathered in a body the one thousand Spaniards crouching behind the walls, and at their head led them forth to whatever fate awaited them. Of the one thousand scarcely one hundred and fifty were armed. Fortunately the Indians let them pass on without an attack, perhaps from fear of Spanish valor, or from hope of being able to make short work of them after a few days' march should have weakened them, or from unwillingness to shed more blood now that they beheld their wish fulfilled—the departure from their land of the detested conquerors.

In a few weeks no Spaniard was in New Mexico north of El Paso. Christianity and civilization were swept away at one blow; churches and convents were burned and razed to the ground; sacred vessels were destroyed or carried off and profaned. The leader of the rebellion, a great medicine-man, Pope by name, proceeded to play, all unwittingly, the part of Antichrist. He forbade the naming of Jesus, Mary, and the saints, decreed that men should put away their legitimate wives and take others to their liking, that none should wear crosses or rosaries, that all be cleansed of baptism by the use of water and soapweed, that the baptismal names be dropped, that the estufas be reopened for the old ceremonies, that the Spanish language be no longer used, and that none but native crops be cultivated and raised. History cannot show a more consummate persecutor, small as is the scale on which he worked. It reminds one, *si parva licet componere magnis*, of Diocletian and his *Nomine Christiano deleto.*

All went well while the excitement of the change lasted. But punishment soon overtook the renegade nation, as, indeed, some of the missionaries, slowly dying amid the tortures only Indian cruelty can invent, had predicted. Pope became a tyrant whose small finger lay heavier than the arm of Spain. Civil discords and bitter wars followed between the tribes. The Apaches saw their chance and came down on them in the midst of their dissensions. Some of the tribes abandoned their former homes and emigrated elsewhere. Nature itself took up arms against them; the streams ran dry; irrigation, without which there can be no cultivation in that country, was neglected. Drought brought on failure of crops and famine. The great Pueblo nation, so prosperous under the flag of Spain, broke to pieces; tribes disappeared, others were reduced. Many of the ruins that now cover the land date from this period, and barbarism darker than that of the aboriginal times seemed to settle on the unfortunate apostates. Meanwhile the refugee soldiers of Spain and of the cross gathered on the frontier at El Paso, awaiting the opportunity to return, in the hope that the natives, prompted to revolt and apostasy by the devil and a few sorcerers, would soon see the error of their ways and be eager for pardon and peace.

The period of growth and prosperity since Oñate's conquest was of eighty-two years' duration (1598–1680). Then followed the rebellion, and twelve years of retreat at El Paso on the part of the Spaniards, of suffering and disorder on the part of the Indians (1680–92). Then came the reconquest and restoration, and a period of tranquillity for the Christian missions of one hundred and fifty years, from 1692 to 1846, when New Mexico ceased to be Spanish, became American, and entered into the church of the United States. We now enter on a brief study of this latter period. The sources and authorities are not so abundant as for the former, nor did the missions attain the prosperity and numbers of that period.

To such a state of weakness had the New Mexican Indians come that the reconquest was an easy affair. In August, 1692, the new governor, De Vargas, set out from El Paso with sixty Spanish soldiers, one hundred Indian auxiliaries, and three missionaries. Santa Fé was occupied by a large body of the rebels. At first they made a show of resistance; but, being assured of pardon on condition of returning to the church, they yielded, were absolved from apostasy, and their children born during the rebellion were baptized. This one instance may stand for what happened at all the pueblos reached during the expedition. On October 16th of that year De Vargas reported to the viceroy that he had reconquered all the Pueblos for thirty-six leagues around the capital, and that one thousand children born in rebellion had been baptized. A month later other Pueblos submitted on the same terms. At Zuni a fact was discovered that shows that all faith had not died out during the twelve years of revolt, but that some Indians remained secretly faithful. Here the sacred vessels had been reverentially saved and preserved, and candles were found burning on an altar in a hidden room. By the month of December De Vargas returned to El Paso. He did not feel safe with the small force at his command, or able to hold the ground he had gained; nor could the submission of the tribes be called anything else than a mere formality so long as the Spaniards did not remain in the country.

One year after (October, 1693) he set out from El Paso with one hundred soldiers, seven hundred settlers, and seventeen Franciscan friars. This time he had to storm the capital and drive out the Indian occupants by force of arms and with much bloodshed. The year was spent in military expeditions in all directions to bring the savages to submission. It was only by the end of 1694 that De Vargas was able to notify the superior of the missions that he might with safety distribute the missionaries among the Pueblos and once more set them to work. Churches and convents had to be rebuilt, the missionaries meanwhile using temporary quarters. The natives had finally made up their minds to submit to the inevitable until a more favorable opportunity should present itself. The missionaries were well aware of this suppressed feeling. In the spring of 1696 the superior warned the governor, called his attention to the defenseless condition of the missions, and asked for details of guards. But, believing that the natives had submitted in good faith, and that the suspicions and fears of the custodio were based on idle rumors, the governor took no precaution, and sarcastically advised the fathers whom fear should overcome to seek refuge in safe places among the Spanish settlers.

The insurrection did come. Six tribes rose, killed five missionaries, some Spaniards, and fled to the mountains. Then followed, in the last year of De Vargas's governorship and the first years of his successor's term (Cubero) a succession of military expeditions to reduce the rebels, during which the work of the missions was more or less at a standstill. It was only in the year 1700 that the submission of New Mexico may be said to have become permanent. The natives were too few and weak, the Spanish and Mexican settlers too numerous, for any successful movement of revolt. Past experience had taught the civil and ecclesiastical powers to live in peace; the Apaches, no less than the Pueblo Indians, had suffered from the trials and struggles of the last twenty years, and were held in check by the increased Spanish power; the heathenish rites and secret ceremonies of the estufas were firmly held in abeyance by the combined watchfulness and action of the custodio and the governor, though here, as elsewhere, eternal vigilance was a necessity, and when the vigilance relaxed the aboriginal superstition would break out fitfully among the tribes.

One tribe there was, the powerful Moqui in Arizona, that stood out from the general submission, and refused to come back to the Christian faith. In October, 1700, they proposed to the governor this treaty of peace, that each nation, Spanish and Moqui, should retain its own religion. But Cubero could allow peace but on condition of return to Christianity. Then the Moqui offered a compromise, that the missionaries should make among them no permanent stay, but visit each one of their pueblos for six years only. Naturally this was rejected as indignantly as the former proposition. War was made at intervals on the audacious tribe, but they held their forts and their old religion. The example, the success, and the counsels of the Moqui excited the Zunis to the same line of conduct, and it may be said that Christianity never regained over them, after the insurrection of 1680, the sway it had before. Thus the two most powerful tribes of the country were lost to the church, the Moqui entirely, the Zunis at least partially.

The archive record for the first half of the eighteenth century is meager and fragmentary. The succession of governors, an occasional political controversy, periodical renewals of efforts to bring back the Moqui to the gospel, some not very important expeditions into the plains or the mountains, rare intercourse with the Texan establishments, fears of French and English encroachments, a few reports of mission progress or decadence, make up the annals of this period.

Of these latter the most important is the account of a visitation of the missions by the Bishop of Durango, Rt. Rev. Benedict Crespo, in 1725. At El Paso and Santa Fé, Spanish settlements, he exercised his functions and administered confirmation without any opposition. But when he would extend his offices to the Pueblo missions, the friars and their superior, under instructions from headquarters in Mexico, objected. The bishop appointed an ecclesiastical judge to reside in the province and to take cognizance in his name of ecclesiastical affairs; again objection was made, and the jurisdiction of the delegated judge was only partially recognized. Thereupon the bishop, in order to compel recognition of his episcopal rights, instituted proceedings against the Franciscan superiors in Mexico under whose order those of New Mexico were opposing him.

At the same time he preferred grave charges against the

missionaries, and chiefly that they did not learn the native languages; that the Indians, rather than confess through an interpreter, did not confess at all, except at the point of death; that the failure to reconvert the Moqui was the fault of the missionaries; that some of them neglected their duties and others caused scandal by their conduct; that the tithes were not properly collected or expended. These charges, if true, prove how absolutely imperative was the need of a resident bishop and a diocesan native clergy in New Mexico. The Christian church had been in existence there a century and a half, but no effort seems to have been made to recruit its clergy from the native population; the Franciscans were all imported from Mexico, and were, for the most part, born in Spain.

The charges were supported by the sworn testimony of twenty-four prominent officials and residents, themselves Spaniards. Of course the missionaries denied the charges, and supported the denial by the sworn testimony of other officials and Spanish colonists. The controversy was referred to the court of Spain. Pending the examination, a royal order sustained the rights of the bishop. We have no evidence that a contrary decision was ever reached or published. The successor of the Rt. Rev. Benedict Crespo in the see of Durango, Bishop Martin de Elizacoechea, made a visitation of New Mexico in 1737, seemingly without any opposition. A record of his visit is graven on Inscription Rock, near Rio Zuni. It runs: "On the 28th day of September, 1737, The Most Illustrious Dr. Don Martin Elizacoechea, Bishop of Durango, arrived here, and on the 29th he proceeded to Zuni." Beyond this we have no account of the details of the visitation.

Three authorities of this period—viz., Villasenor's "Teatro-Mexicano," published in 1748, and reproduced in "Spanish Empire in America," London, 1847; Manchero's manuscript Report of 1744; and Bonilla's "Apuntes," also in manuscript—give some statistics and general information as to the condition of New Mexico at the time. The Spanish population was 3779, distributed between the following towns: Santa Fé, Santa Cruz de la Canada, Albuquerque, Concepcion or Fuenclara; and the following ranchos: Chama, Santa Rosa, Abiquiu, Ojo Caliente, Soldedad, Embudo, Bocas, Alameda. The number of Christian Indians was 12,142, living in the following missions, each mission having one resident missionary: Taos, Jicarilla, Picuries, St. Juan, Santa Cruz, St. Ildefonso, Santa Clara, Tesuque and Pajuaque, Nambe, Pacos, Galisteo, Cochiti, Santo Domingo, St. Felipe, Jemes, Santa Anna, Cia, Laguna, Acoma, Zuni, Isleta, Sandia.

The sources for the history of the missions in the latter half of the eighteenth century are more abundant, but they deal with details so minute that they are of small value for a general account such as I intend making. Yet they throw some light on the mission system, the condition of the Pueblo Indians and the Franciscan friars. In the year 1760 Bishop Tamaron of Durango made a visit to the province and met with no opposition. He confirmed 11,271 persons. This large number of confirmations in a population of 12,142 goes to show that the very great majority of Christian Indians had never been confirmed, even supposing that many of the confirmed were Mexicans. About 1780 famine and pestilence swept the Moqui pueblos. In 1775 they contained 7494 souls; disease reduced them to 798 before the end of the century. A few among them thought this fearful decimation a judgment of God for their obstinacy in apostasy; some thirty families went over to the Spanish settlements and to Christianity; but the remainder declared that if annihilation of their race was to come, they preferred to die in their old home and faith. At the same time smallpox carried off 5100 Indians of the mission pueblos.

In addition to those physical evils there were others, which Padre Juan Agustin Morfi, not a resident of New Mexico, has made known in a manuscript document. The evils he mentions are the lack of order in the Spanish settlements, their houses being scattered, the settlers being beyond the reach of law and religion and exposed to the raids of Indians; a vicious system of trade and dearth of money; the free admission of Spaniards in Indian pueblos, the result being that these adventurers put the Indians into debt and practically make them slaves or drive them to the pagan tribes; and the oppressive tyranny of the Spanish officials. Allowing himself to be carried away by his special pleading, Padre Morfi declares that the New Mexicans are much worse off than they were before the coming of the Spaniards, or than the Moqui, who have maintained their independence. This is too severe.

A minute study of all the sources at hand goes to show that the missionaries could not be charged with cruel treatment of the natives nor with substituting trading to their spiritual duties. But the accusation made against them at a former date stands also at this time, viz., that they neglected to learn the native languages and use them in the instruction of the Indians. Bishop Tamaron, in his visit of 1760, administered severe rebuke on this score. He offered to print at his expense manuals of prayers in the native languages, if the friars would write them. Some promises were made, but no practical result came of them. It was a mistake, committed chiefly by the civil masters of New Mexico, and by them forced on the missionaries, to ignore the vernacular dialects and impose on the Indians the Spanish tongue. This policy had been successful in Mexico, and, not foreseeing that they should ever lose

New Mexico, the Spanish conquerors believed that with time they could make the same policy successful there also. We can see how this hope justified them in their own eyes; but meanwhile the New Mexicans learned to hate the faith that came to them in a foreign garb, and were Christians only in appearance and name, since they could not understand its teachings sufficiently. Yet they loved the padre, so different from the other Spaniards, for he was kind-hearted, a friend of his flock, spending much of the salary the government gave him on them and their churches.

The statistics for the end of the century show a decadence among the Indians. Official reports of 1760 show that the number of the Spaniards had increased to 7666; that of the Indians had decreased to 9104. In the final decade of the century the Spanish population was 18,826, the Indian population, 9732. There were eighteen missions and twenty-four missionaries.

The nineteenth century opened unfavorably for Spain. Bonaparte forced the abdication of the king and put his brother Joseph on the Spanish throne. Confusion prevailed; religion suffered in all the American colonies of Spain.

For the history of New Mexico during the first quarter of the present century the chief authorities are the "Exposicion Sucinta" (Cadiz, 1820), a report of Pedro Bautista Pino, first deputy from New Mexico to the Spanish Cortes; and the "Accounts of Travels of Zebulon M. Pike," a lieutenant of the United States army commissioned to explore the countries of the Red and Arkansas rivers, and arrested by the Spanish authorities as trespassing on their territory. Very little, however, can be gleaned from them regarding the missions. Pino solicited from the Cortes the establishment of a bishopric at Santa Fé, with a college and a system of schools. The order was given for the bishopric, though it was never executed. However, diocesan priests were introduced to take charge of the Mexican settlements in spite of the protest of the Franciscans, and the vicars-general of the Bishops of Durango were doing their best to arrest the decay of religion. The political disorders and revolutions of the times in Spain, Mexico, and the New Mexican colony counteracted all their endeavors. Religious decadence set in. The church of New Mexico had leaned so long on the arm of the state that it knew not how to stand and walk alone when the support gave way.

In 1821 Mexico became independent of Spain, and when Iturbide fell proclaimed itself a republic. The colony New Mexico accepted the fortunes of the parent colony. In January, 1822, its republican birth was celebrated in Santa Fé with great festivity. During this period some schools were established, the first printing-press was introduced, and the first Mexican newspaper was published in 1835—the "Crepusculo," the editor being Padre Martinez. The priests now generally resided in the Spanish settlements, and the Pueblo missions became only out-stations visited occasionally. The report of Dr. Rascon (1830), the vicar-general of the Bishop of Durango, presents a melancholy picture. Churches and priests' residences were falling into ruin, vestments were old, altar-plate scanty; the people, not accustomed formerly to support religion by their own means, could not be induced to do it now; many died without the last sacraments.

The Mexican Congress of 1823 and 1836 talked of putting into execution the order of the Spanish Cortes in regard to the establishment of a bishopric, but nothing was done. In 1833 and 1845 the Bishop of Durango visited the province, but we have no details that might relieve the dark picture drawn by Rascon. The white population had doubled, the

Indian slightly decreased. The total in 1845 was not far from eighty thousand, of which sixty thousand were whites. There were but seventeen priests. Now nothing proves so well how neglected religion was than this disproportion between the population and the clergy. A renewal of life and vigor came to this desolate church when New Mexico became part of the United States, which happy consummation was brought about by the treaty of Guadalupe Hidalgo (1848).

CHAPTER VI.

THE MISSIONS IN ARIZONA AND TEXAS.

ARIZONA (aboriginal, Arizonac) is the name of a mountain range on the frontier line between the present Territory of Arizona and the Mexican province of Sonora, and was applied in the eighteenth century to a Spanish mining-camp in that vicinity. No province of the name was known in Spanish and Mexican times. The early explorers, Father Mark of Nizza, Coronado, Oñate, and Espejo, penetrated into this region. Oñate was the first to visit the Moqui pueblos of the cañon of the Colorado; not, indeed, himself, but the lieutenants whom he detailed to the west of his main line of march. That portion of our present Territory of Arizona lying south of the Gila River was not, in the days of Spanish dominion, a portion of New Mexico, but belonged to Sonora, the northwestern province of the present republic of Mexico, and went by the name of Pimeria Alta: the portion north of the Gila River was known as the Moqui district, named thus from the most prominent Indian tribe dwelling therein. This latter portion was in the province of New Mexico, and was under the civil and ecclesiastical jurisdiction of Santa Fé. After Oñate's conquest the Moqui accepted Christianity from the Franciscans, and were faithful to the new religion until the insurrection of 1680, after which date they never returned to the church, as we have explained in the preceding chapter. We shall deal with the missions in both those portions now constituting the Territory of Arizona.

Father Kino (Spanish for Kühn), from the Mexican province of Sonora, where the Jesuits had flourishing missions, was the first to establish within the boundaries of the present Territory of Arizona, outside the Moqui district, two missions, St. Miguel de Guevavi and St. Francis Xavier del Bac, between Tombstone and Tucson. This was in the year 1687.

He was a most remarkable man, full of energy, and of a zeal that no obstacles could discourage. He learned the different languages of the country, translated the catechism and prayers, composed vocabularies for his fellow-laborers and successors, built houses and chapels, selected sites for missions and towns, traveled more than twenty thousand miles, and baptized thousands—according to Clavigero, forty-eight thousand. On his journeys he carried for food only parched corn, never omitted to say mass, never slept in a bed, and communed constantly with God in prayer or the chanting of psalms and hymns. In a word, he was the Francis Xavier of northern Mexico. As he traversed southern and western Arizona in every direction, he gave saints' names to many places; not that he established missions, but that he hoped the places he named after the saints might become the seats of future missions. In reality, he established within the present limits of the United States only the two missions I have named. He was rather a forerunner and explorer than a resident missionary on our soil. He died in 1711.

It was only in 1732 that two fathers were sent to reside at St. Francis Xavier del Bac and St. Miguel de Guevavi, which became centers of missionary work in the outlying country, and remained under the care of the Jesuits until the suppression and expulsion of the society by the Spanish government in 1767. These central missions and many of the stations had neat adobe churches well supplied with church vestments and vessels, and religious instruction was given in the languages of the natives.

The Moqui, after Oñate's conquest of New Mexico, received the faith from Franciscan missionaries, renounced it during the insurrection of 1680, and never afterward returned to it. The Jesuits, working in Arizona, were anxious to gain back this powerful tribe, and the Moqui were better disposed toward them than toward the Franciscans, back of whom were the military authorities of Santa Fé and of Spain, the main object of their dread and hatred. But the Franciscans were by no means inclined to allow the Jesuits this encroachment in a field that had been their own from the beginning. They must then bestir themselves to make some effort to regain the apostate Moqui. In 1742 two Franciscan missionaries, unaccompanied by any escort of soldiers, made their way to the Moqui towns, and persuaded over four hundred of the Indians to abandon their fortresses and come with them to pueblos nearer the Spanish settlements. Again, in 1745, the Franciscans sent three of their number on a missionary tour through the Moqui district. The Jesuits had offered to convert those Indians, provided the missionaries were guarded by the military; and for a time the king of Spain favored their proposal. But surely, if a few Franciscans, unescorted, without drawing on the royal treasury, could bring out four hundred converts, the Moqui were not so terrible and heathenish a tribe as represented. The previous concessions were withdrawn from the Jesuits, and the viceroy was ordered to support the rights of the Franciscans in the disputed district. We have seen that finally they did not succeed in reclaiming the Arizona tribe.

After the suppression of the Jesuits, the Spanish government turned over the missions of Sonora, and the not inconsiderable property the Jesuits owned in that province, to the Franciscan missionary college of Queretaro, in Mexico. With this transfer went the missions of Arizona. Henceforth we must seek for the history of the Arizona missions in the chronicles of the Santa Cruz College of Queretaro. St. Francis Xavier del Bac was committed in 1768 to the care of Padre Garces. The mission was deserted; the neophytes were scattered and had forgotten their religion. They consented to return if not compelled to work. The official report of 1772 shows a population of two hundred and seventy, and describes the church as moderately capacious and poorly furnished. The present fine church at Bac was completed in 1797. The mission has no later recorded history. From about 1828 there was no resident missionary there. The mission of Guevavi, called in Jesuit times San Miguel and in Franciscan times Santos Angeles, had, at the time these latter came into possession, about one hundred and twenty neophytes. The church was a humble building, and the place was frequently raided by the Apaches. Guevavi has disappeared from our maps. One of its out-stations, San José (Tumacacori) became the central mission. The ruins of Tumacacori are still to be seen near Tubac. I forbear mentioning the smaller stations that depended on those two central missions.

There is, however, one place in Arizona that in our day has become the see of a bishopric, and has a record in the mission period; I mean Tucson. The capital of Arizona lays claim to a high antiquity. Roberts, "With the Invader," p. 116, says: "Tucson is an ancient city. Antedating Jamestown and Plymouth, it was visited by Coronado in 1540, inhabited by Europeans in 1560, and had its first missionaries in 1581. But long before 1540 there was an Indian village on the site of the present city, so that Tucsonians can, if they please, claim an age for their town as great as the Santa Féans claim for theirs." But the truth is, Tucson is not heard of in Spanish annals, even as an Indian rancheria, till the middle of the eighteenth century (1750), and was not properly a Spanish settlement till the presidio was moved there at a still later date. In 1763 it was a station depending on the mission of Bac, and in the last years of Jesuit control it contained three hundred and thirty-one Indians. In 1772 it had neither church nor priest's residence. The Apaches did great damage to the village, for in 1774 it contained only eighty families. At that time, through the efforts of Padre Garces, a pueblo was built, also a church and a priest's house, and the presidio formerly at Tubac was transferred to Tucson. Then (1776) it became a Spanish settlement. The annals of the place are a blank for many years; practically so down to 1840.

Of the Franciscans who succeeded the Jesuits the best known is Padre Garces, who, like the famous Jesuit Kino, became a great traveler in Arizona in the interests of the gospel. The conquest of Upper California to the church by the zealous band of the saintly Serra was an incentive to their Franciscan brothers laboring in the field of Arizona. At that time there was in the presidio of Tubac a military officer who, influenced by the descriptions he heard from Padre Garces, was convinced that the easiest route from Mexico to California was to be found through Arizona. He was allowed by the Mexican home authorities to put his project in execution. Garces accompanied the exploring party of thirty-five men as chaplain. The result of this exploration was entirely satisfactory to the authorities, and it was decided to open up a route through Arizona to California, and protect it by a series of military posts. The Franciscans of Queretaro resolved likewise to push their missionary work in the same direction, and effect a junction with their brothers in California at a point on the Colorado River. But the two missions established there had a short existence. In 1781 the neighboring tribes swooped down upon them, massacred soldiers and missionaries, destroyed and burned churches and presidios; the overland route was abandoned, and communication between Mexico and California continued to take the ocean route.

There is a great lack of record as to the missions of Arizona from 1800 to the time of its annexation to the United States, December, 1853, when the treaty was signed, or 1855, when it was approved. With the Spanish dominion ends the history of the Spanish missions in Arizona; henceforth they become part of the church of the United States.

To the east of New Mexico lay Texas. No definite boundary between them was marked, nor was any definite line drawn to delimitate the French territory lying east of the Spanish province of New Mexico between Texas and Florida. The French did not recognize the Mississippi as a frontier line, and since settlements of both nations did not come into close contact, the delimitation remained vague. The present boundary between Mexico and Texas is the Rio del Norte. South of that river are the Mexican provinces of Nuevo-Leon and Coahuila. This latter was the basis of the military and missionary operations into the country north of the Rio del Norte in the days of Spanish domination. The theater of those operations was not the whole of our Texas, but only its southwestern quarter, as the geographical nomenclature of that State indicates.

In the beginning of the sixteenth century, when Spain was the only European power that claimed and explored the present United States, all the land south of 40° latitude went by the name of Florida. It was to explore Florida that Narvaez sailed (1528), and got wrecked on the Texan coast. De Soto (1541–42) marched through northeasten Texas. In the same year Coronado started from New Mexico in search of Quivira, passing through northwestern Texas. Oñate (1599) followed in the tracks of Coronado, searching, like him, for fabled Quivira. Penalosa, governor of Santa Fé, if we are to take his account, about the trustworthiness of which there is some doubt, marched to the Mississippi in 1662. These are the earliest recorded passages of the Spaniards over Texan soil. The word "Texas," according to H. H. Bancroft, was the name of a tribe, in Spanish, Tejas; according to Shea, it was the aboriginal salutation with which the Spaniards were greeted in that territory, and means "friends."

In 1682 La Salle descended the Mississippi to its mouth. In 1687 he sailed with a fleet from France to establish there a fort and connect the Gulf of Mexico with the St. Lawrence by a series of military posts, thus giving to France control of the interior of the continent. The plan was spoiled by the incompetence or the ill fortune of the naval commander of the fleet. The pilot missed the mouth of the Mississippi, passed beyond it, and the colony was landed on the Texan coast in the present Metagorda Bay, called at the time by the French St. Louis Bay, and later by the Spaniards Espiritu Santo, and also San Bernardo. La Salle was murdered by his own men, and the ill-fated colony lingered and was decimated by death and the Indians until it vanished entirely. Now a deserter from this colony, known, in Spanish, annals by the name of Juan Enrique, made his way southward into the province of Coahuila, was forwarded to Mexico, and told the story of the occupation by the French of what was considered in Mexico as Spanish territory. In consequence Alonso de Leon, governor of Coahuila, was ordered by the Mexican authorities to reconnoiter, expel the intruders, and make good Spain's claim.

This expedition (1689) is the beginning of the Spanish domination and missions in the present State of Texas.[1] With the governor went a Franciscan, Damian Mazanet, with three friars from the apostolic college of Queretaro. The first mission established was called San Francisco de Los Texas. Leaving there his two companions, he returned to Coahuila for more missionaries, and in 1691 came back with nine fathers. The diary of Mazanet ending at this date, we have no further particulars; but it is well ascertained that the missions were abandoned, and that the missionaries departed in 1693 for want of coöperation and protection from the military authorities.

However, the work was resumed in 1716, at which time four missions, and a presidio to protect them from hostile tribes, were established in southwestern Texas, between the Trinity and the Red rivers. The small band of missionaries, five in number, were under the lead of the venerable Father Anthony Margil, who had founded at Zacatecas, in the Mexican state of that name, an apostolic

[1] H. H. Bancroft assigns the year 1689 as the beginning of the Spanish occupation and missions of Texas, and the year 1729 as the foundation of San Antonio. A writer in the "Annual Report of the American Historical Association" (1891) claims that there was an expedition into Texas in 1675 under command of Fernando del Bosque, accompanied by three Franciscan fathers. There is still an earlier date, according to this writer. Father Francisco Freyes makes the colonization of Texas to begin in 1630. A still earlier expedition—that of Urdinola—came to Texas, according to the same writer, in 1575 or 1576; that is to say, thirteen years before Oñate's conquest and occupation of New Mexico. The authority advanced for the above assertions is the archives of Saltillo. Now there is indeed a Saltillo in Texas, but there is also a Saltillo in Coahuila, Mexico. Bancroft gives its history ("New Mexican States and Texas," vol. xv., p. 126). It was the seat of a Franciscan convent; it was founded in 1582, erected into a municipality in 1586. Urdinola was sent thither in 1592 with a military corps of four hundred Tlascaltecs. This Saltillo became later on the basis of military and missionary expeditions into our present State of Texas. The expeditions mentioned above on the authority of Saltillo's archives had for theater northeastern Mexico, not our State of Texas.

college similar to that of Queretaro for the supply of the missions. The missions in charge of the Queretaro friars were San Francisco, on the river known as Trinidad, Purissima Concepcion, eight or nine leagues northeast of San Francisco, Guadalupe, San José, Dolores, and San Miguel de Cuellar. Later on, in 1731, the missions of San Francisco, Concepcion, and San José were united and transferred to San Antonio, near the presidio of Bejar, under whose protection they were. The southern missions were in charge of the friars of Zacatecas and under the protection of the presidio of Pilar.

"The illustrious servant of God," says Shea, "Anthony Margil of Jesus, is one of the most remarkable men in the history of the church in America, whether we regard his personal sanctity, the gifts with which he was endowed, or the extent and importance of his labors for the salvation of souls. His life has been subjected to the rigid scrutiny and discussion of a process of canonization at Rome, so that no national or local exaggeration can be suspected." He pushed his field of work beyond the present State of Texas into Louisiana, founded the mission of San Miguel de Linares, near the sheet of water still called Spanish Lake, in Natchitoches County, and gave to the French of Natchitoches, some fifty miles east of San Miguel, on the Red River, the opportunity of receiving the sacraments, for which kindness the vicar-general of Mobile sent him thanks.

Minute details of the founding, the transferring, and the abandoning of the various missions cannot be given in a general history such as this. We are to conclude from a study of the facts that the missions of Texas were less successful than those in any of the other Spanish provinces. For this there are many reasons. The wandering hostile tribes, Apaches and others, who would not bear sedentary life, or any yoke whatsoever of civilization, were a constant danger. In some missions the small number, in others the total lack, of the military left them open to raids and ruin. The numerous tribes of Texas, the torment of the student at this day, each speaking its own dialect, were an obstacle to the success of the missionaries. After years of experience they had concluded that the only means to overcome this difficulty was to gather various cognate tribes into reservations, on the plan of the Jesuit reductions of Paraguay, and impose on them one common language. But to effect this vast project constant coöperation of the military was needed; and not only was it insufficient, but it was ever grudgingly given. The most serious cause of failure was the misunderstanding between the officers and the missionaries. The missionaries found themselves dependent on the good or the ill will of the military commanders of the presidios. Distance from the central government and difficulty of communication between the center and the extremities have a tendency to make subalterns arbitrary toward inferiors and irresponsible toward superiors. Not only the military failed to give to the missionaries the protection needed, but they often misappropriated the stores and means that should have been devoted to the maintenance of the missions.

In 1729 the Spanish town of San Fernando was founded, close to the mission of San Antonio; in the course of time this latter name prevailed and the former disappeared. The settlement was composed of a certain number of Spanish families sent by order of the king from the Canary Islands. The priests in charge were seculars, and the records of the parish, dating back to 1731, are still extant. The parish does not seem to have flourished. The baptisms were twenty-two in 1733, eleven in 1736. The town was reinforced by a second immigration of Spanish families in

1744, and again the baptisms ascend to the former number and beyond.

In 1759 the Bishop of Guadalajara, Mexico, Francis de San Buenaventura Tejada, visited all the missions of Texas. No doubt his report of the visitation would be most interesting, but, if it exists, it is not accessible. The records of the parish of San Fernando, now in the city of San Antonio, have preserved for us the details of his visitation in that Spanish town. The church had five hundred and eighty-two parishioners, but was found, nevertheless, to be in a deplorable state of neglect, which called forth the bishop's reproof. The Spanish population in Texas at this time consisted of three thousand souls, living at San Antonio, the presidios, and the ranches. There were secular priests at San Antonio, Sacramento, Nacogdoches, and Bahia, and usually a chaplain for the troops.

H. H. Bancroft ("North Mexican States and Texas," vol. xv., p. 631) sums up the condition of the Texan missions about the year 1785, one hundred years after their first founding, naming his authorities, the chief of which is the report by Father José Francisco Lopez, made to the Bishop of Nuevo-Leon or Linares—a see erected in 1777, and including Texas—on the condition and prospects of the missions in the year 1785. From this it appears that while the Spanish population, pure and mixed, was about three thousand, the mission Indians in eight establishments were but five hundred.[1] The whole number of natives

[1] The Spanish settlements and Indian missions are:

San Antonio Bejar.—Presidio, founded in 1718, and San Fernando, villa near by, founded in 1730, the two forming one settlement. Site of modern San Antonio. Capital, and residence of governor. Sixty men in presidio; one hundred and forty houses.

Santa Cruz.—Stockade fort on Arroyo del Cibolo. Guard of twenty men from Bejar. Founded in 1772. Six ranches. Population, 85.

San Antonio de Valero.—Mission opposite Bejar, later called the Alamo. Founded in 1718. Nineteen hundred and seventy-two baptisms down to 1762. Population then, 275; in 1793, 43.

baptized since 1690 was less than ten thousand, and at no one time had the neophytes exceeded two thousand. The few still under the missionaries' care were lazy, vicious, and tainted with syphilis. Nowhere in Spanish America had missionary work been so complete a failure. The buildings and church decorations were the only indications of apparent prosperity in the past, and those that are standing to-day show to what efficiency in handiwork the Indians were trained. In 1798 many of the missions were secularized by the Mexican authorities; that is to say, taken from the Franciscans and turned over to secular priests.

In 1805 Primo Feliciano Marin de Porras, Bishop of Linares, made the episcopal visitation of the Texan missions, San Fernando, the presidio of San Antonio, La Bahia, and Nacogdoches. The revolution of Mexico against the authority of Spain in the first quarter of the century threw the mission work into confusion and disorder.

Puressima Concepcion.—A league from Bejar; founded in 1716 on another site; transferred to present site in 1731. Population in 1762, 207. Number of baptisms from foundation, 792. Population in 1793, 51. Best church in province, cost $35,000.

San José y San Miguel de Aguayo.—Founded in 1720. Down to 1762, 1054 baptized; in that year, 350 Indians. Population in 1793, 114.

San Juan Capistrano.—Founded in 1716; transferred near presidio Bejar in 1731. Baptisms to date, 847. Population in 1762, 203; in 1793, 34.

San Francisco de la Espajada.—Original mission founded in 1690; reëstablished in 1716 near modern Mound Prairie, not far from original site; transferred to San Antonio in 1731. Up to date 815 baptisms. Population, 207.

La Bahia.—Presidio, founded in 1722, on site of La Salle's colony of St. Louis; transferred to the San Antonio River in 1724; again to site of modern Goliad in 1749. Garrison, 53. Population in 1782, 515.

Espiritu Santo de Zuniga.—Founded near the above presidio in 1722; transferred with it. Baptisms to date, 623. Population, 300; in 1793, 33.

Rosario Mission.—Founded in 1754. Up to date 200 baptisms.

Nacogdoches Mission.—Originally of Guadalupe, founded in 1716; abandoned finally in 1773. A new settlement, Bucarelli, founded in 1776 on the Trinidad; transferred three years later to Nacogdoches. Three hundred Indians in neighborhood.

Refugio Mission.—Founded in 1791, south of La Bahia, near the coast. In 1793, 67 Indians.

Some thirteen other establishments, of which four had been presidios, were abandoned entirely or merged into those above named between 1690 and 1790.

State aid ceased; the republican government of Mexico, controlled by Masonic influences, antagonized the church; the missionaries, natives of Spain, were expelled; the Spanish population diminished. As early as 1820 Irish settlers began to arrive, and formed the parish of San Patricio. Other emigrants from the United States—rough, turbulent frontiersmen, not by any means friendly to the Catholic Church—poured into Texas, gradually took into their hands the machinery of government, and finally, in 1836, proclaimed the independence of the republic of Texas, and sealed the proclamation by the victory of San Jacinto. That the missions suffered during those troubled times goes without saying. The Spanish domination in Texas had come to an end. The further history of Catholicity in that province belongs to the second part of this work.

CHAPTER VII.

THE RISE OF THE CALIFORNIAN MISSIONS.

AFTER the conquest of Mexico by Cortez, expeditions to the north by water and by land soon brought to the knowledge of the Spaniards the gulf and the peninsula of California, and opened the latter to permanent occupation, or rather to some settlements on the coast and to missions among the Indian tribes of Lower California. It was much later that the soldiers and missionaries entered upon the territory that is now comprised in the State of California. The name California first appears in the diary of a voyage into the gulf and along the peninsula in 1539 by one Presciado. It was applied not to a whole territory, but to a locality. Soon it was extended to the region, and as the region was supposed to be a group of islands, the name was pluralized into "Las Californias."

The origin of the name has vexed many people, and the etymology of it many more. The origin offers no difficulty since 1862, when Edward E. Hale discovered that the early Spaniards got the name from an old romance, the "Sergas of Esplandian" often printed between 1510 and 1526. In that work is mentioned the island of California, "on the right hand of the Indies, very near the terrestrial paradise," peopled with strange beings, men, and animals. The many expeditions by water that Cortez sent northward were intended to get around to India, with the expectation of finding rich and wonderful islands on the way.

When one of these expeditions returned, in 1536, the disgusted Spaniards applied the name of the fabulous island of the old romance to the discovery reported, and that discovery was the peninsula of Lower California. As to the etymology, it remains a point of ingenious guesswork for the philologist.

Upper California was not occupied permanently until 1769. But many explorations were made before that year along its seaboard. In 1542–43 Juan Rodriguez Cabrillo reached the site of Monterey, and after his death on the coast his lieutenant, Ferrelo, pushed up to latitude 42° 30′, the present northern frontier of California. Francis Drake, roving on a raid around the world, touched (1579) the Pacific coast in 38° 30′, where he found a "convenient and fit harbor," in which he refitted his ship. This was the inlet called to-day Drake's Bay, under Point Reyes; formerly it went by the name of Old San Francisco Bay. In 1584 Francisco Gali, sailing from Macao by way of China, reached the coast in 37° 30′. In 1595 Rodriguez Carmenon, on his way from the Philippine Islands, ran aground in the bay under Point Reyes where Drake had put in. He named it San Francisco, the name it bore until changed to Drake's Bay. Later, when the present Bay of San Francisco was discovered and the name of the saint was given to it, the bay outside the Golden Gate under Point Reyes was christened "Old San Francisco Bay."

In 1602–03 Vizcaino sailed from Acapulco with three vessels, two hundred men, and three Carmelite friars. The work given him to do was, firstly, to find a suitable port in which vessels coming from the Philippine Islands might find refuge and opportunities for refitting; and secondly, to find out if anywhere on the coast there was a waterway to the Atlantic, such as Magellan had found at the southern extremity of America. It is he named the

Bay of San Diego, though Cabrillo in 1543 had christened that harbor San Miguel. Vizcaino's naming has prevailed. While the ships were cleaned here, the friars erected a temporary chapel on shore and celebrated mass. Sailing northward, they bestowed melodious saints' names on islands, harbors, headlands; and when they came to Monterey, so called in honor of the Mexican viceroy, the beautiful river that flows into the bay was christened Rio de Carmelo, in honor of the Order of the Carmel. Here again a stay was made and divine service was held. The fleet sailed as far north as Cape Mendocino; but the Golden Gate was passed unnoticed, and the beautiful Bay of San Francisco remained concealed and unknown behind the hills that stand between it and the ocean. Vizcaino returned without finding a strait, and no port was selected as a place of refuge and rest for the vessels buffeted by the long ocean voyage from the Philippine Islands. After Vizcaino, all interest in Upper California ceased until 1769.

The awakening of the interest was due to many motives: the necessity of a port for ships in the Philippine trade; the probability of a northern interoceanic strait; the encroachments of England and France on the American continent; the consciousness of a duty to convert the natives; above all, the advance of Russia in the Northwest. In 1728 Vitus Behring, in the service of Russia, had set out from Cape Kamtchatka and sailed through the straits that now bear his name, thus proving that the continent discovered by Columbus was separate from Asia. Again, in 1741, he reached Alaska under the towering cone of Mount St. Elias, and claimed for Russia a slice of America larger than France and Germany combined. To check the further advance of Russia, the order came from Spain to Mexico in 1768 to occupy San Diego and Monterey, and the work was intrusted to José de Galves.

He arranged for an expedition by sea and by land, each to consist of two divisions, in order to forestall any failure. The occupation was to be religious as well as military, and Father Juniperro Serra, superior of the missions in Lower California, coöperated with Galves. Three Franciscans were to go by sea, three by land. Serra gave up his position of superior of the lower missions in order to be one of the missionaries in the new field, and joined the land expedition. The personal enthusiasm of Father Juniperro, who from 1769 until his death, in 1784, was at the head of mission affairs, has earned for him a well-deserved reputation for ability and saintliness, a reputation made permanent by the biography that came from the pen of his friend Palou. About his worth as a man and as a Christian there is complete agreement on all sides; his name stands for what is best in religion and for what is most romantic in Spanish annals.

On the 11th of April, 1769, the "San Antonio" sailed into the Bay of San Diego with two friars on board, Juan Vizcaino and Francisco Gomez. On the 29th of April the consort and flag-ship, the "San Carlos," came in with another missionary, Hernando Parron. On the 11th of May the first division of the land expedition arrived with Father Juan Crespi, and on the 1st of July the other division with two Franciscans, one of whom was the spiritual conquistador of this new province, Juniperro Serra. Immediately a small temporary chapel was erected and dedicated, and the first Californian mission, San Diego, was established. Leaving there forty-six persons and three friars, the military commander, Portola, with the rest of the party and two priests, sixty-five in all, started to establish the second post at Monterey.

As they trudged along overland they bestowed beautiful names of saints in sweet Castilian on valleys, rivers, hills, and mountain peaks, many of which names survive to this day. When they came to Monterey, somehow they did not recognize it, though they had in hand the clear and minute description of Vizcaino and the Carmelites. Continuing their search, they pushed on northward, and on October 31st came in sight of the Farallones and of Point Reyes, which they beheld from a spot near the present Point San Pedro. Still ignorant of the existence of the present Bay of San Francisco, which they had not as yet seen, they at once recognized the old port of San Francisco, where Drake and Carmenon had put in. Some of the soldiers happened to climb the hills back of the present city of San Francisco, and for the first time the great bay was revealed to European eyes. A vessel—the "San José"—was to make junction with them in Monterey, but failed; they hoped she would meet them here. Being disappointed of this hope, and running short of provisions, they were forced to return, and reached Monterey by the end of November. Their eyes were not yet opened to recognize it as the port they had set out to find, and so they passed on, after having raised a cross on the shore, with the inscription, "Dig at the foot and thou wilt find a writing." They arrived at San Diego January 24, 1770; but on their arrival, when their report was made and compared with Vizcaino's description, it became evident to them that they had been twice in Monterey and knew not the place.

Discouraged by the failure of this northern trip, by the hostile attitude of the Indians, who during the expedition's absence had attacked San Diego, by the shortness of provisions, which could not last another summer, Portola decided to abandon Upper California if by the end of March a relief ship with stores and men did not arrive. Great was the consternation of Serra and his band. They had come to stay, to do and die in the conversion of the Indians, and, should the others go, they resolved to remain. Nevertheless they hoped that the project of the commander might not be carried out, and they took such means to realize their hope as they had at their command. They betook themselves to prayer. On the feast of St. Joseph, the 19th of March, the "San Antonio" sailed into the harbor with stores and reinforcements. All question of leaving was given up, and it was decided to carry out the second part of the original purpose—that is, to occupy Monterey. This time Serra accompanied the expeditionary corps, which left San Diego in April, 1769, and arrived at its destination at the end of May. On June 3d possession was taken, with the usual festivities, in the name of the king of Spain, and on June 14th a humble chapel was dedicated to God under the invocation of San Carlos Borromeo. Thus were founded the presidio and mission of Monterey.

Encouraged by his good fortune thus far, and anxious to establish other centers of missionary work, Serra applied to the Mexican government for more helpers. In answer to his request ten more Franciscans arrived in Monterey, April 10, 1771. Stimulated by the success of the children of St. Francis in this new field, the children of St. Dominic applied for permission to share in their work. As there might be some inconvenience in two orders under different superiors working in the same region, it was arranged that the missions of Lower California should be intrusted to the Dominicans and those of Upper California to the Franciscans. The transfer of the field of Lower California to the Dominicans was made in 1773. The Franciscans were restricted to Upper California, where, concentrating their forces, they quickly produced the most remarkable effects in the conversion of the natives.

The mission of San Carlos became the residence of the superior and the headquarters for all the other missions.

Serra transferred the mission from Monterey, where it was at first set up, to the valley of the Rio Carmelo, a few miles distant. His pretext was the lack of water and good soil in Monterey; his real reason was to get his neophytes away from daily immediate contact with the troops of the presidio. This was a wise policy. The neighborhood of the military force was undoubtedly advantageous, and frequently necessary for the safety of a mission; the introduction of white colonists in settlements was an important part of the government's plan, and was beneficial in putting before the Indians the lessons of agriculture, industry, and civilization; but whereas soldiers and settlers were not likely to be, at all times, living models of the religion they professed and the missionaries taught in all its ideal purity and severity, it was necessary to segregate as much as possible the newly converted Indians from contact with the Spaniards.

Hence presidio, the military post, pueblo, the Spanish colony, mission, the neophytes' establishment, were always at a distance from one another, yet not so far apart that they could not have speedy intercommunication and mutual support in case of need. When the occupation of California was completed there were four presidios—San Diego, Santa Barbara, Monterey, and San Francisco. The number of soldiers assigned to each was limited to two hundred and fifty, but they were rarely up to that number. From these principal stations a guard of four or five was detached, when required by the fathers, to accompany them in their journeys through the unoccupied portions of the country; and a detail of a few men was attached to each mission to preserve order and defend the mission buildings and their inmates from the sudden attacks of the wild, unconverted natives. The pueblos, after some years, were three in number—Los Angeles, San José, and Banciforte. They were served by the fathers, though not subject to them in the sense that the missions were. Each pueblo was self-governing, having its alcalde, or mayor, and town council.

Within the missions only converted natives resided under the immediate spiritual and temporal government of the fathers. Here was to be found ideal, absolute paternalism in government. The buildings that went by the name "mission" were quadrilateral, each side about six hundred feet in length. The whole consisted of the church, the quarters of the military detail, the fathers' convent, schools for boys and girls, and storehouses. The establishment was under the management of two religious; one attended to the interior, the other to the exterior administration. The female children, under the care of approved matrons, were taught the branches necessary for their condition in life; the more talented were trained in vocal and instrumental music. The boys were taught mechanical and industrial trades. It goes without saying that all were taught the elementary three R's. Morning and evening prayer in common, and daily attendance at mass, gave to the life of the inmates a semimonastic appearance.

Clustered around the mission buildings were the thatched huts in which lived the Indians converted to the faith, whose children were in the schools. They tilled or used as pasturage the land about the mission to the distance of fifteen or twenty miles. The limits seem to have been the equidistances between the settlements, whether missions, pueblos, or presidios. When the secularization of the missions came on, as we shall see, the ownership of those lands became a serious difficulty. The fathers maintained that they belonged to the missions; the Mexican government maintained that they had been given to the missionaries only on trust for the agricultural training of the Indians, but that in reality they were, and remained, the property of the nation, subject to a change of hands under the colonization laws.

The government's idea was that the missions were never intended to be permanent establishments. The time would come when the Franciscans—the pioneers and skirmishers, so to speak—should give way to the regular army of the church, bishop, and diocesan clergy; when the Indians, after having been trained to civilization by the paternal system of the fathers, should be emancipated from civil childhood, and should become, so to speak, men made into individual owners of the land and citizens of the state; when missions should be transformed into pueblos, with the rights and privileges of self-government. Such has been the view held by the Mexican and later on by the American courts as to the mission lands. The mission lands, therefore, were never the property of the fathers, but were held in trust by Spain for the Indians. I say mission *lands*, meaning thereby the tracts, as above described, formerly occupied and used by the Indian converts. Mission *property*—that is, the buildings, houses, vineyards, and orchards in the immediate vicinity of the churches—occupied and used by the missionaries, must be viewed in quite another light and judged by quite a different standard. This kind of property belonged to the Catholic Church in California, in trust to those who represented the church then, the Franciscans; in trust to those who represent her now, the Catholic bishops of California.

Serra founded the mission of San Antonio on July 14, 1771, and that of San Gabriel in August of the same year. The following letter of Serra to a friend, dated "Mission of San Carlos, Monterey, 18th August, 1772," will give an idea of the mission work in California: "Our greatest consolation is the knowledge that from Monterey, San Antonio, and San Diego there are numerous souls in heaven. From San Gabriel there are none as yet, but among those Indians there are many who praise God. However, there are those who think that from lambs they will become tigers. This may be so, if God permits it; but after three years' experience they appear to us better every day. If all are not already Christian, it is only owing to our unacquaintance with the language. This is a trouble which is not new to me, and I have always imagined that my sins have not permitted me to possess this faculty of learning strange tongues, which is a great misfortune in a country such as this, where no interpreter or master of language can be had until some of the natives learn Spanish, which requires a long time." He then goes on to beg for more missionaries, and adds: "Let those who come here come well provided with patience and charity, and let them possess a good humor; for they may become rich, I mean in troubles. But where will the laboring ox go where he must not draw the plow? And if he do not draw the plow how can there be a harvest?"

Not content with asking by letter, Serra resolved to go in person to Mexico for more missionaries, founding on his way to San Diego the fifth mission, San Luis Obispo. The motives of this journey were manifold. Word had come that a new viceroy was in Mexico; it was well to know how he was affected toward the Californian missions. The experience of a few years had proved that certain changes were necessary for the better working of the system; these changes had regard mostly to the relations between the military and the ecclesiastical authorities in California. Then he had charges to prefer against Fages, the military commander: bad treatment and haughty manners toward his men; meddling with the management of the missions; taking into his own hands the punishment of neophytes, whereas only the gravest crimes, such as bloodshed and murder, came under his jurisdiction; refusal to remove from the mission guard soldiers guilty of immoral conduct, irregular and delayed delivery of the missionaries' mail; and other smaller grievances. If the close union of church and state in the early Christianity of California was of some advantage to the church—and that cannot be denied—it was also productive of some disadvantages. It cannot be otherwise when you bring into very close union men of the church and men of the state, so long as human nature is what it is. Cannot? Theoretically the assertion is too strong. At any rate, it has never been otherwise, as history proves on a wider scale. And Spanish California may stand a miniature of all history on this point.

While in Mexico, Serra submitted to a Mexican commission (May 21, 1773) the first official report on the Californian missions. The missions were five—San Diego, San Gabriel, San Luis Obispo, San Antonio, San Carlos. They were in charge of nineteen Franciscans under the jurisdiction of the Franciscan college *de propaganda fide* of San Fernando in the City of Mexico. The military body was composed of sixty men under a commander resident in Monterey; each mission had a guard of six or seven soldiers under a sergeant. As yet there were no pueblos. The results of mission work for the first five years were 491 baptisms and 62 marriages. This small number was owing to the cautiousness of the missionaries, who admitted the natives to baptism only after a long instruction in religion, and to the inability of the missions to feed and clothe a larger number of converts. Agriculture had not yet been adopted on a large scale. There was but a small garden around each mission, and a system of irrigation was needed for further development. The pasturage was good, and each mission began with a small herd of cattle, which had thriven.

The architecture at this time was rude, consisting mainly of stockaded huts. Adobe made its appearance later. Then were erected the mission buildings the ruins of which are even now a prominent and romantic feature in the Californian landscape—huge quadrilaterals with stretching arcades, containing church, workshops, school, and monastery. It is an architecture quite unique; it is Spanish, it is Moorish, but it is also specifically Californian—that is to say, here is a certain originality of design, the outcome of convenience and adaptability to climate and needs. Neither in Spain nor elsewhere in America can anything exactly like it be found.

The Mexican authorities, after examining the complaints and demands of Serra, gave decisions favorable to him on most points. The number of troops was increased; three more presidios were ordered—San Diego, Santa Barbara, and San Francisco. Each mission was to be supplied with a number of servants to be paid from the royal exchequer. To obviate the uncertainty of the relief ships, sent annually with stores, an overland route was to be opened from the presidio of Tubac in northern Sonora, by way of the Gila and the Colorado, to Monterey. We have seen in the preceding chapter that this project was a failure. The commandant was ordered to transfer from the mission guard any soldier against whom the fathers might make complaints of irregular conduct. The missionary was to manage his mission as a father his family. The friars' correspondence was to be sacred, and to be forwarded separately from all other mail. Each mission was to receive an annual stipend of $800. The expenses for the military and ecclesiastical budget were to come from the salt-works of San Blas, Lower California, the revenue of which was $25,000, from the Pious Fund, and, if these sources did not suffice, from the royal exchequer.

The Pious Fund was the aggregate of sums of money donated mostly by individuals for the missions in the northern provinces of Mexico, and principally in Lower and Upper California. This fund was begun in 1697 by the Jesuit fathers, then in charge of Lower California and later of Arizona. In twenty years—that is to say, by the year 1716—it amounted to $1,273,000, of which only $18,000 had been received from the government. Much of this capital was in the hands of the original donors, who paid the interest annually. But failure of one of the donors, causing to the fund a loss of $10,000, induced the Jesuit fathers to call in all the donations and invest them in land and other securities, such as mines, manufactories, or cattle; and the annual revenue of such investments was devoted to the missions. When the Jesuits were suppressed by Spain, the Mexican authorities took charge of the fund as trustees and farmed it out for the benefit of the missions. It was yielding at the end of the eighteenth century an annual revenue of $50,000, half of which went to both Californias and half to other missions, so that the Franciscans of Upper California received as their share but a quarter of this annual revenue. In later years the confiscation of this fund by the Mexican authorities seriously crippled the Californian missions, as we shall see.

The success of Serra's journey to Mexico proves that, if he was a zealous missionary and saintly monk, he was also a prudent administrator, a firm advocate of the rights of the church, and a keen man of business. In the autumn of 1773 he set out from Mexico with an additional number of soldiers for the presidios and of missionaries for new foundations. In consequence the mission of San Juan Capistrano was founded in October, 1775, that of San Francisco in September of the same year, and that of Santa Clara in January, 1777. Serra had applied to Rome through his superiors in Mexico for license to administer the sacrament of confirmation, as the distance and difficulties of the long journey from northern Mexico to Upper California prevented the bishop from coming for that purpose. Clement XIV. granted the privilege to the president of the missions, with the power to subdelegate the same to four other missionaries. The grant was for ten years. It expired in 1784 with the death of Serra. During his life he confirmed 5309 persons. The grant was renewed to his successor, Lasuen, who in five years confirmed 9000. After his death it lapsed entirely.

Though Serra had gained all his points, the controversies between church and state in California were frequent and bitter during this period. For instance, the privilege of confirming raised a difficulty. Under pretext that the privilege had not been sanctioned by the Spanish government, the governor enjoined Serra from the use of it until a decision came from Mexico in 1781 to the governor to let the good father alone. The missionaries were charged by the military with excessive severity and even cruelty in correcting the natives. The Indians, when guilty of misdemeanor, had to be punished, if order was to be maintained; but it cannot be proved that the missionaries inflicted with their own hands the punishment, when it was bodily, or that they allowed the punishment to go beyond the bounds of justice. They were charged with neglecting the spiritual care of the presidios. Now, though they served the troops gratuitously, they never failed to visit them regularly, except when the presidio was so near the mission, as in the case of San Francisco, that the soldiers could without great inconvenience come to the friars for spiritual ministration. They were charged with refusing to sell to the presidios mission produce at the prices fixed by the government. But no tariff had been set by the king, and naturally the price of provisions followed the vicissitudes of the harvest, the periods of scarcity or abundance. It was alleged against them that, without permission of the governor and in defiance of law, they retired from the missions and returned to Mexico, and thus kept up a constant migration to and fro. This is admitted, and it is claimed that full liberty in the change of the missionaries should be allowed to the superiors, as they alone could know and appreciate the reasons for the removal of their subjects. Fault was found that they allowed their neophytes to ride too much and too far, wherein there was danger lest they should become skillful warriors. But there were none but the natives to serve as herdsmen, and herding could not be done over vast ranges except on horseback.

The fathers had their countercharges to make against the governor and the military commanders of the presidios. And one marvels, as he reads the old manuscript accounts, that a handful of Europeans thrown together amid savage tribes far from home could waste their time and energies in quarrels seemingly insignificant. But they quarreled not as men and neighbors, but as representatives of the kingdom of Spain and of the Order of St. Francis. Otherwise their relations were most pleasant. Governors did not weary of testifying to the zeal and success of the missionaries, and missionaries were not slow to recognize that their zeal and labors would have small chance of being effective without the presence and the protection of the representatives and troops of Spain. The recriminations may be forgotten and forgiven in the grand result of their concord.

CHAPTER VIII.

THE DECLINE OF THE MISSIONS.

SERRA died on the 28th of August, 1784, as he had lived, a saint. As such he was held by all, and miracles are said to have been wrought by him alive, and through his intercession after his death. Eight missions had been established by him, and 5800 persons had been brought to the knowledge and practice of Christianity. The reader has now a fair idea of the conditions under which the mission work in California was carried on. It is not within my compass to go into the details of their expansion. Statistics will best tell the results. Forty-three years after the first foundation there were eighteen missions, with two fathers in each, and a Christian native population of 15,500. Fifty-three years after the first foundation there were twenty missions, with a population of 20,900. Sixty-five years after the foundation there were twenty-one missions, with a population of 30,600. At this latter date the missions possessed 62,500 horses, 321,500 head of cattle, large and small, and produced 122,500 bushels of grain.

These results are marvelous, considering the time and especially the people among whom they were effected. H. H. Bancroft[1] gives such a description of the central and southern tribes of California as would place them lower than any Indians met by Spaniards in North America. They were an idle and lazy race, living mostly on fish,

[1] "Native Races," vol. i.

roots, and nuts; not being hunters, they had not the fearlessness, bravery, and independence that are characteristic of our northern Indians. "Digger Indians" is the name given them by our early American settlers. La Pérouse, who visited California in 1785, has much to say of the state of the missions at that time. He narrates in his "Voyage autour du Monde" a visit to the mission of San Carlos. "After crossing a little plain covered with herds of cattle . . . we ascended the hills and heard the sound of bells announcing our coming. We were received like lords of a parish visiting their estates for the first time. The president of the mission, clad in cope, holy-water sprinkler in hand, received us at the door of the church, illuminated as on the grandest festivals." He goes on to present a general view of the system, of the neophytes and the routine of their daily life, of the material civilization created by the zeal of the missionaries, whom he praises in the highest terms for their motives and their complete disinterestedness. Yet he predicts that their training of the Indians is doomed in the end to failure. The neophyte was treated too much as a child, too little as a man, and was not being prepared for self-support and independent existence. The duties and obligations of material life were forgotten in the work of raising him to the privileges of the spiritual, supernatural, and eternal life. The community system, which ought only to be a temporary school for individual citizenship, was seemingly accepted as a perpetual institution. "I have only to desire," he concludes, "a little more philosophy of the missionaries, austere, charitable, religious, whom I have met in these missions."

These strictures were proved true by the event which soon followed the culminating period of the Californian missions. During the first quarter of the nineteenth century (1808–24) took place in Mexico a change of government, the upsetting of Spanish rule and the establishment of the republic. This revolution brought on the secularization of the missions. Secularization meant the confiscation of the mission properties, the breaking up of the mission communities to give way to individual ownership by the Indians, and the expulsion of the Franciscans to make way for a secular clergy, for whom no preparation had been made. The total ruin of the missions, the return of the Indians to savage life and to paganism, were the results of this inopportune policy. Mexico had not learned, it appears, the lesson which the United States government of our day has reaped from a long experience—that it takes years of waiting, of patient toil, of slow training, to turn the red man into a property-owner and an intelligent, self-supporting citizen. We are indeed making that change at present, but not rashly and by the wholesale; rather gradually and man by man.

Though the republic of Mexico effected the secularization, it was Catholic Spain herself that had decreed it. The theory of missions was never vague or doubtful to the Spanish government. The duty of the missionary was to convert the natives, fit them for citizenship, and finally turn them over to the care of a diocesan clergy. Such was the theory. Practically, however, the friars were never ready for the change, the neophytes were never fit for it, because in the Franciscan system there was no room for gradual preparation toward citizenship. More than once the civil authorities had ordered that the Indians of the Californian missions should be essayed in government, without, however, being freed from all control of the fathers, by allowing them the election of certain officials and turning over to them certain minor affairs. But the missionaries were always unwilling to make the essay. For two centuries throughout Spanish America contests between bishops and missionaries of religious orders had been frequent, and many missions had been secularized; that is to say, taken from the religious and given over to a diocesan body of priests, against the will of the pioneer missionaries.

On September 13, 1813, the Cortes of Spain passed a decree that all missions in America that had been founded since ten years should at once be given up to the bishops within whose jurisdiction they were, without excuse or pretext whatsoever, in accordance with the laws. Friars might be appointed, if necessary, as temporary curates. Their business, however, was considered to be to move onward for the conversion and the spiritual conquest of new worlds, which were to be surrendered in turn to the regular hierarchical hosts of the church for permanent occupation. The management of the temporalities was to be surrendered by them, the mission lands were to be partitioned for private ownership among the converted natives, and the neophytes were to be governed by their own town councils under the civil representatives of Spain. This decree applied to California as well as to all Spanish America. But no attempt was made, at the time of its enactment, to execute it in California. At any rate, the missions in the province were not ready for the change. No bishop had ever visited California, or given a thought to gathering a body of diocesan priests to replace the friars there.

The good Franciscans were safe, therefore, when, in 1818 and 1819, they informed the bishop under whose jurisdiction their territory was, the Bishop of Sonora and Sinaloa, that he might put his priests in charge of the southern missions, if he thought the times ripe for the change. The bishop did not find the times ripe. It was some years later (1833) that the republic of Mexico renewed the decree of secularization and set about its execution. But previous to that date the missions had suffered much in their temporalities. The annual revenue of the Pious Fund was lost, as the fund itself had been confiscated to uses of the government. The annual stipend of four hundred dollars to each missionary came but fitfully; the mission vessels with annual stores and provisions ceased to be regular in their visits; the cattle and produce of the mission lands were taken by the troops in the presidios on mere promises to pay, which were never realized. Nothing proves so well on what deep and broad foundations the success and the wealth of the missions were founded and built as that they were able to subsist—nay, to grow and prosper—in the midst of all these losses. It was precisely in the very year the secularization decree was put into operation that the high-water mark of the missions' prosperity was reached, as may be seen from the statistics given above.

The missionaries quarreled with the government not as to the plan itself—it was general throughout the Spanish dominions—but as to the seasonableness, the opportuneness, of putting it into operation. The government was in a greater hurry than the missionaries judged feasible. The missionaries were certainly in good faith; moreover, they were best capable of judging when the times were ripe for the change. Allowing, even, that they thought the old system best and that they fought the incoming of the new, they may have had reasons which were prime with them; and after our long struggle with the Indian problem we should not hurry in blaming them. Civilization is a slow process. How many centuries did it not take to bring the barbarians who overran the Roman empire into Christian civilization? Now to force our civilization upon a race that is in the stage of savagery without due time for absorption is to commit a mistake. The preparation of the Indian for citizenship must be a slow work, the work of centuries. I think that time will show that no more successful plan for this result has ever been devised than that of the Jesuits in Paraguay and the Franciscans in California.

The secularization, because too sudden and preceded by no preparation on the part of the diocesan or the Franciscan authorities, was disastrous to the church in California. Dwinelle, in his "Colonial History," says: "The secularization laws, whose ostensible purpose was to convert the missionary establishments into Indian pueblos, the mission churches into parish churches, and to elevate the Christianized Indians to the rank of citizens, were, after all, executed in such a manner that they resulted only in the plunder of the missions and their complete ruin, and in the demoralization and dispersion of the Christianized Indians. There was an understanding between the government of Mexico and the leading men of California that the government might absorb the Pious Fund, while its representatives in California should appropriate the local wealth of the missions by the rapid and sure process of administering their temporalities."

And so it came to pass. The lands were handed over to the Indians, only to be neglected and to revert to their wild, uncultivated condition. The cattle were divided among them and the administrators for their own personal profit. The Catholic Indian population in 1836 was 30,000; close upon a million of live stock belonged to them; the annual crop was 125,000 bushels of wheat; soap, leather, wine, oil, cotton, hemp, tobacco, salt, and soda were largely cultivated and exported; a million dollars cash, annually flowing into the province, was the reward of industry in those articles, while another million came from other sources. Extensive gardens, orchards, vineyards, that went to the use and comfort of the natives, surrounded the missions. Into these holy retreats were gathered almost all the indigenous inhabitants of southern and central California, Christianized and civilized, and all this was the fruit of the labors of the humble sons of St. Francis during sixty-five years of missionary existence.

No sooner was the decree of secularization reënacted by the Mexican Congress (1833) and put into force by the governor of California (1834) than a great change came over this happy scene. Eight years later the Catholic Indians had dwindled from 30,654 to 4450; for instance, San Rafael could count but 20, San Francisco Solano but 70, yet the former had contained 1250 and the latter 1300. In 1842 there were only 60,000 cattle in the missions, and only 40,000 bushels of wheat were raised. Wilkes, in his "Exploring Expedition," says: "The country was deprived of its religious establishments, upon which its society and good order were founded. Anarchy and confusion began to reign. Some of the missions were deserted, their property was dissipated, and the Indians turned out to seek their native wilds. The property became a prey to the rapacity of the governor, the administrators, and their needy officers."

No arrangements had been made to replace the Franciscans. Many sadly bade farewell to the homes they had made so happy, and retired to convents in Mexico. The neophytes in several instances were abandoned and deprived of the services of religion. Some of the missionaries begged to remain, and were allowed to do so on their taking the oath of allegiance to the republic of Mexico. But poverty, neglect, insult, became their share. The dependents who formerly lived on their charity, the menials of the civil authority, in whose care their temporalities and lands were intrusted for distribution to the Indians, heaped indignities on the friars who remained. Some hardly found means of subsistence; and one, Father Sarria, of the mission of Soledad, is known to have died of starvation in 1838.

Meanwhile the white population, mostly Spanish, was on the increase. In 1790 it was 990; in 1800, 1800; in 1810, 2130; in 1830, 4250; in 1840, 5780. In order to supply these people with the ministrations of the church, and also, no doubt, to stay the total extinction of the missions, the Mexican Congress resolved to put Lower and Upper California in charge of a resident bishop. Had the step been taken earlier the missions might have been saved; for a bishop might have had time to prepare for the change from the religious to the diocesan clergy. The remedy, as far as the Indian missions were concerned, was applied after the agony had set in; that is to say, too late. The choice fell on Don Francisco Garcia Diego, a Franciscan, who had been professor of theology in his convent in Mexico and Commissary Prefect of the missions of Upper California. The appointment was confirmed in 1840 by Gregory XVI. The sum of $3000 was given him for an outfit, and an annual salary of $6000 was promised. He fixed his residence in Santa Barbara, where he arrived in December, 1841, and planned to build a residence, a seminary, and a cathedral. But the funds expected from the government were not forthcoming, and the work lingered until his death (1846). That same year the United States flag was run up in Monterey and San Francisco by Fremont and Stockton, and two years later (1848) California was annexed to the United States.

Our survey of the work of the Spanish church in the territory of the United States is at an end. In time it extended from 1520 to 1840, and covers, therefore, over three hundred years. In space it extended from the Atlantic to the Pacific, south of the thirty-eighth degree of latitude, and covered our present States of Florida, Alabama, Texas, New Mexico, Arizona, and California. Over a hundred thousand of the aborigines were brought to the knowledge of Christianity, and introduced, if not into the palace, at least into the antechamber of civilization. It was a glorious work, and the recital of it impresses us by the vastness and success of the toil. Yet, as we look around to-day, we can find nothing of it that remains. Names of saints in melodious Spanish stand out from maps in all that section where the Spanish monk trod, toiled, and died. A few thousand Christian Indians, descendants of those they converted and civilized, still survive in New Mexico and Arizona, and that is all. It is well worth while to inquire what made the success, what the ruin, of the Spanish missions.

What made their success? I answer: the blood of martyrs; the zeal of missionaries; the reduction of the roving tribes into fixed communities; the industrial training imparted to the Indians; the patriarchal and paternal character of the friars' government; the generosity of Spain in furnishing the temporal means of subsistence; the military protection given the missionaries; the separation of the Indians from the whites even to the difference of their spiritual guardians, the whites, as a rule, being under diocesan, the Indians under religious priests.

What caused their ruin? I name as external causes the wilder roving tribes that remained heathen; the English colonists of Georgia and the Carolinas in the Southeastern missions; the revolution of Mexico, and the consequent confiscation of funds and secularization of missions in the Southwestern missions; in both regions the withdrawal of that military protection that had been so influential in building them up. I name as internal causes the want of gradual preparation in the passage of the Indian tribes from tutelage to independent manhood, and in the transfer of the missions from the religious orders to the diocesan clergy; the tardiness in appointing bishops, who alone could prepare for the transfer and create the diocesan clergy that would take the place of the early missionaries.

This one glorious truth stands prominent: the Spaniards in the United States did not drive the natives from their homes, or oppress them, much less destroy them. These accusations, if made at all, must fall on some other race.

PART II. THE FRENCH MISSIONS.

CHAPTER IX.

FRANCE IN NORTH AMERICA.

THE missionaries of France labored in our Northern States along the line that divides them from Canada. The Eastern missions were in Maine, the central missions in northern New York, the Western missions on the shores of Lakes Huron, Michigan, and Superior. When the French had discovered and descended the Mississippi, they established missions along the river as far south as its mouth, and called the region Louisiana. It is from the southern point of Lake Michigan that their posts trended to the south, cutting in twain the Spanish line of missions from Florida to the Pacific. For convenience' sake we include Louisiana in the Western missions. The head of Lake Superior and the Mississippi are the western boundary-line of the French occupation.

But before detailing the work of the missionaries of France it may be useful to sketch briefly the westward march of her explorers and traders, in order to map out the field of work. When the Cabots in 1497, or, as seems more probable from late researches, in 1494, reached the Western land that they mistook, like Columbus, for part of the empire of the Grand Khan, they touched in reality the island which, at a very early date, was called Cape Breton Island. "This name," says Parkman, in "Pioneers of France in the New World," "found on the oldest maps, is a memorial of very early French voyages." There is a tradition that, in the year 1488, Cousin, a navigator of Dieppe, was blown by winds and carried by currents from Africa westward to an unknown shore, where he descried the mouth of a large river. For this tradition no proof exists beyond the claim of a French writer. The proof, if ever there was any, perished probably in the bombardment of Dieppe (1694). What is more certain is that Norman, Breton, and Basque fishermen frequented at a very early date the banks of Newfoundland. There is reason to believe that this fishing existed before the voyage of Cabot. There is evidence that it began as early as the year 1504. Ever after this date, not only French, but English, Spanish, and Portuguese fishing-fleets made yearly resorts to the banks. In 1506 one Denis of Honfleur explored the Gulf of St. Lawrence; two years later Aubert of Dieppe followed in his tracks; and in 1518 Baron de Léry made an abortive attempt at settlement on Sable Island. These were private enterprises, undertaken without the knowledge and consent of the French crown.

It was Francis I., the rival of the Spanish Charles V., who began the national movement for a share in the transatlantic world. Among the corsairs in the service of France at that time was Giovanni da Verrazano, a Florentine, who in 1523 had captured a Spanish galleon on its way from Mexico to Spain with a freight of gold. Early the next year he crossed the Atlantic with one ship and fifty men, touched the American coast near Cape Fear in North Carolina, skirted it northward as far as latitude 50°, noticing the Chesapeake and the Hudson, and landed on the coast of Rhode Island. A minute description of the voyage exists in a letter of his to the king of France, now in the library of Florence. The Majollo map of 1527, in the Ambrosian Library, Milan, marks the general line of his survey, and an earlier map of 1524, made by his brother, Hieronymus da Verrazano, preserved in the Borgian Museum, is further confirmation of the expedition.

There is frequent mention in French writers of that period of the city of Norumbega. Jean Allefonse (1545) described the river on which this famed city was located, and the description applies to no river on the coast except the Hudson. The claim is urged that French traders, long before the advent of the Dutch, had built some kind of post on the Hudson, where they trafficked in furs with the Indians of the interior. But any one who studies chapter vi. of volume iii. of the "Narrative and Critical History of America," edited by Justin Winsor, will be slow to pin his faith to any identification of Norumbega, much less to adopt the theory lately put forth by Eben Norton Horsford,[1] that it was located on the Charles River, in the neighborhood of Watertown and Waltham, Mass. This mythical city seems to have played in the Northeast the legendary rôle played in the Southwest by the Seven Cities and Quivira.

Among the favorites of Francis I. was Philippe de Brion-Chabot, admiral of France. He conceived the plan of following up the discoveries of Verrazano, and he found in St. Malo, the home of a race of hardy mariners, a fit agent for his design—Jacques Cartier. This bold sailor, in a first voyage (1534), ascended the St. Lawrence as far as the island of Anticosti; in a second voyage, entering the bay he called St. Lawrence from the saint of the day—

[1] "The Discovery of the Ancient City of Norumbega," Houghton, Mifflin & Co., 1890.

a name that passed to the river in 1535—he sailed beyond the site of Quebec, called by the Indians Stadacone, and ascended to a great Indian village, Hochelaga, back of which rose a majestic mound that Cartier named Mount Royal. He had christened Montreal. A rigorous climate, a savage people, a soil barren of gold and grain, rich only in fish and fur, were the sole allurements to this new land.

Yet there was found a nobleman, Sieur de Roberval, anxious to colonize it. He chose Cartier as his captain-general. "We have resolved," says the king in the grant to De Roberval, "to send him [Cartier] again to the lands of Canada and Hochelaga, which form the extremity of Asia toward the west." The object of the enterprise, according to the royal commission, was discovery, settlement, and the conversion of Indians. In May, 1541, Cartier for the third time started for New France; Roberval was to follow with additional ships. Again he ascended to Hochelaga, and beyond to the rapids above that place. But as Roberval was not appearing, Cartier started for home April, 1542, and thus France's first attempt to plant a colony in the New World failed.

We omit, as not belonging to the matter in hand, the French attempts at colonization in the southern portion of the United States, on the coast of Florida; we have seen in a former chapter how they were foiled by the Spaniards. It was fully sixty years after Cartier's final return from the St. Lawrence, when the wars of religion had been brought to an end in France by Henry IV., that France succeeded in planting a colony on the shores of the New World. Happily she found a fit agent in one who was a soldier, a navigator, a courtier, a scientist, an enthusiastic Catholic, a knight as high-minded and brave as Bayard or Duguesclin—Samuel de Champlain. His first voyage to the

Northwest (1613) was made in the service of De Chastes, who had received from the king a patent to colonize New France. This voyage was meant to be one of exploration merely, and extended up the St. Lawrence as high as the rapids above Hochelaga.

On his return (1604) Champlain found his employer dead, and Pierre du Guast, Sieur du Monts, invested with the right and monopoly of the colonization scheme. The patent conceded to this nobleman comprised the country from Montreal to Philadelphia, and named it Acadia, a name that was restricted afterward to Nova Scotia. It was on the Bay of Fundy, first at the mouth of the St. John River, on an island now within the jurisdiction of Maine, and afterward on the opposite coast, at Port Royal (now Annapolis), in Nova Scotia, that Sieur de Monts planted his colony (1604). It was short-lived, for it broke up in 1607. During its existence Champlain, who was a member of it as royal geographer, surveyed our northern coasts as far south as Boston Harbor with most minute accuracy. In 1610 Jean de Biencour, Sieur de Pourtrincourt, renewed the attempt to plant a colony in Nova Scotia, and with some success, as we shall see.

But the great French colony that created a New France in America was to be on the great river, the main artery and the highway of the North American continent—the St. Lawrence; and it was Champlain who laid the foundations of the colony on the rocky eminence of Quebec in the year 1608. During a quarter of a century the population of the new city did not exceed one hundred persons. It was a mere trading-post, with a governor and some soldiers, maintained under a royal patent by a company of French merchants who held the monopoly of the fur-trade. Six years after the founding of Quebec—that is to say, in 1614—four Recollects (a branch of the Franciscan order) came out to New France to attend to the spiritual wants of the settlers and convert the surrounding tribes.

From the very beginning the chief feature of the French colonies is prominent: the triple alliance of the soldier, the trader, and the priest. It was on trade, not on agriculture, that French colonization was based; therein you will find the secret of its expansion when undisturbed, of its weakness when attacked. In 1625 came to Quebec the first band of the Jesuits, whom, it appears, the Recollects had called to their aid. In 1628 Quebec fell into the hands of the English, but was restored to the French in 1632. With the restoration the Jesuits alone returned, and thenceforth made Quebec the center of their work in North America. Ten years later (1644) Montreal was founded by Maisonneuve; with him came the Sulpitians, who made Montreal their headquarters. These two cities and these two religious orders were the sources whence flowed into Canada and overflowed into our northern territory the stream of Catholic truth and life. The tracing of this overflow constitutes the history of the French missions in the United States.

The two main routes by which the Catholic activity of Montreal and Quebec penetrated into the territory of the present United States are plain on our map. The first was threaded by Champlain himself. He ascended the St. Lawrence to the Ottawa, up the Ottawa to Lake Nipissing, thence by a portage and French River into Lake Huron, whence the way was clear and easy to the western end of Lake Superior and the southern end of Lake Michigan; not far from both these points were the sources of streams that flowed into the Mississippi. Had he not feared to encounter on his way the terrible Iroquois, he might have reached the West by another route, the St. Lawrence, Lake Ontario, Lake Erie, Detroit, Lakes Huron, Michigan, and Superior. But this latter highway was practicable only after Frontenac had beaten the Iroquois and La Salle had located his continuous line of posts from the St. Lawrence to the Gulf of Mexico. Thus did the French belt the interior of North America from Quebec to New Orleans with their forts, trading-posts, and missions, and outflanked the English colonies of the Atlantic coast. To the student of geography and history it will ever be an unfailing wonder how that line, broad and solid, along the St. Lawrence, the lakes, the Mississippi, reaching eastward to the head-waters of all the confluents of the great river, was ever broken, and how France surrendered so easily her American empire to the power that snatched from her her Indian empire.

It took years to form and complete that line. Explorers, as adventurous and as lion-hearted as ever was Cortez or Pizarro or De Soto or Coronado or Oñate, contributed each a link during three quarters of a century, from the day when Champlain pushed his canoe into the Ottawa (1613) to the day when heroic La Salle was robbed of life in the swamps of Texas (1687). It will suffice here to name them: Nicollet (1634), who paddled into Sault Ste. Marie, Mackinaw, Green Bay, down the Fox River, and perhaps the Wisconsin, on the way to the Mississippi; Des Groseillers and Radisson, who in 1659 canoed along the southern shore of Lake Superior and visited tribes on the Black, Chippewa, and St. Croix rivers; Joliet, with his no less adventurous companion Marquette, who in 1673 entered the Mississippi by way of Green Bay, the Fox, and the Wisconsin, and floated down to the Arkansas; Duluth, who in 1679 penetrated beyond the western extremity of Lake Superior, where a city immortalizes his name, four hundred miles into the interior of Minnesota, and rescued Hennepin from his Sioux captors; finally, La Salle, the boldest of them all, who, between 1676 and 1687, in theory carried the empire of France from the crest of the Alleghanies to that of the Rockies, and in fact from Lake Michigan to the Gulf of Mexico; who planned a line of posts from the foot of Ontario, through Niagara, Detroit, Mackinaw, St. Joseph, Peoria, and the salient points on the lower Mississippi, to that spot in the delta which in two of our wars proved to be the key to final victory; who did all this amid difficulties that would appall a less brave heart, and died in the doing, bequeathing to his country an empire almost as vast, if not as rich, as the India of Dupleix and Lally-Tollendal.

Such were the western routes that led into the interior of North America and down to the blue, warm waters of the Gulf of Mexico. There was another route from Canada to the Atlantic, as well if not better known in the history of French colonization. Follow on the map the black line running south from the St. Lawrence to New York Bay—a line made by the Richelieu River, Lake Champlain, Lake George, and the Hudson; a continuous water-way, with only a short portage. Along this line were the fortunes of France in America fought many a year with varying vicissitudes of defeat and victory, and finally lost; along this line did American independence waver as the continental troops advanced or retreated. Where the head-waters of the Richelieu and the head-waters of the Hudson meet is the heart of half the continent east of the Mississippi. There dwelt the dreaded Iroquois, the master race of North America. The total population of the Iroquois Confederacy did not exceed twelve thousand souls. Yet their supremacy was recognized by the tribes of New

England; they exacted tribute from those of Long Island; they forayed down on the Chesapeake; they swept the St. Lawrence and the lakes; they drove the Algonquins, Hurons, and Ottawas to the head-waters of the Mississippi; they commanded where Chicago now stands; and the Southern tribes from Georgia to Louisiana trembled at their name and fled at their war-whoop.

Their position had much to do in making them what they were. The head-waters of the Mohawk, which pass through the Hudson to the Atlantic, are interwoven here with streams that flow into the St. Lawrence, with streams that pass through the Susquehanna to the Chesapeake, with streams that pass through the Ohio into the Mississippi, with streams that lose themselves in Lakes Ontario and Erie. Wherever he wished to be—east, west, north, south—the Iroquois had but to launch his canoe, and he was there with the swiftness of current and paddle; from his home nature's roads led him to every quarter of the compass. The European race to which such a people gave its friendship and aid must conquer in the end and drive out the nation that had earned its hostility. The one great mistake that France committed from the start was to earn that hostility.

Little did Champlain dream that he was sealing the fate of France when, on the 29th of July, 1609, at Ticonderoga, between Lake George and Crown Point, he aimed his arquebuse at an Iroquois chief and laid him in the dust. The echo of that shot rang for one hundred and fifty years in wars almost continuous against Iroquois and English, and died out only when Montcalm fell on Abraham's Plains in 1759. France linked her fortunes with the Hurons, England hers with the Iroquois. The Iroquois exterminated the Hurons, weakened the French; England, combined with her savage allies, finished the work, and drove France from North America. But if the domination of France has disappeared from our soil, she has left in the annals of the Catholic Church in North America imperishable monuments of the zeal and the heroism of her missionaries. To these, so far as the United States is concerned, we now turn our attention.

CHAPTER X.

THE MISSIONS IN MAINE.

THE earliest religious establishment on the coast of Maine was founded in 1604, Ste. Croix, on an island now known as Douchet Island; it is a few miles within the mouth of the St. Croix River, which empties into Passamaquoddy Bay. In the latter part of the last century, when the commissioners of Great Britain and the United States were endeavoring to define the St. Croix River, which by treaty had been fixed as the eastern boundary of the American Republic, this island played an important part. The discovery in 1797 of the foundation stones of De Monts's houses on Douchet Island, with large trees growing above them, did away with all doubt as to the site of the colony of Ste. Croix. In a survey of 1798 the island is called Bone Island, and it has been called sometimes, because of its position, Neutral Island.

To Pierre du Guast, Sieur de Monts, was granted a patent by the king of France (1604) to colonize La Cadie or L'Acadie, a region defined as extending from the fortieth to the forty-sixth degree of latitude, that is, from Philadelphia to Montreal and beyond. The foundation of the enterprise was the monopoly of the fur-trade, all former grants being annulled in its favor. Though a Calvinist, De Monts bound himself to have the natives instructed in the Catholic religion, and when he sailed he took with him two Catholic priests; the name of one only has come down to us—Nicholas Aubrey. Champlain, who was attached to the expedition as royal geographer, has left a sketch of the settlement, showing a chapel, cemetery, and priest's house. It is recorded that the Rev. Nicholas Aubrey did no more than attend to the spiritual needs of the Catholic colonists, though no doubt he must have come in contact with the surrounding Indians, and must have tried to instill in their minds some truths of the gospel. After one year De Monts, dissatisfied with the location, packed up the belongings of the little colony, eighty persons all told, and sailed across the Bay of Fundy to a spot on the north side of the Basin, opposite Goat Island, a little below the mouth of the river Annapolis. The new settlement took the name of Port Royal; the location is out of the United States, in Nova Scotia. It was short-lived, for early in 1607 De Monts's grant was rescinded; money spent freely at court by his rivals had broken down the monopoly in the fur-trade on which the grant was based and which gave it all its value. The Port Royal colonists, on hearing the news, sailed for France, and arrived in St. Malo October, 1607. Thus ended the first French attempt to settle in the New World.

Among the colonists was Jean de Biencour, Sieur de Pourtrincourt. To him De Monts had sublet Port Royal under his grant. The subletting, of course, lost all value with the loss of the main grant to De Monts. But Pourtrincourt, undaunted, resolved to make Acadia a New France; and as soon as he landed in France obtained from the king a confirmation of the rights formerly held by him from De Monts. The king, however, insisted as a condition *sine qua non* that the grantee should take out Jesuits with him for the conversion of the natives. Peter Biard was called for this purpose from a professor's chair in Lyons. Pourtrincourt was a good enough Catholic, but did not wish to have the company of a Jesuit in his colony. While Biard was waiting in Bordeaux to be notified that the vessel was ready for sailing, the baron slipped away from Dieppe with a secular priest on board, La Flèche by name. Port Royal was found in good condition; its houses were occupied by the newcomers. The priest at once set to work among the natives, and a pretty full register of baptisms was sent back to France in the returning ship, under command of Pourtrincourt's son, a lad of eighteen. The intent of the baptismal register was to show that good missionary work could be done without the Jesuits.

But they were not to be got rid of so easily. They had at court a powerful patroness, a woman of deep religious spirit, who believed that the best interests of the church required the presence of the Jesuits in the New World. She was lady of honor at court, Antoinette de Pons, Marquise de Guercheville. Pourtrincourt had bargained with two merchants, Huguenots in religion, to equip and load the vessel that was to go back; they were partners in the profits of the enterprise. They swore that the two Jesuits—Biard had now a companion, Enemond Masse—should never sail in any vessel in which they had an interest. Madame de Guercheville stepped in at this point of the proceedings, bought out the interest of the two Huguenots, advanced in addition two thousand livres to Pourtrincourt, and turned her investment over to the Jesuit Province of France for the future support of the missions. In June, 1611, Fathers Biard and Masse set sail for the New World. They were the first of a band of religious heroes who have left on this land the marks of their toil and their blood from Maine to the Mississippi. Already their brothers had preached and died in Japan, had taught astronomy at the court of Peking, had argued and prevailed with the

Brahmans of India, had carried the cross into Abyssinia, preached in Brazil, shed their blood in Florida, created a Christian republic in Paraguay; and now these heroes of the cross were about to renew among the tribes of North America the marvelous deeds with which they had filled the rest of the world. Was ever seen on earth so glorious a band of men as those early Jesuits in the first fervor of their foundation?

While the newcomers proceeded to make themselves at home, and Biard attacked the difficulties of the Micmac language as best he could, Pourtrincourt the elder returned to France to look after his affairs, leaving the colony in command of his son. On his arrival in France he sold to Madame de Guercheville—for he was sorely in need of funds to continue his enterprise—a further interest in his undertaking of one thousand livres, and obtained from De Monts a quitclaim to all his rights in Acadia, and from Louis XIII. a new grant of all the territory from the St. Lawrence to Florida. The next vessel to arrive in the Bay of Fundy had on board, as representative of Madame de Guercheville's interests, a lay brother of the Society of Jesus, Gilbert du Thet. Dissensions arose at once in the colony between the Guercheville and the Pourtrincourt rival interests. The Jesuits resolved to withdraw, but were forcibly hindered from sailing by young Pourtrincourt. Du Thet returned alone to report to his employer, the marquise.

The result of his report was that Madame de Guercheville resolved to start a colony of her own in a more favorable portion of her vast domains. The good ship "Jonas" was chartered, and took on board, with other things needed for the purpose, forty colonists, a third Jesuit father, Du Quentin, and the business manager, Du Thet. La Saussaye was commander of the colony. The vessel left France March 12, 1613, reached Port Royal safely, picked up the two Jesuits, Biard and Masse, glad to escape from the insults and indignities of young Pourtrincourt, and bore away to the southwest for the mouth of the Penobscot. They ran into a large harbor on the eastern side of Mount Desert Island, landed, planted a cross, celebrated mass, and called the island St. Sauveur. The commander, instead of fortifying his position and setting his guns in place, put his men to planting crops. It was a mistake dearly paid for. After a few days a sail hove in sight, and bore down upon the "Jonas" riding at anchor; only a handful of men were aboard, among them Du Thet. As soon as the Frenchmen became aware that the stranger was an Englishman, a few ineffectual shots were fired, to which reply was duly made; most of the men on the "Jonas" were wounded; the lay brother was killed outright. Then the English landed a force, and, finding the settlement empty, had no trouble in capturing it.

The visitors were from Virginia, led by Samuel Argall, who, sailing north to fish off the coasts of Maine, Nova Scotia, and Newfoundland, carried a commission from Sir Thomas Dale, governor of Virginia, to expel all Frenchmen found within the bounds of English territory. Here he found them. While La Saussaye was absent from his hut, the high-minded Argall opened the French commander's trunk and stole his papers. When La Saussaye made his appearance, the Englishman coolly asked to see the commission authorizing him to set up an establishment on English soil, and fumed and raged when La Saussaye could not produce it. Fifteen of the French, including La Saussaye and Father Masse, were cast adrift in an open boat, and were fortunately picked up on the coast of Nova Scotia by two French trading-vessels. The others, including Fathers Biard and Du Quentin, were carried off to Newport News, in the "Chesapeake," the seat of Governor Dale. To save his French captives from the gallows, Argall had to reveal his low trick and show the commission of the French king. The two countries were at peace, and Dale did not dare hang French subjects bearing regular papers for their colonization.

Moreover, if England made claims to North America in virtue of the discovery of Cabot, France made claims to the same in virtue of the discoveries of Verrazano and others before him. It certainly was not for the governor of Virginia to solve the dispute. James I., it is true, by patents of 1606, had granted all North America from the thirty-fourth to the forty-fifth degree to two companies, that of London and that of Plymouth. To the former was assigned Virginia, to the latter Maine and Acadia. But it was not for the governor of Virginia to assert England's right outside his own jurisdiction. And, at any rate, the kings of France had issued patents earlier than 1606 covering the same territory. If we are to go by patents, France was in possession. If we are to go by discoveries, the question was doubtful.

Nevertheless, while sparing the lives of the Frenchmen, the governor ordered Argall to go back and utterly destroy the Mount Desert and Port Royal settlements. The captain, with his own vessel and the captured "Jonas," on which were the Jesuits, set off to do the governor's bidding. Port Royal was burned and the settlers left without a roof. On the way back a terrible western gale struck the "Jonas," drove her to the Azores, and thence she sailed into Pembroke, Wales. The two Jesuits made their way to France (1615). The French court complained to England of the outrage, but in the troubled state of European politics the matter was dropped. Thus were crushed by a lawless and unjustifiable violence the beginnings of the

French empire on our coasts; thus was the current of our history changed. Seven years later, a little south of Mount Desert, landed in Plymouth harbor another colony that was destined to shape the future of North America.

Port Royal had been destroyed, but the colonists remained and kept hold on Acadia. They are the germs of the Acadian race whose happy agricultural life and unhappy exportation by the English a century and a half later are the theme of history and poetry. Port Royal was rebuilt, and plans of more extensive settlement were resumed. England and the English colonists in America seem to have conceded that Acadia was French territory and that it extended to the Penobscot, though France seems to have claimed always the Kennebec as the boundary-line; this claim was allowed by the Treaty of Breda (1667). Intercourse between Acadia and France was brisk. More than five hundred French vessels sailed annually, in the first half of the seventeenth century, to the North American coast for whale and cod fishing and the fur-trade. There is an autograph letter in the "Archives de la Marine" from Pourtrincourt, who had succeeded to his father's estates and titles, written in Port Royal in 1618, and addressed to the magistrates of Paris, in which he urges the importance of establishing fortified posts in Acadia, to defend it against the incursions of the English.

The Recollects were in charge of the French colonists of Acadia in 1619. In 1633 Cardinal Richelieu intrusted the Acadian missions to the Capuchins. They had stations from Chaleurs Bay to the Kennebec, at the points most frequented by French traders; they did not confine their attention to their own countrymen. The fact that Cardinal Richelieu gave them means (1640) to found and maintain an Indian school proves that they were active in the work of converting the tribes. Though Port Royal in Nova Scotia was their central mission, they had stations in Maine on the Penobscot and the Kennebec. The station on the Penobscot went by the name of Pentagoet, as did the river; Pentagoet was on or near the site of the present Castine. In 1863 a copperplate was found there bearing this inscription: "1648, 8, *Jun: F. Leo, Parisin, Capvc; Miss posui hoc fundtm in Hrncm Nræ Dmæ Sanctæ Spei*" ("On the 8th of June, 1648, I, Friar Leo, of Paris, Capuchin missionary, laid this corner-stone in honor of Our Lady of Holy Hope"). That they had a residence, or hospice, somewhere at the mouth of the Kennebec is ascertained from the account given in the "Relations des Jesuites" of a visit made to them in that locality by Father Druillettes, of whom we are to speak presently.

In Maine at that time dwelt a branch of the Algonquin family of Indians. It went by the general name of Abenakis, and contained many tribes; one has left its name to the Penobscot, another to the Androscoggin; at Norridgewock they had a fixed habitation and cultivated the surrounding fields between the seasons of hunting and fishing. The Iroquois were the enemies of this tribe, as of the whole Algonquin race. It is no wonder, then, that the Abenakis felt friendly to the French and always sought to be under the protection of the powers in Canada. They first came in contact with the French when, in 1612, Father Biard visited them on the Kennebec during an excursion down the coast from Port Royal. Later, when the French had settled permanently in Quebec and along the St. Lawrence, Abenakis from Norridgewock paid frequent visits to the mission of Sillery. Some of the visitors were converted and baptized, returned to their homes to become missionaries themselves, and succeeded so well in interesting their tribesmen that a formal deputation was sent in 1646 to the governor of Quebec and the superior of the Jesuits, to ask that one of the fathers be allowed to reside among them.

"A people renowned for their bravery," says Charlevoix, "so situated between the English and ourselves that they might be a great help to us in the future in case of a rupture with New England, was an acquisition that should not be neglected." The deputation was well received, and in August, 1646, Father Druillettes, one of the Jesuits of Quebec, returned with them to Norridgewock. They built for him a rude chapel, and he remained with them some ten months or a year, learning their language, nursing and baptizing their sick, giving such instructions as his imperfect knowledge of their dialect allowed, and winning their respect and love despite the opposition of the medicine-men, the irreconcilable antagonists of the Catholic missionary among the tribes of the North as well as of the South. Three things he demanded of them as previous conditions to admittance into the church: total abstinence from the fire-water of their European neighbors; cessation of war between tribes; renunciation of their manitous and superstitious rites. He was in no hurry to give baptism, unless in danger of death; for a long novitiate and catechising were proved by experience to be best, if not essential The greater number of the tribe were catechumens and attended faithfully the daily religious exercises of the mission.

During his stay he went down the river Kennebec twice, the first time as far as Augusta, and the second as far as the ocean. The purpose of the first voyage was to gain the friendship of an English trader, Winslow, agent for a merchant of Boston, Edward Gibbons, a personage of note, a magistrate of the commonwealth, and a major-general. Winslow, who found his own advantage, no doubt, in the civilizing work of Druillettes among the Indians with whom the trading was carried on, had just returned from Plymouth at the time of the missionary's visit. This colony, as well as Canada and France, claimed jurisdiction over the part of Maine lying below the Penobscot. Winslow had spoken well of the missionary, and brought back from the Plymouth authorities a permission for Druillettes to build a residence, import a few Frenchmen as companions, and pursue his work without fear of interruption. It would seem that the Jesuit, conscious he had come into debatable territory, was well content to have this security from the counter-claimant. The purpose of the second voyage was to acquaint himself with the coast, where he found seven or eight English trading-posts, and to visit the Capuchins on the Penobscot, who received him with the kindness due to a brother religious. Early in the summer of 1647 he returned to Quebec to report to his superiors and get recruits for the mission.

A study of the geography of Maine will give the reason why the French authorities were anxious to attach the Abenakis and cultivate missions among them. The St. John and the Penobscot run up very close to the St. Lawrence; the head-waters of the Kennebec are interwoven with those of La Chaudière, which flows into the St. Lawrence. It was of the last importance for the French to seize and hold these water-routes. The Norridgewock band of the Abenakis, who lived on the Kennebec, and the kindred bands on the Penobscot, the St. Croix, and the St. John, if securely allied to the French, would be a living barrier against English intrusion and Iroquois irruption in this direction. There was no better means to keep them true to France than to make them children of the church and to station missionaries among them.

It was three years before Druillettes returned. Probably the Jesuits of Canada were short of subjects, and older missions claimed their attention. Another probable reason may be deduced from an entry in the Journal of the superior of the Jesuits. It is there stated that the Capuchins of the Penobscot had mildly protested against the intrusion of the Jesuits into their territory. But shortly after, owing to political dissensions and troubles among the colonists of the Penobscot that threatened the closing up of their missions, the Capuchins reconsidered the step and begged the Jesuits to resume charge of the Indians of the Kennebec. In the autumn of 1650 Druillettes again descended the river and arrived at Norridgewock, to the joy of the Indians. This time he came not only as a missionary, but also as a political envoy charged with the negotiation of a treaty. The colony of Massachusetts had asked for reciprocity of trade with Canada. The authorities at Quebec were willing on one condition—an offensive and defensive alliance against the Iroquois. Since the English commonwealth claimed jurisdiction over the Kennebec Indians, it was its plain duty to protect them against their sleepless foes. Druillettes was an envoy of Quebec and of the Abenaki nation to negotiate the treaty. While his friend Winslow forwarded to Boston notice of the missionary's embassy, the work of instructing and converting went on at Norridgewock.

In November he started for the Puritan stronghold, whose chief object in colonizing was "to raise a bulwark against the kingdom of Antichrist, which the Jesuits labor to rear up in all places of the world"—the Puritan stronghold that just three years before had enacted "that Jesuits entering the colony should be expelled, and if they returned, hanged." But the Puritans chose to see in him not the Jesuit, but the ambassador. He was welcomed and fêted everywhere. Edward Gibbons gave him hospitality and a room wherein to say mass; Governor Dudley had him as guest of honor at a dinner graced by the magistrates; Governor Bradford, of Plymouth, also entertained him at dinner, and, as it was Friday, provided fish for him; Eliot lodged him for a night at Roxbury and showed him his Indian pupils; Endicott, at Salem, sympathized with the purpose of his embassy, and advanced him money for his return voyage; and Druillettes himself, we fancy, kept his eyes open and compared the young, bustling, freedom-loving colonies with the feudal colony on the St. Lawrence. He returned to Quebec in June without any definite answer, but with the hope that the object of his mission would meet with success in the near future.

The governor of Quebec and his council heard his report and sent him back to meet the Commissioners of the Four Colonies assembled in New Haven (1651). The Catholic priest pleaded before the assembly—a strange meeting indeed—for a brotherhood of the European nations settled on American soil, and for combined action against the heathen power of the Iroquois. It was in vain. The bait of free trade failed to bring the Puritans to sacrifice their strongest bulwark against French power. Druillettes went back to Canada to report his failure, nor did he ever again revisit his Indian flock on the Kennebec.

For thirty-six years—that is to say, from 1652, date of Druillettes' last visit to the Kennebec, until 1688—the mission work of Maine was interrupted, or rather no missionary resided among the Abenakis. However, frequent visits of the Indians to missions on the St. Lawrence kept them in constant contact with the French and the Jesuits. A certain number of the Abenakis, in order to be under French protection and near their Christian teachers, emigrated to Sillery and fixed their residence in that mission.

Subsequently they were transferred to the mission of St. Francis, on the Chaudière River. These had great influence over their fellow-tribesmen in Maine, and were ever ready to give them hospitality on their visits to the French settlements and authorities, and to take part with them in their wars. The distance from St. Francis to the Abenaki villages on the Kennebec was but a two-weeks' journey. This condition of things explains how Christianity was maintained among them in spite of the absence of a missionary.

In 1688 the Maine missions were reopened at three points—at Norridgewock on the Kennebec, at Pentagoet on the Penobscot, on the St. John River at its mouth. The Jesuits took charge of the Kennebec tribe, the Seminary of Quebec of the Penobscot, the Recollects of the Micmacs on the St. John. As the work of the latter lay mostly to the north of the river, outside the limits of the United States, we dismiss it. The Seminary of Quebec after a few years surrendered its post on the Penobscot. By the year 1700 all the Indians in Maine were in charge of the Society of Jesus, and most of them at that time were Christians.

When the war known in Europe as the War of the Spanish Succession, and in America as Queen Anne's War, broke out, the Maine Indians very naturally sided with the French, to whom they were bound by ties of religion and trade. It was in vain that Dudley, governor of Massachusetts, attempted in May, 1702, at the meeting of Casco, to bring the Abenaki chiefs to an attitude of neutrality; in a few weeks, war, burning, desolation, and death raged all along the frontier. Few incidents in our border history and Indian wars are more pathetic than the attacks on Deerfield and Haverhill. Nothing in all our history more than the cruelties of this war filled the Americans with greater hatred for the French missionaries, whom they held responsible, though without ground, for the fierceness with which Canadians and Indians waged war on the defenseless colonists, respecting neither age nor sex. To the same source may be attributed that contempt for the Indian, that dogged determination to exterminate the race, that have characterized the Puritan and placed him in such unenviable contrast to the New Yorker, Dutch and English, the Pennsylvanian, the Marylander, and the Southern colonists.

This terrible war was ended (1713) by the Peace of Utrecht, which was no less important for America than it was momentous for Europe. It gave to England large concessions of territory hitherto considered as French, and in so far was the entering wedge that split and shattered the American empire of France. England obtained the entire possession of Hudson's Bay, of Newfoundland, and of Nova Scotia or Acadia "according to its ancient boundaries"; and France acknowledged that the Five Nations were subject to the protectorate of Great Britain. This latter concession was big with important conclusions, which were drawn and made practical at a later date. The cession of Acadia "according to its ancient boundaries" raised immediately the question, Which are the ancient boundaries? The St. Croix, said the French, and therefore the territory between the Kennebec and the St. Croix was not ceded; in other words, the Treaty of Utrecht did not give Maine to the British crown. The Kennebec, said the English, and therefore not only the territory now called Nova Scotia and New Brunswick, but also what is now known as Maine, was ceded by the Peace of Utrecht to England; and therefore not only the Five Nations, but the Abenaki tribes also, were English subjects.

To solve this and other disputed questions, commissioners were appointed by both countries who held many meetings; but no solution was found until the war of 1744. While France and England were fighting over maps and charts and relations of early voyagers, to decide which was in possession of Maine, the Abenakis themselves came forward with the assertion that they alone were the rightful owners of their land, and backed their claim by a war of their own making against the English encroachers on their domain. That they were sustained in this struggle by the government of Canada cannot be denied when one studies the original documents of Paris, New York, and Massachusetts. That the Jesuits instigated the war; that they sacrificed to their national sympathies and the political interests of France the lessons of Christianity, the spiritual interests of their flock; and that they used their power over their neophytes only to drive back the English colonists and hold the Abenaki country as a buffer between the Protestant colonies and Catholic Canada, cannot be proved by any original authorities worthy the serious consideration of a grave and impartial critic.

The missionary on the Kennebec at this time was one who in life attracted the hatred of the English colonists, for whom France and Catholicity were one and equally inimical to their interests; who in death is still the target of historical hates hardly less fierce. Sébastien Rale, born in Franche-Comté, France, in 1657, came to the American missions in 1689, at the age of thirty-two. After spending some time among the Abenaki immigrants in Canada and on the Illinois beyond Lake Michigan, he was sent to the Abenakis of the Kennebec, where he was pursuing missionary work when Queen Anne's War broke out. Near the present village of Norridgewock, at a point known then as Narantsouac and now as Indian Old Point, stood his church. Here he lived and labored for a quarter of a century. We have from himself, in letters to his brother and his nephew, a detailed description of his life, than which nothing more apostolic can be found in the history of the church. He was familiar with several Indian languages of the Algonquin family, and knew Abenaki so thoroughly that he wrote a very complete dictionary of it, the manuscript of which is still preserved in Harvard and was published in 1833.

During the war the villages on the Penobscot were raided by Major Church, and those on the Kennebec by Major Hilton (1704–05). Not only were the habitations destroyed, but the church of Father Rale was burned and its sacred contents stolen and profaned. On the conclusion of peace the governor of Massachusetts offered to rebuild the church if the Indians would dismiss the French missionary and receive a Puritan minister. Evidently the governor was not familiar with the temper of the Christian Indian. His offer was scorned. The government of Canada rebuilt the church, and it was so goodly in size and style that, according to Rale himself, it might have passed muster in Europe. At the time there was another church in Maine, on the Penobscot, somewhat above the present Castine, in charge of Father Lauverjat.

This was the condition of the missions in Maine when, soon after the Peace of Utrecht, the Abenakis were informed that France had abandoned them and had ceded their country to England. As if to prove the truth of the news, not only were the English villages destroyed during the war restored, but the Kennebec was crossed, new English settlements and trading-posts were planted on its eastern bank, and forts were raised. But the Abenaki chiefs did not recognize the right of France to give away what God had made theirs—their country; and therefore denied the Englishman's right to occupy it. Canada, it is true, could not openly side with them in a war for their right of possession, since there was peace between France and England; but Canada could secretly encourage and help them to maintain an independence which was of sovereign importance to the integrity of the St. Lawrence.

The colony of Massachusetts was well aware that, if it would have its own way with the Abenakis, the first step was to get rid of the French missionaries, especially of Father Rale. As a direct demand had been more than once made on the Indians for his dismissal and had been refused, only two ways remained to encompass the end—competition or violence. Competition was first tried. A Protestant minister, the Rev. Joseph Baxter, was sent to the tribe to counteract, and in due course of time to destroy, the influence of the Catholic priest. Parkman very frankly says, "With no experience of Indian life or knowledge of any Indian language, he entered the lists against an adversary who spent half his days among savages, had gained the love and admiration of the Norridgewock, and spoke their language fluently. Baxter, with the confidence of a novice, got an interpreter and began to preach, exhort, and launch sarcasms against the doctrines and practices of the Roman Church. Rale came to the rescue of his flock. 'My Christians,' said he, 'believe the truths of the Catholic faith, but are not skillful disputants.'" Thereupon, on behalf of his neophytes, he entered the field of controversy, and sent Baxter a long defense of Catholic doctrines. The paper was in Latin. To prepare an answer and put the answer in Latin, Baxter found it convenient to go to Boston. The answer was short, and, says Rale in a letter to his brother, "of a style so obscure and a Latinity so outlandish that I had to read it more than once to get at its meaning. I finally made out that he complained of my baseless attack on him, and that my arguments were ridiculous and puerile. I rejoined in a second letter showing up his mistakes. After two years I got answer that evidently I was of a scornful and critical temper and was inclined to anger." So ended and failed the attempt at competition.

The attempt at violence came in a short time. Several Indian chiefs, at the instigation of the colonial authorities, were sent to Boston as deputies to arrange amicably the difficulties between the tribe and the commonwealth. They were detained in Boston as prisoners, or rather as hostages, not to be given up until certain outrages perpetrated on the colonists, and valued at two hundred beaver-skins, were made good. The Indians—not that they owned to the outrages and the obligation to compensate for them, but that they wished for the freedom and return of their chiefs—paid the required indemnity. Notwithstanding, the hostages were detained. To this violation of good faith another injury was added. A war-chief, Baron de St. Castin—French on his father's side, and as such holding from the court of Paris a commission as governor of Pentagoet; Indian on his mother's side, and as such a true Abenaki and a chief among them—was seized by stealth and carried off to Boston, where he was treated as a traitor to the English crown, though he was at last set at liberty, for the reason that the Indians were aroused and had begun to burn and kill along the border.

A price was set on Rale's head to tempt the Indians, but without avail. Finally, in midwinter, Colonel Westbrook, at the head of three hundred men, pounced suddenly down on Norridgewock at a time when the warriors were away and Rale was in the village with only the old, the women, and the children. The father, warned of the enemy's approach by some Indians who had seen them coming, had time to consume the consecrated hosts, which he dreaded to leave to profanation, and escaped to the woods, where he was not discovered, though his pursuers came within a few feet of him. His papers fell into the hands of Westbrook, and are still preserved in the archives of Massachusetts. Parkman makes the assertion that they prove beyond all doubt that he had acted as an agent of the Canadian authorities in exciting his flock against the English. And yet he specifies but one letter from Vaudreuil to Rale expressing great satisfaction at the missionary's success in uniting the Indians against the English. If this be the only premise he has for his conclusion, there is more in the conclusion than in the premise. Bancroft contents himself with saying, "The correspondence with Vaudreuil proved a latent hope of establishing the power of France on the Atlantic."

Exasperated by all these insults, the Abenakis resolved to wage a war of extermination. They sent deputies to carry the hatchet and chant the war-song among their friends and allies along the St. Lawrence. The burning of settlements and murdering of settlers went on with greatest cruelty. Rale clearly foresaw that in the end the red men must be conquered. By his advice many families withdrew to the Christian missions on the Canadian border, though this policy did not at all suit that of Vaudreuil and the Canadian authorities, who were unwilling to abandon to the English the rivers of Maine, whose head-waters were so close to the St. Lawrence To the solicitations of his neophytes to seek safety in flight, accompany the refugees to the Canadian missions, and leave the warriors to deal with the English, Rale opposed a constant refusal; he would remain at his post until the very last.

In July, 1722, the government of Massachusetts declared formal war against the Abenakis and raised troops. In March, 1723, Westbrook fell on the Indian settlement of the Penobscot, probably Old Town, above Bangor, and set fire to the village. The fort, every house, and the church where ministered Father Lauverjat were consumed. In August, 1724, Norridgewock was surprised by two hundred and eight men under Colonel Moulton. The Indians did not become aware of the presence of the English until the first volley had been fired within the streets of the village. Fifty warriors—all that were at home—rushed out in disorder, not so much to defend themselves as to give time to the non-combatants to flee to the woods. In the same spirit of heroic self-sacrifice, Rale, well aware that he was the one prey the English were in search of, came forward to draw their attention from his flock to himself. At sight of him a great yell went up from the English ranks; he fell, riddled with bullets, at the foot of the great cross on the village square. When the invaders retired and the Indians came back from their hiding-places to care for the wounded and bury the dead, Rale's body was found "mangled by many blows, scalped, his skull broken in several places, his mouth and eyes filled with dirt." So Bancroft describes the work of the English, or of the Indians that accompanied them.

Thus died one of the noblest members of the heroic band of North American Jesuits, worthy compeer of Jogues, Bressani, Brébeuf, and many another martyr. The story of Rale's death comes to us from the account given by the superior of the Jesuits at Quebec, Father La Chasse, in a letter to the Jesuits of France, dated October 29, 1724, a few months after the event. No doubt he had the story from eye-witnesses, the Abenakis engaged in the fight, "who are," says Parkman, "notorious liars where their interest and self-love are concerned." But what interest and self-love of theirs are particularly concerned in Rale's death? Why call them "notorious liars" when on the very same page we read, "Rale exercised a humanizing influence over his flock; the war was marked by fewer barbarities, fewer tortures, mutilations of the dead, butcheries of women and infants, than either of the preceding wars"? If he could turn these savages into civilized belligerents he could also have taught them love of truth. To call, in a gloriously sweeping style, the eye-witnesses of Rale's death "notorious liars" is to poison the wells of evidence; for the nonce the historian has forgotten himself in the special pleader.

The war went on for some months. But at last the Indians, who, though instigated, were not supported by the French, became painfully aware that they were excelled by the English even in their own method of warfare, and concluded a peace (August, 1726) that was long and faithfully maintained. They became the subjects of England; but they did not for that reason renounce their religion, thus proving that it was a mistake on the part of the Canadian authorities to think that their fidelity to Rome was bound up with their fidelity to Versailles; that the moment they should escape the French protectorate they would fall away from Catholicity. The history of the Abenakis thenceforth proves the contrary.

After the peace the village of Norridgewock was dispersed. One hundred and fifty of the tribe emigrated to Canada, and the remainder found refuge among the other tribes of Maine. The Penobscot settlement rose from its ashes; its chapel was rebuilt, and remained under the care of Father Lauverjat until he was driven away by the immoralities and persecution of the half-breed St. Castines. In 1730 Norridgewock also rose from its ashes. Indians from other parts of Maine and from the missions of St. Francis and Bécancour on the St. Lawrence returned to the Kennebec, and a missionary, Father James de Syresne, or Sirenne, came from Quebec to reside among them. From Norridgewock he extended his visits and care to all the tribes of Maine.

After Father De Sirenne, Father Germain, residing at St. Ann, on the St. John River, near the present Frederickton, visited the Catholics throughout Maine. For many years after 1760 the Indians remained without a missionary. The stern laws of the Puritan colonies against the church were in force. Perhaps, for all we know, priests from Canada made stealthy visits to the scattered Catholic Indians, and no doubt the Indians made frequent visits to the Çanadian missions. The parents baptized and instructed their children. Every Sunday, morning and evening, they assembled in the chapels of their various villages, and before the priestless altars chanted the mass and vespers, the Gregorian melodies being handed down from generation to generation. Thus without priest those faithful red men kept the faith under circumstances that would have annihilated religion among the whites. Outside of Japan I know nothing more admirable in the history of Christianity than the perseverance of the Abenakis in the faith of the early missionaries.

When the War of Independence came on, the Indians of Maine joined the army of Washington. The Penobscot chief, Orono, bore a commission which he ennobled by his bravery. Nor in his wanderings through the colonies did he or his followers forget their religion. To all invitations to join in Protestant worship they made answer, "We know our religion and love it; we know nothing of you and yours." When in 1775 they met at Watertown the council of Massachusetts to agree as to their action in the war, the chief, Ambrose Var, after the political object of the meeting had been disposed of, addressed the commissioners in these words: "We want a black gown, or French priest. Jesus we pray to, and we will not hear any prayer that comes from Old England." The council expressed willingness to get them a priest; but not knowing where to find one, could only offer them a minister, an offer most sternly declined. What a strange scene! Here was a colony that had made it a felony for a priest to visit the Abenakis, that had sought and taken the life of Rale at the foot of the village cross, regretting that it could not give their allies the priest they demanded.

Peace came, and independence, and the organization of the church. Bishop Carroll sent these heroic Indians a missionary. Cheverus, first Bishop of Boston, and his successors, Fenwick and Fitzpatrick, visited them and bestowed their utmost care on this remnant of Jesuit zeal and labors. But this belongs to later history. To-day one thousand descendants of the neophytes of Druillettes and Rale hold the faith and sing the chants of their Catholic forefathers at Indian Old Town, Pleasant Point, and Louis Island, in the diocese of Portland, Me.

CHAPTER XI.

THE MISSIONS IN NEW YORK.

THESE missions were an offshoot, or rather a result, of the labors of missionaries in territory outside the present United States, viz., among the Hurons situated in the peninsula bounded by Lakes Ontario, Erie, and Huron. That territory is the present province of Ontario. It is not my business to recount the birth, the success, the ruin of this Huron mission, the most glorious in the annals of the Jesuits in North America, except in so far as it may be necessary to make plain the history of the missions in New York.

As early as 1623–25 the Recollects Viel, Le Caron, and Sagard went to the Huron country and reached the tribe of the Neutrals, situated on the Niagara River. There is no evidence at hand that they did any more than visit this tribe, or that they made any permanent sojourn among them. After the Recollects of Canada had called to their aid the Jesuits, the Huron missions passed into the hands of the latter, and Brébeuf was in the territory in 1626. The capture of Quebec by Kirk (1628) suspended the work of the Jesuits, whom he ordered back to France. But when Canada was restored in 1632 the Jesuits returned to the Huron country, and continued the mission down to the time of its destruction by the Iroquois in 1649.

Now the Iroquois missions are bound up with the Huron missions in two ways: first, the martyrs of the Iroquois missions were men who had labored in the Huron missions; secondly, after the destruction of the Huron missions a large number of Huron Christians were incorporated into the Five Nations, or the Iroquois Confederacy. The influence of these Christians on their conquerors had much to do in many ways with the invitation extended in after years to the Jesuits by the Iroquois to come to their country.

The fatal expedition of Champlain in 1609 against the Iroquois had left in the hearts of those tribes a hatred that years failed to extinguish. Moreover, the Hurons, whom the Iroquois had been fighting long before the French came, and whom they hounded to final extermination, were the allies and protégés of Canada. From this connection many results followed. The only way to the West which lay open to the French was by way of the Ottawa River; the navigation of the upper St. Lawrence and the lower lakes Ontario and Erie was closed to them, because this avenue was in the hands of the Iroquois. Stretching from the Mohawk River to the Niagara they had two lines by which to swoop down upon the French settlements and intercept their trade with the Western tribes over the Ottawa route. Those lines were, first, Lakes George, Champlain, and the Richelieu River; second, Ontario and the upper St. Lawrence.

Any war waged by the Iroquois against either the Huron or the far Western tribes trading with the French was a war against Canada; for war against those tribes stopped trade, and without trade the French colony was doomed to death. After the destruction of the Huron missions and nation in 1649, a portion of the unfortunate tribe wandered as far as Lakes Superior and Michigan, and there sought to remake their fortunes in alliance with the tribes of the far West; a portion was adopted into the

Five Nations, or the Iroquois Confederacy; a portion sought refuge in the neighborhood of Montreal and Quebec, and was formed into reductions. But the implacable Iroquois, not content with having broken up the Huron nation, were restless until they had absorbed the fragments into themselves; hence either constant forays on the Huron reductions of the St. Lawrence, or wars on them and their allies in the West, or secret intrigues and invitations to them to leave the shelter of French protection and come to live in the Iroquois country. Without these considerations it will not be easy to understand the history of the New York and the Western missions.

Among the Jesuits at work in 1641 on the Huron missions were Charles Raymbault and Isaac Jogues. That same year the great Indian festival of the dead was held. Among the invited allies and relations were some Chippeways from Sault Ste. Marie, at the eastern end of Lake Superior. They solicited the missionaries to visit their people. Raymbault and Jogues were detailed for this purpose. The visit was but a short one. Both missionaries returned to Quebec, Raymbault to recover his shattered health, Jogues to get mission supplies for the Huron work, and mayhap in time to labor in the new field among the Chippeways. In August, 1642, he was paddling his way back with an escort of Hurons, two *donnés* (volunteer servants), Réné Goupil and Guillaume Couture, and a goodly supply of necessaries for his brother religious in the West, when they were suddenly attacked by Mohawks.

At the time all Canada was in terror of these savages. "No man in all Canada," says Parkman, "could hunt, fish, till the fields, or cut a tree in the forest without peril to his scalp." "I had as lief," writes one of the Jesuits, Father Vimont, "be beset by goblins as by the Iroquois. The one are about as invisible as the other. Our people on the Richelieu and at Montreal are kept in a closer confinement than ever were monks or nuns in our smallest convents in France." Armed with firearms which they had purchased from the Dutch of Fort Orange, now Albany, they were a terror to all Indians and more than a match for the French. They despised both as poltroons, and boasted they would wipe them both off the face of the earth. They were masters of the upper St. Lawrence and the junction of the Ottawa. They cut off all trade of the French with the Western tribes, and intercepted the communications of the Quebec Jesuits with their brothers in the Huron country. The spirit of the Algonquin tribes from the Saguenay to the Lake of the Nipissings became broken; they clung for safety to the French. But this very clinging brought down on the French the hatred and enmity of the fierce savages of the Five Nations.

It was in one of their usual forays that they came down upon the canoes of Jogues. The missionary might have escaped, but there were in the hands of the enemy converts not yet baptized. He surrendered to the Iroquois. Then began days of torture and suffering. Not only Jogues and the two Frenchmen, but the Christian Hurons, men and women, were subjected to the refined cruelties of their foes, and bore the torments with the stolidity of the Indian nature and the resignation of Christian martyrs. Guillaume Couture was adopted into the tribe on account of his bravery under torture. Réné Goupil, after much suffering, was tomahawked. Jogues was run through the gauntlet at every village, tied to the stake to be gashed and slowly burned, had his hands mutilated, and was preserved from final death only to be made a slave. He found some work to do among the captive Christian Hurons. He roamed the woods chanting psalms; he carved the name of Jesus on the trees, thus consecrating the land to his Master.

Finally he was released by the kindness and generosity of the Dutch of Fort Orange, whither his captors had taken him on more than one visit. He was sent down the Hudson to Manhattan, where he was welcomed by the population. While awaiting a vessel for Europe he found in New Amsterdam two Catholics, a Portuguese woman and an Irishman. He reached France in January, 1644. The Pope granted him a dispensation to say mass with his mutilated hands. That same year he returned to Canada, undaunted—nay, encouraged—by his former experiences. We shall meet him again among the Iroquois.

In the spring of 1644, Father Bressani, a Roman, met with a fate like unto that of Jogues. He was on his way to the Huron mission when he was attacked and captured by a band of Mohawks. In the July following Bressani wrote from his captivity to the general in Rome: "I do not know if your Paternity will recognize the handwriting of one you once knew very well. The letter is soiled and ill written, because the writer has one finger of his right hand left entire, and cannot prevent the blood from his wounds, which are still open, from staining the paper." He goes on in this humble and moving style to detail his torments. His captors had split his hand with a knife between the little finger and the ring-finger, beaten him with sticks till he was covered with blood, and afterward placed him on one of their torture-scaffolds as a spectacle to the crowd. Here they stripped him, and while he shivered with cold from head to foot, they forced him to sing. The children had their turn—ordered him to dance, at the same time thrusting sharpened sticks into his flesh and pulling out his hair and beard.

These scenes were renewed every night for a week. They burned him with live coals and red-hot stones, forced him to walk on hot cinders, burned off now a finger-nail and now the joint of a finger. They hung him by the feet with chains; placed food for the dogs on his naked body, that they might lacerate him as they ate. "I could not have believed that a man was so hard to kill," writes he in the letter to his superior. Finally he too was ransomed by the Dutch of Fort Orange, and sent back to France. The following year (1645) he returned to Canada and was sent to the Huron missions. Those men were hungry of martyrdom.

While Bressani was undergoing his sufferings in the Mohawk country, three Iroquois, caught in the neighborhood of Three Rivers by Hurons, were having their feet burned and their fingers cut off. The commandant of the fort, Champfleur, prevailed on the Indian torturers to suspend their revenge until Montmagny, the governor of Canada, should arrive and dispose of the prisoners. The governor saw the possibility of using the three captives as a means of concluding peace with their countrymen. They were sent home with a message that Onontio (Big Mountain, Montmagny), the name ever after given by the Iroquois to the governors of Quebec, had given them their lives, and that he still held in his possession two other prisoners formerly captured, whom he should likewise remit if peace were made with the French. Two months afterward came an embassy from the Mohawk nation. Chiefs from the Huron tribe and the neighboring nations along the St. Lawrence were summoned to a grand council, and, after the many mutual presents and speeches usual to Indian diplomacy had been disposed of, peace was concluded. The Mohawk ambassadors took the path homeward, and with them went Jogues, on a political as well as religious embassy, to confirm the peace and to found a mission under the title "Mission of the Martyrs."

He retraced the route every mile of which was marked

in his memory by former sufferings: the Richelieu River, Lake Champlain, Lake George—that he christened Lac St. Sacrement because he reached it on the eve of Corpus Christi; thence by land to Fort Orange, where he visited his friends and protectors, the Dutch traders; thence to the towns on the Mohawk River. A council was held, presents were made, the speeches were spoken, the peace was ratified. His political mission being accomplished, he returned to Quebec. He wished to make his report to the governor, and Mohawk allies had advised him to be off at once, lest the Iroquois of the other tribes who were not parties to the treaty should fail to respect his office of ambassador and his escort of Hurons. After reporting as to the success of his embassy, his superiors ordered him to return to carry out the second part of his work, the founding of a mission among the Mohawks.

Meanwhile a change had come over the spirit of the Mohawks. On his previous visit Jogues had left behind him a small chest containing some personal effects. Pervert Hurons, captives among the Mohawks, hinted that the chest contained a sorcery that would bring evil to them, as the medicine of the Black Robes had brought evil to the Huron nation. This suspicion was rife when a band of Mohawk warriors met Jogues and his one companion, Lalande, a *donné*, south of Lake George. They seized him and led him in triumph to their town; here he was beaten, and strips of flesh were cut from his back and arms. It was in vain that the soberer and better savages raised their voices in his defense. He was doomed, and fell, brained by a tomahawk, and with him his companion. The date of their martyrdom was October 18, 1646, and the scene the present village of Auriesville, Montgomery County, N. Y. A small Catholic chapel marks the spot. The narrative of his sufferings and death was drawn up under the authority of the Archbishop of Rouen, and attested by oath to serve in any process of canonization that might be inaugurated. The Third Plenary Council of Baltimore (November, 1884) formally petitioned the holy see to allow the cause of his canonization to be introduced.

After the death of Jogues there was an end of peace. The war of the Iroquois against the Hurons and Canada continued with unabated fury, and culminated (1650) in the destruction of the Huron missions and the scattering of the Huron nation. Success made the Iroquois bold in the extreme. Montreal, Three Rivers, Quebec, the three chief settlements of the French on the St. Lawrence, were in consternation and daily fear. The fur-trade was ruined. Public prayers and fasting were appointed to obtain a cessation of this terrible state of things. Peace finally came, but not without the price of another martyr's blood.

It was the summer of 1653; Father Poncet, out on an errand of charity, a few miles above Cape Rouge, was surprised by an ambuscade of Iroquois and carried off into the Mohawk towns. He trod the path of Jogues and Bressani; was frequently beaten in the run of the gauntlet, tortured by fire and knife, all but brought to death's door. While he was undergoing this slow martyrdom, sixty Onondagas came to Montreal to treat for peace. This unusual move is accounted for by the fact that the Iroquois were at war just then with the Eries, their western neighbors, and it behooved them to secure themselves on the side of the French. One war at a time was their policy. Clouds rolled away, life returned to the colony, the fur-trade revived. "Yesterday," writes the Jesuit superior Le Mercier, "all was dejection and gloom, to-day all is smiles and gayety. If the Iroquois have their hidden designs, so, too, has God." Of course one of the conditions of peace was Poncet's liberation. He reached Montreal October 21, 1650.

The Iroquois did have their "secret designs," as Le Mercier conjectured. At the very moment they were making peace with the French they were pursuing those designs with their usual cunning. They wished to coax into their own country the unhappy remnant of the Hurons who were living on the Island of Orleans, immediately below Quebec. The Onondagas and the Mohawks were competitors for this prize, and each was jealous lest the other should be the first to get it. Of the two the Onondagas had the deeper scheme and the better chance of success. Among them were already settled many Huron converts. If a Jesuit mission and a colony of French were planted in the Onondaga country, perhaps the Hurons of Orleans Island might be more easily induced to emigrate.

But God, too, had his designs, or rather the Jesuits nourished a bold plan. Their Huron mission had been destroyed. Among the Iroquois were many of their former converts. To care for these was their evident duty. Who knew but that in the providence of God the transplanting of those Christian Hurons was to be the means of bringing the Five Nations to the faith and opening up a new field to Jesuit zeal? It was resolved, before taking any decisive step, to send some one to confirm the Onondagas in their peaceful mood, and ascertain the sincerity of their petition for a mission and a colony. The ambassador chosen was Father Simon le Moyne. He set out July 2, 1653; his route was the upper St. Lawrence and Lake Ontario to the mouth of the Oswego. He was received with due pomp and great joy. Deputies of the Senecas, Oneidas, and Cayugas met him in the chief village of the Onondagas; of the confederacy only the Mohawks were absent. The usual presents and speeches were made by both parties with befitting gravity, and the French were invited to make a settlement on Lake Ontario. On his way back to Quebec to report, Le Moyne was shown a spring of water that was tenanted, so the Indians said, by a bad spirit. Le Moyne found it to be salt-springs, the famous Onondaga springs. His return to Quebec brought joy to the colonists on the St. Lawrence, and the prospect of a period of peace and trade.

However, the Mohawks had not been a party to the treaty. Their allies of the confederacy were busy with war on the Eries; indeed, it was this very war that had brought about the peace with the French. But the Mohawks, taking no part in the Erie war, were free to continue their attacks on the Hurons of the St. Lawrence, and they were doing so at the very time the rest of the confederacy were entering into treaty with Canada. The summer following Le Moyne's return to Quebec a deputation of Onondagas arrived to give further assurances of peace, to insist on the planting of a French colony among them, and to offer the missionaries the most delightful position in their canton. Before sending out a French colony the authorities wisely resolved to establish the mission. Fathers Chaumonot, an old Huron missionary, and Dablon, a newcomer, were detailed for this work. They arrived at Oswego September, 1654, and proceeded thence to Onondaga, the chief town of the tribe. Councils were held, talks were frequent and long, and it became evident to Chaumonot that without the immediate planting of the French colony peace could not be preserved. He sent back Dablon with this information.

Governor and Jesuits finally decided to act accordingly. Major Dupuys, with ten soldiers, thirty French colonists, four Jesuits, Le Mercier, Ménard, Frémin, Dablon, and two lay brothers composed the colony. They were received by the Onondagas with every appearance of joy. A site on Lake Ganentaa, now Onondaga, was allotted to them. Dwellings, or rather huts, storehouses, and a chapel were built and surrounded with a palisade, and the settlement was christened "Mission of Our Lady of Ganentaa." This was the center and base of missionary operations among the Iroquois. West of Onondaga were the Cayugas and Senecas, east were the Oneidas and Mohawks. No better central point could have been chosen. Ménard set out for the Cayugas, Chaumonot for the Senecas, and in the following spring work was begun among the Oneidas.

Of the Five Nations the Mohawks alone held aloof from the missionaries, and pursued their work of war and enslavement along the St. Lawrence. If the Onondagas were about to incorporate into their tribe, as they hoped, the remnant of the Hurons by means of the colony and mission they had solicited and obtained, the Mohawks were bound to get their share of the human plunder in the old Indian fashion. This struggle for the possession of the Hurons was the wedge that split the confederacy. For the missions which the Onondagas had invited, and the other tribes, Cayugas, Senecas, Oneidas, had allowed and accepted, made them friends of France. Years afterward they emigrated to the banks of the St. Lawrence and took sides with the Canadians against the pagan Mohawks and their allies, the English. By a strange fate the Hurons, whom the Five Nations had denationalized, disrupted in their turn the Iroquois Confederacy. History is full of such revenges on a larger scale.

Meanwhile the missions among the Onondagas, Cayugas, Senecas, and Oneidas were giving promise of splendid success. In fact, the Iroquois were receiving the faith more readily than even the Hurons had done. The prisoners and slaves among them were the first to embrace the faith, as in the early centuries of Christianity. The Christian Hurons, especially, by their virtues and patience, wielded a beneficial influence over their conquerors. The Iroquois women were the first to yield to the church, and, as their power was great in the councils of the nation, they were a tower of strength to the mission. So cheering were the tidings reported to Quebec that more laborers were sent to reinforce the little band of missionaries.

However, fair as were the appearances among the tribes that welcomed the missionaries, a secret danger was hatching; the confederacy was seething with impatient desire to break the peace, and the young warriors were planning the destruction of the French colonists. The Canadian governor, D'Aillebout, suspecting the conspiracy, resolved to have hostages in his hands, suddenly seized all the Iroquois found within the limits of the Canadian colonies, and advised the missionaries of the danger that threatened them. The priests and the colonists assembled within the palisade of Ganentaa not any too soon, for immediately around the palisaded fort gathered a throng of Onondaga warriors, impassive, not ready yet to give the blow, but watchful of their imprisoned guests. The reason for the delay is to be found in the embarrassment of the sachems as to the hostages held in Quebec by D'Aillebout.

The position of the Europeans was becoming desperate; the blow might fall at any time; they must bestir themselves; they must first provide means of escape and then make their escape. The first was the easier; timber was abundant, the carpenters were set to work secretly, and enough boats were built to carry off all the French. The second was not so easy at first sight; however, cunning and boldness made a way. Among the many superstitions of the Iroquois was one that concerned dreams and entailed ridiculous consequences. If in answer to a dream Indians were invited to a feast, they were obliged to eat everything laid before them, no matter how large the quantity. One of the young Frenchmen adopted into the tribe was favored conveniently with a dream calling for a banquet. An immense feast was made ready by the French, and the Onondaga warriors had to gorge themselves until they were overcome by the lethargy of a monstrous digestion. The Canadians escaped during the drunken sleep of their jailers and arrived at Montreal April, 1658. The missions were suspended and a long and cruel war followed. Thus ended the first attempt to introduce Christianity among the Iroquois of New York.

An orator, relative of the chief sachem of the Onondagas, Garakontie by name, had listened to the teachings of the missionaries, though he had not embraced openly the faith, had watched carefully the effect of Christianity on the Christian Iroquois and Hurons, and had come to the conclusion that it was a religion necessary for the civilization and preservation of his race. After the departure of the missionaries he became the protector and consoler of the Christians left behind and of the captives brought in during the war that followed. He it was who, in 1660, influenced his tribe to send a deputation to Montreal to ask for the return of missionaries and also for a colony of nuns. Small confidence was reposed by the French in any promise or solicitation of an Iroquois tribe. However, this opportunity was seized to renew, if possible, peace and missionary work. The veteran Le Moyne was chosen for the purpose. He reappeared again in Onondaga in 1660, and for a year ministered to the faithful Hurons and the Iroquois converts of the former mission. But his stay among them was short, there was no lull in the hostilities, and after his departure the war raged as frightfully as ever. But now

Canada was aroused to put forth her mightiest efforts, a large force of regulars was sent from France, one after another the five tribes of the confederacy were worsted, and by the end of 1666 they all sued for peace. This opened a new era for mission work, and the Jesuits thought their dream of the conversion of the Iroquois was about to be realized.

In 1667 were sent to the Mohawks Fathers Frémin, Bruyas, and Pierron. They began work in the village where Jogues had met his death. Two thirds of its population were Christian Algonquins, who, despite the long absence of missionaries, had persevered in the faith; the women especially were remarkable for their strong attachment to the church. As the Jews of old, in the midst of the nations that conquered them, were the providential means of spreading the knowledge of the true God and his revelation, so the Hurons among the pagan Iroquois. Moreover, the blood of the martyrs who had died in this land, no less than that of those who had given their lives laboring in the Huron missions, was pleading with Heaven and was about to spring into a harvest of Christians. The missionaries were solemnly received by representatives of the whole Mohawk tribe in their capital village, Tionnontuguen, a site for a chapel was assigned them, the chapel was built by the Mohawks themselves, and thus was founded the mission of St. Mary of the Mohawks. Father Frémin took charge of it; Father Pierron was dispatched to Albany to conciliate the English authorities, and thence returned to Quebec to report on the success and prospects of the enterprise. Father Bruyas was assigned to work among the Oneidas just west of the Mohawks. He was well received, a chapel was built for him, and the Indians crowded to listen to his teaching. This was the mission of St. Francis Xavier of the Oneidas.

Pierron's visit to Quebec had for immediate result the sending to the Onondagas of Father Julian Garnier. His welcome was cordial, especially on the part of Garakontie, who throughout the war had remained the steadfast friend of the French and the Christians. A chapel was built and regular mission work began. Meanwhile the brave Garakontie, with some French liberated prisoners, set out for Quebec and brought back two fathers: Milet, who was to labor among the Onondagas; and De Carheil, who passed on to the Cayugas immediately west of the Onondagas, and there set up the mission of St. Joseph. Pierron, leaving Milet with the Onondagas, took Frémin's place in the Mohawk country, and Frémin started for the most western tribe of the confederacy, the Senecas, where he built a chapel and founded a mission; thus by the close of 1668 each of the five tribes had its church and missionary.

Meanwhile, villages of emigrated Iroquois, mostly Catholic, had been formed outside the present territory of the United States, at Quinte, on the north shore of Lake Ontario, and at La Prairie, near Montreal. With these and other future reductions in Canada we have not to do. This colonization scheme had been all along the policy of the Jesuits, who sought to withdraw their neophytes from the neighborhood and commerce of the English, whose influence on the savages, especially through brandy, was detrimental to their civilization and religion; and also from commerce with those Indians who remained attached to their medicine-men and old superstitions. The converted Iroquois, desirous of leading truly Christian lives, found it difficult to do so among their pagan relatives, and were only too glad to find peace and quiet in those Christian reductions.

One obstacle to the success of the work of the missionaries were the juggleries of the medicine-men. Another obstacle was drunkenness. French traders themselves were not innocent on this point, though the temporal and spiritual authorities in Canada had made stringent laws as to the selling of liquor to the Indians. But the evil was prevalent, especially among the tribes nearest to the English colonies, who were restrained by no laws in this matter. So crying was the vice among the Mohawks that Father Pierron was forced to appeal to the humane sense of Lovelace, the governor of New York, through a petition he presented in the name of the sachems. The answer of Lovelace was honorable and Christian: "I will restrain by severe penalties the furnishing of any excess to the Indians. I am delighted to see such virtuous thoughts proceed from heathens, to the shame of many Christians; but this must be attributed to your pious instructions, for you have shown them the way of mortification both in precept and practice."

It is beyond the purpose of this work to go into all the minute details that are found in the "Relations" in regard to these missions. The Huron missions had been a glorious field of apostolic zeal, of wonderful conversions, of saintliness among the neophytes; no less glorious a field were the Iroquois missions. Here the Jesuits gave examples of devotedness not to be equaled by their best members in any other quarter of the world; here God's grace produced marvelous holiness in many a child of the forest; warriors proud and cruel were turned into humble and merciful servants of the cross, women and maidens were made as chaste and virtuous as any of the female saints and martyrs of the palmy days of Christianity. The chapels were frequented morning and evening; the hymns and chants of the old church resounded throughout the woods of northern New York. Many who were not admitted to baptism were fervent catechumens and regular attendants at the services. To form an idea of the work done, one would have to read the whole third volume of the "Relations of the Jesuits." Between the years 1668 and 1678—in ten years—there were 2221 baptisms among all the Iroquois tribes. But such statistics give an incomplete idea of the state of religion among them, for the reason that it was the policy of the fathers to lengthen the catechumenate of their dusky disciples; so that the number of attendants at instructions and services was far beyond that of the baptized.

After 1678 a new obstacle arose to interfere with the work of the missionaries; no longer on the part of the Indians themselves, but of two Christian nations, though both at the time were governed by Catholic kings represented in their American provinces by Catholic governors. England and France, New York and Canada, began to quarrel over the possession of the valleys of the Mohawk and the Oswego. To their mutual jealousies the Iroquois missions of northern New York were sacrificed. A few explanations are needed to make the reader understand the cause and the progress of the quarrel.

In September, 1664, the Dutch colonists of New Amsterdam surrendered to the English fleet, commanded by Colonel Nicolls; and the surrender was formally approved by the European powers in the Treaty of Breda, July 21, 1667. New Netherland was rechristened New York. Fort Orange became Albany. From the time of the transfer a rivalry began between England and France for the control of the Iroquois, not unlike that we have seen between Canada and Massachusetts for the control of the Indians of Maine. The foremost of the French governors during this period was Frontenac, and his plan was not only to control the Iroquois, but also all the Western tribes as far as the Mississippi. It was little to have the alliance and the trade of the latter unless he had likewise those of the former. The main question was which way the Western peltries should reach the East: by way of the St. Lawrence and Quebec, or by way of the Hudson and New York. To make himself master of this latter route and keep the canoes of the Western tribes from the waters of the Hudson, Frontenac built on Lake Ontario, at a point where Kingston now stands, a fort to which he gave his name.

This fort was meant to be a rallying-point for Western expeditions, a center of operations against the Iroquois, and a market where both Eastern and Western tribes should meet for trade. It was admirably situated for all these purposes, as a glance at the map will show. The French policy and control were strengthened a few years later (1677) by another fort, built at Niagara by La Salle. Moreover, the Iroquois, since they had obtained firearms from the Dutch, had crushed out two tribes west of them, the Andastes and the Eries, and the profits of the fur-trade which they carried on with New York induced them to extend their forays farther and farther westward. This brought them in collision with the tribes of the Miamis, the Illinois on Lake Michigan, and the Algonquins on Lake Superior. Now these were allies and protégés of the French, and France in honor could not abandon them to the mercies of the Five Nations. To do so would be the destruction of the trade of Canada and the building up of the trade of New York. The governors of Canada were compelled, therefore, to restrain by force the western expansion of the Iroquois, and to defend their Indian allies. This work occupied the administrations of De la Barre, who superseded Frontenac, of Denonville, and again of Frontenac during his second term.

Dongan, the Catholic governor of New York, claimed in the name of England jurisdiction of all the territory south of Lake Ontario, and considered the Iroquois as subjects of the English crown, though that proud people never acknowledged the claim, but constantly asserted its independence of the two European rivals. Dongan held that the French Jesuits were political agents, and that their influence on the Iroquois was disastrous to English interests. His aim was to drive them out of the territory; he was willing to replace them by English Jesuits. Very sharp correspondence passed between Quebec and New York concerning Fort Niagara, the sale of liquor to the Indians, the control of trade in the West, and the political influence of the missionaries. The instructions of the French court to Denonville were to exterminate the Iroquois, sustain the Western allies, and oppose the schemes of Dongan. So Canada waged a vigorous war against the Iroquois; and Dongan could only look on, giving them no support save by advice and surreptitious presents of powder and guns, since France and England were at peace. But after the Stuarts had been expelled and William of Orange had come to the throne of England, war broke out between England and France in Europe, between Canada and the English colonies in America, both sides being helped by their Indian allies; the war lasted until the Peace of Ryswick (1697).

How fared it with Iroquois missions during those years of turbulence? Frémin, Pierron, and Garnier withdrew from the Senecas in 1683. De Carheil was driven by the chiefs of the tribe from the Cayugas in 1684. Only two Jesuits at this date were to be found in the Iroqûois country, at Onondaga; they were brothers, John and James de Lamberville. James was recalled to Canada in 1686, and John remained the sole representative of his church amid the foes of his country. It was from Denonville, the governor of Catholic Canada, that came the blow that put an end to the Iroquois mission, and the blow was a foul deed of treachery. Through Father John de Lamberville he invited the chiefs of the tribes to a conference (1687); when they came unsuspecting, confiding in the Jesuit's word, the governor violently seized them, and sent them in chains to France to become galley-slaves. He had used the missionary for his vile purpose.

More Christian and generous than their European foes, the Iroquois, instead of wreaking vengeance on the Jesuit whose word had led their chiefs into the toils of Denonville, excused him from any part in the treachery, brought him in safety to the nearest French post, and then prepared for war to the death. Nothing shows better than this noble conduct how Christianity had begun to alter profoundly the fierce nature of the wildest Indian race on the continent. With the departure of John de Lamberville in the spring of 1687 closed the Iroquois mission founded twenty years before. Some work, incidental and subsidiary, continued to be done among the Iroquois by the chaplains stationed at the French posts of Crown Point, Niagara, Erie, Waterford, Fort Du Quesne (now Pittsburg), and Fort Presentation (now Ogdensburg), so long as these posts remained in possession of the French. But these were at best but spasmodic efforts; the period of organized mission work among the Five Nations had passed away forever.

The jar of political jealousies and human avarice arrested the work of God when it was in the midway of a progress that promised to reach perfection in time. The Huron missions had been destroyed by the Iroquois, the Iroquois missions were destroyed by Europeans. Something, however, remained of the work of the Jesuits. There were Catholic Iroquois on the banks of the St. Lawrence, whither they had emigrated the better to practice their religion away from the neighborhood of their pagan tribesmen and of the Protestant Dutch and English. They fought by the side of the French against the heathen Iroquois and against the English during the long intercolonial struggles for the mastery of the North American continent. There they are still to be found, at Sault St. Louis or Caughnawaga, at St. Regis or Aquasasne, at Canasadaga or the Lake of the Two Mountains; in these missions the Catholic Iroquois number about three thousand. Some Oneidas and Onondagas, with a considerable number of Senecas and Tuscaroras who joined the confederacy after the mission period, remained in the State of New York. The Mohawks are in Upper Canada, a few Oneidas are in Wisconsin, a few Senecas in the Indian Territory, miserable and degraded remnants of the proudest of tribes. The country they once owned, and whence they ruled the continent, is now the heart of the Empire State of the Union, the great highway over which millions of Europeans have passed to the conquest and occupation of the great West.

CHAPTER XII.

THE NORTHWESTERN MISSIONS.

THE Western missions were located on a line running southward from Lake Superior to New Orleans, on the eastern side of the Mississippi mostly. For convenience' sake we divide them into three main groups: the Ottawa missions, the Illinois missions, and the Louisiana missions.

The country bounded on the east by Lake Michigan, on the west by the Mississippi, on the north by Lake Superior, and on the south by the Illinois River was the home of numerous Algonquin tribes, chief among whom were the Illinois, the Miamis, the Chippeways, the Kickapoos, the Foxes, the Mascoutins, the Sacs, the Menominees, the Ottawas (emigrants from regions situated on the river of that name), and various bands of Hurons, who, after the breaking up of their nation by the Iroquois, sought new homes farther west. In this country were located the missions that go for convenience' sake by the name of one of the tribes inhabiting it, the Ottawa, or as we call them, the Northwestern.

When Cartier came to Hochelaga (now Montreal) in 1535, he was told of Western tribes from whom the Indians on the St. Lawrence received copper in exchange for their goods. An Algonquin chief from the West showed Champlain (1609) a piece of copper a foot in length. Sagard, the Recollect, one of the first band of missionaries imported by Champlain, mentions in his "Histoire du Canada" that two voyageurs, Brulé and Grenolle, returned from the distant West with an ingot of red copper and a description of Lake Superior, that flowed into Lake Huron by a fall which at first was called Sault de Gaston and afterward Sault Ste. Marie. Jean Nicollet, starting from Quebec July, 1634, paddled through Lake Huron, the Straits of Mackinaw, and Lake Michigan into a great bay on the western shore. The people dwelling there were called by the Algonquins Ouinipegous (Winnebagos), "people of the salt or bad-smelling waters;" French voyageurs translated the name into "Puants," and the bay (now Green Bay) was long known in Canadian literature as "La Baie des Puants." Nicollet was told by the natives that, if he followed the watercourses emptying into the bay during three days to a large river (the Wisconsin), no doubt he would come to the sea. Nicollet misunderstood them; they meant the Mississippi.

In 1641 some Chippeways from the junction of Lakes Superior and Huron, the Sault, visited their kindred in the Huron country on the occasion of the great feast of the dead. The Huron missions were just then in a flourishing condition. So impressed were the visitors by what they heard and saw that they invited the Jesuits to their country. Two of the missionaries, Raymbault and Jogues, were detailed to accompany them home. The intention was not to found a mission at once, but rather to reconnoiter the ground. Two thousand Indians gathered at the Sault to see the Black Robes celebrate mass, and to listen to their instructions. After a short sojourn the two fathers departed, with the hope of returning to this promising field at some later time.

The Huron missions were destroyed in 1648, the Hurons were scattered, and many sought refuge in the West. It was ten years and more, however, before the missionaries followed their exiled neophytes and penetrated beyond Lake Huron. In the year 1661, on St. Teresa's day, October 15th, Father Ménard reached a bay on the southern shore of Lake Superior, which he called St. Teresa's Bay (now Keweenaw Bay). Here he began a mission, "composed," he writes, "of a flying church of Christian Indians and of such as God's mercy has gathered in here." A band of Christian Hurons far inland to the south invited him to visit them in the spring. He started with a single servant. The route was full of swamps, streams, and portages; he became separated from his companion, and was never seen again; in all probability he was murdered by some prowling Indian.

Four years later (1665), Claude Allouez, who was sent out to take the place of the luckless Ménard, set up his mission in Ashland Bay, at a spot called La Pointe du Saint Esprit. He traveled constantly from tribe to tribe, came in contact with the Sioux, and wrote home about "the great water, the Mississippi." His labors were hard, his success was small and slow. After two years he returned to Quebec for much-needed supplies, and received as companion Louis Nicolas. The two preached to twenty-five different tribes, but they gathered only few within the church. Were it not for the fugitive Hurons it could hardly be said that they found any Christians to minister to. In 1668 more assistance came—Marquette with a lay brother; and next year Dablon arrived to be the superior of the Western missions; two years later Druillettes and André increased the force. The work in the West was beginning to assume an organized form, and central points were chosen for mission sites.

Such a point was Sault Ste. Marie, a noted fishing-place, for then, as to-day, the rapids were full of whitefish, and Indians from a distance came thither in crowds. Another center was La Pointe (now Ashland). Here were Christian Hurons and Ottawas, fugitives from the rage of the Iroquois, and thither came yearly bands of warriors from many tribes to trade with the French bush-rangers. Michilimackinaw (now Mackinaw) and the great Manitoulin Island at the western extremity of Lake Huron were also refuges of Hurons and Ottawas, and well-frequented places of barter; these too were chosen as mission sites. Of the two, Mackinaw, with its Church of St. Ignatius, was the more important. There was another spot in that Western country famous for fish and game—Green Bay; in its neighborhood were a motley crowd of dusky inhabitants, Menominees, Pottowatomies, Winnebagos, Sacs, Mascoutins, Miamis, Kickapoos, Outagamies. As early as 1669 Allouez founded here the mission of St. Francis Xavier. These were the early mission posts.

While the Jesuits were taking possession of the country for God, French officers were taking possession for the king of France; while the Jesuits were in pursuit of souls, "coureurs de bois" (bush-rangers) were in pursuit of peltries; while Jesuits were bringing to the Indians the pure and elevating teachings of the Gospels, fur-traders were bringing them the immoralities and the fire-water of civilization. In order to take formal possession of the country, Talon, Intendant of New France, commissioned Sieur de St. Lusson as his deputy to meet the Western tribes and raise among them and over them the flag of France. The ambassador was guided by Perrot, one of the most remarkable of French voyageurs, especially for the reason that he has left behind an account of his various explorations. In May, 1671, the representatives of fourteen tribes met, at Sault Ste. Marie, the French commissioner and four Jesuits, Dablon, Druillettes, Allouez, André. A large cross was blessed and planted in the soil, while the Vexilla Regis was sung. Alongside the cross was fixed a cedar post with a metal plate bearing the royal arms; with drawn sword Talon claimed in the name of Louis XIV. all countries from sea to sea, and declared the nations living therein vassals of France. Then Allouez delivered a discourse to the Indians—who of course had no understanding of the meaning of the proceedings—in which he spoke much of the King of heaven and not a little of the king of France.

The missions of the West do not record the bloody martyrdoms that marked those of the Huron and the Iroquois nations. The absence of any cruelties inflicted on the missionaries is evidence that already Christianity, now in contact with the tribes for many years, had gained their respect and was beginning to soften their fierce natures. But here more than elsewhere the missionaries had to suffer from the rigor of the climate, the dangers of long voyages by water and land, the absence of the comforts of civilization as to food, dwelling, society, and from the opposition and obstacles by which their work was impeded: opposition on the part of the Indians—medicine-men and polygamy; on the part of the French traders—immorality and brandy. It is no wonder the success of the missionaries was slow, not only in gaining new converts, but even in keeping loyal to Christianity the former Huron neophytes scattered throughout the Western territory. Moreover, it must be kept in mind, as explained elsewhere, that success is to be measured not so much by the number of baptisms at any one period as by the silent influence of Christian teaching on the Indian nature. It must also be remembered that the catechumens always outnumbered the baptized.

From the "Relations of the Jesuits" a few items are gathered that give some idea of the work done. At La Pointe, Allouez was despairing of making any advance, and was about to leave for more promising fields, when one hundred Indians presented themselves for baptism; they renounced polygamy and the ancestral superstitions, and thenceforward the humble chapel became too small for the attending crowds. When Marquette came, in 1669, to replace Allouez, he found that two villages out of five around his central mission were overwhelmingly Christian. While Marquette was at this mission, its inhabitants, fleeing before the Sioux, the Iroquois of the West, moved to Mackinaw, where the mission of St. Ignatius was founded in 1671. It was from this point that the famous Jesuit set out, in company with Joliet, for the voyage down the Mississippi that has made his name immortal. By the year 1677 Mackinaw counted eighteen hundred Christians; no Christian reduction in Canada could show more piety and virtue or a better attendance on religious duties. The Christians of Manitoulin Island, mostly refugees from the former Huron missions, were numerous enough to occupy the time of one or even two missionaries; we have no data for getting at their exact number. At Green Bay, where the mission of St. Francis Xavier had been founded by Allouez (1670), André was in charge of a community of five hundred souls; this number gradually increased, and in 1676 a fine church was built, due mostly to the generosity of the French traders, and chiefly of Perrot. In 1802 there was dug up at Depere, Wis., a monstrance fifteen inches high, bearing around the base the following inscription in French: "This monstrance was given by M. Nicolas Perrot to the mission of St. Francis Xavier at Bay of Puants, 1686."

At Sault Ste. Marie, Druillettes, who was settled there in 1670, and had the reputation of a saint among the tribes, baptized one hundred and twenty children and three hundred adults; he changed the face of the country, and a wave of Christianity swept over the surrounding region.

An offshoot of the mission of Green Bay was that of St. James, located to the south among a medley of tribes—Illinois, Mascoutins, Kickapoos, Miamis—all of the Algonquin family. Allouez visited them in 1672, was so well received that he founded here a permanent mission, and recorded two hundred baptisms for the first year. To these missions there were many outposts where traders were stationed, which must have been visited occasionally by the missionaries. A map of 1684, supposed to be the work of the voyageur Franquelin, recording the observations of twelve years, shows a Fort St. Croix, at the portage between the sources of the St. Croix and of a stream flowing into Lake Superior; a Fort St. Nicolas, named in honor of Perrot, at the mouth of the Wisconsin, the present site of Prairie du Chien; a Fort St. Antoine, at the lower extremity of Lake Pepin, on the eastern bank, just above the confluence of the Chippewa with the Mississippi. The Minnesota River is marked on the map "Les Mascoutens Nadouescioux," the name indicating that it flowed through the country of the Prairie Sioux. A later map, of 1703, names the Minnesota River St. Pierre, in compliment to Pierre le Sueur, who had explored the river to its headwaters. One of the Jesuits is known to have gone as far inland as Fort St. Antoine; for "on the 8th of May, 1689, at the post St. Antoine," writes Mr. Neill in Winsor (vol. iv., p. 195), "in the presence of Father Marest, Pierre le Sueur, and others, Perrot took possession of the country along the rivers St. Croix, St. Pierre, and of the region of Mille Lacs, in the name of the king of France." It was at a later period that a fort was built midway in Lake Pepin, on the western bank of the river, near the present village of Frontenac, Minn.

Such was the condition of the Western missions when the last "Relation" was written, in 1672. Henceforth our knowledge of Western evangelization must be taken from other sources, mostly incidental allusions of travelers. Meanwhile two voyages had taken place toward the South that opened a new and wider field; and one of these voyages brought back to the American missions the Recollects, the pioneers of the work, who, if they did not stay long and effect much as missionaries, yet acquired great fame as explorers. I refer to the voyages of Joliet and Marquette, of Hennepin and La Salle.

It was on account of his known zeal and success in the conversion of the Indians, and of his proficiency in the languages of the Western tribes, that Marquette was chosen by his superior to accompany Joliet in the duty, assigned to the latter by the Intendant Talon, of exploring the great Western river. In May, 1673, they set out in two canoes, with five men, some Indian corn and jerked meat, and a few bales of goods suitable for presents to the natives. They passed over to Green Bay, up the Fox River, through Lake Winnebago, down the Wisconsin, and emerged on the broad bosom of the Mississippi. The portage from the head-waters of the Fox to the head-waters of the Wisconsin was only two miles at that time. Sixty leagues below the Wisconsin they came to a village inhabited by natives who called themselves Illini or "men," superior men, *the* men; they were also known as Peorias, and belonged to a loose confederation of five or six tribes that went by the general name of Illini; the "ois" termination was added by the French for the sake of euphony. Marquette had already met representatives of this nation, and understood sufficiently their language, a dialect of the Algonquin or Algic family. He promised to visit them on his return and establish a mission among them.

The painted rocks of Alton, revered as manitous, the inflow of the Missouri, the Grand Tower below the Kaskaskia, the confluence of the Ohio, and other remarkable features of the great continental artery were noticed and recorded by the wondering voyageurs, as with paddle and sail, when the wind favored, they floated down until they reached a village conjectured to be not far from the confluence of the Arkansas. They went no farther, being persuaded that the river flowed into the Gulf of Mexico, and not east into the Atlantic, nor west into the Pacific. This discovery of the river's trend was the main purpose of their journey. To go farther would be to expose themselves to fall into the hands of the Spaniards, who were known to hold all the southern country. In July they turned their canoes up-stream. At the confluence of the Illinois they entered that river and paddled up to Peoria Lake, where they made a short stay. "Here," says Marquette, in his "Voyage et Découverte de quelques pays et nations de l'Amérique Septentrionale," published in 1681, "I preached for three days the mysteries of our faith; as we were embarking they brought to me a dying infant, which I baptized at the edge of the water." Higher up the stream they came to another village, called Kaskaskia (not to be confounded with a later Kaskaskia on the Mississippi), containing seventy-four cabins. So cordial was their reception that Marquette promised to come back and instruct them. Finally, by way of the Chicago[1] portage, they arrived at St. Francis, Green Bay, four months after having left it; having traveled within that time twenty-seven hundred miles. Here Marquette rested from the fatigues of the journey, that had seriously impaired his constitution, and meanwhile wrote the journal of his voyage.

In October, 1674, came to him from his superior in

[1] In a relation made by Cadillac (1695) to the governor of Quebec (Margry, vol. v., p. 123), he states that the word "Chicago" means "river of garlic," "because a very great quantity of it grows there."

Quebec the permission to go found a mission on the Illinois River, as he had promised. Winter overtook him at the mouth of the Chicago River. He and his companions moved up its frozen surface about four miles, following the south branch, and built a cabin in which they wintered, the first white habitation on the site of the great city of Chicago. It was a dreary winter for Marquette; the disease that was to carry him off, dysentery, had fastened on him. On the 8th of April he arrived at the village of the Kaskaskias, near the site of the present town of Utica, and began a mission which he named "The Immaculate Conception of the Blessed Virgin." But he could not labor; his illness increased; he decided to return to one of the older missions, St. Francis or St. Ignatius, for rest and repair.

He seems to have traveled homeward by way of the St. Joseph River, and thence skirted the eastern shore of Lake Michigan, as high up as a small stream flowing into the lake from western Michigan. It was not the river that now bears his name, but a smaller stream. Here he must rest; he could go no farther; his companions built a little bark cabin, and made the dying missionary as comfortable as they could. The priest, knowing the end was nigh, heard their confessions; and, when he felt the agony approaching, he placed in their hands his crucifix, made before it his profession of faith, then entered into a silence broken from time to time by pious ejaculations, and expired (May 18, 1675). Before dying he had designated the spot where he wished to be buried, had blessed water with which they were to sprinkle his body and grave, and had given them instructions how to lay out his remains. His sorrowing companions obeyed the directions, and over his grave they planted a rude cedar cross, then wended their way sadly to St. Ignatius, Mackinaw.

Two years afterward (1677) a party of Christian Indians

from Mackinaw, hunting in the vicinity of Marquette's grave, disinterred the remains, cleaned the bones of all flesh, according to their custom, placed them in a birch-bark box, and transported them to Mackinaw. Word reached the mission, through couriers dispatched ahead, of the coming of this strange funeral; hundreds of canoes flew out to join in the train, and thus, amid the doleful strains of the Requiem, the Dies Iræ, and Indian death-hymns, all that remained of the good and heroic Marquette—his fleshless bones—was rowed into the mission harbor, reverently received by his religious brethren, Pierson and Nouvel, and deposited with religious rites under the floor of the log chapel. In the process of time, as we shall see, the mission was abandoned; the tomb was utterly forgotten and unknown until 1877, when it was discovered by a Michigan priest, Father Jacker. A modest fence—nothing more—now surrounds the hallowed spot.

The second voyage that enlarged the field of the Western missions was that of Robert Cavelier, Sieur de la Salle. This remarkable man was born at Rouen, November 22, 1643, and in early manhood, it is said, was teacher in a Jesuit college in France. In after life he was far from bearing them any good will. He sailed for Canada in the spring of 1666, and received from the Sulpitians a grant of wild land ten miles north of Montreal; the place was derisively named by his neighbors La Chine, on account of La Salle's dreams and talk of a western passage to China. From dreaming he soon passed to action, and received from the proper authorities a commission to explore the West and permission to trade on his own account, in order to defray the expenses of his explorations. About the same time the Sulpitians of Montreal were preparing to extend their missionary work toward the West; an expedition for the purpose was fitted out under the management of Fathers Dollier de Casson and Réné de Gallinée. The La Salle and the Sulpitian parties started together July, 1669, and kept together until they reached the southern shore of Lake Ontario, at a village on the Genesee River. Here they parted, for what reason does not concern us. The Sulpitians continued their route northwestward by way of the lakes; but finding at Sault Ste. Marie that the Jesuits had preceded them and established missions throughout the country, they retraced their steps to Montreal. Meanwhile whither went La Salle? It is a debated question; and as it does not concern the subject in hand, we shall not enter into it. We are content with saying that if, as some hold, he descended the Ohio to the present site of Louisville, he opened a new route of trade and laid the foundations of the French claim to the valley of the Ohio and all its confluents.

Joliet and Marquette had well-nigh demonstrated the fact that the Mississippi emptied into the Gulf of Mexico. La Salle wished to see for himself, and, moreover, he conjectured that by occupying the mouth of the Mississippi, and the entrances of Lake Ontario by a fort at Kingston, and of Erie by a fort at Niagara, the first links of a chain would be forged that would give France command of the interior of the continent and shut England to the seaboard east of the Alleghanies. He made two voyages to France (in 1674 and in 1677) to advance his project, received a patent of nobility, was invested with the proprietorship of Fort Frontenac, with a large contiguous territory, was granted privileges of trade that almost amounted to a monopoly, and was commissioned to make further explorations in the West. In his last voyage to Europe he secured an invaluable lieutenant in a Neapolitan, Henri de Tonti, or Tonty, and missionaries in the following Recollects: Louis Hennepin, Gabriel de la Ribourde, Zenobius Membré, Melithon

Watteau. They were natives of Flanders. The choice shows evidently La Salle's opposition to the Jesuits. He knew that the latter were already in possession of the Western field, and that the introduction of another order in the same region would be taken as a mark of hostility.

It is not my province to narrate in detail the voyages, the trials, the final triumph of La Salle. Few pages in history—none in the records of this continent—exhibit a more sublime courage, a more romantic career. I am concerned with the story only so far as the work of the missionaries goes. In November the expeditionary corps were at the outlet of the Niagara channel, where a fort, or blockhouse, was constructed; a garrison was left to man it, a chapel was built, and Father Watteau was detailed from the band to be the chaplain of Fort Niagara. The rest embarked on a small schooner, built in a few months, sail-rigged, and bearing some small guns. Having launched the craft, named the "Griffin," they sailed through Erie, Lake St. Clair (so named in honor of the saint of the day, August 10th), through the Strait of Detroit, past Mackinaw, Green Bay, to the mouth of the Miami or St. Joseph River, a well-known mission and trading-post and one of the routes to the interior. At the mouth of the St. Joseph a small wooden fort, eighty by forty feet, was built by them to serve as storehouse and base of operations for further inland exploration; they called it Fort Miami.

Some years before the Jesuits had set up a mission here, which seems to have been abandoned at this time; some years later, however, a flourishing mission of Pottowatomies and Miamis existed at this point, as we shall see. For the present the Recollects set up a bark chapel, and, while the expedition tarried here, preached and ministered to whites and natives. They named the chapel St. Anthony. On December 3, 1679, thirty-three persons started up the St.

Joseph, crossed a portage to the Kaskaskia, and glided down the Illinois. A mile or more below Starved Rock they came upon an Indian village of four hundred and sixty lodges, found the village empty, the natives being absent on a hunt, landed on New-Year's day, 1680, to hear mass, and then moved down to Lake Peoria, where they found another village of eighty cabins. Here La Salle was well received, though he soon felt among the natives a secret opposition, which he attributes, but on mere suspicions, to the Jesuits laboring in the country immediately north. Nothing daunted, however, he built, on a site not now precisely identifiable, a fort that was named by him Crève-cœur; not because he felt any heartbreaking, but in honor of the fortress of Crève-cœur in Brabant, which shortly before had been taken and demolished by the French; it was a compliment to his Flemish companions.

In the meantime Father Membré devoted himself to the instruction of the natives in the neighborhood. He found the work difficult. In Le Clercq's "First Establishment of the Faith in New France" we find the narrative of the adventures of La Salle's party by Zenobius Membré. "They are wandering," says he of the natives, "idle, fearful, and desolate, almost without respect for their chiefs, irritable, and thievish. They have many wives, and often take several sisters, that they may agree the better; and yet they are so jealous that they cut off their noses on the slightest provocation. They are lewd, even unnaturally so; very superstitious, although they have no religious worship." While Membré was preaching to the Indians and Ribourde acting as chaplain to the French, Hennepin was dispatched to explore the upper Mississippi. We shall have more to say of him presently. No sooner had Hennepin set out than La Salle, taking with him five companions and leaving fifteen behind at Fort Crève-cœur in command of Tonty, started in the dead of winter to go to Fort Frontenac.

When he came back the following August he found the fort dismantled, and there was no trace of his trusted lieutenant. What had become of them? After La Salle's departure five hundred Iroquois swooped down on the Illinois Indians. It was in vain that Tonty, at the peril of his life, tried to make the fierce warriors understand that the Illinois were the children of Onontio, allies of the French, and under their protection. He and his companions were obliged to let the Iroquois do their will, and were themselves compelled to retreat up the stream. During a halt, September 11, 1680, Father Ribourde went into an adjacent grove to say his breviary. He never returned; some prowling Indians tomahawked him; shortly after his breviary came into the hands of one of the Jesuit missionaries. The rest of the party made their way to Green Bay. The laymen spent the winter in the neighboring mission of the Pottowatomies; Father Membré was given most cordial hospitality at the Jesuit house of St. Francis. La Salle, succeeding in finding and getting together his scattered companions, set out from the Illinois River to go down the Mississippi. On April 9, 1682, he reached the Gulf, and took possession of the mouth of the river and the surrounding country in the name of Christ and Louis XIV. Returning to the Illinois, he built a fort on Starved Rock, La Salle County, Ill., and named it Fort St. Louis. His purpose was to gather around the place all the Western tribes, as the only means of protecting and saving them from the Iroquois. In a few months there was a population of twenty thousand Indians under the guns of the fort.

Father Membré returned to France. When La Salle, who also had returned to France to push his project of a French settlement at the mouth of the Mississippi, sailed in July, 1684, directly for the Gulf of Mexico with about two hundred and eighty colonists, Membré once more became his companion, with two other fathers of his order, Anastasius Douay and Maximus le Clercq, and three Sulpitians, one of whom was the brother of La Salle, Jean Cavelier. We pass over the history of the ill-fated expedition, the tragic death of La Salle, the fortunes of the colony he left behind in Matagorda Bay. Of the Recollects, Douay made his way up the Mississippi into Canada; Membré and Le Clercq are believed to have perished at the hands of the savages that prowled about the colony of St. Louis.

It is plain that the Recollects did not do much missionary work, yet they seemed to have regarded the Mississippi Valley as their special field; through their influence the holy see was petitioned to establish there one or more vicariates apostolic, and it also appears that the Propaganda had actually established them. But on protest of the Bishop of Quebec, St. Vallier, who claimed as a portion of his diocese the valley of the great river, because it was discovered by Marquette, a priest of his diocese, and Joliet, a pupil of his seminary, the establishment of the vicariates was revoked. At any rate, after the fateful ending of the St. Louis colony, the Recollects gave up all claim, and the Jesuits were left in undisputed possession of the whole valley.

Let us now turn to Father Hennepin. In the year 1674 Louis XIV., yielding to the appeal of Frontenac, governor of Canada, who was no friend of the Jesuits, ordered that five Recollects be sent to Canada to reinforce the little community of that order already established there. Hennepin was one of the number chosen. On the ship that carried him he had as fellow-passengers François de Laval, recently appointed Bishop of Quebec, and La Salle, with whose fortunes he was to be so closely connected. In the fall of 1676 he was sent with Father Buisset, a brother Recollect, to Fort Frontenac, whence he made a journey to the Jesuit missions among the Mohawks, and to Fort Orange, the Dutch settlement on the Hudson. When La Salle went across Lake Ontario to build Fort Niagara at the foot of the river of that name, Hennepin was a member of the party, gazed on the great falls, and was the first to describe them. In 1679 he sailed with the explorer on the "Griffin" through Lakes Erie and Michigan to the river St. Joseph, and traveled by way of the Kankakee to the Illinois village where Fort Crève-cœur was built. From this point he was sent by La Salle with a small exploring-party down the Illinois and thence to the upper Mississippi. It was on the last day of February, 1680, that he embarked with La Salle's best wishes and Father Ribourde's parting benediction from the water's edge. It was on the 11th or 12th of April that Hennepin and his companions were captured by a war-party of one hundred and twenty Sioux Indians in the neighborhood of the Black River, Wisconsin.

Captors and captives turned their prows northward, and after about twenty days' paddling through some of the grandest scenery on the continent, landed in a cove a few leagues below the falls of the Mississippi, that is to say, three miles below the present city of St. Paul. Thence striking inland, they reached the Sioux villages on Mille Lacs, Minnesota, about the 5th of May. On the whole the missionary was treated kindly; Minnesota was not destined to have its Jogues. But he did not exercise any of his priestly functions; his vestments and altar had been taken from him. Nor did he succeed in making any converts. "I could gain nothing over them," he writes, "in the way of their salvation, by reason of their natural stupidity." On one occasion he baptized a sick child just before its death. After weeks spent among those Isanti Sioux, he accompanied a hunting-party to the Mississippi, and got permission from his captors to row down the river with his French companions in the hope of meeting some traders who, according to a previous arrangement with La Salle, should be about this time at the mouth of the Wisconsin.

Floating down the great river, they soon arrived at the falls, which Hennepin named St. Anthony, in honor of the great saint of his order, St. Anthony of Padua. He described them as from forty to fifty feet high, with an island of pyramidal form lying nearly midway of the stream. They kept on their way a few days more; but having run out of ammunition, and being threatened with famine, they joined a Sioux band that they met at the confluence of the Chippewa below Lake Pepin. While journeying northward with this hunting-party, they met another band journeying southward; it was led by Duluth, who had learned of the presence of some Europeans in this region and was searching for them. The Indians do not seem to have offered any resistance to the liberation of the monk and his companions. In the end of September they left Minnesota, journeyed by way of the Wisconsin and Fox rivers to Green Bay, and thence to Mackinaw, where the Franciscan enjoyed during the winter the hospitality of the Jesuit father Pierson. In the spring he departed for Quebec via Lakes Huron, Erie, Ontario, and the St. Lawrence; by the end of that same year he was in France. There he lived until 1697, when, for what reason we know not, he was ordered by the Minister of War to leave the French soil; he withdrew into his native Holland. It is stated by some writers that before his death he went on a pilgrimage to Rome, was at the convent of Ara Cœli in 1701, and returned thence to die at Utrecht at the age of sixty-two.

On his return to France, Hennepin set about publishing the notes of his voyages. Three books purporting to describe his explorations have appeared over Father Hennepin's name: the first in Paris, 1683; the second in Utrecht, 1697; the third in Utrecht, 1698.

It is only in the second work that we have for the first time the narrative of his descent from the Illinois River to the Gulf. Why did he not mention and describe this trip on the lower Mississippi in his first publication? He makes answer in the preface of the second: "It is true I published only part in 1683 in my account of Louisiana, printed at Paris by order of the French king; but I was then obliged to say nothing of the course of the river Meschasipi from the mouth of the Illinois River down to the sea, for fear of disobliging M. La Salle, with whom I began my discovery. This gentleman wanted to have the glory of having discovered the course of that river; but when he would learn that I had done it two years before him, he would never forgive me, though, as I have said, I was so modest as to publish nothing of it." In the preface to the third book he makes reply to those who doubted the possibility of his having sailed down and up the Mississippi within the time he allowed himself in his former works.

It was after his first and before his second publication that Father Hennepin had been excluded from France and had come under the jurisdiction of the Dutch-English court. It was probably to favor the pretensions of William III. in setting up a claim to Louisiana that he was induced to write his second work. It was to clear away the chronological difficulties created by the second that he put forth the third. But if the two latter works are Hennepin's we are afraid he has prevaricated. In his first work he distinctly states that he did not go down the river: "We had some designs of going down the river as far as its mouth, but the tribes that took us prisoners gave us no time to navigate this river both up and down." The chronological difficulties are of his own making. In his first book he states that he turned out of the Illinois River into the Mississippi northward on the 12th of March, and that he was captured by the Sioux five hundred miles higher up on the 11th of April. This gives him only a month to run down to the Gulf and back again to the point of his capture. The distance gone over would be 3260 miles, an evident impossibility with his means of traveling. In his third book, when he undertakes to explain this chronological difficulty, he gets himself into confusion worse confounded.

Gilmary Shea, in a notice on Father Hennepin annexed to a translation of "Description de la Louisiane" (New York, 1880), exculpates the friar by the statement that he was not responsible for all the fictions published in the second and third works that go under his name. The hand of an anonymous and treacherous editor can be seen in various parts of the book, and alterations were made in it after its first printing, with a view to make the work more salable. This puts another view on the question, and allows us to save the good name of the hero of the upper Mississippi. The only authentic book of Father Hennepin, according to Shea's theory, is the first, and it is the only one for which he ought to be held responsible.

To come back to the missions and their status about the year 1690. Of the old missions noticed heretofore, Mackinaw was in charge of Fathers Enjalran and De Carheil, Green Bay in charge of Father Nouvel, Sault Ste. Marie in charge of Fathers Albanel and Bailloquet. New missions had sprung up, one on the St. Joseph River, in charge of Father Aveneau, and one on the St. Croix River, Wisconsin, in charge of Father Marest. The foundation of the mission of Detroit dates from 1701. At an earlier time some feeble efforts had been made to secure the possession of this important pass; the Jesuits in their journeyings to the West frequently stopped here and baptized what children they found in danger of death. A glance at the map of North America will convince any one that Quebec, Detroit, and New Orleans were the three big rings of the French chain of posts that held the continent, commanding the great inland waterways, the St. Lawrence, the lakes, the Mississippi. La Motte Cadillac was appointed (1701) commander at this new and important post; he brought out from Canada soldiers and settlers, and also a Recollect, Father Delhalle, to serve as chaplain to the post and as pastor to the settlers. A Jesuit, Du Guesles, was engaged to serve as missionary to the Indians. Fort Pontchartrain and a chapel in honor of St. Ann were built. The Jesuit missionary, having learned on his way to Detroit the full details of Cadillac's proposed scheme, renounced his engagement and returned to Quebec.

Cadillac's plan was to gather around this new post all the Western Indian tribes that had no fixed habitation—Hurons, Ottawas, Miamis. Such an arrangement would render completely desert the missions of the Sault, Mackinaw, St. Joseph, and would greatly weaken that of Green Bay. His intention was to secure their trade and prevent it from going northward to the English in the Hudson Bay country. There was a constant tendency on the part of the Western Indians to take their peltries to the English marts on the Hudson Bay in the north or the Hudson River in the east. For this tendency there were two reasons: they received in return goods at a cheaper rate, and they got brandy more freely; for though the French laws on this point were not always executed, yet they were restraints, and the missionaries were ever watchful, and made it uncomfortable for the violators; whereas the English colonies left that trade completely free. Brandy was the irresistible magnet that attracted peltries.

But the Canadian government had a still nobler motive in concentrating the scattered tribes of the lakes around a few central posts: it was to protect them more easily from the Iroquois of the East, the Sioux of the West, and from the incessant quarrels and wars that arose out of their mutual jealousies. Cadillac meant to form these tribes into a military organization, impose on them the French language, and encourage marriage between the whites and the natives. The policy of the Jesuits was the reverse: they had always held that the less contact there was between the Indians and the whites the better for the Christianization and civilization of the former. It was for this reason they had opposed the project of La Salle to make Fort St. Louis, on the Starved Rock, Ill., the center of a large Indian cantonment. Their enemies attributed their policy to another motive—the wish to keep the trade of the mission Indians in their own hands. Such is the accusation brought against them by Frontenac, La Salle, Cadillac, and certain *coureurs de bois;* but the accusation is not borne out by solid proof. The immediate result of Cadillac's settlement at Detroit was to deplete the missions of Mackinaw and St. Joseph. Only twenty-five Indians remained at the former station with Father De Carheil; St. Joseph was entirely abandoned. This desertion induced Fathers Carheil, Marest, and Enjalran to return to Quebec, a proceeding that was severely censured by the French government. After a few years both missions were resumed by Marest and Aveneau. Green Bay alone retained a sufficient number of Indians, and there Nouvel, after forty years of mission work, died in 1702, and was succeeded by Father Chardon.

The growth of Detroit was slow and difficult. In 1703 a conflagration destroyed the little town and the earliest parish registers. The following year the chapel was rebuilt and a new register opened; but only three pages of it are preserved. An uprising of the surrounding Indians, living in three large villages, took place in 1706, and Father Delhalle was shot down while trying to prevent the effusion of blood. He was succeeded by another Recollect, Dominic de la Marche, who remained in Detroit until May 1, 1708. In 1707 Detroit was attacked by a combined army of Foxes, Kickapoos, and Mascoutins, egged on, it appears, by the English; but after a series of desperate engagements they were nearly exterminated by the French and their Indian allies. The Recollects continued to serve the post of Detroit, while the Jesuits were engaged in their former missions, though Green Bay was entirely deserted about the year 1729, and the Miamis moved eastward from St. Joseph to the Maumee in 1721.

Charlevoix made a journey in 1721 from Quebec to New Orleans. He gives the result of his observations on the missions of the West in "Journal d'un voyage," vol. iii. of his "Histoire de la Nouvelle France" (Paris, 1744). At Detroit there were three villages of Indians—one of Hurons from Mackinaw, one of Pottowatomies, and one of Ottawas. There were no Christians among the Ottawas, few among the Pottowatomies; all the Hurons were Christian, but unfortunately no missionary was then residing among these Indians. At Mackinaw there were the fort and the house of the missionaries. They had little to do, because few Indians had remained; but their presence was deemed necessary by the government. At Green Bay there was a fort and a missionary. At St. Joseph were two villages of Miamis and Pottowatomies, mostly Christian; but they had been so long without a missionary "that the one who is there now will have much to do to bring them back to the practice of religion." Thence he went by the Kankakee portage to the Illinois. Besides these stations named by Charlevoix there was one other of some importance in the Northwest.

In May, 1727, a fort, Beauharnois, was established by Laperrière on the western bank of Lake Pepin, six miles above Lake City, Minn. This, however, was not the first attempt at a French settlement on the lake; Le Sueur, it appears, had built a fort there about the year 1696, but it was long since abandoned. Appropriations were made by the government for the support of two Jesuits at this new post. Father Louis Guignas accompanied the expedition that founded the fort: he called this mission St. Michael the Archangel. While attempting to reach the Illinois country in 1728 he was captured by a band of Kickapoos and Mascoutins, and remained a prisoner in their hands for a year. After his liberation he returned to his Sioux mission on Lake Pepin, where he was laboring in 1736. A few years afterward the place was abandoned, and later attempts to reëstablish the post were failures. About the year 1765 there were only two Jesuits in the Northwest, Le Franc and Peter du Launay, in Mackinaw. The suppression of the Jesuits by the French government about this time, and the surrender of New France to England, put an end to the arduous but glorious work which the society had carried on in the Northwest for a period of one hundred years.

The date we have now reached brings us to the period when England became mistress of the French dominions in North America, when the Catholic missions of the territory that is now the United States came within the jurisdiction of a prefect apostolic and shortly after of the Bishop of Baltimore. This was the period of the organized hierarchy, the second part of this work. By that time all the tribes heretofore named—that is to say, all the North American Indians—were more or less extensively converted, all had the gospel preached to them; all, though much diminished in population, still exist, except the Mascoutins. What philological works were composed by the Jesuits in the dialects of Michigan and Wisconsin have perished. It was later missionaries who reduced the Chippeway and Sioux to grammatical form, and left us printed works in these languages.

To-day the two dioceses of South and North Dakota have 4740 Catholic Indians, the diocese of Grand Rapids has 500, the diocese of Green Bay 1400, the diocese of La Crosse 1650, the diocese of Marquette 2500, the diocese of Duluth and the diocese of St. Cloud probably 2000. In the Indian Territory there are Iowas, Kickapoos, Miamis, Ottawas, Osages, Ottoes, Missouris, Peorias, Wyandots, Pottowatomies, Sacs, and Foxes, whose ancestors, when they dwelt on the lakes and the Great River, saw and heard the French Black Robes. The Catholic population of the Indian Territory is given as 5000. The present Catholic population of the tribes that once inhabited the region described in the opening of this section as the "Ottawa missions" is between eighteen and twenty thousand. I doubt whether the whole population of these tribes was much over forty thousand in the days of the French domination.

Such is the result in numbers, but the result in influence was greater: the wild fierceness of the savage was softened; a marvelous respect and love for the priest and the church penetrated so deep into his heart that time and bigotry have not availed to eradicate them. It is a wonder that the success was so great, when one reckons up the causes that should have produced failure: the recklessness and immoralities of soldiers, traders, and bush-rangers; French brandy and English rum; the political and religious quarrels of France and England; the policy of concentration of the tribes adopted in the end by Canada; the contrary policy of the Jesuits, and their unwillingness to work under the plan of the government; polygamy; the superstitions and magic of the medicine-man; the mutual quarrels and the constant wanderings of the tribes. In spite of all these obstacles a great and a lasting work was done.

CHAPTER XIII.

THE ILLINOIS MISSIONS.

UNDER the name "Illinois" I comprise the present States of Illinois and Indiana down to the confluence of the Ohio with the Mississippi. Some features distinguish this mission field from the northern field we have just studied: it contained more and larger French settlements, Detroit being the only French settlement in the North. Here, by the side of the Jesuits, labored also diocesan priests of Quebec, and in fact the latter had more to do with the growth and preservation of the church in this section than the former. At first the Illinois country depended for its civil administration on Quebec; later on it was annexed to New Orleans; but for its ecclesiastical administration it held from the Bishop of Quebec so long as it remained under French domination.

This section was occupied by two Algonquin tribes, the Illinois and the Miamis. Their country lay between the Wabash, the Ohio, and the Mississippi; their population did not exceed eighteen thousand souls. The principal clans of the Illinois were the Peoria, Cahokia, Tamaroa, Kaskaskia, and Moingwena, whose name, curiously transformed, passed to a river in Iowa, the Des Moines, on which they dwelt for some time. The Miamis originally dwelt at Detroit, migrated thence to the mouth of the Wabash, and thence again to the southern end of Lake Michigan, whence they were driven, in the beginning of the eighteenth century, by a Chippeway clan, the Pottowatomies. The principal clans of the Miamis were the Wea, Piankeshaw, Pepikokia, and Kilatak. The Illinois and the Miamis, though distinct races and often at variance, easily intermingled, being of the same nation and language.

The Illinois first came in contact with Christianity on a visit to Chegoimegon Bay, Lake Superior, in the time of Allouez (1667) and of his successor, Marquette. Later Allouez met them again near Green Bay in a village of the Mascoutins. We have seen how Marquette, during his descent down the Mississippi, visited an Illinois village, and again on his return, and how shortly before his death he set up the mission of the Immaculate Conception at Kaskaskia, on the Illinois River, where two thousand Indians lived. Allouez, who preceded him on Lake Superior, succeeded him in this mission. Shea, in "Discovery and Exploration of the Mississippi," gives the father's narrative of his arrival and work in this mission: "In spite of all our efforts to hasten on, it was the 27th of April, 1677, before I could reach Kachkachkia, a large Illinois town. I immediately entered the cabin where Father Marquette had lodged, and the sachems with all the people being assembled, I told them the object of my coming among them. They listened very attentively and thanked me for the trouble I took for their salvation. I found the village very much increased. It was before composed of only one nation. There are now eight. They are lodged in three hundred and fifty-one cabins." To compute the population it must be remembered that there were from three to five fires or families to a cabin; there must have been in the village at this time between six and eight thousand souls. The father further states that on the 3d of May he erected in the village a cross twenty-five feet high in the presence of a great number of the Illinois of all the tribes. The prospects were cheering and the hopes of the missionary were high, when he was warned of the approach of La Salle with four Recollects (1679). Knowing the hostility of the great explorer to his order, and fearing to clash with the new-comers, he withdrew. We have already seen how the Recollects attempted to instruct the Illinois while the expeditionary party dwelt on Lake Peoria, how the Iroquois dispersed the village, how Father Ribourde was murdered, and how the missions were practically abandoned by the Recollects after the journey of La Salle to the mouth of the Mississippi.

In 1683 Tonty, La Salle's lieutenant, rebuilt Fort St. Louis on the Starved Rock; and, as he did not share La Salle's enmity to the Jesuits, he recalled Allouez, who remained at work among the numerous clans concentrated at that spot until 1687. Fort St. Louis continued to be the seat of French power in Illinois down to the year 1702. The dispersion of the surrounding tribes was one reason of its decline; the advantages of the portage of the Fox and Wisconsin rivers over that of the Chicago River was another. When Charlevoix passed by the Rock in 1721 he saw only the remains of its palisade and rude buildings. After the departure of Allouez, Fathers Douay and Gravier paid flying visits to the mission of Kaskaskia. In 1692 Father Rale came to the mission. After laboring here a year or more he was sent back to his original charge, the Abenakis of Maine. We have a most interesting description by himself of his life among the Illinois, in vol. vi. of "Lettres Édifiantes et Curieuses" (Paris, 1781). He found here about two thousand families. However, the faith had made but little progress. The Indians did not object to the instructions of the missionaries, the services were well attended, they freely allowed their children to be baptized (a privilege the missionary availed himself of, especially in cases of imminent death); but they could not be brought to obey the stern requirements of Christian marriage; polygamy stood in the way of practical Christianity.

After the departure of Rale, Father Gravier took charge. He compiled the grammar of the language, but no trace of the work is to be found to-day. A journal covering about one year of his missionary life here is still extant. During that time he baptized two hundred and six, mostly dying infants. Gravier was succeeded in the Illinois country by Fathers Julian Binneteau and Francis Pinet. Bancroft records that Binneteau, having followed his Indians in one of their hunts, sickened, died, and left his bones to bleach on the wilderness range of the buffalo. Pinet went to labor among the Tamaroas, and has the credit of establishing the mission of Cahokia about the year 1700. The place is now a struggling, decayed town, opposite Carondelet, on the Mississippi. His success was unusual, and he soon found his chapel too small for the crowds that came to mass. He seems to have died there in 1704.

About the year 1700 the original Kaskaskia, on the Illinois River, where Marquette had established the mission of the Immaculate Conception, was transferred, by the advice and under the guidance of Father Marest, to the site that now goes by the name of Kaskaskia, on the banks of the Kaskaskia or Okaw River, six miles above its confluence with the Mississippi and two miles east of the latter river. The new settlement was called "Le Village de l'Immaculée Conception des Cascaquias." The motive of this move was double: to get farther away from the ever-threatening Iroquois, and to get into closer communication with the French colony at the mouth of the Mississippi, which had become the supply and trading-center for the missions of Illinois. It was almost a quarter of a century later that

Canadians began to settle in this Kaskaskia. For the first years of its existence it was only an Indian mission station, and its history is to be traced in the parish records, registers of baptisms, marriages, and burials, which continue with varying regularity down to the middle of the present century. Father Marest was master of the Kaskaskia language, in which he compiled a catechism. He died, it is said, near Peoria, September 17, 1715.

In 1707 Father John Mermet had joined him in Kaskaskia. Bancroft (vol. iii.) thus describes the labors of this missionary: "The gentle virtues and fervid eloquence of Mermet made him the soul of the mission of Kaskaskia. At early dawn his pupils came to church, dressed neatly and modestly, each in a deerskin, or a robe sewn together from several skins. After receiving lessons they chanted canticles; mass was then said in the presence of all the Christians, the women on one side, the men on the other. From prayer and instructions the missionaries proceeded to visit the sick and administer medicine, and their skill as physicians did more than all the rest to win confidence. In the afternoon the catechism was taught in the presence of the young and old, when every one, without distinction of rank or age, answered the questions of the missionary. At evening all would assemble in the chapel for instruction, for prayer, and to chant the hymns of the church. On Sundays and festivals, even after vespers, a homily was pronounced; at the close of the day parties would meet in houses to recite the chaplet in alternate choirs, and sing psalms until late at night. Saturdays and Sundays were the days appointed for confession and communion, and every convert confessed once a fortnight."

One more description, that of a missionary trip, is extracted from a letter of Father Mermet in the "Lettres Édifiantes": "I departed, having nothing about me but my crucifix and breviary, and being accompanied by only two savages, who might abandon me from levity, or might fly through fear of enemies. The terror of these vast, uninhabited regions, in which for twelve days not a single soul was seen, almost took my courage away. This was a journey in which there was no village, no bridge, no ferry-boat, no house, no beaten path, and over boundless prairies intersected by rivulets and rivers, through forests and thickets filled with briers and thorns, through marshes in which we sometimes plunged to the girdle. At night repose was sought on the grass or leaves, exposed to the winds and rains, happy if by the side of some rivulet, whose waters might quench our thirst. Meals were prepared from such game as might be killed on the way, or by roasting some ears of corn." Thus labored Father Mermet until his death, in 1718.

There was in the Illinois country another post, which had, however, a short existence. It was established toward the end of 1702 by Sieur Juchereau near the mouth of the Wabash, probably on the site of the more modern Fort Massac. The Mascoutins and the Kickapoos gathered about this post for the purpose of barter. Father Mermet visited them from Kaskaskia, but had no success in converting them. In 1705 the post was abandoned; the French had to fly for their lives on account of the hostility of the Indians. More important and more lasting was the establishment (1719) on the Wabash of a post which still bears the name of its founder, Vincennes. This settlement was about one hundred miles above the mouth of the river, and for many years was a mere halting-place for the missionaries and fur-traders who traveled southward by way of the Maumee and the Wabash. The priests of Kaskaskia and Cahokia visited it occasionally, until it assumed great importance as a Canadian settlement after the year 1725.

There was a mission at Peoria in charge of Father De Ville in 1712, and also at St. Joseph, at the head of Lake Michigan—where lived Miamis and Pottowatomies—in charge of Father Chardon in 1711.

Such, then, were the stations in the Illinois country when Charlevoix, journeying from Quebec to New Orleans, visited them in 1721. He has left his impressions in a journal included in vol. ii. of "Histoire de la Nouvelle France." The Indians at St. Joseph were almost all Christians, but had fallen into great disorders because for a long time they had no resident missionary. He found the Peorias also without a missionary and almost entirely pagan; yet even here he found traces of Christianity and hopes of a brighter future. At Cahokia was a large town composed of two tribes, and here were two secular missionaries who had been pupils of Charlevoix at Quebec. At Kaskaskia he found that "this flourishing mission has been divided into two villages. The most populous is on the river; two Jesuits, Le Boulanger and De Kereben, have charge. Half a league below is Fort Chartres, in command of De Bois-Briant. The intervening space is being rapidly settled by French. Four leagues lower down and one league from the river is a large village of French; their parish priest is a Jesuit, De Beaubois. Two leagues from this farther inland is a second Indian village, in charge of the Jesuit Father Guymonneau." Le Boulanger was the author of a catechism and instructions in the Illinois language, the manuscript of which is, says Shea, in the Carter-Brown Library at Providence, R. I.

We see from Charlevoix's account that secular priests were at work in this section as early as the year 1721. The first Bishop of Quebec, Laval, had been a member of the Seminary of the Foreign Missions in Paris, and had established a branch seminary in Quebec. He destined the subjects of this seminary for the missions of the Mississippi

Valley. Thus it comes that Charlevoix meets them on his journey. Time was when the Recollects threatened to take this field from the Jesuits, the veterans of the Western missions; finally the intruders had come. Dissatisfaction and protests were unavailing, and the bishop went so far in his new policy as to invest one of the seminary priests with powers as vicar-general over all the missions of the Illinois. The move proved to be providential; it provided missionaries to preserve the Christianity created by the Jesuits after the society had been suppressed by France and the Pope.

The palmy period of the Illinois missions was from 1725 to 1750. The center of communication and supply was no longer Quebec, but New Orleans, though the ecclesiastical government and jurisdiction continued on the banks of the St. Lawrence. As early as 1720 the civil administration of the Mississippi Valley south of Lake Michigan passed from Quebec to New Orleans. Communication with the mother country by way of the Mississippi and the Atlantic was far easier and quicker than by way of the Atlantic, the St. Lawrence, the lakes, and the portages into the affluents of the Mississippi.

The great majority of the Illinois were now Christian, excepting the Peorias. They were settled down, cultivated the land, and absented themselves only in the hunting-season. The French intermarried with them freely, and to-day the blood of Illinois chiefs flows in the veins of some of the best French families of Illinois and Missouri. Fort Chartres was built in 1720 by Pierre Duqué de Bois-Briant, the king's lieutenant for Louisiana. This was a wooden building, supplanted later by that expensive stone structure that figures so prominently in the later French history of Illinois, and to-day it is but a shapeless ruin. Here also was built the Church of St. Ann of Fort Chartres. Under the jurisdiction of the priest of St. Ann, chapels were erected subsequently at Prairie du Rocher and St. Philippe's. Part of the ancient records of the parish of St. Ann have been preserved to this day.

The building of Fort Chartres gave an impetus to the settlements of Illinois, and the Canadian population received considerable accessions. The post at Vincennes became the residence of a missionary, Father Meurin, in 1749; he attended to the spiritual wants of the neighboring Piankeshaw Indians and of the French settlers. The latter greatly increased between the years 1754 and 1756 by immigrants from Detroit, Kaskaskia, and New Orleans. Some fourteen French families were settled at Ouiatanon, a trading-post not far below the present site of Lafayette, O.; and also a few at Twightee village, near the site of Fort Wayne. These waifs of civilization, far removed from the great centers, were in a state of almost unlimited ease and freedom, and intermarried with the dusky maidens about them.

But as the white settlements increased and prospered the Indians decreased. Father Vivier, a Jesuit missionary, states in a letter of June 8, 1750, that at Kaskaskia there were three villages of Illinois Indians, with not more than eight hundred souls; whereas the French were eleven hundred, with three hundred black slaves. The whole Illinois tribe at this time could not count more than eight thousand souls. Much smaller was the Indian population at Vincennes—scarcely three hundred. Vincennes and the Indian mission of Kaskaskia were still in the hands of the Jesuits; the French settlements at Cahokia and Kaskaskia and Fort Chartres were in the hands of the Seminary priests. The St. Joseph mission was well-nigh abandoned, and still remained under the civil administration of Quebec. Twelve years later Choiseul, minister of France, suppressed the Society of Jesus and surrendered all the possessions of

France in the New World. The Jesuits of Louisiana, for the most part, became secularized under the immediate jurisdiction of the Bishop of Quebec, and retained their missions.

It was to Spain that France surrendered Louisiana—that is to say, all the region west of the Mississippi and a small territory surrounding New Orleans on the eastern bank. All else east of the river had become English territory. Unwilling to remain under the British flag, the commandant of Fort Chartres, St. Ange, moved with his small garrison up and across the Mississippi to the embryo village of St. Louis. This post had been founded the year before by Pierre Laclède Liguest and Auguste Chouteau. St. Ange exercised the duties of commander here until he was relieved in 1770 by Lieutenant-Governor Don Pedro Piernas, the first Spanish commandant of upper Louisiana.

During the first years of English domination in Illinois there was a large exodus of the French inhabitants to New Orleans, Ste. Geneviève, and St. Louis. In 1770 there were one hundred wooden and fifteen stone buildings in the latter place; there was also a small log chapel (it was only in 1776 that a more decent building was erected). At the close of the year 1765 the whole number of French in Illinois and on the Wabash did not exceed two thousand persons; of the Illinois tribes there were only six hundred and fifty warriors, and the number of Miamis on the Wabash able to bear arms was still less. In 1769 an Illinois Indian of the Kaskaskia band was bribed by an English settler of Cahokia with a barrel of whisky to kill the great Ottawa war-chief, Pontiac, whose vast conspiracy against the English had just ended in a complete failure. The Western tribes, who had loved so well and followed so faithfully the great and luckless conspirator, took a fearful revenge on the Indians of the Illinois country, and the small remnant who survived the carnage forever after sunk into utter insignificance.

In September, 1760, the capitulation, signed at Montreal between General Amherst and the Marquis de Vaudreuil, governor of Canada, giving over to England the territory east of the Mississippi, northwest of the Ohio, and south of the lakes down to New Orleans, expressly stipulated religious liberty for the former French subjects living in the Northwest Territory under the jurisdiction of the Bishop of Quebec, with all the privileges which the bishop and clergy had heretofore enjoyed under French rule. The main provisions of the capitulation were ratified by the preliminary treaty of peace, signed at Fontainebleau in November, 1762, and by the final Treaty of Paris, February 10, 1763. Later on (June, 1768) the Privy Council, in answer to certain questions of the London Board of Trade concerning the interpretation of the religious liberty granted by the treaty to the inhabitants of the conquered territory, gave the following opinion: "That the several acts of Parliament which impose disabilities and penalties upon the public exercise of the Roman Catholic religion do not extend to Canada."

Thus, though France failed to keep in her hands, as she had demanded, the nomination of the future bishops of Quebec, or to secure, as she had asked, for the Jesuits the permanency of their property and of the Indian missions, yet religious liberty and episcopal rights, at any rate, were safeguarded, and it was recognized to be beyond even the power of the king to abolish them in virtue of his supremacy as head of the Anglican Church. These provisions were embodied in a proclamation to the former French subjects of the West by General Thomas Gage, the British commander-in-chief, whereby he informed them that the country was about to be taken possession of by the British forces, and ordered them to take an oath of fidelity and obedience to the English king at the hand of an official sent for that purpose.

There were few missionaries at this time: in Detroit two, one attending the French in the city, the other the Indians across the river; in Indiana and Illinois two, until Father Meurin, an aged Jesuit, arrived from New Orleans (September, 1764) to be the third. Under such circumstances religion was in a decadent state in spite of the guaranties and privileges of the treaty; and such was the embarrassment produced in Canada by the change of government that the Bishop of Quebec could not supply the needed laborers to the Western portion of his flock. In 1768 set out from Canada for the Illinois country, not only with the blessing of his bishop, but also with the consent and good wishes of the English authorities, a priest who was destined to play in our Revolutionary War such a part as entitled him to be called "the patriot priest of the West"—the Rev. Peter Gibault. He took up his residence at Kaskaskia, where he found, besides his French countrymen, Catholic soldiers of the Eighteenth Royal Irish Regiment. In 1770 he blessed a little wooden chapel at Paincourt, our modern St. Louis, and visited Vincennes, where a priest had not been seen since 1763. He found straggling Catholics at Mackinaw, St. Joseph, Peoria, Ouiatanon, and at two places across the Mississippi in Spanish territory, Ste. Geneviève and St. Louis. Of the care of the two latter posts he was relieved in 1772, two Spanish Capuchins having come from New Orleans to take charge of them. Such was the condition of the church in the West when the Revolutionary War broke out.

CHAPTER XIV.

THE LOUISIANA MISSIONS.

CHARLEVOIX says that Louisiana is the name which La Salle gave to that portion of North America watered by the Mississippi and lying below the Illinois River. But the French put no such limits to the vague, undefined country they called Louisiana. In their dreams it stretched eastward to the head-waters of the Ohio, westward to the Rockies, and northward to the Arctic Ocean, on the principle that possession of the main artery carried with it possession of all its affluents. However, the stricter meaning of La Salle is accepted in this work.

The Indians that inhabited this tract are known as the Mobilian family. This family included three considerable confederacies east of the Mississippi: the Chickasaws, faithful allies of the English, bounded on the north by the Ohio; below the Chickasaws, between the Mississippi and the Tombigbee, were the Choctaws, given more than any other tribe to agriculture, and numbering four thousand warriors (these were allies of the French); east of the Choctaws was the confederacy of the Creeks or Muskhogees, extending as far as the Atlantic. The Seminoles of Florida were vagrants from the above-named confederacies, following the chase rather than agriculture. Between the Chickasaws and the Choctaws was the peculiar tribe of the Natchez, supposed, on account of their religion, customs, and advanced civilization, to have wandered northward from Central America. All these tribes combined contained about fifty thousand souls. The descendants of the Chickasaws, Choctaws, and Creeks are to be found to-day in the Indian Territory, almost as numerous as ever, good farmers, with wonderful capacity for self-government and business; they are the civilized nations among the Indians of to-day. West of the Mississippi and south of the Arkansas, extending down into Texas and east of New Mexico, were different nations, or rather remnants of dying nations, not so numerous or important historically as the tribes named above.

After the miserable failure of La Salle's naval expedition to the mouth of the Mississippi, the project of founding any settlement in this new acquisition was apparently abandoned by the court of France. It was only when rumors came that the English were preparing to take advantage of La Salle's discovery to occupy the mouth of the great river, that France awoke to the necessity of heading off her rival, and sent Iberville, in December, 1698, to form a colony at that important point. He made the first settlement at Biloxi, so named from a neighboring Indian band, in Harrison County, Mississippi, February, 1699. With him was Father Anastasius Douay, a Recollect who had accompanied La Salle in his ill-fated expedition to Matagorda Bay, had survived the miseries of the trip, and had made his way back to France. In 1702 the seat of the colony was transferred to Mobile, Ala. It was only fifteen years later (1717) that a point on the Mississippi River was selected for the capital city of Louisiana; at this point New Orleans was founded.

We have seen how the Bishop of Quebec authorized the seminary of Quebec to enter the missionary field of the valley of the Mississippi, and invested with the powers of vicar-general the superior of the band sent out for this purpose. The superior was De Montigny; his companions were Davion and St. Cosme. De Montigny took up his residence among the Taensas (a tribe allied to the Natchez), and erected there a chapel, after having baptized eighty-five children in the first year of his labors. Davion took up his abode in a village (long known as Roche à Davion, afterward as Loftus' Heights, and to-day as Fort Adams) in the State of Mississippi; his labors were also extended to the Yazoo Indians. St. Cosme ascended the river and settled among the Tamaroa Indians at a site that became later on Cahokia. Presently the seminary sent out three more laborers, Bergier, Bouteville, and St. Cosme, Jr., a brother of the missionary at Tamaroa. Bergier settled at Tamaroa, and St. Cosme, Sr., descended to Natchez. De Montigny had vacated this post to go to France in the hope of adjusting difficulties which the arrival of this body of diocesan missionaries had raised between the Jesuits and themselves.

Such was the condition of things ecclesiastical in Louisiana when Iberville returned from France in 1700 with a Jesuit, Father Du Rhu, who ministered to the Indians around Biloxi and Mobile; the French at these posts were in charge of a secular priest. Humble and restricted as were at first this Jesuit father's labors, it was not long before a request was made to the Bishop of Quebec that the exclusive direction of the French posts in Louisiana be committed to the society, and that their superior in the valley of the Mississippi be made vicar-general. The bishop refused, thinking it best that no one religious order should have the monopoly of the field. The matter was appealed to the king, who referred it to the Bishops of Marseilles and Chartres. This commission decided in favor of the Bishop of Quebec and the seminary. The first missionary to lay down his life in the Louisiana missions was Nicholas Foucault, a seminary priest, who was massacred by the Arkansas in 1702. The scene of his death and resting-place is not known. The second victim was St. Cosme, who, on his way from his Natchez mission to Mobile, was massacred by the Sitimachas about fifty miles from the mouth of the Mississippi (1706).

In August, 1717, the regent, Duke of Orleans, transferred, in the name of Louis XV., the proprietorship of Louisiana to the Commercial Company of the West. The fifty-third clause of the transfer obliged the company to build at its expense churches at the places where it should establish settlements, and to maintain the necessary number of approved ecclesiastics, all under the authority of the Bishop of Quebec, who had the nomination of the priests of the colony. Charlevoix, in his voyage from Quebec to New Orleans, was at Natchez in December, 1721. "Though for a time," he says, "a priest lived here, his labors were without fruit among the Indians, and there was no priest there at the time." In fact, from the Illinois River to New Orleans he met with no missionary on the river. It was five years and more since any priest had been among the French settlers at Natchez. They had fallen into a state of indifference. In January, 1722, he arrived at New Orleans. He describes it as a place of a hundred houses, scattered about without any order. Yet he ventures to predict that this would become a wealthy city and the metropolis of a large colony, and he gives good reasons for his prophecy. He does not speak of the spiritual condition of the place. But he must have made a secret report as to the general condition of the colony that caused the Company of the West to bestir themselves.

For Louisiana was divided soon after into three ecclesiastical sections. The section north of the Ohio, the

Illinois missions, was left to the Jesuits and the seminary priests, as heretofore. The second section contained the settlements at the mouth of the Mississippi and the country west of the river as far north as the confluence of the Ohio. This was put under the immediate charge of Bishop Duplessis de Mornay, lately named coadjutor to the Bishop of Quebec, and his vicar-general, who governed this section from France, where he resided. He gave charge of the French settlements and the Indian missions in this section to the Capuchins, to which order he belonged. The third section was the country south of the Ohio and east of the Mississippi. This was confided to the Carmelites; but there is record of the coming to Louisiana of only one father of that order. The Bishop of Quebec turned over this section also to the Capuchins. However, the Capuchins did not have the men to send, and, moreover, felt that they could not do work among the Indians so well as the veteran campaigners, the Jesuits. With the approval of the Bishop of Quebec they gave the country north of Natchez to the Jesuits, and reserved to themselves the region south of that point. Still later (1726) the Capuchins were restricted to the care of the French posts in their district, the charge of the Indian missions going to the Jesuits. Under this arrangement the Jesuits gained a residence for their superior in New Orleans, without any jurisdiction, however, over the whites, and under a Capuchin vicar-general.

The French settlements were growing. Mobile had sixty families, New Orleans six hundred. A great accession to the power of the church in New Orleans came with the Ursulines. Through the influence of Father De Beaubois, the Jesuit superior, these nuns came from France in 1727, and set up a convent and a higher educational institution for girls, the first of the kind within the limits of the present republic. The Catholic Indians throughout the colony were not numerous; the greatest number was to be found among the Appalachees, who fled from Florida to seek protection from the raids of the Protestant colonists of South Carolina and Georgia under cover of the French guns of Mobile. The Jesuits entered zealously into the work of converting the tribes of Louisiana; missions were established by them on the Arkansas River, and among the Choctaws, the Yazoos, and the Chickasaws. These missions, however, were broken up (1729) by the revolt of the Natchez, into which the neighboring Indians were drawn, and in which Fathers Dupoisson and Souel lost their lives. After the quelling of this rebellion by the French forces the missions were again resumed.

From this time on the sources of information as to the history of the missions are scant. This much seems evident: that no great success attended the labors of the missionaries. In New Orleans itself the church was distracted by the maladministration of the Capuchin vicar-general and his unjustifiable enmity to the Jesuits. The Bishop of Quebec finally came to the conclusion that the best interests of religion demanded that the powers of administration should be transferred from the Capuchins to the Jesuits; and thus the office of vicar-general was given into the hands of the latter from the year 1750 until their suppression, which was decreed in Paris in 1761 and executed in Louisiana in 1763. The property of the society in the province was confiscated and sold for $180,000, a large sum at that day. All the fathers, with the exception of a few in the Illinois district, were removed, and the Capuchins, freed from the presence of their formidable rivals, remained masters of the field; but not to the advantage of religion, as we shall see.

At the same time Louisiana passed under Spanish rule.

When the representative of Spain, Governor O'Reilly, came to New Orleans in 1769, the total population of the province, including St. Louis, was 13,238, half of whom were negro slaves. This number does not comprise the Catholic Indian population, an exact account of which it is not easy to get. After the suppression of the Society of Jesus no further steady effort was made for their evangelization. Nowhere in the United States was the success so small. To-day we find traces of the work of the early missionaries among our present Indians who formerly lived in the East and the Northwest, in Florida and New Mexico; but none among the Indians from the lower Mississippi Valley, if we except a small band of Quapaws from Arkansas, now living in the Indian Territory. The blame must be laid to the misunderstanding between the Jesuits and the seculars, the Jesuits and the Capuchins of Louisiana, to the want of zeal in the government for the work of the missions, to the suppression of the society just at the time they were entering this field, and, finally, to the political jealousies and wars of the European nations fighting for the mastery of North America. It is a pity, for the Indians whose former home was in that section are to-day the most civilized, cultivated, and wealthy of the 248,-340 still remaining in the United States, according to the calculations of the Indian Bureau.

Of this total it is hard to say how many are Catholics. Hoffman's "Catholic Directory" of 1894 says 97,850; Sadlier's "Catholic Directory" of 1894 says 58,750; the "Independent" of April 5, 1894, says 45,110; perhaps it will be safe for us to say 50,000. At any rate, this may be said with certainty: that there was not a tribe in all the extent of the United States to which the gospel was not preached by Catholic missionaries from the year 1520 down to the time of our War of Independence; and, again, this: that many a red man fell away from the faith, once held by his fathers, in the inevitable and often cruel flight before the incoming tide of European immigration; and, again, this: that the missionaries of the old church are now once more at work among the aborigines, parked in their reservations, to preserve the fruits of the labors of their predecessors, and to reclaim to Christianity and civilization the sad remnants of a race once the master of this splendid domain.

From the year 1763 Louisiana was under the dominion of Spain until the 30th of November, 1813, when it reverted to France; not for long, however, for twenty days afterward it was formally ceded to the United States. By rescript of September 1, 1805, Pius VII. placed this new acquisition of the republic under the jurisdiction of Bishop Carroll as administrator apostolic. During the forty-two years from 1763 to 1805 the condition of the church in Louisiana was not by any means of the best. The Capuchins who were in charge were not all of them models of ecclesiastical virtues, there was no immediate episcopal supervision, and the missions fell into a sad state of neglect; though the church received at this time a strong reinforcement in numbers from some five hundred Acadians, who from their ruined colony in Nova Scotia escaped to San Domingo and thence to New Orleans.

The province, in passing from the control of France, was no longer under the ecclesiastical jurisdiction of Quebec, but became subject to the jurisdiction of the Bishop of Santiago de Cuba. In 1772 the bishop of that see, James Joseph de Echeverria, sent to New Orleans four Spanish Capuchins, with Father Cyril de Barcelona as superior. But Father Dagobert, the former French superior, roused the people against the newcomers, and the governor, fearing his removal would be disastrous to

Spanish interests under the circumstances, allowed him to retain his position, though his well-known shortcomings rendered him quite unworthy of it. Convinced by this fact and others of like nature that discipline needed the presence of a superior authority, the Bishop of Santiago obtained from Rome the appointment of Father Cyril as his coadjutor, with residence in New Orleans.

The jurisdiction of the new appointee was to embrace the southeastern Spanish possessions from the Mississippi to the Atlantic—that is to say, the States of Louisiana, Alabama, Florida, and others bordering on the western bank of the Mississippi up to Missouri. At this time the church in Louisiana, extending up to St. Louis and Ste. Geneviève, Mo., contained seventeen parishes and twenty-one priests. However, Bishop Cyril did not succeed in restoring discipline to the church under his administration; he fell under the displeasure of the king and of his ordinary—no longer the Bishop of Santiago, but the Bishop of Havana, a new see erected in 1787. The unfortunate prelate was banished by a royal order (1793) to his Capuchin province of Catalonia, in Spain. The growing evils of the church in Louisiana moved Pius VI. to erect that province into an independent bishopric, April 27, 1793. The first bishop of the new diocese was Louis Penalver y Cardenas, a native of Havana, a man of irreproachable life.

He recorded, soon after his arrival in New Orleans (July 17, 1795), his impressions: "As to reëstablishing the purity of religion and reforming the morals of the people, I have encountered many obstacles. The inhabitants do not listen to, or, if they do, they disregard, all exhortations to maintain the Catholic faith in its orthodoxy, and to preserve innocence of life. Because his Majesty tolerates Protestants here for sound reasons of state, bad Catholics, whose numbers are great, think that they are authorized to live without any religion at all. Out of the eleven thousand souls composing this parish [the cathedral] scarcely three or four hundred comply with the obligation of receiving the holy eucharist once a year. Not more than a quarter of the population ever hear mass. Most of the men live in a state of concubinage, and there are fathers who procure mistresses for their sons to divert them from marrying. Their houses are full of books written against religion and the state."

A very sad condition, to be sure—the natural fruit of a clergy that had forgotten the high and sacred duties of their calling. No wonder that the first efforts of reform should be directed by the zealous bishop to the leaders of the flock. With this intent he issued at once, to serve as a rule until a diocesan synod could be held, a document entitled "Instructions for the Government of the Parish Priests of the Diocese of Louisiana." He then set about visiting his diocese. Unfortunately the records of his administration have all perished. We possess, however, a general description of the condition of religion written by him in 1799.

It appears from this description that the source of the religious evils and the great danger to the Spanish power were his American neighbors. "The emigration from the western part of the United States and the toleration of our government have introduced into this colony a gang of adventurers, who have no religion and acknowledge no God; they have made the morals of our people much worse by intercourse with them in trade; they fill the minds of our people with dangerous ideas in harmony with their own restless, ambitious character." He then goes on to advocate a restriction of this kind of immigration. The good bishop was striving unwittingly with the inevitable when he dreamed of rolling back the American tide.

The doom was writ large enough, but he did not see or could not read the handwriting. He was spared the spectacle of the danger he so much dreaded; in July, 1801, he was promoted to the see of Guatemala. Less than two years afterward the control of Spain came to an end, Louisiana became a part of the United States, and the church in that region came under the jurisdiction of the first Bishop of Baltimore, the Right Rev. John Carroll. Its further history belongs to the second part of this work.

PART III. THE ENGLISH MISSIONS.

CHAPTER XV.

THE BEGINNINGS OF CATHOLICITY IN THE COLONIES (1634–48).

THE love and pursuit of religious liberty led to the foundation of Maryland. The penal laws of Elizabeth drove some of her Catholic subjects to seek across the Atlantic a safe haven where they might worship God in freedom. As early as 1584 two hundred and sixty Catholics, under the lead of Sir Humphrey Gilbert, attempted to establish a colony in the country of Norumbega, supposed to be in the present State of Maine. The attempt was a failure. Of the three vessels that sailed, one went down with the leader, the others made their way back to England.

A second attempt was made in 1605, under the patronage of Sir Thomas, Lord Arundel of Wardour, and of Henry Wriothesley, Earl of Southampton; a vessel sent out to select a spot arrived in the Kennebec River. But the project was opposed by no less a personage than the famous English Jesuit, Father Parsons, and it came to naught.

The third attempt was made in 1627, and it, too, failed of success. The leader was Sir George Calvert, clerk of the privy council, knighted in 1617, made one of the secretaries of state in 1618. At an early date he became interested in American colonization: for, besides being one of the councilors of the New England Company, he was also a member of the Virginia Company. He became a Catholic in 1623, and resigned the position of secretary of state. King James I. tried to induce him to remain in office. Failing in this, he appointed him to the privy council and raised him to the Irish peerage as Baron Baltimore of Baltimore in the county of Longford, Ireland. In 1620 Lord Baltimore bought from Sir William Vaughan, who had a patent for part of Newfoundland, his rights over the southeastern peninsula of that island; and the next year he sent out to his purchase a body of colonists. In 1622 he applied for a patent directly to the crown, and all Newfoundland was granted to him. The colony was named Avalon, in commemoration of the spot where, according to tradition, Christianity was first preached in Britain. He visited his colony in 1627, and the next year moved his family thither. But various causes induced him to abandon it. He had serious troubles—even a small naval warfare—with French claimants; one of the colonists, a Puritan minister, complained to the English authorities that Baltimore had brought out with him popish priests and favored the popish worship; above all, he found that the climate was too inhospitable for successful colonization.

Taking with him as many of the colonists as would follow him, he sailed for Jamestown, Va., October 1, 1629. The foundation of Virginia preceded that of Maryland. On the 19th of December, 1606—one hundred and nine years after the discovery of Cabot, ninety years after the first voyage of Ponce de Leon to Florida, fifty-nine years after the foundation of St. Augustine—Jamestown was founded by one hundred and five English colonists. The welcome of the Virginians for Lord Baltimore was by no means cordial. Governor Pott and William Claiborne would not allow him to settle in the neighborhood unless he took the oaths of supremacy and allegiance. In this proceeding they went beyond their powers, and forgot the position Baltimore held in the Virginia Company. But they knew that, as a Catholic, he could not take the oath of supremacy, and cunningly surmised that they could thus get rid of him. He returned to England, and asked for a part of the unsettled region north of the Potomac. This was granted, and at the king's request the new colony received the name of Maryland (Terra Mariæ), in honor of the queen, Henrietta Maria.

The formal document of the grant was issued not to the first Lord Baltimore (he died April 13, 1632, just before it was made out), but to his heir, Lord Cecil, second Lord Baltimore. The boundaries were very precisely defined in the grant: on the north the fortieth parallel of north longitude; on the west a line running south from this parallel to the farthest source of the Potomac, and thence to the Chesapeake Bay; on the east the ocean and the Delaware River and Bay. These boundaries included all the present State of Delaware, a large tract of land now inclosed partly in Pennsylvania and partly in West Virginia, and the State of Maryland. The charter was the most liberal ever issued by the English crown. The other colonies were granted to chartered companies, who managed them on the joint-stock principle; but the grant of Maryland was to an individual, the lord proprietary, with all legislative and executive powers to administer the colony as his private estate, under the sovereignty of the crown, free from all taxation on the part of England, with the exception of the delivery of two Indian arrows yearly and a fifth of all the precious metals found, as an acknowledgment of feudal tenure.

Two vessels were fitted out, the "Ark," of three hundred and fifty tons, and the "Dove," of fifty tons—emblems of happy omen: the one refuge of political, the other olive-branch of religious, liberty. Twenty gentlemen and between two and three hundred laboring-men, mostly Catholics, embarked as colonists. Leaving Gravesend on the 18th of October, they stopped at the Isle of Wight to take on board two Jesuit fathers, White and Altham. It is the "Relatio Itineris" of Father White (discovered, 1822, in the archives of the professed house of the Jesuits in Rome by an American Jesuit, Father William McSherry) that is the chief authority for the early history of Maryland. On March 25, 1634, the pilgrims landed on an island at the mouth of the Potomac, that they named St. Clement's, of which to-day only a sand-bank remains. Mass was celebrated, and a cross was planted, to indicate that the newcomers were Christians and meant to make Christian the land of their choice.

The neighboring Indians, a mild race compared with the near Susquehannas and farther Iroquois, welcomed the strangers cordially. Governor Leonard Calvert, brother of Lord Baltimore, and his lieutenant (for Lord Cecil did not emigrate), went directly to visit the great chief of the region, emperor of Piscataway, was welcomed, and was bidden settle anywhere he chose. After tarrying awhile (according to tradition, at St. Inigoes) the pilgrims ascended the Potomac to the present St. Mary's. The natives there, harried by the Susquehannas, were about to abandon their homes. For some trifling European objects they sold out to the Europeans. Father White was assigned to the chief's hut, which he dedicated as the *primum Marylandiæ sacellum* (the first chapel in Maryland). The relations between the Marylanders and the Indians were always cordial. We have to record in this chapter no wars such as stained the history of Canada and the northern English colonies. The Indians of Maryland have disappeared entirely, not by the violence and cruelties of the whites, rather through what may be called a process of painless extinction, no one knows how. The woes of the colony in her early years came not from them, but from her Virginian neighbors. The story of Claiborne's claim to Kent Island, evidently comprised within the Maryland charter, and the intercolonial warfares that resulted from that claim, belongs to secular rather than to religious history.

In his first colonization in Newfoundland Lord Baltimore, as head of the colony, had brought with him both Catholic and Protestant clergymen. The Protestant clergyman complained of the importation of the Catholic priests and the toleration given to the Catholic worship, and thereby almost brought Lord Baltimore into trouble with the home government. Taught by this experience, Lord Cecil left the colonists free to supply themselves with clergymen. As lord proprietor he took no action in this regard, and thus he was the first American colonizer to put in practice the disestablishment and disendowment of the church and to inaugurate the voluntary system of church support. He informed the English provincial and the general of the Jesuits at Rome that he could offer the clergy no subvention, "nor can they expect sustenance from heretics hostile to the faith, nor from Catholics for the most part poor, nor from savages who live after the manner of wild beasts."

The two fathers who accompanied the emigrants were to go as gentleman adventurers and take up lands on the same conditions as the others. Any colonist of the first emigration who brought with him five men received two thousand acres of land, subject to an annual quit-rent of four hundred pounds of wheat. One who came between 1634-35 bringing ten men had the same allotment of land at the rent of six hundred pounds of wheat; and for those who came later, or brought fewer men, the land given was proportionately less and the rates higher. Under this arrangement Father Philip Fisher, claiming his religious companions as men brought over by him, took his share of land; and afterward the Jesuits, as they came to the colony, acquired more land by the same process. This was the source of their sustenance for themselves and their churches down to the date of their suppression.

Not only did the first fathers minister to the Catholic settlers of St. Mary's—a work that did not take up all of their time—but they also reached out for the Indians, and extended the field of their labors as more priests came to help them in the years following. The superior, Father John Brock, resided at their plantation, apparently St. Inigoes. Father Altham was stationed on Kent Island, off the eastern shore, a great center of Indian trade; Father Fisher was at St. Mary's, the capital of the colony; Father White at first took up his residence among the Patuxents, many of whom he converted, and from whom he received a considerable grant of land. In 1639 he went to the Piscataways residing near the present town of that name, fifteen miles south of Washington. The chief, Chilomacon, was converted, and solemnly baptized in the presence of the authorities of the colony. As the Piscataways were exposed to the inroads of their neighbors, the fierce Susquehannas, Father White removed his residence from their village to the European settlements, and thenceforward made only excursions to the Indian tribes. Almost the whole tribe of the Patuxents was brought at an early date to the faith.

The work of the missionaries extended also to Virginia, and some of the settlers there were converted. In consequence of this inroad of Catholicity an act was passed in that colony, in 1641, that no popish recusant should be allowed to hold any office, under the penalty of a thousand pounds of tobacco, the currency of the times; and thus was a stop put to the work of conversion in Virginia. Meanwhile the population of Maryland was steadily growing. Colonists, attracted by pamphlets and letters of the early planters, came out in numbers and took up manors and plantations. The emigrants were of a kind most desirable for a new colony—men of substance with families, and laboring-men seeking homes. No religious or political tests hampered them; simple allegiance to the lord proprietor in England, and self-government of the broadest kind in their new home, were irresistible inducements. No towns or great agglomerations of population were formed, nor were they needed. The plantations faced on the bay, the rivers, the creeks; so that vessels could load tobacco and unload goods at every man's door, so to speak. Such conditions of life created that patriarchal state of society, that strong family feeling, so characteristic of early Maryland.

Meanwhile trouble was brewing for the Jesuits. On reports from Lewgar, secretary of the colony, Baltimore became prejudiced against them, declared the grant of land made them by the Patuxents to be null and void, objected to their further acquisition of land in that way, and applied to the Propaganda for a prefect apostolic and secular priests. Already the Propaganda had taken steps in this direction (1641), and, though the Jesuits remonstrated in an appeal to the holy see, two secular priests arrived in Maryland (1642). However, a reconciliation between Baltimore and the Jesuits was effected through mutual friends; but the lord proprietor exacted severe conditions. The Jesuits had to give up all lands ceded by the Patuxents, and to promise to accept no more grants of the kind; they were to take up no more lands, except with the permission of the lord proprietor. They were to claim no special exemptions and privileges, except those allowed by the common English law. No new Jesuit recruits were to be sent to the colony without his permission. Any missionary then or thereafter in the colony was to be recalled within the year on his demand. They had to take an oath of allegiance to him. Baltimore was a good Catholic, but he was also a sturdy Englishman. We see in these conditions the fear lest the church should acquire too much real estate; lest the clergy should claim exemptions and immunities of a past age and assert independence of the common law and the constituted authorities.

But a worse storm came from Virginia, and for a time overthrew the missions. Maryland opened her doors and offered hospitality, with civil and religious liberty, to the Puritans persecuted in Virginia. When the royal power in England fell before the Covenanters, the guests of Maryland proved ungrateful and returned evil for good. The inveterate enemy of the Catholic colony, Claiborne, used them as tools to overthrow the authority of the Baltimores and crush out Catholicity. He invaded the colony (1645), drove out Leonard Calvert, looted the plantations of the Catholic gentry and the Jesuits, put in irons Fathers White and Copley, and sent them to England, where they lingered awhile, to be sent afterward into exile. Two other Jesuits, Rigbee and Cooper, hid themselves in Virginia; Father Hartwell, the superior, sank under the blow and died within the year. Not a priest was left in all Maryland.

The Jesuits, within twelve years, had done a noble work. The Indian tribes on the Potomac and the Patuxent had been instructed, and many had been received into the church. Father White had compiled an Indian catechism, still extant in Rome, in manuscript, and also a Maryland grammar and vocabulary, of which no traces have as yet been found. He was undoubtedly the first Englishman to reduce an Indian language to grammatical forms.

The lord proprietary considered his province lost, and had no further hope but to save what he could of his property. Not so his brother, the governor, Leonard Calvert. Toward the end of 1646 he raised a small force, with which he reëstablished once more Baltimore's authority over the colony. He did not live long to enjoy the fruits of his victory, for he died on the 9th of June, 1647. Once more the field was open to the Jesuits; those that had sought refuge in Virginia returned, and others came from England. By this time the Protestants in the province began to increase, and threatened to outnumber the Catholics in the near future; this, no doubt, was the reason why Lord Baltimore, while naming as governor William Stone, a Protestant, reconstructed the council so as to give the Catholics a majority. At the same time he caused to be established by act of the legislature that freedom of conscience which he and his father had advocated and practiced from the beginning. The famous act of toleration was passed in the colonial Assembly, April, 1649. In that body sat eight Catholics and five Protestants, not including the governor. The act was entitled "An Act Concerning Religion." After forbidding, under penalty of death, blasphemy against any Person of the Most Holy Trinity, and making reproachful speeches against the Virgin Mary, the apostles, and the evangelists punishable by fine, it lays penalties upon all who shall call others reviling names, such as "heretic, Puritan, Jesuit, papist, and the like," and then enacts: "Whereas the enforcing of conscience in matters of religion hath frequently fallen out to be of dangerous consequence, and the better to preserve mutual love and amity among the inhabitants of the colony, no person professing belief in Jesus Christ shall be in any ways troubled, molested, or discountenanced for or in respect of his or her religion, nor in the free exercise thereof." Heavy penalties were imposed for so offending. Profanation of the Sabbath or the Lord's day, called Sunday, by swearing, drunkenness, unnecessary work, or disorderly recreation, was also severely forbidden.

This act was an immense advance upon the practice of the age both in Europe and in the English colonies of North America. It was the only sensible position to take in a province inhabited by men of different religious creeds. The evils of an enforcement of any one creed, under such circumstances, were greater than the evil of tolerating what was false; and, like a practical Englishman, Lord Baltimore chose the lesser evil. He had to decide, as the responsible head of a mixed community, not on what was best in theory, but on what was practicable, what was in practice most conducive to the welfare of the community. He was the first to establish by law a *modus vivendi* between conflicting worships, which has since obtained in all civilized countries where Christendom is divided. He saw that the means of healing those divisions was not in the civil compulsion in favor of any one church. Whatever we may think should have been the proper means of preventing the origin and early propagation of novelties in religion, it seems certain that, once they have gained a solid and seemingly permanent foothold, the civil enforcement of any one favored creed as against all others can be no longer the efficacious means of healing the divisions.

This act was no novelty in the policy of the Baltimores; it was but the legalizing of a system followed by them from the foundation of the colony of Avalon in Newfoundland. The oath of office required in the very beginning of the colony from the governors ran thus: "I do further swear that I will not by myself or any other person, directly or indirectly, trouble, molest, or discountenance any person whatsoever, professing to believe in Jesus Christ, and in particular no Roman Catholic, for or in respect of religion, nor his or her free exercise thereof, within the said province; . . . nor will I make any difference of persons in conferring offices, rewards, or favors, for or in respect to their said religion, but merely as I shall find them faithful and well deserving." If toleration had not been embodied heretofore in a legislative enactment of the province, it was because the enactment was not needed; the practice of the proprietary, the governor, and the inhabitants, while Catholics were in the majority, was always against persecution and in favor of equal liberty. That fact is writ large in the history of the first fifteen years of Maryland; the admission of the Puritans from Virginia proves it. Nor can it be said that Baltimore, Catholic though he was, favored the Jesuits beyond measure, since, as we have seen, he confined them within the common law to which all were amenable, and curtailed their ability to grow wealthy. Nor can it be said that he discriminated against Protestants, since he nominated Stone as governor. But when he foresaw that in the near future Protestantism might predominate numerically in the colony of which he was the head, he resolved to make Protestantism continue his policy so far as he could do so, and in advance bound it to that policy by fixing in a legislative enactment the toleration he had practiced and enforced. Alas! the barrier he had then set up against intolerance proved to be too weak for the violence of fanaticism, as the later history of Maryland too sadly proves.

While securing the future peace of the Catholic colonists, Lord Baltimore did not neglect the Indians. In 1651 ten thousand acres around Calverton Manor, on the Wicomico River, were set apart as a reservation for the remnants of the Maryland native tribes; and the dwellers in that reserve were instructed and ministered to by Catholic clergymen. If Baltimore was first in religious liberty, he was also first in that method of preserving and civilizing the Indian which is now the policy of the United States government. Very soon those Indians were received into civilized life; their daughters were educated and frequently married into white families. The blood of some of the chiefs flows to-day in the veins of Maryland's proudest sons. Only a few full-blooded Indians are to be found at present on the Piscataway and on the eastern shore.

This peaceful state of things was rudely broken by an invasion of Claiborne and Bennett, commissioners of the Commonwealth of England for Virginia, who, under pretext that Maryland was royalist and disloyal to Cromwell's Protectorate, undertook a second time to end Baltimore's rule in the colony. The charge was false—Baltimore had accepted the *de facto* government; but the inveterate hatred of Claiborne blinded him. The scenes of the former raid were repeated, and the Jesuits were forced to seek refuge out of the province. An Assembly was convoked, from which all Catholics were excluded. The toleration act of 1649 was repealed, and a new law concerning religion was passed: "It is hereby enacted and declared that none who profess and exercise the popish, commonly called the Roman Catholic, religion, can be protected in this province by the laws of England, . . .

but are to be restrained from the exercise thereof." Governor Stone rallied after the first blow, met force by force, but was defeated in battle on the Severn, March 24, 1655, and was captured and thrown into prison; four of his chief followers were executed in cold blood, three of them being Catholics.

However, in 1656 the government in England, coming to see the injustice done to Baltimore, decided for him against the Virginia commissioners. Once more his rights were acknowledged; his authority was restored, and all acts passed during the rebellion were annulled. It was agreed with the home government that the toleration act of 1649 was to be made perpetual, and a general amnesty to all who had taken part in the rebellion was declared. Baltimore was no less merciful to those whom religious prejudice misled than he was tenacious of his rights and vigorous in defending them; he stands out as the very embodiment of American fair play.

After the restoration the Jesuits were so few in Maryland for many years as to be unequal to the task of attending to the spiritual wants of the Catholic colonists, who were increasing by constant immigration. In 1669 Lord Baltimore complained to Abbate Claudius Agretti, sent from Rome to England on some ecclesiastical business, that there were only two priests in Maryland to minister to two thousand Catholics, and that for the last twenty-four years he had solicited the holy see in vain to send other missionaries to his province. Agretti reported this complaint to Propaganda; the internuncio at Brussels was ordered to make inquiry. The result was that two Franciscans, Father Massey and an associate, were sent to found a mission in Maryland; they arrived, apparently, in 1673. We cannot tell what field was assigned to the newcomers; but in 1677 three more Franciscans came and three more Jesuits, with a certain number of lay brothers. One consequence of this addition to the missionary force of the colony was the opening of a school of humanities by the Jesuits, in which the sons of the planters were given a liberal education. From this school many of them passed to the higher institutions of Europe. With the increase of laborers came an expansion of the field of labor; the seaboard settlements north of Maryland were claiming their attention and services.

In the year 1634 a grant was made out by the English crown to Sir Edmund Plowden, a Catholic gentleman, erecting into a county palatine, under the name of New Albion, lands on the Hudson and Delaware, including what are now known as Long Island and New Jersey. His object, probably, was to found a refuge for oppressed Catholics; but no permanent settlement was made under this grant. After the Duke of York came into possession of New Netherland (now New York), he conveyed a part of his territory, in what is now New Jersey, to the Catholic Earl of Perth. But there was no serious attempt made to found any settlement under this conveyance. However, Catholic individuals gradually found their way into the colonies of New York and New Jersey; for instance, Anthony Brockholls (1674), who was second in authority to Governor Andros; Lieutenant Jervis Baxter, one of the oldest officials of the colony; and William Douglas, who, in 1680, was elected a member of the Assembly of New Jersey, but was not admitted by that body, "the aforesaid member upon examination owning himself to be a Roman Catholic." In 1682 the governor of New York was a Catholic and an Irishman, Colonel Thomas Dongan. He was accompanied from England by the Jesuit father Thomas Harvey. In connection with the departure of Harvey for America, the English provincial,

Father Warner, writes to the general, February 26, 1683: "Father Thomas Harvey, the missioner, passes to New York by consent of the governor of the colony. In that colony is a respectable city, fit for the foundation of a college, if faculties are given, to which college those who are now scattered throughout Maryland may betake themselves and make excursions from thence into Maryland. The Duke of York, the lord of that colony, greatly encourages the undertaking of a new mission." Two more fathers, Harrison and Gage, soon joined Father Harvey. We know from the history of the Iroquois mission that it was the purpose of Dongan to drive the French Jesuits from northern New York and replace them with English fathers, though the purpose was never realized.

There was a small chapel in the fort south of Bowling Green; Dongan kept two chaplains there, who were paid sixty pounds a year. There was a Latin school kept by the Jesuits on the neighboring King's Farm, and the bell of the Dutch chapel in the fort was used to mark the school exercises. In the first legislative Assembly in New York (October 17, 1683) under Dongan's administration it was enacted "that no person or persons which profess faith in God by Jesus Christ shall at any time be anyways molested, punished, disquieted, or called in question for any difference of opinions, or matter of religious concernment, who do not actually disturb the civil peace of the province." The Christian churches were to "be held and reputed as privileged churches, and enjoy all their former freedoms of their religion in divine worship and church discipline." It was this religious freedom, doubtless, that gave the Jesuits hopes of success in their missionary and educational work in New York.

On the 4th of March, 1681, Charles II. granted to the son of Admiral Penn, for the canceling of a debt, a territory in America extending five degrees westward from the Delaware River, with a width of three degrees. This stretch of country (now Pennsylvania) was already occupied by Dutch Calvinists, Swedish Lutherans, and a few Catholics, and was about to receive a large body of Quakers, to which sect Penn belonged. Here, also, liberty of worship was enacted: "All persons living in the province who confess and acknowledge the One Almighty and Eternal God to be the Creator, Upholder, and Ruler of the World, and that hold themselves obliged in conscience to live peaceably and justly in civil society, shall in no way be molested or prejudiced for their religious persuasion, or practice in matters of faith and worship, nor shall they be compelled at any time to frequent or maintain any religious worship, place, or ministry whatever." Knowing for certain that Jesuits passed to and fro between New York and Maryland, we may conjecture that they visited occasionally such Catholics as they met in Pennsylvania and New Jersey; but we have no certain records of the condition or number of Catholics in those two States at that early day.

It was in the reign of James II., in the year 1685, that England received the first Catholic bishop since Elizabeth's reign, Dr. John Leyburn, Vicar Apostolic of all England. Three years afterward the island was divided ecclesiastically into four districts: the London, the Western, the Midland, the Northern. The Catholics of America and their clergy were under the jurisdiction of the incumbent of the London district from this period down to the appointment of the Rev. John Carroll as prefect apostolic in the United States in 1784. The political and religious situation on this side of the Atlantic was full of promise: Maryland, Pennsylvania, New York, were animated by the same spirit of religious freedom; the king was Catholic;

the governors of these provinces were not hostile; episcopal supervision, though distant, was an augury of order and vitality. Yet the progress of the church in Maryland during this period of quiet was astonishingly slow; the Franciscans were few—not more than four at any time—and the Jesuits were thinking of transferring their center of work from Maryland to New York. But the prospect soon lost all brightness, and gloom lowered on the nascent Catholicity of the central colonies. James II. was overthrown, William of Orange came in (1689). At once Leisler seized the government of New York, and Coode that of Maryland; religious liberty was doomed to extinction, and Catholic missionaries to persecution; of all the colonies Pennsylvania alone remained steadfastly true to her original policy of toleration.

CHAPTER XVI.

THE PENAL PERIOD.

One of the first acts of Coode, the usurper of Maryland, was to hold a convention for the defense of the Protestant religion. "Chapels and churches," he writes to the king, "were erected for the use of popish idolatry and superstition; Jesuits and seminary priests are the only incumbents; several children of Protestants have been committed to the tutelage of papists; Jesuit priests and lay papists use every means that art or malice can suggest to divert the obedience and loyalty of the inhabitants from their most Sacred Majestys, and pray for the success of the popish forces in Ireland and the French designs against England." Glad of the opportunity, and having for policy to bring the colonies under the direct action of the crown, William, the king of England, ignored the rights of the lord proprietary, declared Maryland a royal province, and sent out Sir Lionel Copley as royal governor in 1691. He at once convened a legislative Assembly from which Catholics were excluded, and passed an "Act for the service of Almighty God and the establishment of the Protestant religion in this province." The province was divided into Anglican parishes, though there were no clergymen to take charge of them, vestrymen were appointed, and all the inhabitants were taxed annually forty pounds of tobacco for the building of Episcopal churches and the maintenance of Episcopal ministers. Thus Catholics, for nearly a century thereafter, were compelled to support a ministry that was not theirs.

The province, at the time, contained a population of twenty-five thousand, the majority of whom were Protestants, but not Episcopalians. The seat of government was transferred from St. Mary's, mainly because it was the stronghold of Catholicity, and henceforward that original settlement of the Maryland pilgrims declined, until nothing now remains to mark the spot but a few ruins and a Protestant church built at Catholic expense out of the materials of the first Catholic church in the province. A census made in 1696–97 shows two priests, one lay brother, and four chapels in St. Mary's County; three priests, one lay brother, and four chapels in Charles County; one chapel, with no resident priest, in Talbot County. So high ran hostility to the Catholics that the devotedness of the priests during a pestilence in 1697 was turned into a reproach. It appears that their attendance on the sick of all denominations had won some Protestants over to the church. An Episcopal minister complained of this result of their heroic conduct to the governor and legislature, and that body considered the propriety of passing a law "to restrain such presumption"! A rivalry of self-sacrifice, one should think, would have been the proper remedy. They dared not, however, pass such a law, but salved their conscience by enacting, in 1700, that the Book of Common Prayer should be used exclusively in every church and place of public worship.

So far those penal laws bore equally on all denominations other than the Episcopal; but in 1702 toleration was extended to all Protestant dissenters; Catholics alone were outlawed and bore the burden of persecution. Father Hunter, in 1704, for having dedicated a new chapel, and celebrated mass in the old St. Mary's chapel, was summoned before the governor and his council, received a severe and insolent reprimand, and was threatened with direr punishment if he should fall into the same misdemeanor again. St. Mary's chapel was ordered to be locked up by the sheriff, and the key thereof to remain in the possession of that official. In October, 1704, the legislature passed an "Act to prevent the growth of popery within this province." Whoever should baptize a child not of Catholic parents, should say mass or exercise any ecclesiastical function, should endeavor to induce any of his Majesty's subjects to come back to or enter into the Catholic Church, was to be fined fifty pounds and imprisoned for six months. A repetition of the offense entailed transportation to England, to be dealt with there according to the rigor of the laws against popery. The same penalty was decreed against any Catholic keeping school, or educating, governing, or boarding youth. The act further provided that if any popish youth shall not, within six months after he attains his majority, take the oaths prescribed—oaths no Catholic in conscience could take—he shall be incapable of holding lands by descent, and his next of kin, if Protestant, shall succeed him; that any Catholic shall be incompetent to purchase lands; that any Catholic sending his child abroad to be educated in the Catholic faith shall forfeit one hundred pounds. And better to prevent the growth of popery, an act of the same year imposed a fine of twenty pounds on any one who brought in an Irish papist to till the soil of Maryland.

This inhuman legislation has been branded as infamous by all the historians of Maryland. It was the act not so much of the legislature as of the fanatical Governor Seymour, who was incensed at the Catholics for refusing to make up a purse for him. The Protestant colonists themselves, be it said to their credit, were not prepared to go this length of persecution; the legislature declared the law suspended for eighteen months, and Queen Anne abrogated it in 1705. In 1708 the sheriffs of the counties were required to report the number of Catholics in the province. In a population of over forty thousand only 2974 Catholics were found, nearly one half of them in St. Mary's County, seven hundred in Charles County. They were in the care of five Jesuit fathers. The abrogation by Queen Anne of the frightful penal legislation noticed above implied the permission for Catholics to hold divine service in private oratories. The residences of the Jesuits on their plantations, and the manor-houses of a few wealthy Catholics—such, for instance, as the Carroll mansion at Doughoregan Manor—were arranged with a view to this purpose. It was in this private, not to say secret, fashion that Catholicity was preserved in Maryland during many generations.

A sad blow fell on the few Catholics of the colony in 1713. In order to regain personal control of the province, Benedict Leonard Calvert, heir to the House of Baltimore, renounced the religion of his ancestors. Apostasy was the price at which England was willing to restore proprietary rights to the family that had founded the colony. Henceforth the scions of the House of Baltimore were brought up in Protestantism. Naturally the influence of this example was great, and many of the wealthy Catholic planters followed it. Further penal laws fostered apostasy. In 1716 oaths against the supremacy of the Pope and against belief in transubstantiation were demanded from all who would hold office; to join in the service of the mass or receive communion was to forfeit office and become disqualified for election to any political position. In the same year a fine of twenty shillings was imposed on the importation of any Irish papist servant, and the following year the fine was doubled. More than that, Catholics were deprived not only of office, but also of suffrage. "And whereas, notwithstanding all the measures that have been hitherto taken for preventing the growth of popery, it is obvious that not only professed papists still multiply and increase in number, but that there are also too great numbers of them that adhere to and espouse their interest in opposition to the Protestant establishment, it is enacted that all professed papists whatsoever be and are hereby declared incapable of giving their vote in any election of a delegate or delegates."

Yes, the papists seemed to thrive on persecution. Governor Hart, about this time, wrote to Bishop Robinson, of London: "The advantage which the Jesuits have from their [the Anglican ministers in Maryland] negligence is but too evident in the many proselytes they make;" and the same governor, addressing the Anglican clergy in 1718, expressed his great regret that the Jesuits were gaining proselytes, and the assembled ministers admitted the fact. They had a foothold in the capital, Annapolis; for in 1720 the Carrolls had a mansion there and kept a Catholic chaplain. Charles Carroll was, in spite of his steadfast attachment to the faith, the recognized agent of Lord Baltimore in the province; as such he was considered privileged from the penal laws. The number of the Jesuits had increased to twelve by the year 1723; they were in exclusive control of the missions of Maryland and neighboring colonies, the Franciscans having withdrawn from the field in 1720.

The colony of Pennsylvania did not go into the persecutions that were rampant in the other colonies. This liberality induced the Jesuits to establish themselves on the borders of Penn's territory. In 1706 they acquired an estate on the Little and Great Bohemia rivers, Cecil

County, known as St. Xavier's Residence on the Eastern Shore. This became the center of their excursions into Pennsylvania and New York, as well as into Maryland. And here, in 1745, they established a classical school. Among its earliest pupils were Benedict and Edward Neale, James Heath, Robert Brent, Charles Carroll—he of Carrollton—and John Carroll, the future Archbishop of Baltimore. This school was a great success at the time, and called forth the jealousy and anger of the Protestant ministry of the province.

In strong contrast to Pennsylvania stands the colony of Virginia. A few Catholic families had gone over the border to the southern shore of the Potomac at Aquia Creek, Virginia, and priests paid them occasional visits. This intrusion called for a series of penal laws in the legislation of that State, the equal of which is not to be found in history. No Catholic could hold office, under a fine of a thousand pounds of tobacco; no priest was allowed in the colony; all settlers were required by law to attend the services of the Established Church, under a penalty of twenty pounds; Catholics were deprived of suffrage; an attempt to vote by a Catholic was fined five hundred pounds of tobacco; Catholics were incompetent as witnesses before the tribunals against black or white. The Catholic was less than the negro!

The persecution in Maryland, the details of which would take up too much space, grew in severity until the Catholic colonists were compelled in self-defense to appeal to the English throne; and this only a quarter of a century before the American Revolution! Catholics were crushed under double taxation. Every now and then newspapers and pamphlets would call attention to their growing numbers, the increase of their wealth in land, and their schools, as a menace to the province. Matters went so far that the idea of emigrating to Louisiana was seriously considered by some of the wealthiest among the Catholic planters. It seemed to be the public theory or dread that, whenever the colonies got into any difficulty or war with France, the small body of Catholics in Maryland were ready to help the French side; whereas there is no evidence that there was the least disloyalty to England among them, and there is every evidence that they cheerfully bore their just proportion of taxation, and took up arms in defense of England's rights. But their Protestant rulers were not satisfied with a just proportion. Not only were Catholics obliged to pay their forty pounds of tobacco annually to the Episcopal Church, but in times of war they were taxed double the sum their non-Catholic neighbors had to pay.

The temper of the times was clearly shown in the inhuman treatment dealt out to the transported Acadians. It does not come within the scope of this work to tell the story of Acadia's settlement, of its growth, and of its subsequent conquest by England. After the war between England and France that was ended by the Treaty of Aix-la-Chapelle (1748), the English authorities decided to expatriate the Acadians. Their homes were ruined, and seven thousand of them—all Catholics—were scattered from Massachusetts to Georgia: in many cases husbands were separated from wives, and parents from children. A few were able to make their escape to the French colonies of the South and North; the great majority were absorbed into various English colonies, where they lost their nationality, their language, and their faith. Nine hundred of these unfortunates were landed in Maryland. An order was issued forbidding the Catholics of the province to receive the Acadians in their homes; petitions were gotten up to send them once more adrift. However, those who arrived in Baltimore met with kindly people who gave them hospitality, and were consoled by the ministrations of Father Ashton, chaplain of the Carrolls at Doughoregan, who came occasionally to Baltimore to hold services in a private house. The first congregation of that city, the seat of America's cardinal, the metropolis of the Catholic Church in the United States, was composed, one hundred and fifty years ago, of not more than forty families, mostly Acadian refugees.

The city's beginnings were laid in the year 1729. Maryland had never taken kindly to towns. The waterways of the region, making each plantation a port, so to speak, did away with the necessity of any great centers. St. Mary's and Annapolis were the only real towns for a hundred years, and they were rather political than commercial centers. About the year 1729 the planters on the Patapsco, feeling the need of a convenient port, purchased of Daniel and Charles Carroll sixty acres, bounding on the northern branch of the river, in that part of the harbor now called the Basin, and laid out a town. The position had many advantages, yet it grew slowly; after twenty years it had about twenty dwellings and perhaps one hundred inhabitants. The Catholic Church began its existence there when Father Ashton commenced his visits to the Acadian refugees and a few Irish, holding services in the house of Edward Fotteral, an Irish merchant, the first brick structure in Baltimore, at the northwest corner of Fayette and Calvert streets.

About the year 1755 there were fourteen fathers on the Maryland and Pennsylvania missions; the total Catholic population was about ten thousand. "Each father," states a document of that time, "holds services at home in his residence two Sundays in the month; the other Sundays he is in other stations. The extent of their excursions is about one hundred and thirty-five miles long by thirty-five broad. Our journeys are very long, our rides constant and extensive. We have many to attend to and few to attend those many. I often ride about three hundred miles a week, and in our way of living we ride almost as much by night as by day, in all weathers." The residences from which the fathers attended their scattered flocks were: St. Inigoes, one missionary; St. Xavier's at Newtown, three missionaries; St. Ignatius' at Port Tobacco, three missionaries; St. Francis Borgia at Whitemarsh, two missionaries; St. Joseph's at Deer Creek, one missionary; St. Stanislaus' at Fredericktown, one missionary; St. Mary's at Queenstown or Tuckahoe, one missionary; St. Xavier's at Bohemia, one missionary; St. Joseph's at Philadelphia, two missionaries; St. Paul's at Goshenhoppen, one missionary; St. John Nepomucene at Lancaster, one missionary; St. Francis Regis at Conewago, one missionary.

The Jesuit estates not only supported the missionaries and defrayed all the expenses of divine service throughout the colony, but also enabled them to pay the passage of the fathers that came from and returned to England. Time and again it was mooted in the legislature and the press during the penal period to confiscate the property of the Jesuits; it was well understood that this would be the best means of suppressing at one blow Catholic worship in Maryland. The services were of the plainest—no pomp whatever, and in most cases no music. Cemeteries were on the priests' farms or the private plantations of the wealthiest colonists. The whole Catholic population could not hear mass on every Sunday and holy day. It was evident that under such circumstances faith could not be of the liveliest. At any rate, there was lacking one stimulant that experience has proved to be of the utmost service in keeping men interested and steadfast in their religious convictions—the Catholics of Maryland did not contribute of their means to their church. Neither did the clergy take in the lives of their flocks that deep part, and in their hearts that warm attachment, which are created only by a community of temporal as well as spiritual interests, by the voluntary and generous support of the pastor by the flock.

The penal period began in New York in 1700. Then the Earl of Bellomont, governor of New York, succeeded in having an act of intoleration passed through the legislature of that colony. "Whereas divers Jesuits, priests, and popish missionaries have of late come, and for some time have had their residence in remote parts of this province, who by their wicked and subtle insinuations industriously labor to debauch, seduce, and withdraw the Indians from due obedience to His Most Sacred Majesty, and to excite and stir them up to sedition, rebellion, and open hostility against His Majesty's government"—so ran the preamble aimed at the French missionaries among the Iroquois. Now the Iroquois were not subjects of the king of England either in the estimation of Canada or in their own. The history of the Iroquois mission gives the lie to the above indictment. The law goes on to declare that every priest remaining in the province after its passage "shall be deemed and accounted an incendiary and disturber of the public peace and safety, and an enemy to the true Christian religion, and shall be adjudged to suffer perpetual banishment." Any priest imprisoned under the act who escaped from his prison was liable to the penalty of death if recaptured. To harbor a priest was to incur a fine of two hundred and fifty pounds and stand in the pillory three days. The next year papists and popish recusants were prohibited from voting for members of the Assembly or any office whatever. Needless to describe in detail the legislation of a like nature that was enacted in Massachusetts and the other Northern colonies.

On the accession of William and Mary to the throne of England it became necessary for Penn to be prudent and cautious in allowing the religious toleration that had been the first enactment of his colony of Pennsylvania. The penal laws of England were ever repugnant to the spirit of Penn's colonists, and in reality were never enforced in Pennsylvania. In fact, the Charter of Liberty and Privileges of October 28, 1701, reaffirmed liberty civil and religious for all who professed to believe in Jesus Christ; no specified exception was made for Catholics. As a result, Pennsylvania, of all the colonies, became the most favorable and safest field for priests and missionaries, and Catholic settlers began early to make their homes there. In 1708 complaints were sent to the home government that many conversions were taking place and that mass was publicly celebrated in Philadelphia. This was made a subject of accusation against Penn, who wrote from England to his representative in the colony, Logan: "Here is a complaint against your government that you suffer public mass in a scandalous manner." It is not known where, precisely, mass was said, nor by whom.

The first recorded appearance of any priest in Pennsylvania was that of Father Greaton, and his name does not appear on the Maryland mission record until 1721. It was from the residence at Bohemia, founded in 1706, that the Jesuits made excursions into Delaware, Pennsylvania, New Jersey, and New York. There is authority for the statement that, soon after the foundation of the Bohemia residence, Catholicity was first established in Delaware by the foundation of a mission at Apoquinimink; that in 1729 there was a Catholic chapel near the city of Philadelphia, connected with the house of Elizabeth McGawley, an Irish lady who had brought over a number of tenants and settled on land near the road leading from Nicetown to Frankfort; that as early as 1744 Father Schneider visited some Catholics near Frankfort and Germantown. It is claimed, also, that mass was said about 1730 in the residence of Thomas Willcox, at Toy Mills, Delaware County. When the Rev. John Carroll was appointed prefect apostolic in the United States, he sent to the Propaganda an account of Catholicity in his district. From this we learn that about 1730 Father Greaton, a Jesuit from Maryland, laid the foundations of a congregation in Philadelphia, built a chapel (St. Joseph's), and lived there until 1750; that by the year 1741 Catholic German emigrants had come into Pennsylvania, and that two German Jesuits were sent to attend to them. Father Wapeler founded the congregation of Conewago; Father Schneider founded many congregations, and notably that of Goshenhoppen, where a church was built by his exertions.

The Germans in Philadelphia had not, as yet, a resident clergyman, and received only occasional visits; but their number increased so rapidly that by the year 1760 Father Farmer fixed his residence among them. Because of this considerable German immigration, Pennsylvania became a mission district independent of Maryland, with a superior of its own, in 1740. From this new center the feeble and few missions in Delaware and New Jersey were cared for. As to New York, it may be said that at this time it had no Catholics, though occasionally there might be found an individual member of the church, as, for instance, one Leary, who about the year 1740 kept a livery-stable in Cortlandt Street, and imported horses for the officers and others. New England, of course, was completely barred to Catholics by a legislature more severe than that of New York. In the Carolinas and Georgia there were none at all as far as we know. Maryland and Pennsylvania were the only colonies in which Catholics were to be found, with a few in New Jersey and Delaware and northern Virginia. An inquiry instituted by Lord Loudon in 1757 gives the Catholic population of Pennsylvania as 1375, located in Philadelphia, Chester County, Goshenhoppen, Berks, Northampton, and Bucks counties, Lancaster, and Conewago.

Bishop Challoner, the Vicar Apostolic of London, in a report to the Propaganda (1756), says: "There are no missions in any of our colonies except Maryland and Pennsylvania. Of the number of Catholics I have had various accounts. By one account they were about four thousand communicants; another makes them amount to seven thousand. There are twelve missionaries in Maryland and four in Pennsylvania, all of the Society of Jesus. These also assist some few Catholics in Virginia upon the borders of Maryland, and in New Jersey bordering upon Pennsylvania. As to the rest of the provinces—New England, New York, etc.—if there be any straggling Catholics, they can have no exercise of their religion, as no priest ever comes near them." We have the following account of the financial condition of the Jesuit missions about the year 1765: St. Inigoes, a plantation of 2000 acres, revenue 90 pounds; St. Xavier's, 1500 acres, revenue 88 pounds; St. Ignatius, Port Tobacco, 4400 acres, revenue 188 pounds sterling; St. Francis Borgia, White Marsh, 3500 acres, revenue 180 pounds; St. Joseph's, Deer Creek, 127 acres, revenue 24 pounds; St. Mary's, Tuckahoe, 200 acres, revenue 18 pounds; Bohemia, 1500 acres, revenue 108 pounds; Goshenhoppen, 500 acres, revenue 45 pounds; Conewago, 120 acres, revenue 20 pounds; moreover, about 100 pounds received annually from London: total, 13,220 acres, revenue 861 pounds.

CHAPTER XVII.

THE DAWN OF LIBERTY.

THE missionaries in Maryland and the English colonies got their jurisdiction from ecclesiastical superiors in England; at first the archpriests, later the Vicar Apostolic of London. This arrangement was based rather on common law than on any formal document. The first authoritative act in the matter dates from January, 1757, when Benedict XIV. gave to Bishop Petre, then Vicar Apostolic of London, jurisdiction for six years over all the colonies and islands in America subject to the British empire. The same grant was renewed March 3, 1759, for six years more, to Bishop Challoner. It was evident that this arrangement was most inconvenient. Bishop Challoner represented to the Propaganda that, on account of the distance, he could not visit those parts in person; that he could not have the necessary information to know and correct abuses; that he could not provide the colonies with a diocesan clergy for want of funds; that the faithful there lived and died without confirmation. For these reasons the nomination of a vicar apostolic for the English colonies in America was mooted in Rome before our independence. "But," added Bishop Challoner, "this may not be relished by those that reserve the best part of the missions to themselves, and who may, not without show of probability, object that a novelty of this kind might give offense to the governing part there, who have been a little hard on them of late years."

In a report to the Propaganda, August 2, 1763, he states the number of missionaries in Maryland to be twelve, the number of Catholics, including children, to be sixteen thousand; in Pennsylvania the number of missionaries to be five, of Catholics, including children, to be six or seven thousand. He then goes on to suggest that, "now that Canada and Florida are reduced to British sway, the Bishop of Quebec might, with the consent of our court, have his jurisdiction extended by the holy see to all the English colonies and islands in America." This suggestion, however, was not what he desired most; he favored rather the creation of two or three separate vicariates for America. "But I foresee," he writes to his agent in Rome, "the execution will meet with very great difficulties, especially in Maryland and Pennsylvania, where the padri have had so long possession, and will hardly endure a prefect, much less a bishop of any other institute."

There was, however, a grave reason why the Catholics and the Jesuits of America at the time looked on the project with no favorable eye. The colonies had loyally recognized the House of Brunswick; Rome was attached to the Stuarts, and recognized Charles Edward as king of England. His brother, the Cardinal of York, would certainly have great influence in the nomination of any bishop for America. Hence the fear among the American Catholics that some one might be appointed who would not be a *persona grata* either to the court of England or the colonial authorities. Such an occurrence might involve them in political disabilities of a still severer nature. The Jesuits had their own reasons for fearing: Cardinal York was well known to be hostile to the society, and to be active in the proceedings that were then on foot preparatory to its suppression. These fears inspired a remonstrance against the appointment of a bishop for America, signed by the leading Catholics of Maryland and sent by the fathers to the Vicar Apostolic of London; it was not, however, forwarded by him to Rome. Instead, he applied to the Propaganda to be relieved of the care of the American church, and, as his petition was refused, he wrote to his agent in Rome, June, 1771: "It is a lamentable thing that such a multitude should have to live and die always deprived of the sacrament of confirmation. The fathers evince an unspeakable repugnance to the establishment of a bishop among them, under pretext that it might excite a violent persecution on the part of the civil authorities. But it does not seem to me that this consequence can be feared, if the Bishop of Quebec, who is not at so very great distance from those parts, were invited and had the necessary faculties to administer confirmation at least once to these Catholics."

The Jesuits do not seem to have been opposed to visits from the Bishop of Quebec for the purpose of administering confirmation, since Father Hunter, the superior, went to Canada in 1769 to confer with the bishop on this very point. Moreover, Cardinal Castelli wrote the bishop in September, 1771, that it was the desire of the Propaganda that he should, if possible, visit the Catholics of Maryland and Pennsylvania; but no such visit was ever made. The reason probably was that the English government refused permission, lest offense be given to the colonies by the extension to the Catholics of Pennsylvania and Maryland of the tolerance granted to Canada by the Quebec Act. This demands some explanation.

The Northwest Territory, including Ohio, Indiana, Michigan, Wisconsin, and Illinois, was claimed in strips by Massachusetts, Connecticut, New York, Maryland, and Virginia, in virtue of their original charters extending from ocean to ocean. But the people of these colonies not only had not occupied, but had never reached by direct communication and trade, this Western territory, and England did not propose to acknowledge their shadowy claims to it under the vague charters granted in days when little or nothing was known of the geography of the interior. At any rate, the Western territory had been seized and occupied by France, and it was England, not the colonies, that had wrested it from that power. The people living in that territory were subject, after the conquest, directly to the British commander-in-chief, residing in New York, who ruled it through officers appointed by himself. In order to establish some kind of regular organization there, a bill was introduced into Parliament in 1774, known as the Quebec Act.

It annexed the Western country to Canada, thus putting aside the claims of the colonies; it officially recognized the Catholic Church there, with the rights and privileges of the clergy formerly allowed under French dominion; and it decreed that Canada and the Northwest should continue to be governed by French law. All this was done in faithfulness to the Treaty of Paris. After a hot debate, in which Lord North and Edmund Burke were the chief defenders of the rights of the conquered territory, the bill became law, in June, 1774. The Act of Quebec, as it was called, roused the fanatical portion of the Protestant population in England and especially in America. Our Continental Congress in 1774 characterized the act as "in an extreme degree dangerous," as one of those acts that were declared to be "infringements and violations of the rights of the colonies." In an address issued by Congress to the people of Great Britain, September, 1774, it is said: "We think that the legislature of Great Britain is not authorized by the Constitution to establish a religion fraught with sanguinary and impious tenets, and to erect an arbitrary form of government, in any quarter of the globe. By this the Dominion of Canada is so extended, modeled, and governed, as that, being disunited from us, detached from our interests by civil as well as religious prejudices, that by their numbers daily swelling with Catholic emigrants from Europe, they might become formidable to us, and on occasion be fit instruments in the hands of power, to reduce the ancient free Protestant colonies to the same state of slavery with themselves." The author of the address was John Jay. An address to the inhabitants of the colonies, similar in thought, though more moderate in tone, helped to further entertain and extend the excitement. It was an unfortunate agitation; for when the day came that the cause of American independence needed and sought the coöperation of Canada, the remembrance of England's liberal treatment and of America's intolerant attitude caused that province to cast its lot with the mother country; and by so much were the colonies, fighting for liberty, weakened in the contest.

However, much as politicians raved at the Quebec Act, the people at large do not seem to have been much disturbed by it, or to have mistrusted their Catholic fellow-citizens. Facts were stronger than prejudices. As the momentous struggle between England and America arose and pronounced itself, it was found that patriotism was no less warm among the Catholics and their clergy than among the rest of the population. Men like Carroll in the East and Gibault in the West were more convincing by their practical conduct than men like Jay and the Protestant ministers by their rantings, fiery sermons, and pamphlets. The sentiments and deeds of the Catholic ecclesiastical leaders were reflected in the large numbers of the Catholic colonists who were swelling the ranks of the armies raised for independence.

On the whole, then, the Quebec Act produced only a passing effervescence that vanished in words; in only a few cases did it produce deeds of intolerance. Even in Canada the hatred of England was so deep and strong, the spirit of liberty so catching, that in spite of the direst spiritual penalties fulminated by the Bishop of Quebec, in spite of the hard things said in America about the Quebec Act, Canadians flocked to the cause of the colonies, and furnished to the American army two regiments known as "Congress Own." They had a Catholic chaplain, duly commissioned and salaried by the Continental Congress. This instance goes to show that, if the protests against the Quebec Act had never been issued, all Canada would have been with us in the struggle. An evident change was coming over the public spirit; the leading statesmen and soldiers were foremost in the softening of religious prejudices, the toning down of intolerance, and the advocacy of religious liberty. Nothing proves this better than two historic acts of the period, one by Washington, just come to the command of the continental army, the other by the Continental Congress.

Guy Fawkes's day was kept in New England as Pope's day on the 5th of November. On that day a figure representing the Pope was carried through the streets of Boston in mock procession and burned. Informed that the camp was preparing the usual celebration and seeing how impolitic it was when Congress was making every exertion to win over Canada and the Catholics in the Northwest and Maine, Washington issued a general order forbidding it. On the 15th of February, 1776, the Continental Congress resolved "that a committee of three be appointed to repair to Canada" for the purpose of inducing the Canadians to join the American cause. Benjamin Franklin, Samuel Chase, and Charles Carroll of Carrollton were appointed commissioners. John Carroll was invited by Congress to join them. A letter to his mother is extant in which he describes the journey, the reception in Canada, and the result. The American priest found that it was too late to discuss the question of union with the colonies, or even neutrality; the Quebec Act completely satisfied the bishop and clergy, whereas the laws on the statute-books of the colonies and the denunciations of the Quebec Act were taken as proof that only intolerance was to be expected from the colonies. We had spoiled our chances in that quarter, and knew it too late.

On the other hand, the very fact that the former enemies of England were now under English dominion did away with one of the chief reasons for the persecution inflicted on the Catholics of the colonies. Heretofore they had been suspected and accused of sympathizing and secretly conniving with France whenever intercolonial war arose. From the time, therefore, of England's triumph on the American continent began for Catholics a new and better era, a period of toleration that had its crowning a few years later in the American Revolution. Still brighter times came with the resistance of the colonies to the Stamp Act. Among the native clergy, of whom Carroll was the most prominent member, patriotism was strong; and those of German extraction, without being so ardent in their opposition to England, nevertheless cast their lot with their flocks. The feeling of bigotry evoked by the Quebec Act soon passed away; "popery" ceased to be heralded as dangerous to colonial interests. The necessity of presenting a united front to the coming danger brought about a kindlier spirit; religious liberty gained in public opinion, and presently became the theme of public discussion. Under these favorable circumstances the missions were extended, and churches were erected and publicly opened in cities like Baltimore, New York, and Philadelphia, as well as in country places, without exciting the former animosities.

In July, 1773, there fell on the American missionaries a blow that came nigh shattering the missions; it was the bull *Dominus ac Redemptor*, suppressing the Society of Jesus. In October, 1773, Bishop Challoner, the Vicar Apostolic of London, notified formally the Jesuit missionaries of America under his jurisdiction of the act of Clement XIV., and required their individual subscriptions to its acceptance. They were transformed into diocesan priests; their former superior became the diocesan vicar general of the Vicar Apostolic of London; all the fathers on the American missions—there were nineteen at the time—remained at their posts. The bull of suppression had made very precise arrangements as to the property of the society, and each bishop was empowered to carry them out in his diocese. The Vicar Apostolic of London took no action on this score; left free in the matter, the American fathers, in order to secure the former property of the society for the support of the missions, formed themselves into a legal corporation for the purpose.

In the same year (1773) that Clement XIV. pronounced the suppression of the Society of Jesus the men of Boston took the first historic step toward independence by the unloading of a cargo of English tea in the harbor; the following year the first Continental Congress met in Philadelphia; and in the spring of 1775 was fired at Lexington the first shot for liberty that rang continuously in the land until October 19, 1781, when Cornwallis yielded his sword to Washington at Yorktown. In that memorable war Catholics joined the army and the navy in numbers out of all proportion to their quota of the population; and to both they furnished not only sturdy privates, but brilliant leaders, whose names make a long and glorious roll. In 1776 the House of Lords appointed a committee of inquiry on the American war. Joseph Galloway, who was an officer in high command on the royalist side, testified before that committee that one half of the troops in the service of Congress were Irish, one fourth English and Scotch, one fourth natives of America. Before the same committee Major-General Robertson, in reply to a question from Lord George Germain, said, "I remember General Lee telling me that half the rebel army came from Ireland." The authority we have for the above is a letter to the "Monitor" of San Francisco from M. W. Kirwin, of Los Angeles, Cal., who asserts that he went to the British Museum for the purpose of ascertaining if there were any record of the Irishmen who served in the Revolutionary armies, and found there the statements just given.

We do not claim that the Irish one half were all Catholics; but, granting any justifiable amount of paring down, we do claim that the number of Catholics in the war was considerable. So that after the struggle Archbishop Carroll could write: "Their blood flowed as freely, in proportion to their numbers, to cement the fabric of independence as that of any of their fellow-citizens. They concurred with perhaps greater unanimity than any other body of men in recommending and promoting that government from whose influence America anticipates all the blessings of justice, peace, plenty, good order, and civil and religious liberty. The Catholic regiment, 'Congress Own,' the Catholic Indians from St. John, Me., under the chief Ambrose Var, the Catholic Penobscots under the chief Orono, fought side by side with their Protestant fellow-colonists. Catholic officers from Catholic lands—Ireland, France, and Poland—came to offer their services to the cause of liberty." In February, 1778, France made a treaty of amity and commerce with the new republic, thus formally recognizing its independence as a nation; the following year Catholic Spain declared war against England and sent a representative to the United States, thus acknowledging them to be a nation.

Our first diplomatic circle was Catholic, made up of the ministers of those two countries. This accounts for the solemn church services, introduced to the American people, to which the federal authorities and high military officers were invited on great national occasions. Then to our shores came French fleets and French regiments, with chaplains and religious services for the Catholic soldiers and sailors of France. In this toleration, not to say triumph, of the Catholic Church the Tories found an excuse for their opposition to the American cause and their sympathy with England. They preferred political enslavement to liberty gained with such aid, *non tali auxilio.* Listen to the traitor Arnold in a proclamation issued to the officers and soldiers of the continental army, October 20, 1780: "And should the parent nation cease her exertions to deliver you, what security remains to you for the enjoyment of the consolations of that religion for which your fathers braved the ocean, the heathen, and the wilderness? Do you know that the eye that guides this pen lately saw your mean and profligate Congress at mass for the soul of a Roman Catholic in purgatory, and participating in the rites of a church against whose antichristian corruptions your pious ancestors would have witnessed with their blood?"

The attempt made by England in 1778 to form a Catholic regiment of Americans and give them Father Farmer as a chaplain failed most miserably. The recruits were not forthcoming, and the venerable priest refused to lend the influence of his name and office to the enemies of American independence. Among the signers of the Declaration of Independence were the Catholics Thomas Fitzsimmons, Thomas Sim Lee, the war-governor of Maryland, Daniel Carroll, the brother of the future Archbishop of Baltimore, and Charles Carroll, who by the affix to his signature, "of Carrollton," pledged his fortune to the cause. Toward the end of his long and noble life he wrote to a descendant of the Washington family, G. W. P. Custis, February 20, 1829: "When I signed the Declaration of Independence I had in view not only our independence of England, but the toleration of all sects professing the Christian religion, and communicating to them all equal rights. Happily this wise and salutary measure has taken place for eradicating religious feuds and persecution, and become a useful lesson to all governments. Reflecting, as you must, on the disabilities, I may truly say on the proscription, of the Roman Catholics in Maryland, you will not be surprised that I had much at heart this grand design founded on mutual charity, the basis of our holy religion."

That the times were changing and that a spirit more tolerant was coming over the nation was proved not only by the publicity and almost official recognition given to the solemn services of the church on certain occasions, not only by the freedom with which the missionaries penetrated to the camp, the fleet, the settlements of Catholics all along the seaboard States, but much more by the constitutions adopted by the States immediately after declaring their independence of England. Not all of them, it is true, inscribed on their charters religious liberty at this time; bigotry dies not quickly. But, at any rate, the first

Continental Congress (1774) had sounded the key-note: "As an opposition to the settled plan of the British administration to enslave America will be strengthened by a union of all ranks of men within this province, we do most earnestly recommend that all former differences about religion or politics . . . from henceforth cease and be forever buried in oblivion." Many of the States—Pennsylvania, Delaware, Maryland, Virginia, Georgia, Connecticut—caught up this spirit, removed former restrictions on the Catholics, and admitted them to all rights of citizenship. This movement toward religious equality became universal and complete, however, only after the Philadelphia Convention of 1787, in which was adopted the present Constitution of the United States. The dawn had come; yet a little while and the full sun will shine above us.

CHAPTER XVIII.

THE PREFECTURE APOSTOLIC.

DURING the Revolutionary War direct correspondence between England and the States had ceased and indirect correspondence was difficult. After the death (January, 1781) of Bishop Challoner, the Vicar Apostolic of London, his successor, the Rt. Rev. James Talbot, held no intercourse whatever with the church in America. In 1783 he refused faculties for the American missions to two Maryland priests, John Boone and Henry Pile, belonging to the suppressed society, who at the end of the war wished to leave England for home; and he declared to them that he would no longer exercise jurisdiction in the United States. These two priests stated their case to the Propaganda, from whom they solicited the faculties refused by the bishop, and thus the abnormal condition of the church in this country was made known to Rome. Left to themselves, the Maryland clergy made no attempt to restore their dependence on the Vicar Apostolic of London, lest they might excite the prejudices of their fellow-colonists, and began to move for a local superior chosen from themselves, who should be subject directly to the holy see. It behooved them to bestir themselves, for they had now no formal connection with any section of the European church, nor with Rome, nor had they any organization of their own; and, moreover, having no hopes of further accessions to their ranks from England, they were thrown upon their own resources to perpetuate their body—a pressing need, for death was fast thinning their number.

The situation was critical and demanded a rearrangement. Until the holy see should make provision for this state of things, the Maryland clergy took steps to secure their former property and maintain some kind of discipline. A preliminary meeting for this purpose was held at Whitemarsh, June, 1783, and a formal meeting in September of the same year, at which met duly chosen and accredited delegates of all the clergy in Maryland and Pennsylvania. Among them was the vicar general, Mr. Lewis, and John Carroll. The final adoption of the plans discussed was postponed to a future meeting; the only outcome of the present assembly was a petition to the Pope asking that Rev. Mr. Lewis be formally constituted superior, with power to administer confirmation, and with other privileges not strictly of the episcopal order.

As, on second thought, it was considered that the first petition, already sent, might give offense, a second one, with slight alterations and a milder tone, was drawn up, and sent by Father Carroll to a friend in Rome to be presented to the Pope. A remarkable feature in Carroll's letter is that he states to his friend in Rome that he will have this move aided by "a recommendation from our own country and the minister of France," and "you will know how to avail yourself of so favorable a Russian minister at Rome." Here is shown a tendency to bring into church matters the influence of the civil power. Evidently the non-interference policy of the United States in religion was not fully comprehended or outlined at that time; the European ideas of the relations of church and state still possessed Carroll, brought up in Europe, and, what is more strange, possessed that pure American, Benjamin Franklin, as the following facts show.

Franklin at that time represented the United States in Paris, and Prince Pamphilio Doria, Archbishop of Seleucia, was the papal nuncio there. The latter was approached on the subject of the American project, and wrote to Franklin that it was a matter that ought to be arranged between Congress and the French king, and that a Frenchman residing in Paris ought to be chosen the ecclesiastical superior of the colonies. This scheme, it appears, had been hatched in the French embassy at Philadelphia. It meant the de-Americanizing of the church in the United States at its very birth, and making it a dependency of the church of France. That country had rendered us political services, and was about to render us religious services for which we cannot be too grateful, but not at the cost of our ecclesiastical independence. Franklin for a moment forgot his American spirit, fell in with the scheme, wrote the prime minister of France, Count de Vergennes, in the sense of the nuncio's note, and then referred the matter to the Continental Congress.

No Catholic sat in that body at the time, nor did the American clergy know what was going on; therefore the answer of Congress did not come from Catholic influence or dictation. The answer was, "That the subject being purely spiritual, it is without the powers and jurisdiction of Congress, who have no authority to permit or refuse it, these powers being reserved to the several States individually." It was not long before the intrigue came to the knowledge of European clergymen, former associates in the Society of Jesus of the Maryland Jesuits, and of Carroll. They hastened to open the eyes of Franklin to the dishonor thus inflicted on the American clergy, and especially on Carroll, whom he knew well; for the intrigue implied, and Marbois, the French minister in New York, had plainly enough asserted, that the American priests were not worthy of trust, and had no one among them fit to guide the American church. Franklin saw at once his mistake, and thenceforward exerted his influence in an unofficial way for the nomination of Carroll. At any rate, what between the refusal of Congress to touch the matter and Franklin's refusal to go on with it, the French scheme fell through. It stands at our cradle as a lesson and a warning to us to beware how we invoke the interference of the civil powers in our church affairs.

While Paris was thus busying itself with us, Rome, without heeding the intrusive busybodies, was also engaged with the same matter. The memorial of the Maryland clergy to Pope Pius VI. was referred by him to the Congregation of the Propaganda, which, before coming to any decision, wrote to Carroll for a complete report on the actual condition of the American missions. But the Congregation did not await Carroll's report; there were other sources at hand from which it could get the information, viz., the former reports of the vicars apostolic of London, especially of Challoner, and the archives of the English province of Jesuits. The upshot was that the Propaganda proposed to the Pope the name of John Carroll as the superior of the church in the thirteen United States of North America, with power to give confirmation. The nomination was confirmed by the Pope June 6, 1784. The decree making the church of the United States a distinct body from that of England, and appointing the Very Rev. John Carroll prefect apostolic, was issued by Cardinal Antonelli, prefect of the Congregation of the Propaganda, June 9, 1784. By letter of June 19th the cardinal prefect notified the Vicar Apostolic of London of this step, and by that official act was terminated the jurisdiction of the English over the American church. Carroll was given jurisdiction over the thirteen States; but it was not at all clear from the document that he had jurisdiction over those portions of the new republic which heretofore had been under the jurisdiction of Quebec, such as the Maine Indians and the Catholics in the Northwest Territory. In time this doubt was cleared up, and all the country over which floated the stars and stripes came under his jurisdiction.

A few words here about the early life of John Carroll. It was in the days that France was exploring and occupying the interior of the continent, and English colonial statesmen were viewing with alarm the thin, long line of French posts gradually stretching along the lakes and the Mississippi from Quebec to New Orleans; it was on the eve of the long intercolonial struggle for the possession of this country between France and England, a struggle lasting over half a century; it was, I say, at this crucial period in the history of our land that John Carroll was born, on the 8th of January, 1735, at Upper Marlborough, Prince George's County, Md. His father, a native of Ireland, had married Eleanor Darnall, a woman of most refined education, of remarkable mental and moral qualities, fitting her to be the mother of noble children. At this time the Jesuit fathers had a school at Hermon's Manor of Bohemia in Cecil County; nothing of the building remains to indicate the site of the first seat of Catholic education in the State save an old chapel. Thither, at the age of twelve, the boy was sent, and there he had for fellow-student another lad, a relative and namesake, Charles Carroll, who became in the political sphere as great and illustrious as John in the ecclesiastical; Charles Carroll, who gave to Carrollton on the charter of the nation a renown as immortal as John gave to Baltimore on the pages of church history.

After a year spent in this school John Carroll was sent

abroad; for there was not yet in this land any institution —at least Catholic—in which a higher education might be safely obtained by a Catholic boy. Nor was there in England any such institution; the Protestant Reformation had turned into nurseries of Protestantism all the glorious homes of learning which Catholic faith and generosity had set up in the preceding centuries. But in France, Spain, and Portugal Catholic English refugees, secular priests and religious, had provided houses of education where the sons and daughters of the persecuted Catholic gentry of England might receive, without danger to faith, that instruction their country denied them, at the great price, however, of exile from home. Such was St. Omer's College in France, to which young Carroll, at the age of twelve, was sent. He was not to see again the beloved faces of parents and relatives, nor the green fields and fair streams of his Maryland, until he was a man of forty. It was in foreign lands that he spent the better part of his life, student for six years at St. Omer, novice for two years in the Jesuit house of Watten, ecclesiastical student again in the Jesuit college at Liège, priest at the age of twenty-eight, professor in Jesuit colleges at Liège and Bruges for fourteen years.

In 1773 was given to the world the famous bull of Clement XIV., that suppressed and dissolved the Society of Jesus. Carroll's career as a member of that famous order came to an end. Invited by Lord Arundel to make Wardour Castle in England his home for the future, he refused to lose himself in the refined and comfortable life of a nobleman's palace. No doubt he felt that his American manhood demanded he should be the people's, not the nobleman's, priest; and, at any rate, as he had kept himself constantly in touch with his native land, he knew and foresaw that the day was not far distant when the colonies should arise as one people, and claim at the sword's point, if need be, their national independence. Stirring times were ahead, freedom was at stake; what might be the outcome for country and church was doubtful; it behooved him, like a loyal American, to be on the field, and share his people's fate, and give his aid to the nascent church of America through the coming ordeal. But, whatever Carroll's motives, God had his views and was leading him. He was destined to be in our land the providential man of Catholicity as Washington of democracy; in these representative leaders Catholicity and democracy were to join hands and give to the Old World on this new field of human life, wrested two hundred and fifty years before by Columbus from the terrors of the ocean, the spectacle of the old faith and of a new political form growing side by side in wonderful strength and harmony. The year 1774 saw Carroll, in the prime of manhood, back in his mother's home in Rockville, Montgomery County, Md.

It was only November 26, 1784, that the official documents of his appointment as prefect apostolic reached Carroll, though as early as the preceding August he had been privately informed, and the news was generally known in the country. But before the documents came the postponed meeting of the clergy of Maryland and Pennsylvania for the getting up of a plan of church government was held. The priests, suppressed Jesuits in Maryland and Pennsylvania, were to form a body corporate, which was to hold, until restoration of the Society of Jesus, the property formerly held by the individuals of that society in those two colonies. The affairs of the corporation were to be managed by a chapter elected by the members thereof. The chapter was to name a procurator to have charge of the property. The person who should be invested with spiritual jurisdiction in the colonies should not, as such, have any power over or in the property. The superior in spiritualities was, however, to receive from the chapter an annual salary of one hundred pounds, with a servant, a chaise, and a horse. It was also decided that "a bishop is at present unnecessary," but that a superior with power to give confirmation, bless oils, grant faculties and dispensations, was sufficient; that, if a bishop was sent them, he should not be entitled to any support from the present estates of the clergy.

By those proceedings, which had no authorization from Rome, a double superiorship was set up, one in temporals, another in spirituals; the superior in spirituals was put at a disadvantage, not to say at the mercy of the clergy, if he did not prove agreeable to the corporation; and the appointment of a bishop, as far as in them lay, was barred. At the bottom of it all lay the idea and hope of the restoration of the society. It was Barbé de Marbois, the French ambassador residing in New York, the originator of the French intrigue, who first notified Carroll of his appointment as prefect apostolic. The formal decree reached him November 26, 1784. The decree states that Carroll was appointed "to please and gratify many members of the Republic, and especially Mr. Franklin, the eminent individual who represents the same Republic at the court of the Most Christian King." The arrangement, it goes on to say, was temporary; a bishop would soon be appointed as vicar apostolic. In the meantime the Propaganda wanted to know what was the condition in spirituals and temporals of the country.

This gave the church in the colonies independence from any other center but Rome at the very time we had gained political independence. By a clerical oversight a clause was put in the document of Carroll's appointment that cramped his administration for a while; it was that the prefect should give faculties to no priests coming to this country except those sent and approved by the Congregation of the Propaganda. Now, as the Propaganda did not intend to send any priests, and as those priests who might come could not very well return to Europe for the approval of the Congregation, the predicament was rather an awkward one. It so puzzled and vexed Carroll that he hesitated whether he should accept the position. He feared, as letters of his to friends in Europe show, that this very strict subordination in the choice of priests to a foreign congregation might create difficulties and suspicions on the part of the colonial authorities. But since the prefecture was expected to pave the way to some more satisfactory and permanent arrangement, and since, on the other hand, his refusal might result in the imposition of a foreigner as prefect on the Catholics of America, Carroll yielded to the arguments of his fellow-priests and decided to take up the onerous office.

On the 27th of February, 1785, he wrote Cardinal Antonelli to notify him of his acceptance and return his thanks. In this letter may be seen in many passages his fear lest the country should look with disfavor on the too close connection of the church with the Congregation of the Propaganda. He was hinting, no doubt, at the unlucky clause. "In most places," he writes, "Catholics are not admitted to any office in the State unless they renounce all foreign jurisdiction, civil or ecclesiastical. . . . The Most Eminent Cardinal may rest assured that the greatest evils would be borne by us rather than renounce the divine authority of the holy see. . . . The Catholic body, however, think that some favor should be granted to them by the Holy Father, necessary for their permanent enjoyment of the civil rights which they now enjoy. . . .

From what I have said and from the framework of public affairs, your Eminence must see how objectionable all foreign jurisdiction will be to them; . . . and we hope that some plan may be adopted by which hereafter an ecclesiastical superior may be appointed for this country, in such a way as to retain absolutely the spiritual jurisdiction of the holy see, and at the same time remove all ground of objecting to us, as though we held anything hostile to the national independence. . . . I know with certainty that this fear will increase if they know that an ecclesiastical superior is so appointed as to be removable from office at the pleasure of the Sacred Congregation de Propaganda Fide, or any other tribunal out of the country, or that he has no power to admit any priest to exercise the sacred functions, unless that Congregation has approved and sent him to us." He urged specially the removal of this latter restriction. Indeed, so fearful was Carroll of difficulties from the authorities and public opinion that he notified only the clergy and not the laity of his appointment.

Accompanying this letter was a "Relation on the State of Religion in the United States." In Maryland were fifteen thousand eight hundred Catholics; in Pennsylvania seven hundred; in Virginia two hundred; in New York fifteen hundred; in the territory bordering on the Mississippi many Catholics, number not ascertainable, who were destitute of priests. These were formerly under the jurisdiction of the Bishop of Quebec. "I do not know," writes Carroll, "whether he wishes to exercise any authority there now that all those parts are subject to the United States. The small number of priests is cause why the Catholics here cannot attend worship, receive the sacraments, hear the Word of God, as frequently as they should or as is customary in Europe. There are nineteen priests in Maryland and five in Pennsylvania. They are maintained chiefly from the proceeds of the estates held by the clerical corporation. There is no ecclesiastical property held by the church as such."

As prefect, Carroll met in the government of the church difficulties which seemed impossible to master with such dignity and powers as he had, and which hastened the appointment of a bishop. The chief difficulty was trusteeism, and the scene of the trouble was New York. Since the end of the Revolutionary War New York was looming up as an important center of Catholicity. It was at the time the capital of the United States, and the foreign ministers, many of whom were Catholics, resided there, thus giving a high standing to the church. In 1785 the "Trustees of the Roman Catholic Church in the City of New York" were incorporated, and purchased a site on Barclay Street for a church. These trustees, not content to hold and administer the church property, which indeed was within their powers, encroached upon the spiritual administration, and undertook to appoint and dismiss pastors at their will. They held that the congregation, represented by its trustees, had the right not only to choose its pastor, but to dismiss him at pleasure; and that the ecclesiastical superior, bishop or prefect, had no right to interfere. These assumptions are what is known as trusteeism.

"If ever such principles," wrote Carroll to the New York trustees, "should become predominant, the unity and catholicity of our church would be at an end; and it would be formed into distinct and independent societies, nearly in the same manner as the Congregational Presbyterians. Your misconception is that the officiating clergyman at New York is a parish priest, whereas there is yet no such office in the United States. I cannot tell what assistance the laws might give you; but allow me to say that you can take no step so fatal to that responsibility in which as a religious society you wish to stand, or more prejudicial to the Catholic cause." Meanwhile the church edifice in New York had been completed, and dedicated November 4, 1786. The Spanish minister, and the Spanish residents of the city, who furnished much of the means to build the church, entertained at dinner on the occasion the President of the United States and his cabinet, the members of Congress, the governor of the State, and the representatives of the foreign powers.

Nationalism was another difficulty that faced the prefect. It was to Ireland mainly that Dr. Carroll looked for recruits to the American clergy. In a letter to Archbishop Troy, of Dublin, November 9, 1789, he expresses his wish in this regard, and adds: "But one thing must be fully impressed on their minds, that no pecuniary prospects or worldly comforts must enter into the motives for their crossing the Atlantic to this country. Labor, hardships of every kind, and particularly great scarcity of wine, especially out of the towns, must be expected. Sobriety in drink is demanded from clergymen to a great degree. That which in many parts of Europe would be esteemed no more than a cheerful and allowable enjoyment of a friendly company would be regarded here in our clergy as an unbecoming excess." However, at this time it was not so much from Ireland as from Germany and France that came the pioneer clergymen of the American church, and the varieties of nationality among the clergy, even at this early period, resulted in dissensions. There was, moreover, some jealousy on the part of the newcomers toward the former members of the suppressed Society of Jesus.

Worse still, it was claimed that each nationality ought to have its own churches and priests selected by itself. Against this movement, which made its appearance in

Philadelphia, Dr. Carroll opposed at first strenuous resistance; but in the course of time he acknowledged that foreigners who did not understand English were entitled, when in sufficient number, to have a church in which their own language should be used. For this reason he approved the opening of the Church of the Holy Trinity for Germans in Philadelphia, November, 1789, the first instance on record of a congregation using a language different from that of the country. These troubles among the clergy and the laity induced the body of the clergy in Maryland to petition (March 18, 1788) the holy see for a bishop. The petition was signed by John Carroll, Robert Molyneux, and John Ashton. In a meeting (November, 1786) in which, at the instigation of Dr. Carroll, steps were taken in the project of a college—the beginnings of Georgetown College—it had been decided that a bishop was required by the wants of the American church. But these views came to naught at the time because of the resistance of some of the clergymen. The opponents, however, who up to the present had stood out against the appointment of a bishop, now yielded, in view of the dangers that threatened the church.

"To omit other very grave reasons," states the petition, "we experience more and more, in the constitution of this very free Republic, that if there are, even among the ministers of the sanctuary, any men of indocile mind, and chafing under ecclesiastical discipline, they allege as an excuse for their license and disobedience that they are bound to obey bishops exercising their own authority, and not a mere priest exercising any vicarious jurisdiction. This was the boast of the men who recently at New York sought to throw off the yoke of authority, and alleged this pretext, which seemed most likely to catch the favor of Protestants, contending that the authority of the ecclesiastical superior whom the Sacred Congregation had appointed was forbidden by law, because it not only emanates from a foreign tribunal, but is also dependent on it for its duration and exercise." The holy see acted promptly on this petition, and Cardinal Antonelli, by letter of July 12, 1788, informed Dr. Carroll that permission was given to the priests on the mission to select the city, and, for this case only, to name the candidate for presentation to the Pope. There were twenty-six priests entitled to vote; Baltimore was chosen for the see, and twenty-four votes were given to Dr. Carroll as the candidate. All this was ratified by the Congregation of the Propaganda on September 14th, and the necessary bull was issued November 6, 1789. When the news reached England, Thomas Weld, of Lulworth Castle, a personal friend of Carroll, invited him to allow the ceremony of consecration to take place in his private chapel. Carroll accepted the invitation, sailed for England in the summer of 1790, and was consecrated, August 15th, by the Rt. Rev. Charles Walmesley, senior Vicar Apostolic of England.

If great events were taking place at this time in the sphere of religion, events no less important were happening in the sphere of politics. The convention that met in Philadelphia, May, 1789, laid in the Constitution of the United States the broad and deep foundations of religious equality by the sixth article, abolishing religious tests as a qualification for any office or public trust; and the first Congress in the same year affirmed the incompetency of the federal government in religion by the passing of the first amendment: "Congress shall make no laws respecting an establishment of religion, or prohibiting the free exercise thereof." In bringing about those wise enactments Dr. Carroll had no small share. He drew up a memorial to Congress, representing the necessity of some constitutional provision for the protection and maintenance of civil and religious freedom, for which so much blood and treasure had been spent. Through the influence of Washington the memorial was favorably received; he, more than any other man, brought about the happy result. The States—some freely and at once, others reluctantly and after some delay—agreed to the clauses, and thus the penal period for Catholicity closed forever, never to be reopened so long as the Constitution retains the respect and love, and remains the chart, of this land.

The grateful Catholics presented to Washington, after his election to the Presidency (1789), an address signed by Bishop Carroll on behalf of the clergy, by Charles Carroll, Daniel Carroll, Dominick Lynch, Thomas Fitzsimons, signers of the Declaration of Independence, on behalf of the laity, to which "the father of his country" made a reply that is among the classics of the land and one of its most precious heirlooms. It is a singular, not to say providential, coincidence that Washington and Carroll came to their offices at the same time (Washington was inaugurated April 30, 1789; Carroll was consecrated August 15, 1790), and that our political organization was fully fashioned in the very year that our church organization was perfected; coincidence emblematic of that amity and concord that have hitherto existed between the church and the republic—amity and concord which, instead of being obliterated, are emphasized by the clean-cut distinction made in our fundamental law between the two spheres, the political and the religious.

BOOK II. THE ORGANIZED CHURCH.

I DIVIDE this portion of my work into four parts, basing the division on prominent facts proportionately spaced: first part, from the consecration of Carroll (1790) to the First Provincial Council of Baltimore (1829); second part, from the First Provincial Council of Baltimore (1829) to the First Plenary Council of Baltimore (1852); third part, from the First Plenary Council (1852) to the Second Plenary Council (1866); fourth part, from the Second Plenary Council (1866) to the establishment of the Apostolic Delegation (1893).

If I were asked to characterize each one of those four periods by some prominent event within them, I should say that the first (1790–1829) is the period of trusteeism; that the second (1829–52) is the period of native Americanism; that the third (1852–66) is the period of the Civil War; that the fourth (1866–93) is the period of centennials. Of this latter part I shall have little to say, for obvious reasons.

The Catholic Church is papal in its head, hence a general history of the church resolves itself into a history of the papacy; but in its body the church is episcopal and sacerdotal, hence the particular history of the church in any one country resolves itself into an account of the development and administration of the episcopate in that country. The narrative of the following pages is the growth of the hierarchy, implying a corresponding expansion of the clergy and the laity, in the United States.

Part I. The Growth of the Church from the Beginning of the Hierarchy to the First Provincial Council of Baltimore (1790–1829).

CHAPTER XIX.

THE EPISCOPATE OF CARROLL (1790–1815).

The return of Bishop Carroll from England to Baltimore (December, 1790) was marked by a reception that was like a triumph. And truly there was good reason for rejoicing, since the young church in the United States was in a much better condition than the parent church in England, that still remained under the government of Vicars Apostolic. A diocesan clergy is not less necessary to the life and growth of a church than a hierarchy. The older missionaries in the colonies, mostly members of the suppressed Society of Jesus, were fast passing away. One of the first cares of the new bishop was to supply their places, if possible, with a native clergy. For priests from abroad, of many nationalities, tongues, customs, habits, and trainings, could not but import into the nascent church varieties and antagonisms that might impair its growth, especially at a time when immigration was not the mighty flood it became afterward, when the Catholic population was essentially one as to nationality, and the field to which the church looked for increase was a non-

Catholic body whose language was English and whose spirit was American.

Meanwhile God, who knows how to draw good out of evil, made the Revolution in France serve his purposes for the church in the United States. Fleeing from the persecution which was foreseen in 1790 and broke out with terrific fury a few years later, some priests of the congregation of St. Sulpice, Paris, France, came to Baltimore, at the invitation of Bishop Carroll, and established in 1791 the ecclesiastical seminary which since that time has been a fruitful nursery of good and great ecclesiastics. Here was the possibility of solving the question of a native diocesan clergy; a few short years would bring the complete solution, when the stream of young priests would begin to flow from the newly founded seminary.

The diocese of Baltimore in 1790 comprised all of our present States east of the Mississippi, with the exception of a district around New Orleans, of Florida, and of the country in the neighborhood of Detroit, which was still in dispute between the United States and England. Those excepted parts were, as to the South, under the jurisdiction of the Bishop of Havana, as to the North, under that of the Bishop of Quebec. Within the diocese of Baltimore thus delimited there were about thirty-five priests and thirty churches, with a number of outlying stations visited from time to time by the nearest clergymen. The most remarkable among the priests, because the first convert to take orders, was the Rev. John Thayer, in charge of the church in Boston. He was a native of that city. His conversion from Protestantism was brought about by an investigation he made while in Rome of the miracles attributed to St. Benedict Labre. Though a man of great talent and blameless life, the Rev. John Thayer was by no means a success as an administrator and a leader of men.

Difficulties that arose in Boston necessitated a visit of the bishop to that city in the spring of 1791. We refer to the visit mainly because of the reception with which he met; it proves how highly he was esteemed and how quickly Puritan prejudice was passing away, the result, no doubt, of the patriotism displayed by Catholics in the Revolutionary War, and of the spirit of tolerance that the Constitution had created throughout the land. "It is wonderful," he writes, "to tell what great civilities have been done to me in this town, where a few years ago a popish priest was thought to be the greatest monster in creation. Many here, even of their principal people, have acknowledged to me that they would have crossed to the opposite side of the street rather than meet a Roman Catholic some time ago. The horror which was associated with the idea of a papist is incredible; and the scandalous misrepresentations by their ministers increased the horror every Sunday. If all the Catholics here were united, their number would be about one hundred and twenty." North of Boston were the Catholic Indians of Maine, who persevered, in spite of the absence of any missionary, in the faith preached to them by the early Jesuits. At their request Bishop Carroll sent them a priest, the Rev. Francis Ciquard, one of the Sulpitians who had come to Baltimore.

Next to the establishment of a seminary the convening of his widely scattered clergy in a diocesan synod was considered by the bishop to be of the highest importance. The synod was opened on the 7th of November, 1791. This assembly, the first of the kind in the country, had great influence in shaping our church legislation. On this occasion there gathered about the Bishop of Baltimore some twenty priests, representing no less than five nationalities. The synod discussed the appointment of a coadjutor. It was felt that a bishop should be, so to say, in permanence, because, in case of the death of the ordinary, the distance from Rome and the slowness of communication in those days might leave the church in a long and disastrous widowhood. Fortunately, too, Rome, for the sake of unity of discipline, favored the appointment of a coadjutor rather than a division of territory and the erection of a new diocese.

The bishop was instructed by the holy see to choose a subject, with the advice of his older priests, to be presented to the Pope. Accordingly the Rev. Lawrence Graessel, a German, was chosen, and his name forwarded to Rome. He did not live, however, to bear the honor; the yellow fever, which raged along the coast in 1793, carried him off. His selection is evidence that Carroll's Americanism was not of the narrow sort, and was not blind to merit, wherever it might be. A second choice fell on the Rev. Leonard Neale, a native of Maryland. The appointment was approved by the holy see in April, 1795, and the bulls were issued and expedited at the time; but owing to the troublous times in Europe, they did not reach Baltimore until January, 1801.

One of the topics that engaged the deliberations of the synod, and occupied a large place in the pastoral letter issued by the bishop after its close, was the support of the churches and the clergy. As we have seen, in the colonial days the properties of the Jesuits bore this burden, and no appeals were made to the generosity of the faithful in Maryland. But it was foreseen that immigration would soon bring into the States many Catholics from Europe, and, moreover, the new recruits to the clergy were shut off from any participation in the revenues from the lands of the earlier Maryland and Pennsylvania missions. It became necessary, therefore, to impress on the people the duty of giving voluntary support to religion. Carroll was the first to preach this duty, which since his time has become the glory and the strength of the American church, and the subject of unfailing wonder to the state-endowed churches of Europe. In colonial mission times the services of the church, held for the most part in small chapels attached to the residences of the Jesuits or the manorial houses of the richer colonists, were simple in the extreme. The arrival of priests who had witnessed the gorgeous ceremonial of the church in France, Germany, and other lands untouched by penal laws, changed this simplicity of the early days, and the services began to improve in solemnity.

Synod, coadjutorship, voluntary support, solemnity of service, though but premonitory signs of a later glorious development, were in the line of progress. Contemporaneous with them appeared in many cities, and notably in Philadelphia, a movement which was to be for many years the bane of our young church—schism issuing from trusteeism. The Rev. Father John Nepomucene Goetz was assistant to Father Helbron in the Church of the Holy Trinity, Philadelphia. Intriguing with the trustees, Goetz got them to expel the legitimate pastor, and to elect and recognize himself instead. It was in vain that the bishop suspended and excommunicated the usurper. The trustees upheld him, rejected the authority of the Pope "as of foreign jurisdiction," and maintained in court, into which they brought the case, that as Germans they were outside of his jurisdiction, and that he was the bishop of the other nationalities only. It was in vain that Carroll appealed to them in letters of the greatest forbearance and charity; they turned a deaf ear, would recognize no bishop but one of their own race, and claimed the right to give, by the very fact of choice and nomination by themselves, jurisdiction to their pastors. It was only in 1802 that they were induced to end the schism by an explicit recognition of the authority of the Bishop of Baltimore.

A similar trouble was caused in Baltimore by Germans and a German priest, who claimed to have powers from Rome to set up a church independent of the bishop, and got up a petition to the holy see to erect in the United States a German diocese for Germans. Accordingly they built St. John's Church, ran it without any authorization, and forcibly prevented the entrance of the bishop. Carroll, to settle the question once for all, obtained from the court a mandamus to compel the trustees to receive him. Their defense was that the members of a church had the sole and exclusive right of nominating and appointing the pastor; that no other person, whether bishop or Pope, had the right to appoint a pastor without the assent or approbation of the congregation. This plea was based on no laws of the church that they could produce, and the case was decided against them in May, 1805.

Meanwhile the vineyard of the Lord was extending day by day, and the laborers were presenting themselves rapidly for the doing of the work. The Sulpitians were not only teaching and training the future clergy of America in the seminary of Baltimore, but also were acting as missionaries in Maryland, in New England among the Indians, and in the West among the descendants of the early French colonists and the miserable remnants of the Illinois tribes. The Augustinians were beginning their glorious career of apostolate in Delaware and Pennsylvania. The Dominicans were preserving the work of the early missionaries in the city of New York, and were completing the Church of St. Peter. The surviving Jesuits, who had continued in the American field as diocesan priests of Baltimore, were following the while with wistful eyes and anxious hearts the fortunes of the small band of refugees under the protection of Elizabeth of Russia, who kept alive the hopes and spirit of the suppressed society. When appeared in March, 1801, the bull of Pius VII., *Catholicæ Fidei*, recognizing the society as then preserved and existing in Russia, the American ex-Jesuits sought to connect themselves with it, received recruits from Russia, reopened their novitiate in Georgetown (1806), and entered again into possession of the properties held by the clerical association which had been formed in Maryland after their suppression for the purpose of securing what the society had possessed in the English colonies.

Other priests were coming year by year to Carroll's help from France, Germany, and Ireland. On the 18th of March, 1795, Bishop Carroll raised to the priesthood a student of the seminary of Baltimore who was known throughout his missionary career as Father Smith, the Anglicized form of Schmidt. But he was none other than the Russian Prince Dmitri Gallitzin, son of Prince Dmitri Alexievitch Gallitzin and the Countess Amalia von Schmettau. He abandoned the religion and the military or diplomatic service of Russia to which his birth destined him for the Church of Rome and the missions of America. His priestly labors were begun at Conewago, whence he extended his visits to Taneytown, Hagerstown, and Cumberland in Maryland, to Chambersburg and Huntingdon in Pennsylvania.

Likewise the field was extending. In the State of New York, between Albany and Fort Stanwix on the Mohawk, there were four hundred Catholic families; and in September, 1797, the corner-stone of the first Catholic church in Albany was laid. In New England two remarkable men, both French, were giving to Catholicity an impulse which has gone on increasing to our days: the Rev. Francis A. Matignon and the Rev. John Cheverus. From their reports we find that in the year 1798 the Catholics in all New England were: in Boston, 210; in Plymouth, 15; in Newburyport, 21; in Salem, 3; in Maine, the Penobscot tribe of Indians 300, the Passamaquoddy 150. At Hartford the Rev. John Thayer had officiated for a few Catholics in 1790, and for a time the Rev. John Ambrose Sougé resided there as chaplain to Vicomte de Sibert-Cornillon. In all New England there was no building worthy the name of church until Dr. Matignon, in 1800, began the erection of one, eighty-one by fifty-eight feet, on Franklin Street in Boston, to the building of which John Adams, President of the United States, and other Protestant gentlemen, gave generous contributions.

Respected as were the two French priests, Matignon and Cheverus, for their admirable qualities, it was only as individuals, not as ministers of a barely tolerated religion. Two occurrences prove that the spirit that dictated the penal legislation of the colonial days was not quite exorcised. Cheverus had married two Catholics in Maine. Now Maine at the time was annexed to Massachusetts, and the law of the latter colony prohibited marriage except by a minister or a justice of the peace. Although Cheverus, after the religious ceremony, sent the parties to the justice of the peace to have the marriage ratified, he was dragged before the court first in a criminal action, with the result of a verdict of not guilty, thus escaping the pillory; then in a civil action immediately afterward, which for some reason or other never came to a hearing. But it was generally held that the constitution of the commonwealth did not recognize Catholic priests as empowered to marry, because the word "Protestant" was to be understood before the word "minister."

The other occurrence is stated thus by Father Cheverus: "Mr. Kavanagh, a respectable merchant living at New

Castle, in the county of Lincoln, district of Maine, has fitted up at his own expense a small neat chapel, and with his partner, Mr. Cottril, has subscribed one thousand dollars for our new church. He thought in consequence he would be free from paying taxes to the Congregational minister of his township; but the judges of the Supreme Court now sitting in Boston declared unanimously that he must pay for the support of the said minister, even if he had a priest always residing with him. The constitution obliges every one to contribute for the support of Protestant ministers, and them alone. Papists are only tolerated, and as long as their ministers behave well they shall not be disturbed; but let them expect no more than that."

Another lawsuit with a different ending deserves to be recorded. The Rev. Theodore Brouwers had been in charge of the missions of Westmoreland County, Pennsylvania. Before his death, which happened in 1788, he bought a farm known as "Sportsman's Hall," and left it by will to "the Catholic priest who should succeed him in the said place, and the priest shall transmit the land so left him to his successor." A certain German Franciscan, Father Francis Fromm, without any authorization from the bishop, left his appointed field of labor to go to Westmoreland County and assume control of the estate, coolly informing the bishop that he had been chosen by the congregation and that he was in possession. A lawsuit followed, not between the bishop and the intruder, but between the intruder and the congregation, who soon tired of him and sought to oust him from the property. The jury gave a verdict against the intruding priest under the following charge of the judge of Common Pleas of the Fifth Circuit of Pennsylvania:

"The Bishop of Baltimore has, and before and at the time of Fromm's taking possession of the estate had, the sole episcopal authority over the Catholic Church of the United States. Every Catholic congregation within the United States is subject to his inspection, and without authority from him no Catholic priest can exercise any pastoral functions over any congregation in the United States. Without his appointment or permission to exercise pastoral functions over this congregation, no priest can be entitled under the will of Brouwers to claim the enjoyment of this estate. Fromm had no such appointment or permission, and is therefore incompetent to discharge the duties or enjoy the benefits which are the objects of the will of Brouwers." This was the first case of the kind that came before a civil tribunal in the United States; it established in the courts the authority of a Roman Catholic bishop in the government of the church and in the holding of church property. The property in litigation has since become the site of the great Benedictine Abbey of St. Vincent.

The growing city of Pittsburg stood where was once Fort Du Quesne. As yet no church was there, and the few Catholics of the place received only the occasional ministrations of the missionaries traveling to the farther West; for the Ohio was then the highway to the missions on the Mississippi, in the Northwest Territory, and in the new settlements of Kentucky. In 1783 a strong movement of emigration from the Atlantic to the lands west of the Alleghanies commenced. Even as early as 1774 Catholics from Maryland set out for Kentucky: twenty-five families settled on Pottinger's Creek in 1785; the next year another party settled on Hardin's Creek; and in 1787 a cluster of Catholic families made their home at Bardstown. At first these settlements received but occasional visits of priests, as of the Carmelite, Rev. Paul de St. Pierre, in 1784, of the Dominican, Father William de Rohan, who in 1787 erected the Church of the Holy Cross at Pottinger's Creek, the cradle of Catholicity in Kentucky, and of Rev. Charles Whelan, in 1790.

To this derelict portion of his diocese Bishop Carroll sent, in 1793, the Rev. Stephen Badin, who had come from France as a seminarian in 1792, and had been ordained in Baltimore May 25, 1793, the first seminarian to receive holy orders in the United States. For three years this young missionary labored all alone amid appalling difficulties, but with an energy and zeal that nothing could relax. He received an auxiliary (1797) in the Rev. Michael Fournier, who died in 1803; in the Rev. Anthony Salmon (1799), who died very soon after; and in the Rev. John Thayer, who retired from the field of American missions (1803) and went to England, where he died. In July, 1805, there came to the help of Badin in Kentucky a Belgian priest whose name has become famous in the history of Western Catholicity, the Rev. Charles Nerinok. He arrived in Baltimore October, 1804, and was at once assigned to work in the West. These two missionaries not only labored among the Catholic settlements of Kentucky, where four humble churches, log and frame, were erected by them, but also pushed their journeys as far as Vincennes, which was then without a priest. In 1806 Father Fenwick, of the Order of St. Dominic, purchased a plantation of five hundred acres near Springfield, Washington County, Ky., was joined by some fellow-religious the year following, and erected the Church of St. Rose of Lima. In 1806 a novitiate was opened near by, which became the cradle of the Dominican order in the United States. Farther south, on the Mississippi, Natchez and Vicksburg, which had been lately relinquished by Spain to the United States, came under the jurisdiction of Bishop Carroll, and, at a request made by him to the Spanish

Bishop of New Orleans, Rt. Rev. Louis Penalver, were attended to by the nearest Spanish clergyman.

When Jay's treaty (1796) put an end to the occupancy by England of Michigan and other Northwestern points, Bishop Carroll found his burden increased by the duty of providing priests for this new accession, as well as for the missions along the Mississippi formerly under the jurisdiction of the Bishop of Quebec. The latter at once recalled to Canada the priests who had been laboring in this district. Father Gibault, the "patriot priest" of the West, had retired in 1791 from the French missions to the Spanish territory across the Mississippi. Thus by the year 1796 the region that is now Illinois, Indiana, Ohio, and Michigan, and was known then as the Northwest Territory, was left on the hands of Bishop Carroll without a resident priest. Fortunately the Sulpitians, just arrived in Baltimore in greater number than the work of the seminary needed, came to the rescue. The Rev. Mr. Levadoux labored at Kaskaskia from 1793 to 1795, and after him the Rev. Gabriel Richard till 1796. In 1799 the Rev. John Olivier was stationed at Cahokia, and his brother, the Rev. Donatien Olivier, at Kaskaskia and Prairie du Rocher. The Rev. Benedict Joseph Flaget, the future Bishop of Bardstown, arrived at Vincennes in December, 1792. He found for a church "a very poor log building, open to the weather and almost tottering. The congregation was, if possible, in a still more miserable condition. Out of nearly seven hundred souls, only twelve could be induced to approach holy communion during the Christmas festivities."

This description might be applied to all the Canadian missions of the West. The uncertainties created in the ecclesiastical government of these far-away posts by the Revolutionary War, and its consequent changes in the civil and religious spheres, had produced a great neglect in the practice, and even some falling off in the profession, of the faith. To Father Flaget, obliged by ill health to return to Baltimore, succeeded, in 1796, the Rev. John Francis Rivet. This zealous missionary's labors were ended by his saintly death at Vincennes in the winter of 1804. In 1796 the Rev. Mr. Levadoux took charge of the church of Detroit, from which the Bishop of Quebec had recalled the former incumbent; and to his aid was sent the Rev. Gabriel Richard and the Rev. John Dilhet. After Mr. Levadoux's recall to France by his superiors in 1801, Father Richard became the pastor of Detroit. Father Dilhet's field of labor extended from Sandusky to St. Joseph River at the head of Lake Michigan, and as far south as Fort Wayne. From Detroit and Sandusky the two zealous missionaries paid occasional visits to Mackinaw, Sault Ste. Marie, and other Northwestern posts where were to be found the fast-decaying descendants of former Canadians and of Catholic Indians.

In the South the Rev. John Dubois, another of the French pioneer priests, who became afterward Bishop of New York, visted Richmond, Va., in 1791, gathered together the few Catholics of the city, and held services in one of the rooms of the capitol. But he did not remain long there, and for many years only fitful visits were made to the faithful of the present episcopal see of Virginia. Before the year 1799 a church was begun in Norfolk, but here, as elsewhere, trusteeism held sway and retarded the progress of religion. Alexandria had a log chapel from colonial days. In 1796 a better church was begun on ground donated by a Protestant gentleman; but it was never completed, as the site was considered to be too distant from the center of the town. Father Leonard Neale at first attended this congregation from Georgetown. It was only in 1805 that it began to have a resident clergyman.

About the year 1786 a vessel bound for South America put into the port of Charleston, S. C. A priest was on board. At the request of a few Catholics who heard of this welcome arrival, he celebrated mass in the house of an Irish citizen before a congregation of twelve persons. In 1788 the Rev. Mr. Ryan was sent there by Bishop Carroll. After two years' labor, when ill health compelled him to retire, he had succeeded in getting together a flock of two hundred souls, most of whom up to that time had kept their religion concealed. They worshiped in a half-ruined meeting-house which they hired. The Rev. Mr. Keating, who succeeded Father Ryan, withdrew discouraged at the end of a few months. The next incumbent, the Rev. Mr. Gallagher, was a detriment rather than an aid to the church by his unclerical life. In vain did Bishop Carroll try to get him to resign; the refractory priest appealed to Rome and went thither to argue his case. On his return he drove from the altar the priest, Rev. Mr. Le Mercier, whom the bishop had sent to assume charge of the parish. The trustees took sides with Gallagher, though he was suspended by his ordinary, and Le Mercier was compelled to take up his residence in Raleigh, N. C., in which State there were but a handful of Catholics. In New Berne, N. C., lived a Catholic family, the Gastons, in whose house, about 1784, the Rev. Patrick Cleary, of Funchal, Madeira, celebrated the holy sacrifice of the mass before a few Catholics. He had come to claim an inheritance, and was detained by the law's delays until 1790, when he died.

Georgia in colonial days was closed to the church by stringent penal laws. A certain Abbé Le Moine labored there—how long is not known—and died in 1796. In 1803 arrived in Savannah the Rev. Anthony Carles, who attended to the few Catholics there and in Augusta. Such was the condition of the vast diocese of Baltimore in the first years of the century.

On the death of Washington (1799) Bishop Carroll ordered the 23d of February to be celebrated as a day of mourning. Of late years some Catholic writers have claimed that Washington died a Catholic. At most we may perhaps say that he was thinking of such a step before death overcame him; for Carroll—our authority for the statement is Gilmary Shea—compares him to "the young Emperor Valentinian, who was deprived of life before his initiation into the church." Carroll's discourse on the occasion of Washington's death was considered at the time a masterpiece, and is undoubtedly one of the finest eulogies ever pronounced on "the father of his country." These two great men were bound by ties of mutual respect, and none could speak more understandingly and feelingly of the great general and President than the great priest and bishop; both are types of our earliest and our best Americanism. Mr. Custis, the adopted son and heir of Washington, described the relations of Carroll and Washington in a letter to Dr. White which is to be found in the appendix to Darras's "History of the Church": "From his exalted worth as a minister of God, his stainless character as a man, and, above all, his distinguished services as a patriot of the Revolution, Dr. Carroll stood high—very high—in the esteem and affections of the *pater patriæ*."

The city of Washington was called into existence by acts of Congress (1790 and 1791) setting apart as the District of Columbia a tract of ten square miles, taken partly from Maryland and partly from Virginia. In this space were the village and college of Georgetown. The Catholics of the village had hitherto depended mainly on the chapel of the Young family as a place of worship; it was only in 1792 that the Church of the Holy Trinity was erected. Within the limits of the new city—planned by a Catholic, L'Enfant, and governed by three commissioners, of whom the brother of Bishop Carroll, Daniel, was one—the Catholics secured a site (1794) on which was built a church dedicated to St. Patrick. The first pastor was the Rev. Mr. Caffrey, who ruled it until 1805. The second was the Rev. Mr. Mathews, who ruled it for fifty years. At a point near the present navy-yard was St. Mary's Church (known as Barry's Chapel, because it had been erected by a Mr. Barry), the corner-stone of which is now shown in the walls of the present St. Dominic's Church. Another Daniel Carroll, of Dudington, cousin of the bishop, proprietor as well as the bishop's brother of part of the site of the capital, donated for a church a piece of land, now in St. Peter's parish, long known as the cathedral lot.

The coadjutor, Bishop Neale, was yielding to the influence of years faster than Carroll, and was less able than he to undergo the hardships of long journeys. The necessity of erecting new sees was urgent, and was treated by Carroll in his correspondence with Rome as early as 1802. A political event made this move still more necessary. It was the acquisition by the United States of Louisiana (1803), and the addition of this new province by the Propaganda (September, 1805) to the jurisdiction of Carroll, inasmuch as he was made the Administrator Apostolic of the diocese of New Orleans, with power to name for it a vicar general. This diocese at the time of cession had twenty-one parishes. Of the twenty-six priests who were laboring there when the Spanish domination ceased, only a few agreed to continue in service under the American flag. The first vicar general named by Bishop Carroll was Rev. John Olivier, who had been at work in the missions of Illinois. He found matters in New Orleans in a sad state, and was thwarted in his administration by one of the Capuchins, the Rev. Antonio Sedella, an unworthy ecclesiastic, who had been in the past and continued to be for many years the curse of the church in Louisiana, where his influence over the trustees of the cathedral enabled him to resist the ecclesiastical authorities. Age and sickness rendered the Rev. Mr. Olivier unfit to cope with the evils, and in 1810 the bishop sent to New Orleans as his vicar general the Rev. Mr. Sibourd; but he, too, found that Sedella and his unworthy assistants would not be brought under discipline nor be changed from their scandalous lives.

Again did Carroll urge the erection of new sees, and sent to Rome the names of the clergymen he deemed fittest for the honor and burden of the episcopate. The recommendations were accepted by Rome, with one exception. Carroll had advised that the contemplated see of New York should for the time being remain unfilled and be placed under the care of the Bishop of Boston. Another influence than that of the American church was at work in Rome, and succeeded in filling at once the see of New York with an Irish Dominican, Father Richard Luke Concanen, who had resided many years in the Eternal City as the agent of the Irish bishops. We shall have more to say presently of this foreign influence. The bulls dividing the see of Baltimore and erecting the sees of New York, Philadelphia, Boston, and Bardstown are dated April 8, 1808, and signed by Pope Pius VII. The diocese of New York was to comprise that State and the eastern part of the State of New Jersey; the diocese of Philadelphia was to comprise the States of Pennsylvania and Delaware and the western and southern parts of New Jersey; the diocese of Boston was to comprise Massachusetts, New Hampshire,

Rhode Island, Connecticut, and Vermont; the diocese of Bardstown was to comprise Kentucky, Tennessee, and the Northwest Territory. The new sees were made suffragan to the metropolitan church of Baltimore, which was left with Maryland, Virginia, the Carolinas, and Georgia as its diocesan territory. The see of Baltimore had also, for the time being, the administration of the diocese of New Orleans, which comprised Alabama and Florida, the Isle of Orleans, and the whole country west of the Mississippi as far north as the northern boundary of the United States, as far west as the Spanish possessions in New Mexico and Upper California, a boundary-line so vague at the time that no one could well trace it. Such, then, was the ecclesiastical division of the United States nineteen years after the erection of the see of Baltimore.

The Bishop elect of New York, Concanen, who was consecrated in Rome April 24, 1808, was intrusted with the bulls for the other bishops elect; but he was prevented from finding passage for America owing to the troubled politics of the time, and died in Naples, vainly waiting for a ship and a passport, June 20, 1810. How much more time might have elapsed before Bishop Carroll could have proceeded to the consecration of the bishops elect it would be hard to say, had not Bishop Concanen fortunately forwarded, before dying, to Rev. Mr. Emery, superior of St. Sulpice, Paris, authentic copies of the bulls. It was on these copies of the original documents, brought to the United States by Mr. Flaget, that Bishop Carroll acted. The consecrations took place in the following order: that of Dr. Egan, Bishop elect of Philadelphia, on October 28, 1810; that of Dr. Cheverus, Bishop elect of Boston, on November 1st; that of Dr. Flaget, Bishop elect of Bardstown, on November 4th. Between the issuing of the bulls and the consecrations more than two years had passed.

Before separating, the suffragans, with their metropolitan, held a meeting in which were discussed the church interests of the country, and a pastoral letter was drawn up embodying their views. The statistics at this time, as far as they can be made out, show seventy priests and eighty churches in the United States, exclusive of the diocese of New Orleans; we have no means of stating precisely the Catholic population; a fair guess would be seventy thousand. It had been agreed among the bishops in their first meeting that a Provincial Council should be held not later than November, 1812; a few years of administration in their respective dioceses would have shown them by that time the needs of the church. But the difficulty, not to say impossibility, of holding communication with the Pope, then a prisoner in the hands of Napoleon, made the project impossible of realization. And, at any rate, the War of 1812 between England and the United States broke out, bringing disaster to the country on the Chesapeake, on the northern frontier of Michigan, and on the Mississippi at New Orleans.

By this time the country that had formerly made up the diocese of Louisiana passed from the jurisdiction of Bishop Carroll. He succeeded in inducing the holy see to name as Administrator Apostolic of Louisiana and the Floridas the Rev. William du Bourg. He was a learned and brilliant man, but had not the courage and perseverance necessary to oppose and overcome the rebellious Capuchins. The cathedral remained closed to him; he even took to flight before the commotion raised among the followers of Sedella by his suspension of that unworthy priest. However, he is to be commended and remembered for his patriotic action in the war. While the British forces attacked the city he ordered prayers to be said in the churches; and after General Jackson's glorious victory he threw open his pro-cathedral for a solemn service of thanksgiving, at which the "hero of the two Floridas" was present.

Of all the clergy under the jurisdiction of Carroll, the most useful were the Sulpitians, who not only trained in St. Mary's Seminary, Baltimore, the rising generations of native priests, but also took charge of neglected missions in the East and the distant West, when no one else of the diocesan and regular clergymen could be found free or willing to undertake the arduous task. It looked at one time (1803) as if the American church was to lose those heroic auxiliaries. Better times for religion in France and dissatisfaction among some of the Sulpitians in the United States induced their superior general, Mr. Emery, to order the return of all his American subjects. To Bishop Carroll, who spoke of them always as the best priests he ever knew, the prospect was disheartening. Already some had obeyed the order and others were preparing to do so, when Mr. Emery, who hesitated on the representations and protest of Carroll, laid the matter before Pius VII., then in Paris for the coronation of Napoleon. "My son," answered the Pope, "let this seminary subsist. To recall the directors in order to employ them in France would be stripping St. Paul to clothe St. Peter." Thus was America providentially spared the disaster of being deprived of an institution and of men that have rendered to the church of this republic services the value of which Heaven alone can appreciate and reward.

Four years after the installation of Bishop Egan in the see of Philadelphia he died, sickened and discouraged by the opposition he found in the trustees and the priests of his cathedral. New York and Philadelphia were now vacant. As it was known that Bishop Concanen before his death had petitioned the holy see to name as his coadjutor the Rev. Ambrose Maréchal, Archbishop Carroll and his suffragans, who approved that choice, gave themselves no further concern about filling the vacancy made by Concanen's death, considering Maréchal's nomination as good as settled. To their utter astonishment they learned that certain European influences were at work in Rome, viz., the Archbishop of Dublin and other Irish bishops, urging for the see of New York the priest who had been the great opponent of Bishop Egan in Philadelphia, Father Harold; and, though they succeeded in having that gentleman thrown out of consideration, it was with no small wonder and dissatisfaction that they saw their own nominee, the Rev. John B. David, set aside, and the nominee of the Irish influence, Dr. Connolly, a subject of the country with which the United States was actually at war, appointed and consecrated Bishop of New York in November, 1814.

It is proper that we should say a word in regard to the Irish Cahenslyism—a word introduced by the Standard Dictionary—that tainted our infancy and threatened our future. No sooner had the United States become an independent nation than lay and clerical authorities in various foreign countries considered it fair spoils and an open field for their intrigues. We have already seen how the French minister to the United States, Barbé de Marbois, concerted with the papal nuncio, and inveigled good Benjamin Franklin into the scheme to set over the Catholics of the United States a French prefect, or vicar apostolic, or bishop. Another French attempt was made in 1775. A certain adventurer, Pierre Penet, trafficking among the Oneida Indians of New York, induced them to apply to the French minister for a French priest, a Rev. Mr. Perrot, who arrived there in 1789 and received from the tribe a glebe of three hundred acres. A few years afterward

(1790) another French adventurer, professing to be the agent of the Oneida Indians, addressed a petition to Pius VI., through the nuncio in Paris, asking the establishment of a bishop at Oneida, "a great territory between the United States and Canada;" and presented to his Holiness as nominee "the Rev. John Louis Victor le Tonnelier de Coulanges, whom the Oneida nation and the chiefs of the Six Nations have chosen as Bishop of Oneida and Primate of the Six Nations." The petition is in the archives of the Propaganda. The scheme never came to realization.

In 1791 an Irish priest, the Rev. Edmund Burke, a professor in the seminary of Quebec, called the attention of the Propaganda, through Archbishop Troy, of Dublin, to the sad condition of the missions in the Northwest, and proceeded thither to carry out certain reforms of his own. He thus expresses his views: "I am the Administrator of Upper Canada, with every episcopal power except what requires episcopal order; yet I find a very great want of power, for here the limits of jurisdiction are very uncertain and unsettled, the country being in dispute between the Bishops of Quebec and Baltimore. I know no jurisdiction certain but that of his Holiness. Besides, confirmation is a sacrament totally unknown here." He then urged Archbishop Troy to get the Propaganda to establish a mission independent of both bishops; but this was never done.

Yet another project is recorded—French this time. The Scioto Company, an association of real-estate speculators, founded a colony on the Scioto River, and actually got the Propaganda to create a prefecture apostolic before even the colony had come into existence. When, a few years afterward (1790), a few hundred French immigrants reached the Ohio and founded Gallipolis, Dom Didier, a

Benedictine monk who accompanied them, was appointed superior with ample powers, but under the jurisdiction of the Bishop of Baltimore, "if the contemplated colony would be located in that diocese." Gallipolis dwindled away, and Dom Didier, an estimable man, ended his days in St. Louis. So ended the prefecture apostolic of Scioto.

In 1808 the Archbishop of Dublin and other Irish bishops brought about, as we have seen, independently of Bishop Carroll and the American clergy, the nomination of Father Richard Luke Concanen to the see of New York, and in 1814 the nomination of Father Connolly as his successor. In the same manner and through the same agencies Philadelphia received a successor to Bishop Egan (1819) in the Rev. Henry Conwell, Vicar General of Armagh; Richmond was given for bishop (1820) the Rev. P. Kelly, president of St. John's Seminary, Kilkenny; and in the same year Charleston received as bishop the Rev. John England, a priest of the diocese of Cork, Ireland. It looked in the first quarter of this century as if home rule were to be taken from the church of the United States through foreign interference.

Now the one thing that Carroll fought for during his whole life was the independence of the American church from any control and dictation but that of the holy see. It was for him a sorrow, embittering his last years, that other influences had a predominating voice in our destiny, and that Rome seemed to withdraw confidence from him and his fellow-bishops, and prefer to their counsels those of aliens who could not have a correct knowledge of the needs of the United States.

In the summer of 1815 he showed signs of breaking up; the end came to him December 3d of that year. The progress of his episcopate had been wonderful, a fit pledge of the still more marvelous development about to take place within a few years. An archbishopric, four suffragan sees, and one at the mouth of the Mississippi not under the metropolitan jurisdiction of Baltimore; a seminary, a novitiate and scholasticate, colleges, convents, institutions of charity; the beginnings of a Catholic press and literature; a clergy increased to at least one hundred priests; an extension of the church southward and westward by means of an immigration small, as yet, compared to the coming flood; a wider liberty for the church in the constitutions and the rulings of the courts in the various States—such is the noble record that is to be placed to his credit. He came on the scene when the sky was darkest for the church; he departed with the full light and warmth of success shining on it. A great American and a great churchman, he molded the diverse elements of the American Catholicity of his day into a unity which the vicissitudes of time and the seemingly adverse influence of a vast foreign immigration have not destroyed. The Americanism of Carroll is a precious heirloom and a lasting inspiration to the churchmen of to-day.

CHAPTER XX.

THE PROVINCE OF BALTIMORE (1815-29).

AFTER the death of Archbishop Carroll the administration of the diocese of Baltimore fell to his coadjutor, Bishop Neale, who for fifteen years had lived in Georgetown and continued to live there, visiting the episcopal city only when business of the diocese required his presence. Troubles with the trustees of Norfolk and Charleston embittered the two years during which he survived his predecessor. He had, however, the consolation of receiving from Rome the canonical erection of the Visitation Convent of Georgetown, and also of restoring to the Society of Jesus, of which he had been a member, the old missions that the fathers had founded and attended in colonial days.

Ambrose Maréchal, elected to succeed Archbishop Neale, was a Sulpitian who came to the United States in 1792, had been professor of philosophy in Georgetown, of theology in St. Mary's Seminary, Baltimore, and had refused the miter of Philadelphia. One of his first efforts was to settle the disordered condition of the churches of Norfolk and Charleston. But the obstinacy of the trustees and the rebellious priests, upheld by a laity ignorant of ecclesiastical law, paralyzed his efforts; and, worse still, false representations made to Rome brought forth orders from the Propaganda that gave for a while approval and courage to the rebels, pain and discouragement to the archbishop and the defenders of correct discipline. Bishop Connolly, of New York, who was a stranger in the country, and could not know at such a distance how matters really went in Virginia and the Carolinas, was unwittingly led to take sides with the men, cleric and lay, who ignored the rightful authority of the Archbishop of Baltimore, and was mainly instrumental, through the hierarchy of Ireland and their agents in Rome, in fostering the opposition and foisting on the church of America important decisions from Rome, some of which were proved by the events to be unwise and unfavorable to progress.

Archbishop Maréchal petitioned the holy see to erect in the Carolinas and Georgia a diocese, with the bishop's see at Charleston. He did not propose any candidates, as no fixed mode of episcopal elections had been settled as yet for the United States, and as he knew that certain prejudices against the former archbishops of Baltimore existed in Rome. Now it is a strange fact to state at the present day that the proposed plan of Maréchal was altered, two dioceses being erected while he asked for one, a large and wealthy State being cut off from his own jurisdiction while he requested and hinted no such curtailing; a strange fact that as bishops to the new sees thus created—Richmond and Charleston—men were appointed foreign to the country, unknown to the American clergy—the Rev. Patrick Kelly and the Rev. John England; and strangest fact of all that this originated with the rebel element in Norfolk and Charleston, men without religion, who had thought at one time of recurring to the Jansenistic bishops of Holland to effect their independence of Baltimore. This element misled the Irish hierarchy, which in turn, through its Roman agent, misled the Propaganda into taking such important measures without, I will not say the consent, but even the advice of the American hierarchy.

The singular feature about this move was that the new sees split the diocese of Baltimore in two parts, viz., Maryland and the District of Columbia in the northeast, Alabama and Mississippi in the southwest. Evidently the Irish bishops and the Propaganda were not well up in the geography of the United States. Maréchal protested, of course, but it was too late; the thing was done. Particularly unfortunate was the appointment of the Rev. Patrick Kelly to the see of Richmond. He took possession of his diocese in January, 1821, fixing his residence in Norfolk, the hotbed of discontent and rebellion. One of the reasons given in Rome for the erection of Virginia into a separate diocese was its immense distance from Baltimore. It took Bishop Kelly just twenty-four hours to sail down the Chesapeake from that city to the place of his residence. The very men who had clamored for independence from the metropolitan see turned against him, and he was compelled, in order to maintain himself, to open and run a school. Finally he left Virginia in July, 1822, for Waterford, Ireland, to which diocese the Pope in mercy transferred him. Of the new Bishop of Charleston we have a different story to tell. His coming turned out a blessing; he became the great American prelate of his generation, and his name is forever enshrined in the history of the church of the United States.

Though compelled by want of means to complete the cathedral begun by Archbishop Carroll with less grandeur than had been originally intended, yet Maréchal had the consolation of dedicating that building—a noble one for the time, a noble one still to-day—in May, 1821. This done, he went to Rome to fulfil the obligation that rests on every bishop to visit from time to time the Holy Father and the threshold of the apostles. He laid before the holy see a statement of the condition of his diocese and province. He estimated the Catholic population of his province and of Louisiana at two hundred and forty-four thousand. The number of Catholics in Baltimore, the largest center at the time, was ten thousand. For the education and supply of future priests he had St. Mary's Seminary, Baltimore, in charge of the Sulpitians, the seminary at Emmitsburg, and the Scholasticate and Novitiate of the Society of Jesus at Georgetown. For the higher education of Catholic boys there were the College of St. Mary, Baltimore, in care of the Sulpitians, and Georgetown College, in care of the Jesuits. For the higher education of girls there were the Visitation Academy, Georgetown, in care of the Visitation nuns, and St. Joseph's Academy, Emmitsburg, in care of the Sisters of Charity founded by Mother Seton.

While in Rome the archbishop brought to the attention of the holy see some questions concerning the property that had been formerly held in Maryland and Pennsylvania by the Jesuits in colonial times. The bull *Dominus ac Redemptor*, by which the Society of Jesus was suppressed under Clement XIV. (July, 1773), forbade the members of the suppressed society from purchasing or selling any house, goods, or estates. The encyclical *De abolenda Societate Jesu*, issued about a month afterward (August 18, 1773), required each bishop to take and retain possession of the houses and colleges of the extinct order in his diocese, and of their goods, rights, and appurtenances of what kind soever. At that time the church in the United States was under the jurisdiction of the Vicar Apostolic of London, Bishop Challoner. He made known the above-named documents to the Jesuits of Maryland and Pennsylvania, and received their written adhesion thereto. As to their properties he took no steps, for the Jesuits, as a corporation, could not at that time hold property in England or its dominions, and therefore their lands in the

American colonies were held by individuals. Perhaps Challoner knew not how to enforce the Roman provisions under the circumstances, and, at any rate, the war soon came to break off his intercourse with the American church. In December, 1792, the individual ex-Jesuits who held in their names the properties in question transferred them, as trust property, to a corporation—formed under an act of the legislature of the State of Maryland, and made up of the former members of the extinct society—"Corporation of the Roman Catholic Clergymen." When Carroll was made Bishop of Baltimore the revenues of one of the plantations were assigned to him and continued to his successor, Neale, both having been Jesuits. But when Maréchal became archbishop the payment of the revenues of the plantation was discontinued for the reason that he had not been a member of the Jesuit corporation.

Now Maréchal's contention in Rome was that the bull erecting the see of Baltimore vested in the bishop of that see all the properties formerly held by the Jesuits in Maryland, and, moreover, that certain of the estates had been originally given not to the society, but to the Catholic Church. The matter was referred to a commission of cardinals, and on their recommendation Pius VII. issued a brief (July, 1822) requiring the general of the society and the Maryland fathers to transfer to the Archbishop of Baltimore one of the estates, Whitemarsh, or its equivalent, the rent of the other properties to remain in their hands. The Maryland Jesuits delayed compliance with the order and protested; the Propaganda again insisted on the exact execution of the brief. Meanwhile the affair had been laid by parties favorable to the Maryland fathers, if not by themselves, before the President of the United States, Monroe; and so strong were the expostulations from Washington that the Pope accepted a compromise proposition made by the general of the society to pay Archbishop Maréchal annually the sum of eight hundred Roman crowns. At the bottom of the decisions by the holy see lay the principle that the property of the society at the time of its suppression vested in the Pope, who could dispose of it to the best interests of religion.

The interference of the hierarchy of another country in American church affairs, and the urgency of some fixed mode of appointment to American bishoprics, was another important matter which the Archbishop of Baltimore laid before the holy see. "We freely confess," he writes in a document to the Pope, "that we have no right to present bishops for the province of Baltimore; . . . yet it is certain that they must be nominated by some one. But who, seeing the distance of North America from Rome, is to present capable and worthy subjects? The Irish bishops cannot do so with advantage; it is utterly impossible for them to nominate men who suit our States." In consequence of this plea the Pope granted to the Ameircan hierarchy the right of recommending suitable persons for vacancies in the episcopate. This was a first step in home rule and a blow to Irish intermeddling in the government of the church in the United States. In immediate exercise of this home rule, the archbishop renounced his jurisdiction over Alabama and Mississippi; Alabama, with the addition of Florida, was then erected into a bishopric, the see being Mobile, and Mississippi was erected into a vicariate apostolic, and was put for the nonce under the care of Bishop Du Bourg, of New Orleans. By these acts the diocese of Baltimore was limited to the territory over which it has had jurisdiction even to our day, Maryland and the District of Columbia. In addition to the diocese proper of Baltimore, Maréchal was the Administrator *pro tem.* of the diocese of Richmond, left vacant by the transfer of its first incumbent, Bishop Kelly, to the see of Waterford, Ireland.

Two other dioceses in the United States became vacant: that of Boston by the translation of Bishop Cheverus to the see of Montauban in France, October, 1823; and that of New York by the death of Bishop Connolly, February, 1825. Acting on the privilege granted by the holy see, the bishops of the province of Baltimore recommended the Rev. Benedict J. Fenwick, S.J., for the vacant see of Boston, and the Rev. John Dubois, president of Mount St. Mary's College, Emmitsburg, for the vacant see of New York. The former was consecrated in the cathedral of Baltimore, November 1, 1825, and the latter, October, 1826. As the field of labor of Archbishop Maréchal was too extensive, and his health too impaired by age and the hardships of his former missionary life, to allow him to fulfil all the duties of his office, he solicited and obtained the appointment of a coadjutor with the right of succession. The bulls, however, did not arrive before the venerable metropolitan's death (January 29, 1828). He was a worthy successor to the great American prelate, John Carroll; he achieved the one great object for which Carroll labored throughout his administration—freedom of the American church from any influence and control but that of the holy see. No greater proof of thorough Americanism could be demanded even from a child of the soil, and the achievement was all the more remarkable that Maréchal was not by birth, though he surely was at heart, an American.

The Most Rev. James Whitfield, the coadjutor elect, was consecrated in the cathedral of Baltimore, May 25, 1828. For eleven years he had been laboring as a priest in that parish, having come from England, his native country, in September, 1817. It is the special glory of his episcopate that he convoked and presided over the First Provincial Council of Baltimore, which in a sense might be called plenary, since all the bishops of the country were present as members of that assembly; but which in reality was only provincial, since there was in the country but one province. The project was one that Carroll and Maréchal had cherished. The necessary authorization came from Pius VIII. in the first year of Whitfield's administration, and the assembly was convoked by him for the first day of October, 1829. His diocese at that time contained about seventy-five thousand Catholics and fifty-two priests; the diocese of Richmond, of which he, like his predecessor, was administrator, counted scarcely one thousand Catholics and two or three priests.

We have seen elsewhere how it came to pass that the Rev. John England, parish priest of Bandon, Ireland, was chosen (July 11, 1820) to become the first Bishop of Charleston. He was a man of great native talents and wide experience in many departments of priestly labor. His ancestry had suffered for church and country, and England himself had inherited their spirit of faith and love of liberty. Two facts prove this: he opposed the movement to allow the British government a veto on the nomination of Irish bishops; he refused to take the usual oath of allegiance to the king of England at his consecration in Cork, September 21, 1820. Rather than take such an oath, he declared he would seek consecration elsewhere, for he meant to become an American citizen as soon as possible after landing in the United States. He arrived in Charleston, December 30, 1820, and from that moment no man in the land was a greater and truer American than John England.

His diocese comprised the two Carolinas and Georgia.

In Georgia there were but three points where a few Catholics were to be found—Savannah, Augusta, and Locust Point—and only two priests were resident in the State. In South Carolina, outside of Charleston, the only place where Catholics were found was Columbia, the capital, and they were in such small number that they could not support a priest. In North Carolina the only points that had any Catholics were Santee River, Wilmington, New Berne, Washington, Plymouth, Elizabeth; and so few, indeed, were they that only at Wilmington and New Berne was there any possibility of the erection of churches. In his travels through these States the bishop was the missionary and the good shepherd. Administering baptism and confirmation, hearing confessions, preaching in Catholic churches, where there were any, else in Protestant churches or public halls, going out of his way to seek some stray family reported to have been or to be Catholic—such were the ordinary occupations that made his life of visitations one worthy of the apostolic days.

The wants and dangers of his diocese, being now well known to him, set his active mind in search of supplies and remedies. The Catholics in his charge were few; they were scattered; they were sinking by the very force of circumstances into indifference and loss of faith. Priests were scarce, and, had they been more numerous, how could the feeble aggregations of faithful support them? Bishop England had recourse to the press as a substitute for the priest, organized a book society, and founded the "United States Catholic Miscellany," the pioneer of Catholic newspapers, which lasted until the Civil War. The works of Bishop England testify to his own literary activity, reveal the vast extent of his learning and interest in religious and national questions, and show what a power for good he was in the land.

In the South as in the North trusteeism was a present evil and a threat for the future. England did not stop to quarrel with the trustees of the one church he found in Charleston on his arrival. He quietly ignored them, and having secured an eligible site, proceeded to erect a temporary chapel for a cathedral, and, alongside of the church, the Philosophical and Classical Seminary of Charleston, an institution that attained some fame and flourished for years, in which the bishop at first was not only president, but professor of almost all the departments. Adding legislation to action, he ordained that as to churches to be thereafter erected no priest should be allowed to officiate therein unless a deed to the bishop of the diocese was first executed. Then shortly he took a further step, and seeking to secure the protection of the law for the church's rights, he drew up, after long study and deliberation, the "Constitution of the Roman Catholic Churches of the States of North Carolina, South Carolina, and Georgia; which are comprised in the diocese of Charleston, and province of Baltimore, U. S. A." The object was to lay down the general principles of the law of the Catholic Church as to the mode of raising, vesting, and managing church property; to fix the special manner in which the great principles that are recognized by the church should be carried into practice in this country. This was done by consultation, discussion, and arrangement between the bishop, the clergy, and the laity in several meetings. Acts of incorporation embodying these views were passed between the years 1823-25 in the legislatures of the three States comprised in the diocese of Charleston; and thus the plague of trusteeism that was eating out the church's heart in the North was removed from the South.

The action of the bishop in regard to the property rights of the church reveals how thoroughly he understood the conditions in which he lived, the character and temper of the government and people of the United States. He was truly, in his loves, his views, his modes of proceeding, a thorough American. The whole country did him the justice to acknowledge this. Let one fact among many stand as proof. In the winter of 1825–26, while in Washington, he was invited to address the members of Congress from the floor of the Hall of Representatives. He accepted, and on Sunday, January 8th, preached to them a discourse which is to be found among his works. Such an honor has been rare in the history of Congress. When the Provincial Council was about to convene, Bishop England, after gigantic efforts in his diocese, had small success to show in material results, though no member of the hierarchy stood higher in public esteem for talents and energy. The South, because of slavery, was not then and has not yet become the field in which Catholicity was to flourish. Three churches in South Carolina, three in Georgia, two in North Carolina, eight in all, about as many priests—that was all in the material order after years of labor.

The diocese of Boston, comprising New Hampshire, Vermont, Rhode Island, Connecticut, and Massachusetts, which at the time included Maine, was erected by the bull *Ex debito Pastoralis Officii* of Pius VII., December 8, 1808. The first bishop was John Lefebvre Cheverus, a native of France, who for twelve years previous to his promotion had labored zealously among the few and scattered Catholics of New England. In his vast diocese there were but three churches—Holy Cross, his cathedral in Boston, St. Patrick's at New Castle, Me., and a log chapel in the Indian village of Pleasant Point, Me. The Catholics in Boston numbered about seven hundred souls; smaller communities were to be found at various points—Salem, Newburyport, Damariscotta, Portland, Portsmouth, Bristol, Providence, and Pawtucket, not to mention again the Indian missions of Maine.

Much of his time was given to episcopal, or rather missionary, visitations of those widely separated congregations; his moments of rest in his episcopal city were spent in a most simple and mortified mode of life. A single apartment was his sleeping and reception room, "his episcopal palace open to all the world." His dress and table were of the plainest; he was his own servant, and was known on occasions to become the servant and nurse of his neighbors in distress and sickness. His apostolic life no less than his strong and eloquent preaching preserved and encouraged his flock, brought to the faith converts from Protestantism, and gradually softened prejudices. Such was the success of his labors that in 1820 his flock numbered 2120 in Boston and about 1000 in Maine.

Those results were due also in no small degree to the few zealous priests he had gathered about him, one of whom deserves to be mentioned—the Rev. Francis A. Matignon, a Frenchman, whose death in 1818 was a severe blow to the bishop and an irreparable loss to the diocese. The trying labors of the American missions had impaired the health of Cheverus. His friends at home, as well as the French minister in Washington, hoping that the air of his native land might restore, or at least prolong, a life so useful to the church, procured, much against his will, his translation to the see of Montauban, France. In 1823 he left Boston, followed by the love of his flock, the esteem of his non-Catholic friends and admirers, and the regret of the whole community. For two years the affairs of the diocese were in the hands of an administrator, the Very Rev. William Taylor, until the consecration (November 1,

1825) of the Rt. Rev. Benedict Joseph Fenwick, who had been recommended to the holy see by the Metropolitan of Baltimore and his suffragans as a fit successor to the saintly Cheverus.

Fenwick was a native of Maryland, a lineal descendant of one of the original settlers under the charter of Lord Baltimore, and was one of the first band of six who entered the Jesuit novitiate at Georgetown after the reorganization of the Society of Jesus in this country and its affiliation to the remnant of the society preserved in Russia. On taking possession of his see he described the situation in a memorandum: "The diocese of Boston comprehends all the New England States. The Catholics reside principally in Boston. At present there are in all the diocese but eight churches, all of which, with the exception of the cathedral, scarcely deserve the name." He had but three priests in his vast diocese, one near him in Boston, and the others hundreds of miles away. Happily, two more priests came to him, whom he sent, one to the Indians of Maine, the other to Salem. Presently three young men presented themselves as candidates for the priesthood; they were the first seminarians of Boston. The bishop himself took in hand their training, and became superior of seminary and general professor of theology. What between his lessons to the seminarians, his parochial work, his duties as chaplain to the Ursuline nuns, his occupation as architect and builder of an addition to the cathedral and of a convent, his life was a busy one when in Boston; and, naturally, no less busy was it when he was out of his episcopal city on the visitation of his diocese. Catholics were increasing faster than the clergy. He found them in greater or lesser number in the principal towns of New England—Lowell, Fort Adams, Newport, Fall River, Windsor Locks, Taunton, Providence, Hartford. To provide these small groups of faithful with churches or places of meeting was a heavy task. It is a remarkable fact that within one year (1827) he secured church buildings in three cities that to-day are sees of flourishing dioceses—Hartford, Portland, and Providence. But to provide the growing communities with priests was a still harder task. For this purpose he addressed himself to New York, Baltimore, Quebec, but without success; for the same dearth affected the rest of the country. He had greater happiness in the results of his own labors; in December, 1827, he ordained three of the seminarians he had trained. The statistics of the year 1828 tell better than any details I might give what had been since his consecration the progress of the church in his diocese. It contained in 1828 14,000 Catholics, of whom 7,000 were in the city of Boston, 16 churches, 8 priests, 7 or 8 schools, with an Ursuline Academy for the higher education of girls in Boston. To these institutions we may add a weekly newspaper, the "Jesuit," founded by the bishop in September, 1829. Such was the condition of his diocese when he set out for the First Provincial Council of Baltimore.

The diocese of New York, comprising the State of New York and the eastern part of New Jersey, was erected, April, 1808, by his Holiness Pius VII. Father Richard Luke Concanen, of the Order of St. Dominic, residing in Rome at the time, as the agent of the Irish hierarchy, was chosen for the see through the influences I have already mentioned, and consecrated in Rome, April 24, 1808. But he never reached the shores of the United States. The political condition of Italy was disturbed by the French occupation. Vessels sailing from Italian ports for America were rare, and difficulties were raised as to the bishop's passports. He fell ill of fever in Naples, and died there, June 19, 1810.

Meanwhile the administration of the affairs of the diocese was in the hands of Father Anthony Kohlman, S.J., appointed to this charge by Archbishop Carroll. He found the parish of St. Peter's to contain fourteen thousand souls. Deeming a second church absolutely necessary, he purchased ground between Broadway and the Bowery Road, then on the outskirts of the city, and thereon was built St. Patrick's Cathedral. Father Kohlman, during the years of his administration, had as co-laborer Father Fenwick, who afterward became Bishop of Boston. Both came into a strange relation with the famous infidel, Thomas Paine. It was their visit to his death-bed, at the invitation of the dying man, who imagined they might relieve his bodily sufferings. They tried to bring him to Christian sentiments, but did not succeed in their missionary attempt.

While he was in New York as administrator, before the bishop's arrival, Father Kohlman became the hero of a *cause célèbre* which implied the rights of a Catholic priest in regard to the secret of the confessional. A man and his wife were indicted for receiving stolen goods, but before trial the owner of the property acknowledged that he had received his property back from the hands of Rev. Anthony Kohlman. The clergyman was subpœnaed to appear at the trial as a witness against the supposed thieves or receivers of the stolen property. When called to the witness-box, Rev. Mr. Kohlman asked to be excused from answering, and said: "Were I summoned to give evidence as a private individual (in which capacity I declare most solemnly I know nothing relative to the case before the court), and to testify from these ordinary sources of information, from which the witnesses present have derived theirs, I should not for a moment hesitate, and should even deem it a duty of conscience, to declare whatever knowledge I might have. But if called upon to testify in quality of a minister of a sacrament, in which my God himself has enjoined on me a perpetual and inviolable secrecy, I must declare to this honorable court that I cannot, I must not, answer any question that has a bearing upon the restitution in question; and that it would be my duty to prefer instantaneous death, or any temporal misfortune, rather than disclose the name of the penitent in question. For, were I to act otherwise, I should become a traitor to my church, to my sacred ministry, and to my God. In fine, I should render myself guilty of eternal damnation." The court, through the Hon. De Witt Clinton, who presided, carefully reviewed the whole case, and decided that a priest could not be called upon to testify as to matters which he knew only through the confessional.

Though consecrated in Rome, November 6, 1814, Bishop Connolly did not reach New York until a year or more later. We were at the time at war with England, and Connolly, being a British subject, feared to come to the United States until peace was signed. His arrival was the signal for the departure of the few Jesuits in New York; only four priests remained in the vast diocese, two of whom were with the bishop in the city, which contained at the time fourteen or fifteen thousand Catholics. Even then Catholic emigrants were beginning to come to the United States; the larger number, indeed, to drift farther inward, not a few, however, to remain in the port where they landed. Great was the bishop's concern, and not very successful his appeals to Ireland and the other states, to provide clergymen for this constantly increasing population.

Small as was the number of his priests, yet Bishop Connolly had to suffer from some of them a violent opposition, backed by the rebellion of the trustees of the two churches of the city, St. Peter's and St. Patrick's. "The whole affair," says Gilmary Shea, "was a sad commentary on the introduction of national preferences into the affairs of the church. Bishop Connolly had been selected to appease the complaints made to Rome by unworthy priests and pretentious laymen; he had drawn into his diocese none but priests of his own nationality; yet he found himself denounced by his own to the Propaganda, and found a fellow-countryman aiming to supersede him." Bishop Connolly succumbed, February 6, 1825, to a disease contracted at the burial of one of his priests.

After a year and a half's vacancy, during which interval the diocese was administered by the Very Rev. John Power, New York received its third bishop in the person of John Dubois, consecrated in Baltimore October 29, 1826. Born in Paris, August 24, 1764, educated at the College of Louis le Grand with such school-fellows as Desmoulins and Robespierre, ordained in Paris August 22, 1787, John Dubois labored in the parish of St. Sulpice until 1791, when, fleeing from the terrors of the Revolution, he came to the United States with letters of recommendation from Lafayette to the leading American statesmen of the day. Adopted into the diocese by Bishop Carroll, he labored in various missions around Baltimore, built a college at Emmitsburg, and there devoted himself to the training of the clergy.

On his arrival in New York he estimated the Catholics in the city at twenty-five thousand, and throughout the diocese at one hundred and fifty thousand. Churches, priests, and schools were wanting for this large number of faithful. New York City had but six priests; the diocese outside the city had but four. It is strange to read in the account of his first episcopal visitation that Albany, Rochester, and Buffalo seventy years ago, though containing each a few hundred Catholics, were without resident clergymen; that Newark, Paterson, and New Brunswick were only then moving to the first steps for the building of small churches; that the one modest chapel in Brooklyn, built in 1823, was visited occasionally by priests from New York.

In every effort that the bishop made to erect churches and schools he was hampered by the trustee system, which claimed that he must surrender the whole control of the newly formed congregations to a board of laymen; a system which, as we have already seen, had produced evils in other places, and was yet to inflict irreparable woes and losses on the church in the United States ere it gave way before the persevering opposition of the hierarchy. To find some remedy for this deplorable condition, as well as to secure a seminary for the supply of clergymen to the fast-increasing number of the faithful in his diocese (he had at this time but eighteen priests for one hundred and fifty thousand Catholics), Bishop Dubois felt compelled to forego attendance on the Provincial Council about to convene in Baltimore, in order that he might repair to Rome and lay the state of his charge before the Propaganda, which, at any rate, had requested his presence in the Eternal City at an early date.

At the time of its erection (1808) the diocese of Philadelphia comprised Pennsylvania and Delaware. The first bishop, recommended by Archbishop Carroll and confirmed by the holy see, was the Rev. Michael Egan, of the Order of St. Francis, who had been for some years on the missions in Pennsylvania. When the see of Philadelphia was established there were in the city four churches attended by six priests, and outside of the city seven priests residing near as many churches. The first episcopal visitation made by Bishop Egan revealed to him the absolute need of a greater number of clergymen if the scattered Catholics of his charge were to be preserved in the practices of their faith. "Without some timely aid," he wrote to his metropolitan, the Archbishop of Baltimore, "from Europe, particularly from Ireland, I know not how to provide for the necessities of this diocese."

But a greater evil than the lack of priests threatened his administration—the rebellion of the trustees of his cathedral, the disobedience of the priests supported by them, and a schism that destroyed the faith of many and for years paralyzed the progress of the church in Philadelphia. The trustees of St. Mary's, the cathedral, had promised Archbishop Carroll, previous to the consecration of Dr. Egan, to secure to the new bishop one half of an annual salary of eight hundred dollars. But no sooner was he settled in his see than the trustees, claiming to be the owners of the cathedral, refused to pay the salary, and demanded the removal of one of the two assistant priests on the ground that there were not sufficient funds for his entertainment. This action precipitated the war. The bishop appealed to the pew-holders; the trustees stood out against the bishop and the pew-holders. The worry of it all hastened the bishop's death (July 22, 1814).

There was no little difficulty in finding a man willing to assume the onerous task of governing so troublesome a diocese as Philadelphia proved itself to be. The Rev. Ambrose Maréchal was first appointed, but he declined and returned the bulls. The Rev. John David, afterward Coadjutor of Louisville, refused the nomination. The Very Rev. Administrator of the see pending the vacancy received bulls of appointment in 1818; but he, too, refused the honor, through a sense of deep humility and of the difficulties of which he was having a sad experience

Finally, in November, 1819, the Very Rev. Henry Conwell, Vicar General of Armagh, Ireland, was chosen by the holy see, and consecrated in London, August 24, 1820. He was at the time seventy-four years of age, too old for the severe struggle that lay before him; moreover, he lacked knowledge of the character of the people he had to deal with; we shall see, too, that he did not possess that keenness of judgment and firmness of will without which it is impossible to succeed in a conflict with human pride and obstinacy.

Soon after his installation Bishop Conwell withdrew from the Rev. William Hogan, one of the priests of the cathedral, the faculties that had been temporarily granted to him by the Very Rev. Administrator during the vacancy. The reason for his action is stated to have been that Hogan openly ridiculed the bishop from the pulpit for his simplicity and a slight hesitation in speech. Thereupon began between the bishop and the trustees of the cathedral an ecclesiastical war that lasted nine years and inflicted great evils on the church in Philadelphia. Rev. William Hogan had the trustees on his side. They called a public meeting, which adopted an address to the bishop, asking the restoration of Hogan. The bishop, in a mild but firm reply, declared that in suspending Hogan he acted under a sense of duty. Hogan then issued an address attacking the character of the bishop, and went on to cite extracts from the "Corpus Juris Canonici" to prove that he was a parish priest and that canon law was established in this country, when in fact it never had been. He also called upon Archbishop Maréchal to convene a Provincial Council of all the bishops to examine his case, and forged an absurd pastoral letter, ascribed to Bishop Conwell.

This was forcing on the war with a vengeance, and so

Bishop Conwell gave notice to the congregation of the canonical steps he had taken in the case of the refractory priest, and warned them against employing his ministry or attending any service that he might attempt to hold while suspended. Bad as Hogan was, the men who supported him were far worse. Bishop England says of them that they never discharged a single duty of their religion; that they and the other members of their party were not only negligent in the performance of positive duty, but, either from ignorance of the principles of the religion which they professed, or from an utter dislike for them, were hostile to Catholic discipline. Hogan declared later on to Bishop England that he never intended opposing his bishop, but that the trustees prevailed on him to do so, and that the dread of their vengeance and exposure kept him in a place which was to him the worst species of slavery, and from which he was anxious to escape. They persuaded him to continue his functions in St. Mary's Church, though he declared that he had no longer any faculties in the diocese of Philadelphia. Bishop Conwell gave him written notice that he would be excommunicated on his first attempt to perform any ministrations as pastor of St. Mary's; but Hogan disregarded the warning and went on with his pastoral functions. This was nothing less than schism, and Bishop Conwell, after giving Hogan another monition, proceeded to the step of final excommunication, which was formally pronounced in St. Augustine's Church on the 27th of May, 1822.

Aware that there were turbulent men like themselves in New York, Norfolk, and Charleston, the Philadelphia ringleaders, Leamy, Ashley, Meade, and others, endeavored to make the schism general in the church in the United States. They issued an address which stands as a perpetual monument of their iniquity. It was entitled

"Address of the Committee of St. Mary's Church of Philadelphia to their Brethren of the Roman Catholic Faith throughout the United States of America, on the Subject of a Reform of Certain Abuses in the Administration of our Church Discipline." "Owing," they write, "to the arbitrary and unjustifiable conduct of certain foreigners, sent among us by the Junta or Commission directing the Fide Propaganda of Rome, we are imperiously called upon to adopt some measures by which a uniform system may be established for the future regulation of our churches and the propagation of our holy faith by the nomination and selection of proper pastors from our own citizens, from whom alone ought to be chosen our bishops, without our being compelled to depend on persons sent to us from abroad, who have uniformly shown themselves hostile to our institutions." After stigmatizing the bishops of the country as "a disgrace to our religion," who attempted to introduce "superstition and ignorance," they had the effrontery to speak for the Catholics of the United States and assume to represent them. It is needless to say that this anti-Catholic and revolutionary appeal met with no encouraging response from any part of the United States. It was in vain that Bishop England interposed his good offices to bring about a cessation of the scandal. The trustees were relentless and Hogan was their blind tool.

After this the tide of public opinion was set against the trustees, who saw many of their deluded adherents fall away, and felt their position growing insecure. Soon Hogan himself proposed to leave Philadelphia on being absolved from censure by Bishop Conwell; but his good resolution was prevented by the trustees. At the time when the unfortunate priest was thus throwing away his last hope of being able to persevere in his vocation and ministry, the Holy Father, Pope Pius VII., by his brief

Non sine magno, addressed to Archbishop Maréchal, his suffragans, all boards of trustees, and the faithful in general, condemned Hogan for his attack on the bishop, for withdrawing the faithful from their lawful pastor, for calling a council of bishops to depose his bishop, and, finally, for intruding himself into the cathedral church, from which he had expelled the bishop. The sovereign pontiff expressed astonishment and indignation that "in so manifest a contempt for all law he could find any followers, supporters, and defenders of his pride and contumacy." The Pope declared all the acts sacrilegiously and daringly performed by Hogan to be null and void. The immoderate right which trustees or the administrators of the temporal properties of churches assume, independently of the diocesan bishops, unless it be circumscribed by certain regulations, may prove an eternal source of abuses and dissensions. Trustees ought to bear in mind that the properties which have been consecrated to divine worship, for the support of the church, and for the maintenance of its ministers fall under the power of the church; and since the bishops, by divine appointment, preside over their respective churches, they cannot by any means be excluded from the care, superintendence, and administration of these properties. The lay element has a place and office in the administration of temporalities described and sanctioned by the Council of Trent. If the trustees in the United States were to administer the temporalities of the church in conformity to the council's decrees, and in union of mind and heart with the bishop, everything would be performed peaceably and according to order. But trusteeism in the United States has not been of this character. "In order, then, to avoid the dissensions and disturbances which frequently arise from the unbounded power of trustees, we have provided, venerable brothers, that certain regulations and instructions concerning the choice and direction of trustees should be transmitted to you. If these be observed, all things, we hope, will be settled rightly, and peace and tranquillity will again flourish in these regions."

Rev. Mr. Hogan, when the brief was made known to him, showed a disposition to submit and put an end to the schism; but the malign influence of the trustees again prevailed for a while over the unfortunate priest's better sentiments. Wearied finally by the struggle, he resigned. The trustees accepted his resignation and proceeded, in the very face of the brief of Pope Pius VII., to appoint as pastor of St. Mary's Church an unworthy adventurer, Rev. A. Inglesi, who had imposed upon Bishop Du Bourg, of New Orleans, and whose career had been fully exposed at Rome. But he came in that city with means, secured the support of the Sardinian consul in that city, and pleased the trustees, who did not even go through the form of presenting him for the bishop's approval. But soon finding Inglesi not suited to their purposes, they invited from England a certain Rev. Thaddeus J. O'Meally, and, though Bishop Conwell declined to receive him as a priest of the diocese, they prevailed upon him, in spite of the bishop's formal prohibition, to officiate in St. Mary's. He persisted in his sacrilegious course for more than a year.

Since the laity, the clergy, the hierarchy of the United States, the cardinals of the Propaganda, and the sovereign pontiff himself declared them to be in error, the trustees began to realize the fact that they must yield. They opened negotiations with the bishop, actually agreeing to recognize him as Bishop of Philadelphia, to acknowledge him as senior pastor of the church, and to admit his right to appoint priests to St. Mary's Church; but they proposed that, in case they objected to the bishop's selection of clergymen, the matter was to be decided by a committee composed of the bishop, two priests chosen by him, and three trustees selected by the board. To this Bishop Conwell, for the sake of peace, agreed. But the dishonest leaders, without the bishop's knowledge, it appears, entered on their minutes a protest virtually nullifying the agreement, in which they declared that they did not recognize the bishop as the chief pastor of St. Mary's Church, or renounce their right to appoint the clergy. When the agreement between Bishop Conwell and the trustees, and their protest nullifying what they had apparently recognized in the agreement, reached Rome, the Propaganda, to which the trustees transmitted them, made them the subject of a special meeting of cardinals. This body gave as its judgment "that the said agreement and declaration, which were the subject of debate, were to be altogether reprobated," which decree was approved by the Pope. It was a condemnation of the course adopted by Bishop Conwell, who humbly published the decree, was ordered to report to Rome, and thereafter ceased to administer the diocese. The diocese of Philadelphia contained the State in which from colonial days religion had been comparatively free, where Catholics were numerous and better endowed with the goods of this world than in most other dioceses. But the unholy war waged by the trustees of a single church against two successive bishops had this result: that in 1829 the diocese was without a seminary, a college, a convent academy for the education of young ladies, and with only a single asylum, few schools, and a disheartened people. The loss of souls to the church had been great.

CHAPTER XXI.

THE NORTHWEST AND THE SOUTHWEST (1808–29).

BARDSTOWN, once, but no longer, the see of a bishop, is a town of some two thousand souls in Nelson County, Kentucky. Pope Pius VII. erected (April, 1808) Kentucky and Tennessee into a diocese, with the episcopal see at Bardstown, and appointed as its first bishop the Rev. Benedict Joseph Flaget, a native of France and a member of the Society of St. Sulpice. With two priests and three seminarians he traveled overland to Pittsburg, descended the Ohio in a flatboat, and reached his episcopal city June 4, 1811. Nothing whatever in the shape of a church was to be found there. His installation in his cathedral was a fiction of law. Besides Kentucky and Tennessee, that formed his diocese, he had the temporary administration of the "Northwest Country," now divided into the States of Illinois, Indiana, Michigan, Wisconsin, and Ohio. In the "Northwest Country" there were small scattered Catholic communities at Kaskaskia, Cahokia, Prairie du Rocher, Ill.; Vincennes, Ind.; Detroit, Raisin River, Mackinaw, Mich.; Green Bay, Wis.; and Sandusky, O.; and all these communities were attended by three priests.

This field was not unknown to him; he had labored in it as a missionary between the years 1793 and 1795. The diocese proper of Bardstown, that is to say, Kentucky and Tennessee, was poorly provided in 1808, for it contained only ten churches—all but one of logs—and six thousand Catholics served by six priests. In 1813 the zealous bishop made a visitation of the Northwest Territory. Of this visitation he speaks in a letter to Archbishop Carroll, October 10, 1814: "My visit through the French settlements has been very laborious, but a hundred times more successful than I would have expected; I have confirmed about twelve hundred people, though I confirm none but those who have made their first communion. At least eight or ten priests are wanting in these immense countries, and if some could be put among the Indians who would be willing to receive them, ten more would scarcely do. Pray that God may send me proper ministers to convert or support so many souls that run to perdition for want of assistance." The bishop heard of certain small Catholic congregations, which he was unable to visit on account of the disturbed condition of the country. Chicago was one of these; another was Prairie du Chien, on the upper Mississippi. The southeastern part of the diocese, Tennessee, contained at most twenty-five Catholic families, scattered over a territory extending from the western border of North Carolina to the Mississippi River.

On the 11th of April, 1815, he addressed a touching letter to the sovereign pontiff, rendering an account of the diocese and district committed to his care. He was able to report that he had in Kentucky nineteen churches and ten priests. Because of the fluctuating character of the population it was not easy to fix the number of Catholics, but he estimated it at ten thousand. There was much to be done and no means to do it with. He estimated the Catholics in Ohio at fifty families, without a priest, and therefore menaced with a gradual loss of faith. As to Indiana, Vincennes had one hundred and thirty families, which, had there been good will, might easily support one or two priests; as it was, the place could only get an occasional visit from Kentucky. In Illinois he estimated the population of the three Catholic parishes, Kaskaskia, Cahokia, and Prairie du Rocher, at one hundred and twenty families. Detroit had fifteen hundred souls in St. Ann's parish, and there were five hundred on Raisin River under Rev. Gabriel Richard. There were under his jurisdiction Indian tribes among whom some traces of the faith formerly preached by the Jesuit fathers still lingered; and stretching away to the Rocky Mountains, beyond the Mississippi, were other tribes who were asking for Black Robes, and afforded a field worthy of the zeal of the Society of Jesus, just restored by his Holiness.

Feeling the burden of this diocese too heavy a weight for him to bear, Bishop Flaget asked of the holy see a coadjutor, and the Rev. John Baptist David was appointed such July 4, 1817. Not content with this relief, the bishop recommended the erection of two dioceses in the Northwest Territory, one at Detroit, the other at Cincinnati. Deeming the erection of a see at Detroit inexpedient just then, the holy see established only that of Cincinnati, and appointed thereto the Rev. Edward D. Fenwick, O. S., making him also Administrator Apostolic of Michigan and the eastern part of the Northwest Territory. Now that he was relieved of part of his former charge, and had a sufficient clergy to attend the larger congregations in Kentucky, Bishop Flaget set out in May, 1821, to visit Tennessee. The Catholics he found in and around Nashville were estimated at sixty, and not more than half as many more were in the rest of the State.

In a letter to the holy see, January, 1826, he gives a lengthy description, which may be summed up thus: Kentucky had fourteen log churches and ten of brick, two bishops, twenty-two priests, and three houses of study to which the church might look for a future supply of priests.

In Indiana the church was directed by Rev. Mr. Champaumier, struggling hard to put it on a better footing, aided by the schools of the Sisters of Charity. Other stations in Indiana were visited from Kentucky; while the priest in Breckenridge County, Kentucky, at least once a year, but as a rule more frequently, pushed his visits a hundred and fifty miles to Nashville, the only spot in Tennessee that could boast a Catholic congregation. Such was the condition of Catholicity in the diocese of Bardstown and annexed territory when Bishop Flaget set out to meet his brother bishops in the First Provincial Council of Baltimore.

By the bull *Inter Multiplices* of June 19, 1821, Ohio was erected into a diocese, with the see in Cincinnati. To the diocese was annexed the apostolic administration of so much of the Northwest Territory as is now comprised in the States of Michigan and Wisconsin. The chosen candidate, the Rev. Edward D. Fenwick, of the Order of St. Dominic, a native of Maryland and cousin to B. J. Fenwick, Bishop of Boston, was consecrated by Bishop Flaget in St. Rose's Church, Kentucky, January 13, 1822. A poor little chapel two miles outside of Cincinnati was his cathedral; a rented house of two rooms (one for himself and the other for his two priests) was his episcopal residence. As early as 1749 a Jesuit, Joseph de Bonnecamp, had traversed northern and eastern Ohio with De Blainville, who at that time was taking possession of the valley of the Ohio in the name of France. In 1751 another Jesuit, Armand de la Richardie, established a mission station at Sandusky. In 1795 the Rev. Edmund Burke began a mission, which did not last long, near Fort Miami on the Maumee River, for a few scattered bands of Ottawa, Chippeway, and Pottowatomie Indians. In 1790 a French settlement was attempted at Gallipolis, but came to naught, as we have seen elsewhere. In 1811 Bishop Flaget found a few Catholics in Cincinnati, Chillicothe, Lancaster, and Somerset, and prevailed on the Dominicans of Kentucky to take charge of them. In 1818 a log church, St. Joseph's, erected in Somerset County, and a two-story log cabin, became the cradle and nursery of Catholicity in Ohio. Gradually small congregations were formed, as emigrants from the East crossed the Alleghany Mountains, in Zanesville, Lancaster, Dungannon, and Cincinnati, which were visited by the fathers of St. Joseph. Such was the state of Catholicity in Ohio when Bishop Fenwick took possession of his see.

Wisconsin and Michigan since 1642 had been the theater, as we have seen in the first part of this history, of the heroic and romantic labors of the Jesuit missionaries. In 1822, when this territory came under the administration of the new Bishop of Cincinnati, the old mission stations were still Catholic centers, containing a population of about forty-five hundred souls. The principal points were Detroit and neighboring settlements, Mackinaw, Green Bay, and Prairie du Chien. In this extensive district there were Indians of the Ottawa, Pottowatomie, and Wyandot tribes still attached to the Catholic faith, whose number might be estimated at six thousand. That the tribes among whom the Jesuits had labored so successfully one hundred and seventy-five years before had not forgotten the devotion of the missionaries and the teachings of their religion, is made evident from a touching appeal which they sent at this time to the federal authorities for priests such as had come in former times to their forefathers.

The field was vast, the laborers few. Bishop Fenwick resolved at once to go to Rome to report this condition of things and get what help he might in men and means. His exertions obtained three priests as recruits and ten thousand dollars. He was thus enabled to replace the small chapel that served as cathedral in Cincinnati by a brick church of statelier dimensions, and to build alongside of it a residence for himself and a seminary that went by the grand name of Athenæum. It was opened May, 1829, with ten pupils, four in theology and six in the preparatory class. Meanwhile churches with congregations were beginning to spring up all over the State, and Catholicity had made a fair start on the way to progress when Bishop Fenwick departed for the First Provincial Council of Baltimore.

The Very Rev. Louis du Bourg was the Apostolic Administrator of Louisiana. He had but ten priests, and the cathedral of New Orleans was in rebellion against him. The sad condition of his charge demanded the authority and rule of a bishop. Du Bourg in 1815 proceeded to Rome to lay the dangers and the remedy before the holy see. In September of that year he was named Bishop of New Orleans and consecrated in Rome. Before his return he secured for a contemplated seminary some priests of the mission commonly known as Lazarists; inspired in a few pious ladies of Lyons a project that issued in the Association for the Propagation of the Faith, and which has since done noble work for the foreign missions; gathered funds for his diocese; got together a band of five priests, four subdeacons, some seminarians, three brothers of the Christian Schools; and with them sailed from Bordeaux June 28, 1817, in a frigate put at his disposal by the king of France. They landed at Annapolis, traveled overland to Pittsburg, descended the Ohio, remounted the Mississippi to St. Louis, where the bishop arrived January 5, 1818, and was installed in his cathedral, a poor wooden church in a ruinous condition.

He had resolved, since the trustees of New Orleans and

their tool, the Capuchin Sedella, continued in their rebellion and held the cathedral against him, to make St. Louis, in the upper portion of his diocese, then comprising all the territory known at the time as Louisiana, the center of his administration. The seminary under the charge of the four Lazarists who had preceded him was settled at the Barrens, Perry County, Mo. The Ladies of the Sacred Heart, under the superiorship of the saintly Mme. Duchesne, were established at St. Charles, and soon after at Florissant. When the Jesuits came to the West from Maryland they established themselves also in Florissant. A church and an episcopal residence, both costing twenty-five thousand dollars, were erected in St. Louis.

However, lower Louisiana was by no means neglected. New churches were built in the old parishes and the number of priests was increased. The people of New Orleans soon began to realize the mistake they had made in allowing an unworthy priest and a few irreligious laymen to drive away their bishop, with the result of raising in the upper country a rival to the old French capital. Penance followed upon punishment, and the strange spectacle was seen of the Bishop of New Orleans invited and begged to celebrate Christmas day in his cathedral. While in New Orleans the bishop held a synod to consider needs and devise means. Much had already been done, but much more remained to be done. Appeals for clergymen were constantly reaching him from all parts of his immense diocese, even from the banks of the Columbia in far-away Oregon, where lived fifteen hundred Catholics who had never seen a priest in their Western home. Moreover, Florida, since its cession to the United States by Spain (February, 1819), had been added to his charge and placed under his jurisdiction, temporarily at least, by the holy see. Bishop England, of Charleston, was in nearer communication with eastern Florida than was the Bishop of New Orleans. In consequence the latter begged the former to attend to the administration of St. Augustine and its neighborhood.

Bishop Du Bourg, conscious of his inability to give proper attention, single-handed, to the interests of his vast diocese, petitioned Rome for relief. Various plans, such as the creation of new sees in the Floridas and Louisiana and the erection of New Orleans into an archbishopric, were in turn presented to and rejected by the holy see; and it was finally decided to give Bishop Du Bourg a coadjutor in the person of the Rev. Mr. Rosati, one of the Lazarists who had founded the seminary of the Barrens. He was named Bishop of Tenagra, *in partibus infidelium*, and consecrated March 25, 1824. Bishop Du Bourg remained in New Orleans in charge of lower Louisiana. Bishop Rosati returned to St. Louis, took up his residence there, and assumed charge of upper Louisiana, that is to say, of Missouri and Arkansas, and also of western Illinois, which really belonged to the jurisdiction of Bishop Flaget, but which Bishop Rosati consented to administer at the request of the overworked Bishop of Bardstown.

Bishop Du Bourg, though relieved, at his request, of most of his cares, became discouraged, and offered his resignation to the holy see; it was accepted. He found Louisiana in a most destitute condition; he left it with twenty parishes well provided with priests, churches, and schools. It was not the state of his health that compelled him to resign, nor overwork, but opposition; as he himself declared, "It was evident my presence would be more prejudicial than useful." "It was time," writes one of his priests, "to put an end to his sufferings, and just, above all, that in the decline of his life he may enjoy a little peace and repose. The prejudice against him is so strong in this city, this sewer of all vices and refuge of all that is worst on earth, that, in spite of all his sacrifices and all his exalted ability, he could not have effected any good here. The very name of Du Bourg has an irritating sound in the ears of a great portion of this new Babylon." No such prejudice existed against his coadjutor, and Bishop Du Bourg felt that in retiring he rendered an essential service to the church. He bade farewell to New Orleans, which beheld him depart without the slightest sign of regret or repentance. He was made Bishop of Montauban, and died Archbishop of Besançon in France.

Before Bishop Du Bourg had sent in his resignation a decree issued from Rome, restricting the diocese of New Orleans to Louisiana, and annexing temporarily to New Orleans the administration of the vicariate apostolic of Mississippi. By the same decree (March 20, 1827) St. Louis was erected into a see, with upper Louisiana—an indefinite territory—as a diocese. After the resignation of Bishop Du Bourg, Rosati, now Bishop of St. Louis, was appointed Administrator of New Orleans until an incumbent should be named for that see. Meanwhile he lived in St. Louis, rivaling his brother bishops in the other sections of the republic by his apostolic zeal, energetic efforts for progress, and his wide missionary travels. The diocese of St. Louis embraced Missouri with the territory of Arkansas. In St. Louis the church begun by Bishop Du Bourg during his former residence there was still unfinished, financial troubles having driven away some and prevented others from meeting their subscriptions. Carondelet, Florissant, St. Charles, Ste. Geneviève, the Barrens, and New Madrid were the principal points where Catholics were to be found, and religious institutions were established. The Catholic population was largely of French origin, with a small Spanish sprinkling.

In western Illinois, the temporary administration of which Bishop Rosati had assumed at the request of Bishop Flaget, Kaskaskia had one hundred and fifty families; Prairie du Rocher had one hundred, the church there being under the care of Rev. Donatien Olivier, now seventy-five years old and almost blind; O'Hara's Settlement had a growing English-speaking flock, eager for a priest; and Cahokia, an old French village, had a church and an aged priest. In 1824 Rev. John M. Odin, accompanied by Rev. John Timon, then in subdeacon's orders, set out on a missionary journey, their definitive point being Arkansas Post, where the Catholics had long been without mass or sacraments. Near Davidsonville and at Little Rock they found Catholics who had never seen a priest. On the Arkansas River was a cluster of sixteen Catholic families, who reported that mass had twice been offered there. Arkansas Post was the only place where there were enough Catholics to maintain a clergyman. Everywhere the missionaries had to begin by teaching grown-up children the elementary doctrines, practices, and prayers of religion. The parents had endeavored to keep up the faith, and had given private baptism to their children. The celebration of the mass was for the children a strange ceremony, for the parents one they welcomed back with joy.

The period of Bishop Rosati's administration of New Orleans was marked by a new condemnation of trusteeism by Rome, and by the passing away of the unfortunate clergyman who for years had been the bane of the church in lower Louisiana. The trustees of St. Louis' Cathedral in New Orleans endeavored to secure the passage of a law vesting in them the right to appoint and remove priests. We have seen that a similar claim made at Philadelphia had been condemned by Pope Pius VII., and that Bishop Conwell had been reproved for even indirectly admitting it. Moreover, the New Orleans trustees claimed ownership of the cathedral, as representing the Catholics of the city, though they had not bought the ground or erected the church, since the site had been given by the king of Spain, and the church had been built by Señor Almonaster under an agreement with the king. Bishop Rosati laid the matter before Pope Leo XII., who in answer issued the brief *Quo Longius*, confirming the letters apostolic of Pope Pius VII. against the trustees of St. Mary's Church, Philadelphia. The fomenter of the troubles in the church of New Orleans, the Capuchin Anthony Sedella, soon after passed away. He died apparently in full communion with the church, but his funeral was turned into an anti-Catholic demonstration, and the city lodges of Freemasons accompanied it by a special order of the Grand Lodge of the State.

The bulls appointing the Rev. Michael Portier to the newly erected vicariate apostolic of Alabama and Florida found that clergyman presiding over a college in New Orleans and unwilling to accept the charge. But he had to yield to renewed orders from Rome, and was consecrated in St. Louis, November 5, 1822. In Alabama there was the old French settlement of Mobile, with a resident priest, a church much in need of repair, and about ten thousand Catholics. There were also a few scattered Catholics at Huntsville, Florence, and Tuscumbia. In western Florida there was the old Spanish town of Pensacola, with a resident priest and a small congregation. The bishop visited both these centers, then made his way to Tallahassee, where he found but a few Catholics, and thence to St. Augustine, which had been deprived of the services of a priest for years. Here for two weeks he preached a mission to the faithful. One hundred and twenty-five persons received the holy eucharist, and sixty children were baptized. In the old Spanish part of Florida, along the coast, and especially in St. Augustine, the greater number of the Catholics were Minorcans. A word about them.

By the treaty of 1763 Florida passed from Spain to England. The former Spanish subjects, under the impression that the change was to be of brief duration, gave no indication of retiring from their homes. But the harsh administration of the English officials caused them soon to change their mind, and they emigrated almost in a body. In violation of the treaty made at the time of the surrender, the property of the Catholic Church—churches, convents, hospitals—was seized without compensation and turned to secular uses. All trace of former Catholicity was swept from the soil of Florida. A few years later, in 1768, fourteen hundred Minorcans, Italians and Greeks, were imported into Florida and located at Mosquito Inlet by an English company chartered for the raising and manufacturing of sugar and indigo. There a church, San Pedro of Mosquito, was erected into a parish by the Bishop of Santiago, under whose jurisdiction the province continued, and was served by two priests who came with the colonists to minister to their spiritual wants. The treatment of this colony by the English company was cruel, nine hundred perishing in nine years. Goaded to desperation by the ill treatment of their English employers, they rose in resistance (1777) and made their way—six hundred of them, including two hundred children born in Florida—to St. Augustine. The governor, Moultrie, having become convinced of the justness of their cause, assigned to them a part of the city of St. Augustine. None of the churches or religious houses of Spanish days were given them, some being in ruins, others being occupied by troops; so that they were compelled to hold services in private houses. It was the descendants of these refugees who formed in great part the congregation of St. Augustine in the first quarter of the century.

On his return to Mobile, Bishop Portier was pained to find that the two priests of Mobile and Pensacola had left their posts for the diocese of New Orleans, to which they originally belonged. He was now without a priest of his own in his vast vicariate, and without resources of any kind. He embarked for Europe to seek the aid he needed.

Let us now resume the history of the progress of this period (1790–1829). At the opening of the First Provincial Council of Baltimore (October 4, 1829) the hierarchy of the United States was constituted thus: (*a*) the province of Baltimore, containing the sees of Baltimore, Boston, New York, Philadelphia, Bardstown, Charleston, Cincinnati; (*b*) outside the province of Baltimore three dioceses having no center in this country, but depending directly upon the Propaganda in Rome—New Orleans, St. Louis, the vicariate of Alabama and Florida. It was only the incumbents and the coadjutors of the sees within the province of Baltimore that were the regular, the canonical members of the council. The incumbents of the outside dioceses, Bishops Rosati and Portier—New Orleans was vacant—were invited to take part in the general consultations as to the best means of advancing religion in the United States; however, before the council was concluded, Bishop Portier was made a suffragan of Baltimore. The collective letter of the fathers of the council to Pius VIII. sums up the progress and the condition of the church at the time; we transcribe it:

"Not two centuries have elapsed since, in a remote and obscure corner of Maryland, a little band of Catholics, guided by a few missionaries, exiles from their native land, flying from the cruel persecution inflicted on them for adhering to the faith of their forefathers, laid the foundation of this American church. It is scarcely forty years since this body of the faithful in the United States of America was found sufficient to demand, in the opinion of the sovereign pontiff, the erection of the first episcopal see of Baltimore. Not twenty years have rolled by since a decree of the holy pontiff, Pius VII., exalted the church of Baltimore to the dignity and rights of a metropolitan; and, like a joyful mother of children, she has beheld in recently erected suffragan dioceses, quickened by a heaven-bestowed fruitfulness, an offspring in new churches which she has borne to Christ. We see so many blessings bestowed by God on these rising churches, such increase given to this vineyard, that those who planted and those who watered, and those who harvested and tread the overflowing wine-press, are compelled to confess and admire wholly the finger of God.

"The number of the faithful increases daily; churches not unworthy of divine worship are everywhere erected; the Word of God is preached everywhere, and not without fruit; the hatred and prejudice spread against the church and faithful vanish; holy religion, once despised and held in contempt, receives honor from her very enemies; the priests of Christ are venerated even by those without; the truth and divinity of our faith is proclaimed and vindicated from the calumny of heresy and unbelief, not only in churches and from pulpits, but from the press in widely scattered periodicals and books. Six ecclesiastical seminaries, the hope of our churches, have already been established, and are governed in holy discipline by pious and learned priests; nine colleges under ecclesiastical control have been erected in different States to train boys and young men in piety, arts, and higher branches of science; three of these have been chartered as universities by the legislatures; thirty-three monasteries and houses of religious women of different orders and congregations—Ursulines, Visitandines, Carmelites, Sacred Heart, Sisters of Charity, Loretto, etc.—are everywhere established in our dioceses, whence emanate not only the observance of the evangelical counsels and the exercise of all other virtues, but the good order of Christ in the pious training of innumerable girls; houses of religious of the Order of Preachers and the Society of Jesus, of secular priests of the Congregation of the Mission and of St. Sulpice, from which, as centers, priests are sent out to missions; many schools where the poor of both sexes are taught gratuitously; hospitals carried on by religious women, who daily give signs of heroic charity, to the great benefit of souls and of religion. These, Most Holy Father, are the signal benefits which God has bestowed upon us in a few years."

Yes, there was prosperity, thanks to the innate life and vigor of the church herself, and also to the liberty guaranteed by the Constitution. Since the declaration and acquisition of independence they had helped to secure, Catholics had remained true and loyal to the United States and its institutions. There was nothing in their record to justify a revival of the colonial spirit of opposition and persecution. Yet that evil spirit had not been entirely laid and exorcised in the land; it remained as a smoldering fire ready to burst forth at the first fanning of the embers. Such a fanning came from the violent anti-Catholic literature called into existence in England by the movement for Catholic emancipation. A religious and political storm, which was finally to burst upon us as Know-nothingism, was steadily looming up, a menace to the friendliness and peace that had heretofore reigned between all classes in the United States, a menace to the inalienable rights of the church and of Catholics, a menace to liberty, life, and property. We shall see, as we approach the middle of the century, how our hierarchy was forced to take notice of this movement and counsel their flocks to calmness and patience in the presence of the danger.

Part II. The Growth of the Church from the First Provincial Council of Baltimore to the First Plenary Council (1829–52.)

CHAPTER XXII.

BALTIMORE AND ITS SUFFRAGANS (1829–52).

The year 1829 is generally accepted as a turning-point in the history of the United States. The Presidency of Andrew Jackson was the culmination of a process of material growth and institutional expansion. The population of the country had increased from about four millions to almost thirteen millions within the forty years that had elapsed since the formation of the federal government in 1789. The nation had succeeded in planting new homes and creating new States in the territory which lay between the Eastern mountains and the Mississippi. A new nation had been born and nurtured in the West; the old Eastern colonies could no longer expect to dictate the politics of the republic. In the increase of the population since 1789 immigration had not been a prominent factor; but after 1829 the incoming of Europeans became a marked characteristic of our growth, to an extent so vast as to excite the jealousy of the descendants of the former colonists and call into existence the semi-political, semi-religious movement known in our history as Native Americanism, which degenerated by a natural process into Know-nothingism. Of this strange movement, which was not American, but originated with disappointed and turbulent men thrown on our shores by the European revolutions of 1848–50, much will be said in the following pages.

Since 1811 the steamboat, after 1830 the railroad, facilitated the distribution of immigrants throughout the West, and by easier transportation assured the predominance of the great agricultural States beyond the Alleghanies. It was precisely in the same direction that the church found her greatest growth and progress. Within the period of little more than nine years, from 1812 to 1821, seven States were admitted to the Union. The aggregate population of the States which had been created in the West was almost half as great as the aggregate population of the States which had formed the Union in 1789. It was not a period of great civic agglomerations, but of rural communities. Not many manufactures had been developed; the people were absorbed in conquering nature—felling the forests, plowing the prairies, and erecting homes. Everything was conditioned by the newness of the country—literature, schools, and social manners. The general characteristics of the national life will be found also in the Catholic life of the period.

One more suffragan see was erected since the holding of the First Provincial Council, that of Detroit. It was represented by its bishop, the Rt. Rev. Frederic Résé, in the Second Provincial Council, held in October, 1833. This Second Provincial Council asked the sovereign pontiff to erect a see at Vincennes, the diocese to embrace Indiana and eastern Illinois, and to reunite canonically Virginia to the diocese of Baltimore by suppressing the see of Richmond. A plan for nominating candidates to vacant or new sees was proposed to the sovereign pontiff. When the acts of the council reached Rome, it was not deemed best to suppress the see of Richmond, but the other suggestions of the council were approved. Pope Gregory XVI., by the bull *Benedictus Deus* (June 17, 1834), fixed more exactly, the limits of the several existing dioceses and the Congregation de Propaganda Fide prescribed the mode to be observed in nominating to vacant sees, which is not described here because it is no longer in use, having been superseded by another system which will be noticed in its place.

The pastoral letter issued by the council alluded to the calumnies current against Catholics in the press of the time: "We advise you to heed them not, but to continue, whilst you serve your God with fidelity, to discharge honestly, faithfully, and with affectionate attachment your duties to the government under which you live, so that we may, in common with our fellow-citizens, sustain that edifice of rational liberty in which we find such excellent protection. We notice with regret a spirit exhibited by some of the conductors of the press engaged in the interests of those brethren separated from our communion, which has within a few years become more unkind and unjust in our regard. Not only do they assail us and our institutions in a style of vituperation and offense, misrepresent our tenets, vilify our practices, repeat the hundred-times-refuted calumnies of the days of angry and bitter contention in other lands, but they have even denounced you and us as enemies to the liberties of the republic, and have openly proclaimed the fancied necessity of obstructing our progress, and of using their best efforts to extirpate our religion. It is neither our principle nor our practice to render evil for evil, nor railing for railing, and we exhort you rather to the contrary, to render blessing; 'for unto this are you called, that you by inheritance may obtain a blessing.'"

In view of his declining health, Archbishop Whitfield asked that a coadjutor be given him in the person of Rev. Samuel Eccleston, president of St. Mary's College. The holy see acceded to the request, and the consecration of the candidate took place September 14, 1834. About a month later (October 19th) Archbishop Whitfield passed to his eternal reward. In 1837 Archbishop Eccleston convened and presided over the Third Provincial Council of Baltimore. It was attended by Bishops Rosati of St. Louis, Fenwick of Boston, Kenrick, Coadjutor of Philadelphia, Purcell of Cincinnati, Chabrat, Coadjutor of Bardstown, Clancy, Coadjutor of Charleston, Bruté, Bishop of Vincennes, and Blanc, Bishop of New Orleans. Bishop Dubois, of New York, was unavoidably absent. Pope Gregory XVI. acceded to the requests made by this council for the erection of the sees of Pittsburg, Nashville, and Dubuque.

The Fourth Provincial Council of Baltimore assembled on the 16th of May, 1840, under the Most Rev. Samuel Eccleston, and was attended by Bishops Flaget of Bardstown, Rosati of St. Louis, Fenwick of Boston, Portier of Mobile, Kenrick of Philadelphia, Purcell of Cincinnati, Blanc of New Orleans, Loras of Dubuque, Miles of Nashville, De la Hailandière of Vincennes, and also by Mgr. Charles Augustus Joseph de Forbin-Janson, Bishop of Nancy and Toul, Primate of Lorraine, who happened to be in America at the time and was invited to the council. Of the infamous anti-Catholic literature that was being poured on the country the pastoral letter issued by this council said: "The miserable libels have had their day;

their compilers and the unfortunate and degraded instruments of their guilt, if not already fallen to their proper level, are fast sinking in the estimation of those whom they sought to delude." But though dishonest attacks were still made on Catholics and their faith, they were urged to bear the persecution patiently, to pray for their enemies, and to avoid all temptation to retaliate. The council requested the holy see to restore autonomy to the diocese of Richmond, and recommended for that see the Rev. Richard Vincent Whelan; advised the erection of a see at Natchez, and proposed for it Rev. John J. Chanche; and proposed Rev. John M. Odin as Coadjutor and Administrator of the diocese of Detroit, left vacant by the resignation of Bishop Rèsé.

The Fifth Provincial Council was held in the Cathedral of Baltimore, May, 1843. The fathers of the council solicited from the sovereign pontiff the erection of sees at Hartford, Chicago, Little Rock, Milwaukee, and Oregon. They also proposed candidates for the see of Charleston and coadjutors for Boston and New York. The flood of Native Americanism was steadily mounting, and though it had not yet broken out into overt acts of persecution, still the Protestant public was being educated by a campaign of calumnies. The council alludes to this dangerous state of things in its collective letter: "To you we trust for the practical refutation of all those atrocious calumnies which deluded men, severally or in odious combinations, constantly circulate by every possible means against our holy religion. Your strict integrity in the daily concerns of life, your fidelity in the fulfillment of all engagements, your peaceful demeanor, your obedience to the laws, your respect for the public functionaries, your unaffected exercise of charity in the many occasions which the miseries and sufferings of our fellow-men present—in fine, your sincere virtue—will confound those vain men whose ingenuity and industry are exerted to cast suspicion on our principles and evoke against us all the worst passions of human nature."

Each Provincial Council added to the number of dioceses and bishops, as the following list of attendants on the Sixth Provincial Council shows: Archbishop Eccleston, Bishops Portier of Mobile, Purcell of Cincinnati, Chabrat, Coadjutor of Louisville, Blanc of New Orleans, Loras of Dubuque, Hughes of New York, Miles of Nashville, De la Hailandière of Vincennes, Chanche of Natchez, Whelan of Richmond, Kenrick of St. Louis, Odin, Vicar Apostolic of Texas, O'Connor of Pittsburg, Byrne of Little Rock, Quarter of Chicago, McCloskey, Coadjutor of New York, Tyler of Hartford, Reynolds of Charleston, Kenrick of Philadelphia, Henni of Milwaukee, and Fitzpatrick, Coadjutor of Boston. The progress of the church was mainly in the North Atlantic States, Maryland, and the West. The State of New York, with part of New Jersey, had hitherto been one diocese, and the State of Ohio also one diocese: The former, at the commencement of 1846, contained a Catholic population of two hundred thousand, with one hundred and nine priests and one hundred and fourteen churches. Bishop Hughes, believing that the good of religion demanded the erection of new sees in his district, solicited in this council the establishment of bishoprics at Albany and Buffalo. With the same view, Bishop Purcell, who had in his diocese sixty priests and seventy churches, with sixty-five thousand Catholics, solicited the erection of a see in Cleveland. These proposals were adopted by the fathers of the council and laid before the sovereign pontiff for his approval.

Up to the year 1846 the Archbishop of Baltimore was the only metropolitan in the United States; but in that year a rival archiepiscopal see arose in the farther Northwest, and the erection of this second metropolis entailed the creation of a third one. The diocese of St. Louis had no fixed limits to the west; it was regarded as extending to the Pacific coast, and, in fact, sent missionaries to the Rocky Mountains and beyond. England, however, claimed the territory on the Pacific north of California. The holy see, apparently unaware of the ultimately recognized claims of the United States, treated Oregon as British territory, and on the 1st of December, 1843, erected there a vicariate apostolic, connecting it virtually with the hierarchy of Canada. In July, 1846, Oregon City was made an archiepiscopal see, and suffragan sees were erected at Walla Walla and Vancouver Island, while other neighboring districts were laid off for future dioceses. The Bishop of St. Louis thus beheld a whole ecclesiastical province created in a region that he had always considered as being within his own diocese. When the authorities in Rome came to see their mistake and recognized that Oregon was United States territory and therefore within the jurisdiction of St. Louis, this latter was made a metropolitan see by Pius IX. (October, 1847), with Dubuque, Nashville, Chicago, and Milwaukee as suffragans.

This made three ecclesiastical provinces in the United States. There was a general wish that the archbishops and bishops of the three provinces should meet in a council embracing and representing the whole country. To carry out this view, Archbishop Eccleston issued (September 23, 1848) letters to the Most Rev. Archbishops and Rt. Rev. Bishops, convoking a Plenary Council. The original plan was not carried out, however, as the Archbishop of Oregon City and his suffragans represented that on account of the great distance they could not very well attend. The council held in May, 1849, was accordingly styled the Seventh Provincial Council of Baltimore, though among its members were the two Archbishops of Baltimore and St. Louis. It was therefore improperly called a Provincial Council, and yet was not a Plenary Council, since the province of Oregon was not represented. It resolved to solicit the holy see to make the following metropolitan sees: New Orleans, with Mobile, Natchez, Little Rock, and Galveston as suffragans; Cincinnati, with Louisville, Detroit, Vincennes, and Cleveland as suffragans; and New York, with Boston, Hartford, Albany, and Buffalo as suffragans. The erection of more dioceses was solicited, viz., of Savannah and Wheeling, to be included in the province of Baltimore; and of St. Paul and the vicariates of New Mexico and the Indian Territory, to be included in the province of St. Louis.

The holy see acceded to the requests of the council. The ecclesiastical province of Baltimore, which heretofore had contained all the dioceses of the country, or, to be more exact, all the dioceses east of the Mississippi, was thus narrowed down to the dioceses of Baltimore, Philadelphia, Pittsburg, Richmond, Wheeling, Charleston, and Savannah. Baltimore, at first the original diocese, then the original archbishopric, had gradually branched out into other dioceses and provinces. We shall see that in the course of time these new provinces were in turn subdivided and brought forth other provinces. It was by such an evolution that the present administrative condition of the church in the United States was reached, viz., fourteen ecclesiastical provinces or archbishoprics, containing seventy-one suffragan dioceses, with the prefecture apostolic of Alaska.

Archbishop Eccleston died in May, 1851; in the following August the Rt. Rev. Francis Patrick Kenrick,

Bishop of Philadelphia, was transferred to the see of Baltimore and was named by brief (August 19, 1851) apostolic delegate, with power to convoke and preside over a Plenary Council which was to convene in May, 1852. Though an archbishop may without special authorization convoke to a Provincial Council his own suffragans, he needs authorization from the holy see to convoke to a Plenary Council other archbishops and their suffragans. The era of Plenary Councils begins.

Richmond had been erected into a diocese in 1820 without the knowledge or consent of the American hierarchy, as we have already explained. So little was the new diocese prepared for the maintenance of a bishop that the first incumbent was unable to find support, and was transferred in 1822 to a diocese in Ireland, the country of his birth and of his priestly career. Since that time Richmond had been annexed to Baltimore, and recovered its autonomy only in 1841, when some hope was given that it might be able to maintain a bishop. The candidate chosen for the restored see was Richard Vincent Whelan, a native of Baltimore and a zealous missionary of that diocese. The Catholic population of Virginia did not exceed six thousand, under the care of five clergymen.

Wheeling, in the western part of the State, was giving promise of a quicker and larger growth than Richmond. Climate, soil, a great natural highway, the Ohio, and above all the comparative absence of slave labor, invited emigration. On the representations of Bishop Whelan the Seventh Provincial Council of Baltimore requested the holy see to form Western Virginia into a new diocese, with Wheeling as the episcopal see. So it was done in July, 1850, and Bishop Whelan was transferred from Richmond to Wheeling. He was succeeded in Richmond (November

10, 1850) by the Rev. John McGill, a native of Philadelphia and a priest of the diocese of Bardstown.

The increase in Catholic population and the progress of the church had never been so marked in the Southern as in the Northern and Western States. Many causes might be assigned for this fact. Let it suffice to name one. Emigration did not flow in the direction of the South, mainly because of slavery. Charleston was not, therefore, a fit field for a man of the temperament and gifts of Bishop England. His ideas were large, his projects vast, his activity relentless, but his environment cramped him. No American bishop of his day journeyed more frequently to Rome, and none was better known there and exercised more influence.

However, a wider field than his own slowly progressing diocese was opened to the boundless energy of the "steam-bishop," as he was called in Rome. The holy see appointed him apostolic delegate to visit Hayti and arrange with the government of that island for a reorganization of the church which would revive religion and morality. Bishop England sailed (December 18, 1833) for Hayti, where an archbishop had once presided with metropolitan jurisdiction over the West Indies and our southern coast. England was requested to report on its religious condition and to give his advice as to the best policy to be pursued. He found there about seventy priests, governed by vicars appointed by the last archbishop. After visiting Guadalupe and St. Thomas he returned to his diocese, and in April, 1834, set out for Rome to give an account of his Haytian mission. The sovereign pontiff was so well satisfied with the report that he reappointed Bishop England apostolic delegate, with more ample powers to make definite arrangements between the holy see and the President of Hayti for the proper reorganization of the church. As this would entail a long absence from his diocese, the bishop solicited the appointment of a coadjutor. Among the names proposed by him was that of Dr. Cullen, then superior of the Irish College. Failing to obtain the future Cardinal of Dublin, he proposed Rev. William Clancy, a native of Cork and professor of theology in Carlow College, who was accordingly appointed. This appointment was a sad mistake. Bishop Clancy was a complete stranger to the United States and never became American either in thought or sympathy. His temper was difficult, and he saw in our institutions only matter for censure. In less than a year he solicited his transfer to another field of labor.

The end of Bishop England's career was worthy of his long and active life. In 1840, on a homeward journey from Europe, he contracted ship-fever while attending to the fever-stricken steerage passengers, and reached Charleston in a state of great prostration. His stirring life came to an end April 11, 1842.

So passed away one of the most remarkable men in the history of the church in America. Thoroughly devoted to his duties, he never spared himself; he was constantly traveling through his diocese or abroad for its good. His general learning was great, he was fond of literary and scientific studies, and his mind retained and classified all it acquired. With little leisure at his command, he was a prolific writer, able and cogent in controversy; an eloquent speaker, ready to address any audience—the Congress at Washington, a learned society, the humblest of his own flock, or a congregation of non-Catholics—with such a flowing tide of eloquence, such a rich fund of illustration, that all minds and hearts were swayed. He was prudent and practical, and in the councils of the church here and at Rome acquired an influence which could not be accorded to one not really great. His works, collected and published by his successor, Rt. Rev. Dr. Reynolds, remain one of the great treasures of our literature.

After his death the diocese of Charleston passed into the hands of an administrator, the Very Rev. R. S. Baker, until the consecration of Bishop England's successor, the Rt. Rev. Ignatius Aloysius Reynolds (March 19, 1844). The three States contained in the diocese of Charleston at the time of his consecration had a population of two million, out of which twelve thousand were Catholics; "but few wealthy," he states, "and of those few some are only nominal members of the church." The diocese was burdened with a debt, small in itself and according to our present views, but heavy for such a small population and the circumstances of those times. In 1845 Bishop Reynolds went to Europe to seek relief, but met with very little encouragement or success. The financial forces of his clergy and people were taxed to the utmost to sustain the seminary and build the cathedral. Not for long, however, could he carry the burden of the seminary; it ceased to exist in 1851, with a glorious record, nevertheless, for it had furnished many priests to the church since its establishment by Bishop England.

Notwithstanding the small number of Catholics in the southern section of the country, the Seventh Council of Baltimore judged it expedient to ask the erection of a see in Savannah, with jurisdiction over Georgia and Florida east of the Appalachicola River. The diocese of Charleston was in consequence left with the two Carolinas and a Catholic population of about eight thousand. The candidate for the new diocese was the Rev. F. X. Gartland, born in Dublin, but brought up from childhood in the United States. He was consecrated in Philadelphia,

November 10, 1850. The new diocese contained small chapels at Savannah, Augusta, Locust Grove, Washington, Mason, Atlanta, Columbus, and St. Mary's in the State of Georgia; and at St. Augustine, Key West, and Tallahassee in Florida. Bishop Gartland attended the First Plenary Council of Baltimore, but did not survive long; he died, a victim to yellow fever, September 20, 1854.

The most important in size, numbers, and wealth of the suffragan dioceses of Baltimore was Philadelphia. The trustee schism had given it a sad prominence in the preceding period (1808–29). A violent and disastrous outbreak of Native Americanism gave it a no less sad prominence in the present period (1829–52). The Very Rev. William Mathews did not remain long burdened with the administration of the diocese of Philadelphia; for on June 6, 1830, the Rev. Francis Patrick Kenrick, named by the holy see coadjutor to the Bishop of Philadelphia and administrator of that diocese, was consecrated with the title of Bishop of Arath, *in partibus infidelium.* He at once assumed the administration of the tormented diocese, and struck at the center of all the evils that had afflicted it in the past, the board of trustees of his cathedral, St. Mary's Church. After maturely considering the state of affairs, he resolved to assume the pastoral charge of St. Mary's, and notified the trustees of that church "that being duly and exclusively invested by the apostolic see with episcopal jurisdiction for the government of the diocese of Philadelphia, he should himself act as chief pastor of the Church of St. Mary's," and that he appointed Rev. Jeremiah Keily as his assistant. The trustees asked him to reconsider his resolution, threatening to maintain against him the rights of the congregation as they understood them.

Thereupon Bishop Kenrick addressed a letter to the pew-holders (April 12, 1831), announcing that it would be his duty, in compliance with the decrees of the Council of Baltimore, to interdict the church, "unless all opposition be forthwith withdrawn, and the Catholic principles of church government be unequivocally admitted." An evasive answer came from them, and Bishop Kenrick ordered the cessation of all sacred functions in St. Mary's Church and its burial-ground after twelve o'clock of April 16th, unless the trustees signed a distinct disclaimer of their pretensions. This they explicitly declined to do, and the church was formally interdicted. "A small and contemptible faction," Bishop Kenrick wrote in a pastoral letter, "by intrigues and misrepresentations has succeeded in resisting my pastoral rights, and has forced me to have recourse to a measure of severity to which no bishop more than I can be averse. The gates of St. Mary's open every Sunday morning to receive a few murmurers, who amidst the tombs utter their plaints, because the consolations of religion have been withdrawn from those who in defiance of its authority sought to establish a tribunal of eight laymen to approve or reject at pleasure episcopal appointments. This just measure, which was imperiously demanded, has humbled and mortified the party, and gratified the great body of Philadelphia Catholics, who are sincerely attached to the doctrine and government of the church. There has hitherto been no excitement, the Catholics worshiping peaceably in the other churches." The trustees, failing to entrap Bishop Conwell, living in retirement in the city, whom they sought to use as a tool against the coadjutor and administrator, finally submitted. Then Bishop Kenrick reopened St. Mary's Church, and thus Philadelphia's long period of schism and rebellion came to an end.

Having thus overpowered the one great enemy to the church's progress, he turned his attention to the clergy, which naturally enough had been neglected during the struggles of trusteeism. He convoked a synod for May 13, 1832, which was preceded by a spiritual retreat. Thirty priests attended; nine were absent from age, ill health, or other valid excuses. Wise statutes were enacted securing ecclesiastical discipline; but the bishop knew that the one great means to such a desirable end was the training of his own priests in a diocesan seminary. This became the main object of his thoughts and labors. He recommended the project to his people, he sought aid for it abroad. In thanking the Leopoldine Association for its generosity in aiding the seminary, Bishop Kenrick estimated the Catholic population of his diocese at one hundred thousand, one fourth of them being in the city of Philadelphia. He had only thirty-eight priests—twenty-nine diocesan, the others being Jesuits, Augustinians, and Franciscans—to attend to fifty churches and many stations. Several of the priests were yielding to the influence of age and infirmities, so that it was vitally important to train young Levites to lighten their labors and in time succeed them. He was able to realize his wish in 1835, when the seminary was opened in his own residence and directed by himself.

The reader, however, must not imagine that all the energies and time of the bishop were given to the city of Philadelphia and the internal administration of his diocese. He devoted not less than three months of every year to visiting even the remotest parts of his charge. These visitations proved to him that the diocese was far too extensive for one bishop conscientiously to fulfill all the duties of supervision and detail. He explained to the Congregation de Propaganda Fide the immense labor required, and earnestly urged the erection of a see at Pittsburg, a city with eight thousand Catholics and two churches. The Congregation de Propaganda Fide yielded to the views of Bishop Kenrick; but, when the matter was laid before the Pope, canonical objections raised by Bishop England prevailed against the advice and wish of not only Bishop Kenrick, but the whole hierarchy of the country. Thus was he left to bear alone for nearly ten years more the heavy and daily increasing burden. In 1840 the Catholic population in the diocese of Philadelphia was estimated at one hundred and twenty thousand, with about seventy churches. However, the Fifth Provincial Council of Baltimore succeeded in persuading the Propaganda of the necessity of a division. The bulls erecting the diocese of Pittsburg were issued August 7, 1843, and the Rev. Michael O'Connor was consecrated its first bishop in Rome, whither he had gone to be freed, if possible, of the burden of the episcopate.

The territory left to Philadelphia after this division embraced the eastern portion of the State of Pennsylvania, the State of Delaware, and the western portion of New Jersey. In the diocese thus reduced not many new settlements grew up; the immigration that came was easily incorporated in congregations already organized, until they grew by acquired and natural increase to such a size as to require division. Though for a period newly erected churches were not frequent, yet there was a growth and increase of religion in stricter ecclesiastical discipline, in better provisions for the spiritual needs of the faithful, in educational and charitable works. The diocese of Philadelphia, as reduced by the diocese of Pittsburg, contained fifty-one churches in Pennsylvania, four in New Jersey, and three in Delaware, attended by twenty-nine diocesan priests, seven Jesuits, and four Augustinians.

We have frequently alluded in the preceding pages to the anti-Catholic sentiment that was sweeping over the country, and to the wise and mild precautions the hierarchy had been taking against it by advising to their flocks patience and calmness in the presence of calumnies, threats, and dangers. The spirit of political bigotry, however, was not to be balked by the spirit of Christian forbearance. The time was ripe for action; only a pretext was wanting. The City of Brotherly Love furnished the pretext and became the theater of fierce Know-nothing riots.

In the schools of Philadelphia the Protestant version of the Bible was used. The bishop petitioned the school board to allow to the Catholic children the use of the Catholic version. The petition was misrepresented and made the occasion of a violent pamphlet. In a card issued on the 12th of March the bishop explained himself: "Catholics have not asked that the Bible be excluded from the public schools. They have merely desired for their children the liberty of using the Catholic version in case the reading of the Bible be prescribed by the controllers or directors of the schools. They only desire to enjoy the benefit of the Constitution of the State of Pennsylvania, which guarantees the rights of conscience and precludes any preference of sectarian modes of worship. They desire that the public schools be preserved from all sectarian influence, and that education be conducted in a way that may enable all citizens equally to share in its benefits, without any violence being offered to their religious convictions."

But it was impossible to so present the question that the public would view it calmly. The Native American party, already well organized, caught readily at the opportunity. Meetings were held in which Protestant ministers took an active part, and thousands were induced to believe that Catholics wished to prevent Protestant children from reading their own Bible, when, in fact, Catholics asked merely that the Protestant Bible should not be forced upon Catholic children. As the election time approached a plot was formed to provoke a disturbance in Philadelphia, and, under cover of it, to destroy the Catholic churches. A Native American meeting was called in which violent language was used against the Irish. A storm of rain compelled the crowd to seek refuge in a neighboring market-house. In the rush collisions took place, blows were struck, and firearms were used. At ten o'clock that night the Native Americans gathered a mob and began an attack on the houses occupied by Irish families in Franklin and Second streets. The inmates fled, and the mob, after destroying all they could lay hands on, set fire to the buildings, which were soon consumed. An attempt was made by those who were attacked to defend their lives and property, and some of the rioters were slain. Then the cry was raised, "To the nunnery!" A rush was made for the house which was occupied by a little community of Sisters of Charity on the corner of Second and Phœnix streets; but a volley from a few defenders drove the rioters off for a time.

The riot thus far had resulted in the death and wounding of several men and the wanton destruction of private property. Ever a friend of peace, Bishop Kenrick next day printed and posted conspicuously throughout the city this card:

"*To the Catholics of the City and County of Philadelphia:*

"The melancholy riot of yesterday, which resulted in the death of several of our fellow-beings, calls for our deep sorrow, and it becomes all who have had any share in this tragical scene to humble themselves before God and to sympathize deeply and sincerely with those whose relatives and friends have fallen. I earnestly conjure you all to avoid all occasions of excitement, and to shun all public places of assemblage, and to do nothing that in any way may exasperate. Follow peace with all men, and have that charity without which no man can see God.

"FRANCIS PATRICK,

"*Bishop of Philadelphia.*"

But the conspirators had no wish for peace. This placard was torn down, and a meeting was called, which, after being roused to the highest pitch of violence by the speakers, moved in a body to Kensington. There they attacked the Hibernia hose-house, which was soon destroyed, with its contents, and twenty-nine houses inhabited by Irish people were set on fire. Such was the condition of affairs when the First Brigade and two companies of the Third Brigade under General Cadwalader appeared on the scene; further violence was prevented, but the fire department made no effort to save the burning houses.

The next day a mob gathered at St. Michael's Church and set it on fire, as well as the priest's residence. No attempt was made by the militia or firemen to prevent the deed or check the fire, though the militia were on the ground. St. Augustine's Church, in Fourth Street, was threatened. Here some show of protection was made. Mayor Scott stationed the City Watch in front of the building, and took up his position in the rear with a posse of citizens. Undeterred by these, the mob gathered in the morning and made an attack with bricks, stones, and other missiles. The mayor was knocked down senseless, the watch and posse were scattered. Only then did the military appear. The First City Troop rode by at a gallop, but made no effort to disperse the mob. The church was fired, and the rise of the destroying flames was hailed with cheers, which redoubled when the cross fell. Between four and five o'clock in the afternoon the mob assembled again and renewed the attack on the house of the sisters in Second and Phœnix streets, where these pious women had attended Protestant and Catholic alike in the days of the cholera. That building too was soon a blazing mass.

The bishop, with the seminarians and many of the clergy, sought shelter in the houses of friends, and even the orphan asylums were not deemed safe from the mob. Seeing his flock threatened in their homes, seeing the menace of destruction hanging over every church in the city, Bishop Kenrick felt it a duty to resort to the extreme measure of suspending all public religious services. He issued the following card:

"*To the Catholics of the City and County of Philadelphia:*

"BELOVED CHILDREN: In the critical circumstances in which you are placed I feel it my duty to suspend the exercises of public worship in the Catholic churches which still remain, until it can be resumed with safety, and we can enjoy our constitutional right to worship God according to the dictates of our conscience. I earnestly conjure you to practice unalterable patience under the trials to which it has pleased divine Providence to subject you, and to remember that affliction will serve to purify us, and render us acceptable to God, through Jesus Christ, who patiently suffered the cross.

"FRANCIS PATRICK,
"*Bishop of Philadelphia.*

"May 10, 1844."

That a peaceful and numerous community of American citizens should be deprived of the opportunity of assembling for the exercises of religion in a State guaranteeing equal rights to all denominations is something that no sophistry can explain. A grand jury was packed to consider the riots. Its finding falsely ascribed them to "the efforts of a portion of the community to exclude the Bible from the public schools." It represented those who were killed while burning houses as "unoffending citizens," and never mentioned the fact that two Catholic churches and a seminary had been given to the flames. In this "outpouring of frenzy which swept over this city in 1844," says Rt. Rev. Michael O'Connor, "which laid in ashes some of our churches and institutions, and threatened all the rest, as well as the lives of the clergy and people, many blamed Bishop Kenrick for not opposing to it a bolder front. He considered it more conformable to the spirit of the gospel to bend to it and suffer. He thought it best even to retire for a few days from what was evidently a momentary outburst, lest the tiger, tasting blood, might become more infuriated. Events justified his course. The torrent that, if resisted, would have accumulated its waters, and eventually swept on with greater fury, rolled by and spent itself. His order to suspend divine service was the severest rebuke the fanatics could have received. The tramp of the sentinel pacing before the house of God, deserted on the Lord's day, with this order pasted on the walls, was a comment that roused the better minded."

In April, 1845, Bishop Kenrick set out for Rome. He was received in the Eternal City with the honor due to his reputation for piety and learning. In a memoir to the Congregation de Propaganda Fide on the condition of his diocese he reported that of a population exceeding a million the Catholics in his diocese scarcely numbered one hundred thousand. There were few direct apostasies from the faith, but where immigrants settled far from churches, their children often grew up in ignorance of religion and strangers to the Catholic worship. Children whom poverty or loss of parents left at the mercy of Protestant or State institutions as a rule were perverted. The diocese contained sixty churches, ten of them in Philadelphia. His priests numbered fifty, and the Seminary of St. Charles Borromeo had twenty-six candidates preparing for holy orders. When the metropolitan see of Baltimore was left vacant by the death of Archbishop Eccleston the holy see transferred Bishop Kenrick from Philadelphia to Baltimore (August, 1851). To him was reserved the task and the glory of presiding as apostolic delegate over the First Plenary Council of Baltimore.

Western Pennsylvania was the somewhat vaguely delimited territory, cut off from the jurisdiction of Philadelphia by the brief *Universi Dominici* (August 11, 1843), to be erected into the new diocese of Pittsburg. It was agreed that the bishopric thus formed should embrace Bedford, Huntingdon, Clearfield, McKean, and Potter counties, with the country west of them. The clergyman appointed to the new see, and consecrated August 15, 1843, in Rome, whither he went to ask exemption from the burden of the episcopate, that he might enter the Society of Jesus, the Rev. Michael O'Connor, was a man remarkable for learning, and stands out in the roll of American bishops as a strong and striking figure. He found in his diocese thirty-three churches, fourteen priests, and forty-five thousand Catholics. His efforts in organizing education and charities and in introducing religious orders were unrelenting and successful. At the time of the First Plenary

Council of Baltimore, in 1852—that is to say, nine years after the erection of the see of Pittsburg—such had been the increase of Catholicity within its limits that Bishop O'Connor proposed its division by the formation of a new diocese with the see in Erie.

CHAPTER XXIII.

NEW YORK AND ITS SUFFRAGANS (1829–52).

WE have seen that Bishop Dubois, instead of going to the First Provincial Council of Baltimore, had departed for Rome on a call from the Propaganda. In his report to the Congregation de Propaganda Fide he estimated the Catholic population of his diocese at one hundred and fifty thousand, scattered among three millions of non-Catholics. To attend to this flock he had but eighteen priests; eight of these had been received within two years; but notwithstanding careful examination, he found himself often deceived as to the real usefulness of the applicants. The faithful, as a rule, were poor, struggling hard to build churches or free from debt those already built. The diocese could not prosper or have such a body of priests as it required until a theological seminary was established. Church extension and the increase of the clergy were hampered by the general reluctance of Catholics possessed of means to make contributions unless some of themselves, as trustees, had entire control.

When Bishop Dubois returned from Europe (November 20, 1831) he found his episcopal city poorer in churches than when he left it; for St. Mary's Church, Sheriff Street, after being robbed, had been burned by incendiaries. He set out to make a diocesan visitation. In no fewer than eighteen places in the northern and western parts of the State he found Catholics numerous enough to establish churches and maintain resident priests, whom he did not have to send. This condition of things stimulated him to make heroic efforts to build up a seminary, for experience taught him that he could not expect a supply of priests of the right kind from abroad. As his means were insufficient to obtain a suitable site in or near the city, he purchased a farm of one hundred and sixty acres at Nyack. The building planned for a seminary was carried on actively during the year 1832; but the completed portion was destroyed by fire before it was occupied. However, the seminary was opened in the old farm buildings on the ground, with Rev. J. McGerry as president, Rev. John McCloskey as professor, and five students in theology.

In addition to temporal losses the bishop had to suffer from the evil that desolated almost all the dioceses formed out of the old colonies; for, strangely enough, it was within that territory that trusteeism prevailed, as if it were the outcome of the spirit that ruled in colonial times, when the church of the country was in its mission state and without hierarchical organization. The trustee power had always been strong in New York, and aimed to control all the institutions in the diocese. A slight circumstance in 1834 brought on a conflict which lasted as long as Dr. Dubois had the administration of the see of New York. For some years the relations between the bishop and the Rev. Thomas C. Levins, of the cathedral, had been strained. This clergyman was a well-read theologian, an able controversialist, thoroughly versed in all branches of mathematics and natural philosophy, a mineralogist and a lapidary, was very popular, and was looked upon as a champion of the Catholic cause. Soon after the return of the bishop from his visitation in 1834, in consequence of a disrespectful reply to an order of the bishop, though it was obeyed, Rev. Mr. Levins was suspended. The difficulty might easily have been settled, but unfortunately the trustees of the cathedral took up the cause of the priest and so embittered the situation that a removal of the suspension became impossible without a recognition of their assumed powers. A regular ecclesiastical war ensued. The trustees appointed the suspended priest rector of the parochial schools, while they annoyed the bishop in every possible way, and even threatened to take away his salary.

The period was one of violent anti-Catholic prejudice, as we have frequently remarked in the preceding pages. In New York, before coming to acts of violence, the prejudice showed itself in literature. Early in 1836 a work appeared which, though not relating to the church in this country, was a vile attack on Catholicity, and turned out to be for Know-nothingism what "Uncle Tom's Cabin" has been for the abolition movement.

A wretched girl, Maria Monk, after leading a life of shame, had been placed by her mother in a Magdalen asylum at Montreal, from which she was dismissed or escaped by the aid of one of her old lovers. She was the tool employed by bigotry. Unscrupulous plotters got her to pretend that she had been not a penitent in a Magdalen asylum, but a nun in the Hotel Dieu. A narrative was drawn up in her name charging the devoted nuns with immorality, harshness, cruelty, and murder. The infamous book was offered for publication to the Harper Brothers, well-known publishers in New York. The firm, lured by prospective profits, undertook to issue it, but from a sense of shame published it under the name of Howe & Bates, two persons in their employ. Circulated at a time when ministers and newspapers were assailing the Catholic Church, purporting to prove that priests and nuns were monsters of vice, it was greedily received, and read more widely, perhaps, than any book ever before published in this country.

Several New York ministers and zealous members of Protestant churches took up the wretched woman, paraded her, and maintained the truth of her story. The profits of the fraud must have been very great, for the conspirators quarreled. Maria Monk sued in the Vice-Chancellor's Court for her share of the profits as author and holder of the copyright. The Harpers denied her authorship and her ownership of the plates and the copyright. Vice-Chancellor McCoun declared the case one for a jury, when "the motives of those who have prompted and promoted the publication will be duly considered." William K. Hoyt also brought suit against Rev. J. J. Slocum and Maria Monk in the United States Circuit Court for his share in getting up the book. Meanwhile those who received the wretched woman into their houses soon became disgusted with her vicious manner and language; she sank lower and lower, and died in one of the city institutions. In Montreal her wretched life was known to many; the superior of the Magdalen asylum to which she had been committed recognized her pretended descriptions of the Hotel Dieu as partly correct descriptions of the asylum. As applied to the Hotel Dieu, they were pronounced utterly false by a committee of Protestant clergymen and other gentlemen who visited it book in hand.

Though all this was made known to the public, Rev. J. J. Slocum, one of the conspirators, brought out a second book to defend the "Awful Disclosures." Whereupon William L. Stone, editor of the "Commercial Advertiser," a man by no means favorable to Catholics, went to Montreal with the original book in his hand, and was allowed to make a thorough and complete examination of the Hotel Dieu. After visiting every room and closet from the cellar to the attic, Mr. Stone wrote: "The result is the most thorough conviction that Maria Monk is an arrant impostor, that she was never a nun, and was never within the cloister of the Hotel Dieu, and consequently that her disclosures are wholly and unequivocally, from beginning to end, untrue; that they are either the vagaries of a distempered brain, or a series of calumnies unequaled in the depravity of their invention and unsurpassed in their enormity."

Age and hardship induced Bishop Dubois to seek the aid of a coadjutor. The Second Provincial Council of Baltimore, before which he laid his desire, forwarded to Rome for the coadjutorship of New York a list of three names, out of which was chosen the Rev. John Hughes, a former Emmitsburg pupil of Bishop Dubois, and at the time of his nomination pastor of St. John's Church, Philadelphia. The consecration took place in New York, January 7, 1837. The coadjutor had come none too soon. Before the end of January Bishop Dubois was struck down with paralysis, and though he rallied for a while, yet his inability to manage the affairs of the diocese became manifest. He survived till December 20, 1842.

And now had come on the scene a great and strong churchman who was to leave the impress of his mind and will on the church not only of New York, but of the whole country. Early in the year 1839 an event occurred which convinced Bishop Hughes that a struggle between himself and the trustees could not be avoided. A civil officer, by virtue of a written instrument from the trustees of the cathedral, expelled from the Sunday-school a teacher appointed by the bishop. After waiting two weeks for some official expression of regret or some explanation, Bishop Hughes issued a pastoral address to the congregation of the cathedral in the name of Bishop Dubois, who was still nominally in charge of the diocese. "Is it your intention," he asked, "that such powers may be exercised by your trustees? If so, then it is almost time for the ministers of the Lord to forsake your temple and erect an altar to their God around which religion shall be free, the Council of Trent fully recognized, and the laws of the church applied to the government and regulation of the church." He then passed in review other invasions of ecclesiastical power by the trustees, who made the right of the bishop to appoint priests a nullity by refusing them means of subsistence, and assumed the right to appoint and remove teachers and all officials who attended the altar or chanted the divine service.

He backed the pastoral letter by explanations from the pulpit, and, carrying the war, so to speak, into Africa, he advised his hearers to refuse all further contributions to the trustees. When the bishop, he added, and his clergy shall think it necessary to appeal to the faithful for means of support, he knew that the response would be generous. After this sermon the collection-plates went down the aisles empty and came back as they went. Before leaving the sanctuary the bishop called a meeting of the pew-holders of the cathedral for the same afternoon. A large audience assembled; he appealed to the sacrifices their ancestors had made for the faith, and exhorted them not to yield the discipline of their church and the rights of their families in the house of God to a power conferred by the State with a view to their good, but perverted by illegal interference with the legislation and spiritual authority of the church established by Christ. A preamble and resolutions introduced by him were adopted, and he felt that he had won the people.

He followed up the victory by submitting a series of questions to his assembled clergy; they unanimously sustained the pastoral letter, declaring that its principles could not be denied without heresy or schism. The trustees made an ineffectual effort to oppose the will of the congregation. As the next election for trustees would legally decide the matter, Bishop Hughes began in April an electioneering campaign with a series of lectures on the connection between the Catholic religion and the system of secular incorporation of lay trustees, which had never realized the anticipations of Archbishop Carroll, whom circumstances compelled to tolerate it, but, on the contrary, had produced havoc in many parts of the Catholic fold. He traced its history in different States and convinced the faithful of its dangerous character. When the election came off the new members elected represented the bishop, the clergy, and the faithful. The opposition was broken forever in New York; in Buffalo, however, it lasted for some years longer.

Bishop Hughes was full of projects, for his was a mind that could see in the questions and events around him the important bearings, and his was a will that knew no fear and stopped at no obstacle. In order to study systems of education and means of advancing religion he undertook a voyage to Europe (October, 1839), leaving his diocese in the hands of his vicars general. During his absence there arose in New York a movement which, had he been present, might have been guided on other lines and have reached a different conclusion. Under the School Act of 1812 the Catholic schools of New York, with other denominational schools, received a ratable proportion of the school fund. But a private corporation, the Public School Society, which had been growing up for some years past, was allowed to gradually absorb the school fund, and the Catholic as well as other denominational schools no longer received their share. As the schools of the Public School Society and their school-books were offensively anti-Catholic, the Catholic body, feeling that an injustice was done them, moved to obtain a restoration of the old system; that is, they moved to put out of the way the Public School Society. This action brought into the arena of public opinion a difficult question that has not yet been settled—the combination of secular and religious education. Though the Baptists had been the first to advocate religious instruction in the schools as against the secularism of the Public School Society, yet as soon as Catholics advocated it and asked a return to the old New York system, the Protestant denominations arrayed themselves solidly against them on this vital point.

At this time there were free schools attached to each of the eight Catholic churches in the city, and more than five thousand children attended them. The State superintendent called the attention of the legislature to this fact and to the apparent injustice of excluding Catholics from the benefit of a fund to which they contributed. The petition of the Catholic schools to the Common Council was rejected, and a general meeting of Catholics was held March 20, 1840, in which a memorial to the legislature was adopted and circulated for signatures. It was not long before the matter was taken up by politicians and made an issue. Such was the condition of the question when the bishop arrived. Two days after his return from Europe he attended a meeting that had been previously called, and in a careful speech made himself the controlling spirit of the movement. "An Address of the Roman Catholics to their Fellow-citizens of the City and State," from his pen, set forth distinctly the grounds of the Catholic appeal, and presented clearly the fact that the Public Society schools, while avowedly non-sectarian, were thoroughly Protestant, and used books in class and library in which Catholics and their religion were coarsely assailed. "These passages were not considered as sectarian, inasmuch as they had been selected as mere reading-lessons, and were not in favor of any particular sect, but merely against the Catholics. We feel it unjust that such passages should be taught at all in the schools, to the support of which we are contributors as well as others. But that such books should be put into the hands of our own children, and that, in part, at our own expense, was in our opinion unjust, unnatural, and at all events to us intolerable."

The address excited much attention, and a "Reply" to its arguments appeared, issued, evidently, by the Public School Society. On the 21st of September a meeting of Catholics adopted a petition for relief, which was at once presented to the Board of Aldermen then in session. This petition showed the Public Society schools to be such as would not permit Catholics to send their children to them, and asked the Common Council that the eight Catholic schools of the city should be put on an equality with the Public Society schools, and be designated as "entitled to participate in the Common School Fund upon complying with the requirements of the law, and the ordinances of the corporation of the city." With this petition and counter to it were presented to the Common Council a remonstrance from the Public School Society and a protest from the Methodist Episcopal Church. On the day appointed for the debate before the Board of Aldermen on the Catholic petition and the opposing documents, Bishop Hughes stood alone for his side. Two able lawyers, Theodore Sedgwick and Hiram Ketchum, were arrayed against him, with Rev. Drs. Bond, Reese, and Bangs of the Methodist Church, Rev. Dr. Spring of the Presbyterian, and Rev. Dr. Knox of the Reformed Dutch Church.

The bishop began by explaining the Catholic petition and the grounds of the prayer for relief; he then analyzed the counter-documents and showed that they avoided the real question and raised false issues. Mr. Sedgwick rose in defense of the Public School Society, treating its history at length, and taking the legal ground that the Common Council had no power to grant the petition. He spoke with courtesy, but Mr. Ketchum, who followed, drifted into a strain of virulence and personal invective, eying the bishop as if he were some degraded culprit at the bar, and charging the Catholics with the intent to drive the Bible from the schools. Bishop Hughes in reply said, and truly: "I conceive the true point has not been touched. Not one of our objections or scruples of conscience has been considered. When I gave reasons for our objections, I thought some argument would have been urged fairly against them; but the only end the gentleman has in view is the preservation of the Public School Society."

Dr. Bond took the floor next day and argued that to grant the petition was to give money for sectarian teaching; he then launched into a general attack on the Catholic Church as a persecuting church. He was followed by Rev. Mr. Reese in the same strain, treating the schools of the society as though they were government institutions and not those of a private association. Rev. Dr. Knox, of the Dutch Reformed Church, insisted that public schools were Protestant institutions, and held that Protestants could not yield to any Catholic claim.

Bishop Hughes summed up for the petitioners. He cited historical instances to show the tolerant action of the church. In regard to the Bible he said: "They have represented us as contending to bring the Catholic Scriptures into the public schools. This is not true. . . . They have represented us as enemies to the Protestant Scriptures.

Now if I had asked this honorable board to exclude the Protestant Scriptures from the schools, then there might have been some coloring for the current calumny. But I have not done so. I say, gentlemen of every denomination, keep the Scriptures you reverence, but do not force on me that which my conscience tells me is wrong. I see the question stands precisely where it did before the gentlemen began to speak, and I see the same false issue—and I challenge any gentleman to say that it is not a false issue—persevered in to this very hour, so that our argument has not been moved one iota; there must therefore be something powerful in our plain, unsophisticated statement, when all the reasoning brought against it leaves it just where it was before." In a speech lasting three hours and a half the bishop reviewed and answered his opponents, defending the church from their attacks, and narrowing the subject down to the question at issue.

In regard to religious teaching in the parochial schools, he was willing to have it after regular school hours; he even offered to conform the system of secular teaching in the parochial schools to that of the Public School Society, and make the parochial schools subject to State supervision. The compromise was of no avail; it was evident that the question was prejudged. As Bishop Hughes well said: "Eight or nine hours were wasted in the discussion of a theological tenet, but not one half-hour was given to the only questions which the Common Council should have permitted to come before them, namely, Are the rights of this portion of the citizens violated or not? If so, is there in our hands the means to apply a remedy?" The committee of the Common Council reported against the claim of the petitioners. The Catholics then forwarded to the legislature petitions representing their grievances and asking redress. The matter was referred to Hon. John C.

Spencer, Secretary of State, who reported against the exclusive power given to the Public School Society in New York City, and recommended that the State system should be extended to that city. The upshot of the struggle was that a school bill, introduced by William B. Maclay, extended to New York City the provisions of the general act in relation to common schools. It passed April 9, 1842, and the Public School Society went out of existence. No substantial gain had been acquired by Catholics by this struggle. Their schools were as far from relief as ever; but instead of a society absolutely hostile to them and controlled by their religious enemies, the State itself, in the election of whose officers they had at least a voice, became the controller of the public schools. This at least was a change for the better.

The future supply of priests was the object of serious thought with Bishop Hughes, as it had been with his predecessor. The first foundation of a seminary had not been successful. In 1840 a second foundation was made in Fordham, and in 1842 there were thirty students in the house, nineteen of whom were pursuing the theological course. Meanwhile congregations and churches were fast increasing throughout the diocese. The diocesan synod of August, 1842, was attended by fifty-four priests. The burden was becoming too heavy for Bishop Hughes to bear alone, especially as much of his time was taken up by literary work and a very extensive correspondence. In the Fifth Provincial Council of Baltimore he solicited the aid of a coadjutor, and recommended for the position the Rev. John McCloskey, president of St. John's College, Fordham. The request was granted by the holy see, and on the 10th of March, 1844, the appointee was consecrated Bishop of Axiern, *in partibus infidelium.*

By the firmness and boldness of Bishop Hughes the city

escaped the disgraceful and terrible riots which, as we have seen, caused a reign of terror in Philadelphia. The situation in New York was critical. The Native American party had elected as mayor one of the publishers of Maria Monk's book. Confident in the support of the incoming chief magistrate, they called a public meeting. Its object was arson and murder. Bishop Hughes was a man of decision. When appealed to by some of his flock for advice, he inquired if the law of New York provided compensation for damage done by rioters. A lawyer assured him it did not. "Then," said he, tersely, "the law intends that citizens should defend their own property." The "Freeman's Journal" (Catholic) immediately issued an extra. "If," said the "Journal," "as it has already appeared in Philadelphia, it should be a part of Native Americanism to attack the houses and churches of Catholics, then it behooves Catholics, in case all other protection fail, to defend both with their lives. In this they will not be acting against, but for the law. . . . In no case let them suffer an act of outrage on their property without repelling the aggression at all hazards." The bold words told. It was the turn of the leading Native Americans to become suppliants. They rushed to the outgoing mayor, Morris, to solicit protection. They found that he had made provision to quell any riot by stern and decisive measures. In an hour the city was placarded with posters revoking the call for the Know-nothing meeting announced for that afternoon. New York escaped a terrible danger, for a large Irish society, with divisions throughout the city, had resolved that in case a single church was attacked, buildings should be fired in all quarters and the great city should be involved in a general conflagration.

In 1846 the diocese of New York had one hundred and fourteen churches, one hundred and nine priests, a seminary, a college, and in the city itself there were over a hundred thousand Catholics. Two new dioceses were erected out of the original one in 1847: the diocese of Albany, to which was transferred the Coadjutor of New York, the Rt. Rev. John McCloskey; and the diocese of Buffalo, to which was appointed the Rev. John Timon, of the Congregation of the Mission. These new erections reduced the diocese proper of New York to the counties in New York State south of the forty-second degree and to the eastern part of New Jersey. Thus reduced it had eighty-eight priests, a theological seminary with twenty-two students, a Jesuit college, an academy of the Ladies of the Sacred Heart, eleven institutions, such as schools and asylums, in the care of the Sisters of Mercy and Sisters of Charity; the city had seventeen churches, which were far from sufficient for the number of Catholics.

The Tractarian movement in England, that had brought into the Catholic Church the brightest lights of the Anglican Church, had about this time its counterpart in the United States. Rev. Mr. Bayley was led to the church by the study of the early fathers. Others, guided in the same direction by the influence of the English movement, renounced worldly prospects to enter the church. Rev. Messrs. Ford, Preston, Jedediah V. Huntington, F. E. White, Donald McLeod, with many others, became Catholics. Earlier still, in 1844, the deep thinker and vigorous writer, Orestes A. Brownson, had come into the church. The effect of these conversions was great, for submission to the authority of the church was an act of moral heroism, an acceptation of a most unpopular faith from pure motives of conviction and duty, in the face of popular prejudice. Other notable converts of this period in New York were Isaac T. Hecker, A. F. Hewit, who had been an Episcopalian minister in Maryland, Clarence Walworth, son of

Reuben Hyde Walworth, Chancellor of the State of New York, and Edgar P. Wadhams.

The time had come when the church in the United States had outgrown its cradle, Baltimore. The Seventh Council of Baltimore, considering the great increase of the Catholic flock, solicited the holy see to erect new provinces within the ecclesiastical domain which had formed at first the diocese and then the province of Baltimore. The action of the sovereign pontiff was delayed for some time by the political troubles of Italy. But when more peaceful times came, New York was erected by Pope Pius IX. (July 19, 1851) into an archiepiscopal see, with the Bishops of Boston, Hartford, Albany, and Buffalo as its suffragans. On receiving the official notification of his promotion, Archbishop elect Hughes proceeded to Europe to receive the pallium from the hands of the sovereign pontiff himself. The prominence which the archbishop had attained led to the report that our government, which then had a representative in Rome, solicited from the Vatican his appointment to the cardinalate. It seems certain that the authorities in Washington, through their Roman minister, suggested to the sovereign pontiff the advantage of having this country represented in the senate of the Pope, the College of Cardinals.

The diocese of Albany, created in 1847 by his Holiness Pope Pius IX., comprised that portion of the State of New York lying north of the forty-second degree and east of Cayuga, Tompkins, and Tioga counties. It was a district with a past famous in the annals of the church and of the border wars; it was the Iroquois country. The diocese contained about twenty-five churches, attended by thirty-four priests, but had no institutions except an orphan asylum at Albany and one at Utica under the Sisters of Charity, with free schools at Utica and East

Troy. Dr. McCloskey, appointed to this see, was already invested with the episcopal dignity as Bishop of Axiern. He was duly installed by Bishop Hughes, whose coadjutor he then ceased to be, September 19, 1847. Such was his activity and such the inflow of immigration into his diocese that four years afterward he could report to the Leopoldine Society that the Catholic population of his diocese was seventy thousand, with sixty-two churches and fifty priests, having gained in two years fifteen priests and twenty churches. He was laboring to give Albany a cathedral worthy of the capital of the State of New York, where fifteen thousand out of a population of fifty thousand were Catholics, at the time that the First Plenary Council was convoked (1852).

The see of Buffalo was established April 23, 1847, by Pope Pius IX., who detached from the diocese of New York all that part of the State lying west of the eastern limits of Cayuga, Tompkins, and Tioga counties. It contained forty thousand Catholics, sixteen priests, and the same number of churches, though some of them were humble enough to be styled huts. For this new see the sovereign pontiff selected the Very Rev. John Timon, Visitor of the Congregation of the Mission, a priest of learning, energy, and experience, who, as superior of a body of missionaries and as Prefect Apostolic of Texas, had displayed great ability.

The spirit of discontent and rebellion, fruits of trusteeism, was rife in the city of Buffalo. Bishop Timon had to meet this foe of religion at the very beginning of his administration. He had taken up his residence at the Church of St. Louis, the largest congregation in the city. He was notified by the trustees to leave, and was actually turned out of doors. Originally made up of different nationalities, this congregation became in time exclusively

German, and maintained toward the bishop the spirit of revolt and schism that has characterized trusteeism in our history. The bishop wished to place the church in charge of the Jesuit fathers, but the trustees refused to admit them. They issued libels against him, charging him with the design to take their church from them and give it to the Irish. The bishop called upon the congregation to show their fidelity to the discipline of the church, warning them that if they sustained the trustees they must cease to be Catholics. But a majority did sustain their leaders, expelled the pastor, and profaned the church with forms of service unauthorized by the Catholic religion. Bishop Timon accordingly placed the church under an interdict and warned the faithful to take no part in the unhallowed rites; this extreme measure, however, did not at once put an end to the schism.

Not only was Bishop Timon an energetic man, as his treatment of the St. Louis trustees shows, but he was a zealous missionary, untiring in his diocesan visitations. The statistics of Buffalo for the year 1852 indicate the results both of his apostolic work and of the Catholic immigration, which was then swelling to vast proportions. They show seventy churches, fifty-eight priests, twelve ecclesiastical students, an academy for girls, a hospital, three orphan asylums, and parochial schools in the more important towns of the diocese.

From 1829 to 1834 the administration of Bishop Fenwick, of Boston, is remarkable for his ceaseless visitations throughout New England and the constant increase of Catholicity in new congregations and churches. To go into details, naming places and persons, would be beyond the scope of a summary such as this work is intended to be. At the close of 1836 there were in the diocese thirty-five priests, thirty churches, and a Catholic population of about forty-five thousand. While the church and the true faith were steadily gaining ground in New England, giving just offense to none, interfering with no rights of others, an incident occurred which, though trifling in itself, led to one of the greatest calamities in our history, the destruction of the Ursuline convent of Charlestown.

One of the ladies of that institution, Sister Mary John, of a well-known Boston family, holding a high position in the community as a teacher of music, had been overworked in the preparation of her pupils for the exhibition day of the academy. She was finally prostrated, and in her delirium left her room, ran from the convent to the house of a neighbor, Mr. Runey, and asked to be taken to the residence of a Mr. Cutter, whose daughters had been her pupils. Word was sent to Bishop Fenwick, who drove to Mr. Cutter's house to persuade her to return to the convent. Failing to see her, he called on her brother, Mr. Thomas Harrison. Together they returned to Mr. Cutter's house, found the poor nun evidently unnerved, and succeeded in persuading her to return to the convent. A physician was summoned, and under his treatment her reason returned and her health began to mend.

Rumors were industriously spread by malicious persons and circulated by the press, notably by the "Mercantile Journal," that Miss Harrison was detained in the convent against her will and was subjected there to harsh treatment. On the night of the 9th of August, 1834, a number of evil-disposed men, the dregs of the city, assembled around the convent. After shouting "Down with the convent! Down with the nuns!" they called for the superior and demanded to see Miss Harrison in order to learn from her own lips if she were detained in the house against her will. She assured them that she was not detained, but could go when she liked. The Messrs. Cutter, who were present, perfectly satisfied with this announcement of the sister, endeavored to undeceive the public and made a statement to that effect; but the assurances came too late to do any good.

In view of the threatening aspect of public opinion it may seem strange that the bishop and the Catholic community made no call on the authorities to protect the nuns and their property from insult and violence. But it should be remembered that although, Catholics themselves, their beliefs and practices had been frequently assailed with the coarsest virulence, yet no actual violence had been offered them, and they believed defenseless ladies to be as safe in their home under the protection of the laws of Massachusetts as though they were guarded by the armed ranks of a devoted soldiery. Even when Bishop Fenwick was vaguely informed that the convent might be attacked, he did not credit the rumor. Parents, non-Catholic as well as Catholic, who had daughters in the academy seemed lulled into a like confidence. But bigotry was rousing the wildest fanaticism, regardless of the lives of the nuns and of the fifty-five young ladies under their care. Inflammatory sermons were preached, and meetings were held to organize the work of destruction. In the dead of night the mob came, unchecked by any authority, shouting roars of hate and rage. Not an officer, not a defender, was there to protect defenseless women and children roused hastily from sleep and driven half-dressed into the night. Musket-shots rang above the shouts. The door was broken in; the mob entered and drove the inmates, shrinking and trembling with fear, to the upper stories. Then began a demons' revel. The fences and outhouses were used to light up bonfires fed with barrels of tar and other combustibles. Casks of liquor were opened, and rum nerved the frenzied mob to the work of plunder and incendiarism. The superior, seeing no hope of relief, marshaled her sisters and pupils and left the building. Then the rioters, undisturbed masters of the situation, took possession, smashed furniture, profaned the chapel, stole garments and jewelry, and applied the torch. As the fire died away the mob withdrew unchecked, unhampered, unpursued, exultant in a noble deed gloriously, heroically done.

Boston was startled in the morning by the report of the destruction of the Charlestown convent. In the first impulse of honest indignation and shame a meeting was called in Faneuil Hall, at which Theodore Lyman, Esq., mayor of Boston, presided. Addresses were made by the best citizens, and resolutions were adopted in which the attack on the convent was declared to be a base and cowardly act, a high-handed violation of the law. The mayor was requested to appoint a committee to investigate the whole affair and to consider the expediency of providing funds to repair the damage done to the sisters. A meeting held at Cambridge expressed similar feelings. As the news spread outside the city, Irish Catholic laborers employed on the railroads came pouring into Boston, bent on vengeance. They might have done violence had not Bishop Fenwick sent his clergy to dissuade them from any attempt at retaliation.

The moment was full of danger; the cathedral, the house of the Sisters of Charity, and other Catholic property in Boston were threatened for several days by menacing crowds. The riot might break out anew at any minute. In view of the dangerous state of affairs the infantry of the Third Brigade, Colonel Prescott, was called out and kept under arms, and respectable citizens prepared to support the authorities. The committee appointed at the Faneuil Hall meeting made a report showing the groundlessness of the rumors circulated against the nuns. The report did something to disabuse a few of those who had been misled, but the larger number would not yield to its testimony.

Meanwhile Governor Davis issued a proclamation offering a reward for the detection of the offenders. A number were arrested and committed, and preparations were made to bring them to trial, which began in the Supreme Judicial Court of East Cambridge on the 2d of December. It soon became apparent, however, that the State was taking no means to secure a conviction. No witnesses were called to connect any of the accused with a conflagration witnessed by at least a thousand. The counsel for the defense appealed to the religious prejudice of the jury by cross-examining Catholic witnesses as to their religion. The argument of the attorney general, James T. Austin, presented the evidence strongly, but Judge Shaw charged that the accusation of arson could not be sustained. The jury returned a verdict of "not guilty." The acquitted criminals became the lions of the hour. Emboldened by the acquittal, the rioters threatened churches in Boston and the convent in Roxbury. As there seemed to be no disposition on the part of the city and State authorities to give protection, and as the federal authorities instructed Commodore Elliott not to interfere in case of a riot, but to leave matters solely to the officials of the city and the State, the bishop called on the Catholics to prepare for resistance. Well might he write: "We live in awful times. All this movement on the part of the lower classes of people is occasioned by their jealousy of the Catholic religion. Their object is to put it down if they can." Application was made to the General Court of the legislature of Massachusetts for indemnity for the destruction of the convent; but although a committee reported in favor of granting in compensation a sum of money, nothing came of it. The matter was again brought up in 1842, with a similar result—a favorable report, but justice withheld. Yet Judge Thatcher, in his charge to the grand jury of Sussex County (December, 1834), said: "In the destruction of the Ursuline convent on Mount Benedict it was seen that a portion of the people could wage war equally against political liberty, the sacred rights of property, and religious charity. The just and enlightened everywhere will look to the justice of the country and to its liberality to the sufferers to efface the foul disgrace." It was never effaced.

Bishop Fenwick began to feel the weight of his long labors in the priesthood and the episcopate. A coadjutor and a division of the diocese were absolutely needed. He laid these matters before his fellow-bishops in council in Baltimore, and a petition was forwarded to the holy see requesting the erection of Rhode Island and Connecticut into a diocese, with the see at Hartford, recommending Rev. William Tyler as the bishop, and asking the appointment of Rev. John B. Fitzpatrick as Coadjutor of Boston. Bishop Tyler was consecrated in the Cathedral of the Holy Cross, Boston, by Bishop Fenwick, and Dr. Fitzpatrick in the Chapel of the Visitation, Georgetown, in the year 1844.

Much had been accomplished during Bishop Fenwick's administration in the face of the violent opposition from Know-nothings without and trustees within the church. Twenty-five churches had been erected, nineteen priests had been ordained, a college, an orphan asylum, and parochial schools were well on the way of organization. The diocese of Boston, now shorn of Rhode Island and Connecticut by the erection of the see of Hartford, comprised Maine with 5240 Catholics and 5 priests, New Hampshire with 1370 Catholics and 2 priests, Vermont with

5311 Catholics and 2 priests, Massachusetts with 51,872 Catholics and 21 priests. It was, then, with a record made glorious by energetic toil and hard-earned success that Bishop Fenwick passed from the scene of his labors to eternal repose, January 11, 1845. A more beautiful eulogy could not be pronounced on him than these words of Dr. Brownson: "Take him all in all, he was such a man as Heaven seldom vouchsafes us. It will be long before we look on his like again. But he has been ours; he has left his light along our pathway; he has blessed us all by his pure example and his labor of love, and we are thankful. We bless God that he gave him to us; we bless God that he has seen fit to remove him from his labors to his rest."

His successor, the Rt. Rev. John Bernard Fitzpatrick, was a native of Boston, had received his early education in the schools of the city, and was therefore well fitted to carry the church of New England safely through the stormy period of Know-nothingism. His thorough Americanism, his learning, his indefatigable activity in the administration and visitation of his diocese, brought it in a few years to a high degree of efficiency. On the eve of the First Plenary Council of Baltimore (1852) the diocese had seventy-two priests, seventy-three churches, with many others in progress of erection; a more than doubling within seven years.

Connecticut and Rhode Island, which had formed part of the diocese of Boston for thirty-five years, were erected into a separate diocese in 1844, with the episcopal see in Hartford. The first bishop was the Rt. Rev. William Tyler, a native of Vermont. The diocese of Hartford at this time contained a Catholic population of about ten thousand, a little more than half being in Rhode Island. There were churches at Hartford, New Haven, New London, Bridgeport, Newport, Providence, Pawtucket, one nearly completed at Woonsocket, and one begun in Middletown. These churches and the annexed stations were attended by six priests. As Providence contained the largest Catholic population and two Catholic churches, Bishop Tyler selected it as his residence and made the Church of St. Peter and St. Paul his procathedral. The expectations raised by the appointment of a man so well fitted as was Bishop Tyler for the upbuilding of a new diocese were foiled by his untimely death, which occurred the 13th of June, 1849, after a short episcopate of five years. His successor, the Rt. Rev. Bernard O'Reilly, was consecrated November 10, 1850. Immigration just then was giving an impetus to the church in New England which can best be estimated from the following statistics. The diocese of Hartford, when Bishop O'Reilly was installed, contained a Catholic population of 20,000 souls, 12 churches, and 14 priests. One year later the Catholic population was estimated at 40,000, the priests were 28, the clerical students were 23. These figures show to what a tide had risen the immigration of those days.

CHAPTER XXIV.

THE PROVINCES OF CINCINNATI AND NEW ORLEANS (1829–52).

BISHOP FENWICK, of Cincinnati, did not long survive the close of the First Provincial Council of Baltimore. In the autumn of 1832 the cholera then prevailing in the country seized on the bishop while he was on a visitation, and caused his speedy death. In the month of May, 1833, news came that the successor of Bishop Fenwick was to be the Rev. John Purcell, and that a new diocese was to be detached from Cincinnati, having its see in Detroit and comprising Michigan and the undefined country to the west. Bishop Purcell was consecrated in Baltimore October 13, 1833. The diocese of Cincinnati, now restricted to the State of Ohio, contained about thirty thousand Catholics, seventeen priests, nine brick and eight wooden churches. Immigration was beginning to pour into the State, and it needed constant and heroic efforts on the part of the few priests to furnish the newcomers with opportunities to worship and receive the sacraments, and on the part of the bishop to provide the new settlements springing up daily with the needed clergymen. In a letter (1838) to the Leopoldine Association, which had contributed generously to the missions in Ohio, the bishop gives a glimpse of the growth of five years. At that date he had thirty priests and thirteen students of philosophy and theology in his seminary. His churches numbered thirty-five, most of them poor and rough. He had parochial schools and a girls' orphan asylum in Cincinnati.

Statistics of five years later (1843), given in a second letter of the bishop to the Leopoldine Association, show that the growth continued to be rapid and that the population was not outstripping the clergy. At the close of that year the diocese of Cincinnati contained fifty-five churches, with fifteen in course of erection, forty-two priests on the mission, and twelve otherwise engaged. The population of the diocese was estimated at fifty thousand. At the end of the year 1845—a year memorable in the history of Cincinnati because of the dedication of its cathedral—that is to say, two years after the above report, another letter to the Leopoldine Association claims for the diocese seventy-five thousand Catholics, seventy churches, sixty-six priests, five orphan asylums, and many schools. Such were the results of the mighty flood of immigration that was covering the West.

As his episcopal see was at the southern boundary of the State, Bishop Purcell felt that the time had come for the erection of a new diocese in the northern part of Ohio. Before the holding of the Sixth Provincial Council of Baltimore he made his views and wishes known to the metropolitan. When the council convened in May, 1846, the assembled bishops approved the plan and solicited of the holy see the erection of a see in Cleveland. The sovereign pontiff created the new bishopric, embracing all the State of Ohio north of a line drawn across the State at 40° 41′. As reduced by the bull erecting the see of Cleveland, the diocese of Cincinnati comprised eighty churches and chapels, nine of them in the city of Cincinnati, seventy-seven priests, and a Catholic population of one hundred thousand. Such magnificent growth, indicating where lay the future expansion of the nation, induced the Seventh Provincial Council of Baltimore (May, 1849) to solicit the erection of Cincinnati into a metropolitan see, with Louisville, the original diocese of the West, Vincennes, Detroit, and Cleveland as suffragans.

Bare and lifeless on this printed page are the statistics we have just given; but to the imagination of the historian how eloquent they are! They tell of heroic feats of apostolic zeal, of hardships and perils by water and land, of lives spent and deaths incurred in the pursuit of souls; they tell of brave men and women crossing mountains and pláins, floating down great rivers, in search of homes; they tell of the settler's hut, of forests cleared, of all the weak beginnings and mighty struggles out of which was born our great Western commonwealth. They are the outlines of a story—the Making of a Nation—fit subject for one of humanity's grandest poems.

After the First Provincial Council of Baltimore, Bishop Flaget believed that his period of active usefulness was past, and in this spirit he wrote to the sovereign pontiff asking to be relieved of the burden of his diocese. In view of the advanced age and infirmities of his coadjutor, Bishop David, Dr. Flaget proposed that Rev. Guy Ignatius Chabrat should be made bishop and administrator of the diocese. His resignation was not at first deemed best for the good of religion, but his constancy finally prevailed. Late in the year 1833 information came from Rome that his resignation had been accepted. But the holy see, while allowing the retirement of Bishop Flaget, did not take any such action as he had proposed in regard to the administration of the diocese. Rt. Rev. Dr. David became, by right of succession, the Bishop of Bardstown. Now he was more infirm than Rt. Rev. Dr. Flaget, and had become so corpulent that it was utterly impossible for him to make the long journeys on horseback required by the visitation of the churches.

The first act of his administration was to appoint Bishop Flaget his vicar general, with the most ample powers he could confer, and the next was to transmit to Rome his resignation of the see of Bardstown, with a clear statement of the causes which unfitted him for the discharge of the duties demanded by the position. He advised the reappointment of Bishop Flaget. In May, 1833, the documents arrived by which Bishop David's resignation was accepted and Bishop Flaget's reappointment to the see was decreed. No sooner was this done than Bishop Flaget solicited the appointment of Father Chabrat as his coadjutor, which request was granted, the consecration taking place in Bardstown July 20, 1834. Bishop Flaget had long urged the erection of an episcopal see in Indiana, and his desire was gratified when Pope Gregory XVI., by bull of the 6th of May, 1834, established the diocese of Vincennes. Thus was he relieved of all the territory north of the Ohio River, which originally had been annexed to Bardstown, but was now committed to the care of the Bishops of Cincinnati, Detroit, and Vincennes. His diocese was growing slowly but steadily, gaining less than the Northern dioceses by immigration, but comparatively well supplied with churches, priests, schools, and asylums.

In April, 1837, Bishop Chabrat attended the Third Provincial Council of Baltimore and explained to the fathers the desire of Bishop Flaget for the formation of the State of Tennessee into a diocese. In the fifth private congregation the assembly decided to petition the sovereign pontiff to erect a see in Nashville, with Tennessee as the diocese. Pope Gregory XVI., complying with the desire of the American episcopate, erected that see on the 25th of July, 1837. By this action the diocese of Bardstown was reduced to the State of Kentucky. Louisville had by this time grown to be a city of twenty thousand inhabitants, and its Catholic institutions had so developed that Bishop Flaget concluded it was the proper residence for the head of the diocese; though he was reluctant to leave Bardstown, the cradle of Catholicity in the West, and the institutions which had been so laboriously built up during thirty years of his episcopate. The matter was presented to the holy see, and a rescript of the Pope authorized him to remove the see to Louisville; however, he was to retain the title of the former see and style himself "Bishop of Louisville and Bardstown."

In 1843 a new trouble, of a painful character, afflicted the heart of the venerable bishop. The staff on which he leaned was yielding; his coadjutor, Bishop Chabrat, showed an alarming decline of health and was threatened with the complete loss of sight. Convinced that his days of usefulness in the episcopate were ended, and anxious to give way to a younger and abler man, the afflicted coadjutor forwarded to Rome his resignation, which after consideration was accepted. To be thus left alone in his extreme old age, with infirmities fast growing upon him, was indeed a severe trial for Bishop Flaget, who had already endured so much and had reached the age of fourscore. Naturally he turned in his distress to his vicar general, Very Rev. Martin J. Spalding, who, after a brilliant course of studies in Rome, had labored in Kentucky for fourteen years with great ability and judgment. An American of old lineage, learned, eloquent, earnest, manly, he was well fitted for the see of his native State. He was appointed Bishop of Lengone, *in partibus infidelium*, and Coadjutor of Louisville, with the right of succession.

Greatly relieved in mind, though extremely weak in

body, the aged bishop performed his last public official act in the consecration of his third coadjutor on the 10th of September, 1848. After that he gradually grew too weak to offer the holy sacrifice, and in the summer of 1849 symptoms of an alarming character appeared. He sank so gradually as to excite little immediate alarm until February, 1850. His last words were expressions of attachment to his clergy, religion, and people, and his last act was an effort to give them his episcopal benediction. While the "Sufferings of Christ" were read to him he calmly expired, February 11, 1850. "He died as he had lived—a saint," wrote Bishop Spalding; "and the last day was perhaps the most interesting and impressive of his whole life. Tranquilly and without a groan did he fall asleep in the Lord, like an infant gently sinking to its rest." With him ended the last tie that bound the prosperous church of the middle of the nineteenth century with the nascent church of the first years of the century, when three newly consecrated bishops, Egan, Cheverus, and Flaget, gathered in Baltimore around Carroll, the patriarch of the American church, and started thence for Philadelphia, Boston, and Bardstown to begin the glorious conquest we are narrating.

Gregory XVI. erected the see of Detroit, detaching it from Cincinnati, by bull of March 8, 1833. It embraced the State of Michigan and the territory extending northward to the boundary-line between the United States and the British territory and westward to the Mississippi River. It was classic ground for the church; it had been the theater of the early Jesuit missions. The bishop elect was the Rev. Frederic Rèsé, a native of Hanover, Germany, who was consecrated in Cincinnati October 3, 1833. The faithful in this diocese were mainly of French origin, few persons of other nationalities having as yet settled there. Within the limits of his diocese were fourteen priests, scattered from Detroit to Green Bay. It was a noble field of work, soon to become the most flourishing portion of our Northwestern States. But Bishop Rèsé was a failure from the start; he was arbitrary, quick, and impulsive. Seriously affected in health and completely discouraged, he resolved to resign. Leaving the diocese in charge of Very Rev. S. T. Badin and Very Rev. John de Bruyn as his vicars general, he left Detroit early in 1837.

He was in Baltimore at the time of the Third Provincial Council. He did not attend its sessions, but from St. Mary's Seminary he addressed to the assembled fathers a letter in which, after declaring that he had accepted the episcopate reluctantly, had learned by experience that it was a burden beyond his strength, and had frequently entertained the intention of resigning, or at least of soliciting a coadjutor, he stated that he now desired to do so, having left his diocese in charge of two vicars general. The fathers of the council yielded to his wish, and addressed a letter to the sovereign pontiff advising that the resignation be accepted and proposing the names of clergymen worthy to succeed him. Dr. Rèsé was summoned to Rome, where he was known and esteemed. He reached that city in very feeble health, and it was soon found that softening of the brain had set in. The Pope therefore decided to appoint a coadjutor and administrator.

The choice fell on the Rev. Peter Paul Lefevre, who was consecrated in Philadelphia November 21, 1841. He made an extended visitation of his diocese in 1842, and found the temporal affairs greatly confused; and to add to his sorrows turbulent men gave him so much trouble in Detroit that he threatened to withdraw from the old French Church of St. Ann. The diocese in 1843 contained St. Ann's Cathedral, Holy Trinity Church in Detroit, twenty-three churches and chapels in the rest of the diocese, sixteen priests, ten schools, and two charitable institutions. The Catholic population was estimated at twenty-five thousand. Immigration was only beginning to reach Michigan. The diocese was vast and somewhat vague in its western limits, since Prairie du Chien, La Pointe, Sinsanawa Mound, Wis., and St. Paul's Chapel, near the Falls of St. Anthony, Minnesota, were all regarded as being within the jurisdiction of Detroit. By the erection of the sees of Dubuque and Milwaukee, in 1849, the diocese of Detroit was limited to the State of Michigan. Thus reduced it contained twelve churches—ten more in course of erection—fifteen priests, as many schools, and a Catholic population of twenty-five thousand. To the gratification of Bishop Lefevre the Cathedral of St. Peter and St. Paul was completed in 1848 and consecrated by Archbishop Eccleston, who came from Baltimore to honor the old French town of the Straits.

After that year the general progress of the diocese was remarkable and felt the impetus of the great wave of Western immigration. In 1852 it had forty churches completed and thirteen in process of building, thirty-two priests, two academies, twenty-four schools, and eighty-five thousand Catholics.

It was in 1834 that the diocese of Vincennes, containing Indiana and eastern Illinois, was detached from the diocese of Bardstown. The bishop chosen was one of the most learned and saintly priests in the country, Simon William Gabriel Bruté de Rémur, a native of France, a descendant of a noble family, a graduate of the Polytechnic School of Paris, a schoolmate, friend, and correspondent of the famous Lamennais. He accompanied Bishop Flaget to the United States in 1808, and thenceforward labored as a missionary in Maryland, as a professor in Mount St. Mary's Seminary, and as president of St. Mary's College, Baltimore. He was consecrated in St. Louis October 28, 1834. The cathedral he found in Vincennes was a "plain brick building, one hundred and fifteen feet long and sixty feet broad, consisting of four walls and the roof, unplastered, and destitute even of a place for preserving the vestments and the sacred vessels." The Catholic population of Vincennes was poor, generally ignorant, and requiring much instruction and rousing. He found that the pew-rents and subscriptions would amount in all to about three hundred dollars a year—enough for a self-denying missionary, hardly enough for the expenses of a bishop and the constant calls that he might expect.

To form a definite idea of the scattered congregations in Indiana and Illinois he set out to visit his diocese. He found small congregations at Washington, Box's Creek, Rivière-au-Chat, Columbus, and Shelbyville. In Chicago there were about four hundred Catholics. At Paris, Edgar County, Ill., he found some Catholics, at Fort Wayne six or seven hundred, along the canal about two thousand. A few families were in La Porte, Michigan City, Logansport, and Terre Haute; and at Desselles there was a village of six hundred and fifty Catholic Indians. For this widely scattered flock Bishop Bruté had only a few priests, who, like Father St. Cyr, residing in Chicago, belonged to other dioceses. Practically he was without a clergy and without financial means either to educate priests or to import them from abroad. He resolved to make an appeal to Europe, and left in July, 1835.

Cheered and encouraged by his reception in Austria, Rome, and France, he returned to America, landing in New York July 20, 1836, and reaching his cathedral a month later. By the aid given him he established a diocesan seminary, an orphan asylum, and a free school at Vincennes, completed the so-called cathedral, and aided in erecting several small churches. But he brought back what was more important than money—nineteen priests and seminarians, many of them Bretons, resolute, hardy, full of faith and zeal. The priests were soon stationed at the points of greatest need, and the bishop, resuming his old life of professor, undertook the training of the seminarians in ecclesiastical learning and especially in that spirit of piety and self-sacrifice which he could so well inspire. They, too, gradually entered into the field of labor. The whole Western country awakened to a new religious life, and the apostolic bishop, by his personal visitations as well as by his councils and virtues, kept that life constantly vigorous and growing.

Amid the labors and hardships of his charge his health began to give way; but the strong will prevailed long after the body had grown feeble. Shortly before his death, while in a distant part of his diocese, he actually fainted on his way to the bedside of a patient. On Trinity Sunday, 1839, he celebrated the thirty-first anniversary of his first mass, being assisted on that occasion by two of his clergy, who supported him at the altar. When he was at last compelled to take to his bed he continued to be the missionary by his devotion, his humility, and his patience. On the 26th of June he surrendered his saintly soul into the hands of his Creator. Blessed is the land that has such patriarchs in its origin as Flaget, David, and Bruté. Their names are held in honor, their memories are an inspiration.

The successor of Bruté was the Rt. Rev. Celestine René Lawrence Guynemer de la Hailandière, a native of France, Vicar General of Vincennes at the time of the venerable bishop's death. He was consecrated in Paris August 18, 1839. In a letter to the Propaganda (1841) he estimated the population of his diocese to be twenty-five thousand to thirty-five thousand, attended by thirty-three priests. Undoubtedly the great glory of Bishop de la Hailandière's administration was the foundation, on the 26th of November, 1842, by a young member of the Brothers of the Holy Cross, the Rev. Edward Sorin, of the institution now known as the University of Notre Dame, Indiana. Though active to an extreme degree, no less than Bruté, unlike Bruté, Bishop de la Hailandière lacked a quality as essential as energy—prudence. He managed to excite among priests and people such an opposition that in the autumn of 1845 he was compelled to go to Rome to offer his resignation. It was not at once accepted; but having induced the other members of the hierarchy in the United States to confirm his request, he was relieved of his charge in the summer of 1847.

The clergyman chosen to be his successor was the Rev. John Stephen Bazin, a native of France, Vicar General of Mobile, who was consecrated in that city October 24, 1847. He was but installed in his see when he was seized with a disease that carried him off in the spring of 1848. The vicar general, Very Rev. J. M. Maurice de St. Palais, of an ancient and noble French family, was consecrated his successor January 14, 1849. The energy of which he was known to be possessed, and which he displayed in the visitation of his diocese immediately after his consecration, infused into all a new spirit of hearty activity. He found under his jurisdiction thirty-five priests attending to thirty thousand Catholics. He visited Europe in 1849, made his way to the great Benedictine Abbey of Einsiedeln, and induced the abbot to send him a colony of the monks of his ancient order.

As constituted by the bull erecting it (April 23, 1847), the diocese of Cleveland embraced about the third of the State of Ohio that lies north of the parallel of latitude 40° 41′. Pope Pius IX. chose for bishop of the new see the Rev. Amadeus Rappe, a native of France, whose piety, zeal, and energy as a missionary priest in Toledo proved him worthy and able to organize a new diocese. He was consecrated in Cincinnati August, 1847. He took possession, within a week after his consecration, of the only church in Cleveland, St. Mary's on the Flats, too small for the combined English and German speaking Catholics, whose numbers had increased to nearly four thousand. Besides this procathedral the diocese contained forty-two churches, attended by twenty priests. In September, 1849, he went to Europe, where he received generous assistance and secured several priests and seminarians and a colony of Ursuline nuns, for whom the residence of Judge Cowles, on Euclid Avenue, was purchased. Bishop Rappe came back to his see in August, 1850, full of courage and hope. The future was most promising for Ohio, the prospects for the church were bright. At this time Father Mathew, the great apostle of temperance, was in the United States. Bishop Rappe wrote a stirring pastoral in favor of temperance, and invited Father Mathew to preach and lecture on the subject in Cleveland. It is to be regretted that Father Mathew's visit to this country did not produce the good that was expected and should have come of it. He was accused by his countrymen and co-religionists of having allowed himself to be entrapped by a committee of fanatics and having appeared in public in a way that shocked Catholics by his seeming to take part in Protestant services. This apparent departure from Catholic discipline (surely Bishop England's example was forgotten) made the bishops hold aloof from his movement. It is to the credit of Bishop Rappe that he stood by the great apostle of temperance. We have made progress in our ideas about great social movements since then; we realize that preaching temperance even in Protestant churches is not taking part in Protestant religious services.

When Bishop Rappe was summoned to the Plenary Council in 1852 the new diocese of Cleveland could show a creditable progress: fifty-five churches and chapels built or in course of construction, forty-two priests, and a Catholic population estimated at thirty thousand.

After the resignation of Bishop Du Bourg the Rt. Rev. Joseph Rosati, Bishop of St. Louis, was transferred by the holy see to New Orleans; but on his representations the transfer was not effected and he was allowed to remain in St. Louis. The Rev. Leo Raymond de Neckère, a native of Belgium and a well-known missionary in Louisiana, was chosen for the vacant see of New Orleans and consecrated in the cathedral of that city May 16, 1830. He lacked one of the most necessary qualities for a bishop in those early times, bodily health, and was unable to endure the hardships of episcopal visitations. He did what good he could from his home in the city by the example of his virtues and by his wise legislation for the clergy. The year was one of cholera and yellow fever. Priests and Sisters of Charity gave their lives heroically in the service of the sick; the bishop himself was carried off by the fever on the 5th of September, 1833.

The Rev. Anthony Blanc, a native of France and vicar general of the diocese, was consecrated its bishop November 22, 1835. Nowhere, perhaps, had trusteeism done so much harm to religion in the beginning of the century as in New Orleans. Since the death of Sedella, its leader, this uncatholic system of church administration had been quiescent; but under Bishop Blanc it awoke to life and made a last desperate effort for supremacy. In 1842 the trustees of the cathedral refused to recognize a clergyman appointed as pastor by the bishop, and in justification of their action they claimed the right of patronage formerly enjoyed by the king of Spain. Presenting a petition full of misstatements, they brought suit against the Bishop of New Orleans in the parish court of the city. Their only real title to the property was based on the forcible seizure of the church in the year 1805. The right of patronage had never been transferred to them by the Spanish monarch, and could not be conferred by either the federal or the State government. Judge Maurian decided against the trustees. They appealed to the Supreme Court, which confirmed the decision of the parish court. Judge Bullard declared: "The right to nominate a curate [parish priest], or the *jus patronatus* of the Spanish law, is abrogated in this State. The wardens . . . cannot compel the bishop to institute a curate [parish priest] of their appointment, nor is he, in any legal sense, subordinate to the wardens of any one of the churches within his diocese in relation to his clerical functions." A rehearing, claimed by the wardens, was refused. The Supreme Court thus upheld the decision given by the holy see in the case of Philadelphia.

Of the progress of the church in Louisiana during this period we find but one item: in 1844 there were fifty-four priests in the diocese; this number may be taken as indicating a Catholic population of seventy-five or one hundred thousand. Yielding to the wishes of the fathers of the Seventh Provincial Council of Baltimore, Pope Pius IX., on the 19th of July, 1850, made New Orleans a metropolitan see and promoted Rt. Rev. Dr. Blanc to the archiepiscopal dignity. The province of New Orleans embraced the archbishop's diocese, with the suffragan dioceses of Mobile, Natchez, Little Rock, and Galveston. The pallium, which is the symbol of archiepiscopal jurisdiction, was conferred on the archbishop elect on the 16th of February, 1851, by the venerable Bishop Portier, of Mobile.

The see of Mobile, made suffragan to New Orleans in 1850, dated in a certain sense from the year 1826, when Bishop Portier was named Vicar Apostolic of Alabama, with residence in Mobile. From his voyage to Europe in 1829 he returned with two priests, four subdeacons, and two clerics. With these recruits not only was he able to provide the scattered flock in Alabama with the ministrations of the church, but he also laid the beginnings of Spring Hill College, that since then has become famous. St. Augustine, Fla., was under the care of a good priest, Rev. E. F. Mayne, whom Bishop England had sent there at the request of Dr. Portier. The trustees of the church in the ancient Catholic city drove their pastor from the sacred edifice in May, 1830, and when the case came before the court Judge Smith decided that the right of presentation vested in the congregation and not in the bishop, and that the treaty ceding Florida transferred to the congregation, through the United States government, all the rights which the king of Spain had possessed. This strange ruling was in direct contradiction to the rulings made in like cases by the other States of the Union. The States in the diocese of Mobile—Alabama and Florida—gained very slowly by immigration; in 1850 the Catholic body was estimated at ten thousand. Having met the most pressing wants of his flock, Rt. Rev. Dr. Portier could only await what did not come, an increase of numbers.

The see of Natchez, made suffragan to New Orleans in 1850, had been erected July 28, 1837, by his Holiness

Pope Gregory XVI., at the instance of the Provincial Council of Baltimore, with the State of Mississippi as a diocese. The clergyman first proposed for the new see, Very Rev. Thomas Heyden, after some hesitation declined the miter, and it was not till December 15, 1840, that the Rev. John Joseph Chanche, president of St. Mary's College, Baltimore, was selected and accepted the bulls. He was consecrated in the cathedral of Baltimore March 14, 1841, by Archbishop Eccleston, assisted by Bishops Fenwick of Boston and Hughes of New York. John Joseph Chanche was born in Baltimore October 4, 1795, his parents having fled from the horrors of the negro insurrection in St. Domingo. Educated by the Sulpitians in Baltimore, he became a member of that order, was made a professor in the seminary, and in 1834 succeeded Rev. S. Eccleston, the Archbishop of Baltimore, as president of the college.

Nearly the whole State of Mississippi was originally included in the diocese of Baltimore, although it was not till 1796 that Bishop Carroll obtained control of Natchez. It was made a vicariate apostolic and placed under the Bishop of New Orleans in 1825. This State had been the scene of French occupation in the end of the seventeenth century, and of the labors of missionaries from the seminary of Quebec and later of the Jesuit fathers. Under the French rule there was generally a priest at Natchez; and under the Spanish rule there was a chapel, if not a resident priest, at Villa Gayoso. After the vicariate apostolic of Mississippi was erected, Bishop Du Bourg exerted himself to meet to some extent the spiritual wants of the faithful there, and the Catholics of Natchez were occasionally visited by a clergyman from New Orleans until the diocese of Natchez was erected.

Bishop Chanche reached his episcopal city on the 18th of May, 1843, and, after ascertaining the needs of the diocese, visited the Northern States to solicit aid for the district committed to his care. Bishop Chanche returned encouraged by the liberality he had met; so much, indeed, that in February, 1848, he laid the foundation-stone of a Gothic cathedral sixty feet wide and one hundred and thirty feet long. The organization of the diocese of Natchez was a slow and difficult task. Although some points, like Biloxi and Natchez, were comparatively ancient settlements where churches once existed, the Catholic population had disappeared, leaving scarcely a vestige of religion. Being a slave State, Mississippi offered small inducements to immigrants, and the few who did come scattered far and wide. Writing in 1845, Bishop Chanche declared that when he took possession of his see he had not a single church or institution. After providing as well as he could for the little Catholic flock at Natchez, he planned churches at Biloxi, Pass Christian, and Yazoo. Hard as he had labored, yet he could show in 1848 only five priests and six poor churches as the result. A journey to Europe procured for this derelict diocese a half-dozen generous missionaries, who in their apostolic trips throughout the State unearthed more Catholics than any one had ever supposed were there.

Though an offshoot of the diocese of St. Louis, Little Rock was made a suffragan of New Orleans in 1850. On petition of the Council of Baltimore (1843) the State of Arkansas was detached from St. Louis and erected into a diocese, with the see at Little Rock. The Rev. Andrew Byrne, elected for the new diocese, was consecrated in New York March 10, 1844. Arkansas, like Mississippi, had been the scene of early explorations and missions under the French and Spanish rules. The French frontiersmen, however, were not models of attachment to the faith or the practice of their religion. A chapel erected at Arkansas Post was attended at intervals, but neither under French nor Spanish rule did it ever possess a zealous or growing congregation. After Bishop Du Bourg was appointed to the see of New Orleans, attempts were made to revive the faith among the scattered Catholics in Arkansas, and the missions were renewed by Bishop Rosati; but the prevailing ignorance and vice were deplorable and almost insurmountable. Being a slave State, with no inducement to immigration, Arkansas attracted but few Catholics from Europe or the Eastern States.

After proceeding to his diocese and searching for Catholics throughout the length and breadth of the State, Bishop Byrne wrote: "I can assure you that within the whole diocese of Little Rock there exist no means to erect a single altar. The Catholic population does not exceed seven hundred souls, and they are scattered in every county in the State." There were not at any one point Catholics enough to erect a church or maintain a priest. In fact, the diocese had but a single priest and two churches, loaded with heavy debts. Bishop Byrne appealed to the missionary societies of Europe and obtained some aid from them. He was also assisted by his friends among the clergy and laity of New York. He was thus enabled to obtain a site in Little Rock to build a church. "You may judge of my position," he wrote, "when I state that since I came to Arkansas I have received only twenty dollars toward my support. I have expended the money from Europe in purchasing lots and building a few small churches." Yet he did not give up, disheartening as the prospect was. He kept on at his work with a zeal worthy of a larger and more conspicuous field. At the beginning of 1852 the diocese had ten clergymen, eight churches, and two chapels; but the Catholic population was not estimated at more than one thousand.

In the first part of this work we have studied the rise and decline of the missions of Texas. The territory that went by that name had originally been part of the Spanish possessions in America. In 1821 Mexico broke away from Spain and declared its independence; in 1824 it adopted a federal form of government, of which a State composed of the former provinces of Coahuila and Texas became a constituent member. But presently immigration transformed Texas from a Spanish into an American community. By the year 1833 the Americans had become so numerous that they made bold to take matters into their own hands and form a new constitution after their own pattern. In 1836 Texas seceded from Mexico, and eight hundred Texans assured their secession and their independence by the battle and victory of San Jacinto (April 21, 1836), won by General Sam Houston against the Mexican President, Santa Anna. Texas then set up for an independent republic, and was recognized as such by the United States, England, France, and Belgium. It was only a question of time, however, when it should enter into the Union; it was annexed by Congress March 3, 1845.

We may well fancy that the missions of Texas, and consequently religion, had fallen into a sad condition, especially after the secession of Mexico from Spain and the influx of American immigrants. When the wretched state of religion in Texas became known to Pope Gregory XVI., a letter was addressed from Rome to the Bishop of New Orleans requesting him to send a capable priest to examine and report on the actual situation. Bishop Blanc selected Very Rev. John Timon, Visitor of the Congregation of the Mission, to undertake the task. When his statement reached Rome, the sovereign pontiff, by the advice of the Congregation de Propaganda Fide, resolved to establish a distinct jurisdiction in Texas. Documents were forwarded appointing Very Rev. John Timon prefect apostolic and investing him with power to administer confirmation. Father Timon accepted the charge and at once sent to Texas one of his fellow-religious, the Rev. John M. Odin, as vice-prefect. After a journey through the territory, Father Odin estimated the Catholics in Texas at ten thousand. In December the prefect himself, Father Timon, arrived in Austin and presented to President Lamar letters from Cardinal Fransoni, Prefect of the Propaganda, officially recognizing the new republic in the Pope's name. The Congress, by a special act, confirmed to the chief pastor of the Roman Catholic Church in the republic of Texas the churches of Nacogdoches, San Antonio, Goliad, Victoria, Concepcion, San José, San Juan, Espada, Refugio, and the Alamo, with the contiguous grounds, not to exceed fifteen acres. The prefect and vice-prefect then traversed the country to ascertain where the Catholics could be most easily gathered into congregations. Meanwhile Rome, having by this time received fuller information of the condition of the church in Texas, concluded that a prefecture was a less honor than the republic deserved. A bull erecting the republic of Texas into a vicariate apostolic was issued by Pope Gregory XVI. on the 16th of July, 1841, and the Rt. Rev. John M. Odin, C.M., was appointed to the newly constituted vicariate, with the title of Bishop of Claudiopolis, *in partibus infidelium.*

In his mission tours through Texas Bishop Odin found many Catholics who had not seen a priest since they had left their European homes. The field was immense, the laborers few. He went to Europe for aid, and returned in the spring of 1846 with some priests and seminarians. Meanwhile (March 3, 1845) Texas became part of the

United States, and war with Mexico followed. Naturally immigration into Texas stopped during the conflict, and the priests and sisters had much work to do in camp and hospital. After the war, ended by the Treaty of Guadalupe Hidalgo (February 2, 1848), prosperity returned to Texas. Before proceeding to the Plenary Council of Baltimore (1852), Bishop Odin had in the diocese seventeen priests and twenty churches.

CHAPTER XXV.

THE PROVINCE OF ST. LOUIS AND THE PACIFIC COAST (1829–52).

As early as 1830 Bishop Rosati set about erecting a cathedral worthy of his growing diocese, but, owing to the difficulties which environed him, it was not completed till 1834. It was regarded as a remarkable piece of architecture at the time. This building still bears the name of cathedral in the city of St. Louis and does service as such. It is venerable by many a grand ceremonial performed in it since the day of its consecration. In 1838 Bishop Rosati could report nine stone churches, ten of brick, twenty-five of wood, attended by twenty-four Jesuits, twenty Lazarists, one Dominican, and twenty-three secular priests. He solicited from the holy see the appointment of a coadjutor, and proposed for the office Rev. Peter Richard Kenrick. It was not, however, till he visited Rome in 1840, after attending the Fourth Council of Baltimore, that he obtained the appointment of that learned clergyman as Bishop of Drasis, *in partibus infidelium*, and Coadjutor of St. Louis. The coadjutor was needed, for the sovereign pontiff laid a new burden on the shoulders of Bishop Rosati by charging him with an important mission to Hayti. On his return from Rome to the United States he consecrated his coadjutor in St. Mary's Church, Philadelphia, and then prepared to sail to Hayti to fulfill the duties imposed upon him. His departure from St. Louis (April 25, 1840) was really a last farewell to his diocese. After successfully arranging with President Boyer, of Hayti, the terms of a concordat, and administering confirmation to hundreds, he hastened back to Rome. His report gave great satisfaction, and he was deputed to return to the island and consummate the proposed arrangements. At Paris his condition became so critical that he was obliged to go back to Rome, where he died, September 25, 1843, honored for his virtues, piety, zeal, learning, and the ability he displayed in the government of his diocese, in the councils of the church, and in delicate negotiations with the civil powers.

At the time that the diocese came into the hands of Bishop Kenrick the city of St. Louis had five churches for the accommodation of sixteen thousand Catholics, who were attended by twenty-five priests. The diocese comprised the State of Missouri, with about fifty churches outside the episcopal city, the western part of Illinois, with about thirteen churches, Arkansas, with two, and Indian missions among the Pottowatomies and the Flatheads. The Catholic population of the whole diocese was estimated at one hundred thousand. But its limits—and therefore the number of its clergy and laity—were reduced to the State of Missouri and the territory west of Missouri when the sovereign pontiff, at the petition of the Council of Baltimore, erected (November, 1844) the sees of Chicago and Little Rock. This division left to the diocese of St. Louis a Catholic population of fifty thousand. Bishop Kenrick attended the Baltimore Council of 1846, which solicited the erection of St. Louis to an archbishopric; and on the 8th of October of the following year Pope Pius IX., by his apostolic brief of that date, raised St. Louis to that dignity. At the petition of the Seventh Provincial Council of Baltimore, which Archbishop Kenrick attended in 1849, the Bishops of Dubuque, Nashville, Chicago, Milwaukee, and St. Paul were made suffragans of the Archbishop of St. Louis. A diocesan synod held August 25, 1850, showed the number of priests in the diocese of St. Louis to be forty-three.

The State of Tennessee had been included in the diocese of Bardstown since the first division of the diocese of Baltimore. The progress of the faith in that State had been slow; Catholics were few and widely scattered. Like North Carolina, from which it sprang, Tennessee had a population that had not come in contact with Catholicity and was little disposed to welcome the church. The conviction that a devoted resident bishop, ready to endure trials and hardships, could ultimately build up Catholicity there led to the erection of the diocese of Nashville. The establishment of that see was recommended by the Provincial Council of Baltimore in April, 1837, and was decreed by the bull *Universi Dominici Gregis*, of Gregory XVI., July 28, 1837. The arduous duty of organizing and directing the diocese devolved on Father Richard Pius Miles, of the Order of St. Dominic, a native of Maryland, born in Prince George's County May 17, 1791. He was consecrated in the cathedral of Bardstown September 16, 1838.

The city of Nashville contained at that time about one hundred and thirty Catholics; Murfreesborough had but one Catholic family; in the neighborhood of Athens there were about a hundred Catholics, chiefly men employed in building a railroad, and a few at Fayetteville, Mount Pleasant, and Columbia. After a journey of four hundred and sixty miles on horseback in search of Catholics, the bishop estimated his flock, including a few families at Memphis and other places not yet visited, at not much more than three hundred; and this little body was widely scattered. It was surely a poor diocese, with slight immigration, a difficult mountain country, and a population filled with strong prejudices against the church.

On the 28th of July, 1837, was erected the see of Dubuque, a city four years old. The new diocese contained within its jurisdiction the territory north of the State of Missouri lying between the Mississippi and Missouri rivers; in other words, Iowa, Minnesota, and part of the two Dakotas. The priest selected for the see was Rev. Mathias Loras, a native of France and a missionary for some years in the diocese of Mobile, in which city he was consecrated December 10, 1837. Within his vast diocese there was one priest and a half-finished church. At once he went to France for auxiliaries and means. In October, 1838, Bishop Loras arrived from Havre with two priests and four subdeacons, the nucleus of his clergy. Meanwhile Father Mazzuchelli, the one priest in the diocese at the time of its erection, had completed a residence for the bishop, who reached Dubuque on the 18th of April, 1839, and was duly installed on the third Sunday after Easter. He began a visitation of his diocese, and found that Davenport, mainly by the liberality of Mr. Anthony Leclaire, had already a fine brick church with a schoolroom attached to it, and that in Burlington the Catholics were at work on a church. The town of St. Peter, in the northern part of his diocese (now Mendota, Minn.), next claimed his attention; there he was welcomed by nearly two hundred Catholics. At Prairie du Chien he found seven hundred, and started a church which Father Mazzuchelli undertook to build. Returning to Dubuque, he dedicated his cathedral under the patronage of St. Raphael the Archangel, on the 22d of August, 1839.

In 1840 he could report five churches—his cathedral,

St. Patrick's in Makoquata, St. Anthony's in Davenport, St. Paul's in Burlington, and one building in St. Peter. After another year there was a brick church in Iowa City, a German church in West Point, and Catholics were busy erecting churches in Bloomington and Fort Madison. As Wisconsin was temporarily placed under his care, he visited that territory, establishing a mission among the Menominees, and organizing a congregation in Milwaukee that undertook to erect a church on some lots given by Solomon Juneau. No contrast could be greater than that between the State of Alabama, where Bishop Loras had lived, with its decayed congregations and its apathy, on the one hand, and the busy, pushing, active Northwest to which he was now come, on the other, with immigration pouring in, largely of Catholics, all active, stirring, energetic, building houses, factories, schools, and churches. But Bishop Loras showed himself to be eminently a man of work; he was in his element.

As he was himself a man of energy and apostolic zeal, so he expected the priests under him to be. His solicitude extended to the Indians as well as the whites. In 1842 he sent Rev. Remegius Petiot to the Winnebagos, Rev. Mr. Pelamourgues to the Sacs and Foxes, Rev. Augustine Ravoux—who still lives in St. Paul, the model and the glory of that province—to the Sioux above the Falls of St. Anthony, the scene of Hennepin's adventures. The erection of the dioceses of Chicago and Milwaukee relieved Bishop Loras of the district east of the Mississippi, though it deprived him of a few priests. The bishop's great struggle was to keep pace with the Catholic immigration, then pouring in a steady stream all over Iowa; and though by December, 1843, he saw twelve new churches erected, yet as many more were needed. New settlements were constantly springing into existence that required the visits of priest and bishop; there was no rest for either. But fast as was the pace of Western immigration—and Bishop Loras never ceased to encourage it—the increase of churches and clergy seemed not to lag behind. The bishop was untiring, ubiquitous, and withal shrewd, keen, and far-seeing in securing in all new settlements ground and property for the church. It is on the foundations he thus laid that has risen the greatness of the province of Dubuque.

The see of Chicago was erected November 28, 1843. It contained the State of Illinois. This was classic ground in the early mission period for the voyageur and the missionary. Chicago then was the point where converged all the lines of Indian and Canadian explorations, travels, and commerce, just as Chicago now is the hub of all our inland routes of trade. In 1804 the United States government established at Chicago Fort Dearborn. Gradually a few whites settled there, Ouilmette and Beaubien being among the pioneers. The Rev. Gabriel Richard, of Detroit, visited Chicago in 1821 and said mass in Colonel Beaubien's house. He also preached to the garrison in the fort. In 1833 the Catholics, headed by Thomas J. B. Owen and J. B. Beaubien, sent a petition to Bishop Rosati asking him to give them a resident priest. The Bishop of St. Louis, acting as vicar general of the diocese of Bardstown, under whose jurisdiction Illinois was at the time, appointed Rev. J. M. J. St. Cyr to the charge of Chicago. He reached his post, and said mass in Mark Beaubien's house May 5, 1833. The next year a lot was purchased on Lake and State streets, and a little church twenty-five by thirty-five feet was erected. Rev. Mr. St. Cyr was recalled in 1837; after him came Revs. Leander Schaffer, O'Meara, and Maurice de St. Palais, who opened St. Xavier's Academy, and soon after began the erection of a brick church on

Madison Street and Wabash Avenue which cost four thousand dollars.

Such was the condition of the Catholic Church in the city of Chicago when Pope Gregory XVI. made that city an episcopal see, and appointed as its first bishop Rt. Rev. William Quarter, who was consecrated in St. Patrick's Cathedral, New York, on the 10th of March, 1844. The priests who were at the time in Chicago belonged to the diocese of Vincennes and were recalled by the bishop of that see. Bishop Quarter at once exerted himself to obtain priests to fill the vacancies, and to such purpose that by the close of the year he had twenty-three priests in his diocese. The Catholic population of the State was estimated at more than fifty thousand.

Full of that spirit of energetic go-aheadativeness that is said to have characterized the city of Chicago from the very beginning, Bishop Quarter was ceaseless in stimulating congregations to build churches, and seemed to reach out in all directions for the priests needed to keep pace with immigration. But the vast and constant labor had overtasked his strength and energies, though neither he nor those around him saw anything to excite alarm. He lectured in his cathedral throughout the Lent of 1848, and after preaching on Passion Sunday seemed to be greatly exhausted. He retired early to rest; during the night his moans summoned Rev. P. T. McElhearne to his room, and he was found seated on the side of his bed, complaining of excruciating pain in his head. A physician was summoned and the last sacraments were administered. With the cry "Lord, have mercy on my poor soul!" he sank into a comatose state and soon expired (April 10, 1848).

The successor of Bishop Quarter was a Jesuit father, a native of Belgium, who since his ordination (1827) had been on the mission in Maryland and Missouri, the Rev.

James Oliver van de Velde. He was consecrated in St. Louis February 11, 1849. Chicago at that time had four churches—the cathedral, St. Joseph's Church on Chicago Avenue, St. Peter's on Washington Street, and St. Patrick's on Randolph Street; a theological seminary, with eighteen students; a university, St. Mary of the Lake; and a convent of the Sisters of Mercy, with its academy. There were in the diocese forty-eight other churches or public chapels, and forty priests to minister to a constantly increasing body of eighty thousand Catholics. Bishop Van de Velde was zealous and energetic, but a rheumatism, from which he had long suffered, became extremely severe in the damp and chilly climate of Chicago. At the earliest moment that he could communicate with the sovereign pontiff he tendered his resignation. Though refused at first, he did finally succeed in getting himself transferred to the see of Natchez.

Wisconsin and eastern Minnesota—that is to say, the part of Minnesota east of the Mississippi—were classic ground in the history of our early missions. This was the territory included in the diocese of Milwaukee, erected November 28, 1843. Though it was an offshoot of Vincennes, and therefore of Cincinnati, Bardstown, and Baltimore, Milwaukee, for territorial convenience, was made suffragan to St. Louis in 1849. The new bishop was the Rev. John Martin Henni, a native of Switzerland, a missionary in the United States since 1828, and at the time of his appointment Vicar General of Cincinnati, where he was consecrated March 19, 1841. Bishop Henni, after being installed in the one little wooden church of Milwaukee, which required three masses to hold the three congregations, French, English-speaking, and German, found in the diocese twenty congregations, about fourteen churches, and six priests. Under the impulse given by him the faithful were soon busy improving or erecting churches throughout the diocese. Indeed, before the end of the year 1845 no fewer than twenty churches were in progress. The great difficulty was to obtain clergymen for these willing congregations. Conscious that he could not depend on priests from other parts, he projected from the outset a theological seminary, and resolved to establish it on a firm basis. In forming the plan of his seminary and directing it he was greatly aided by Rev. Michael Heiss, who afterward became his successor. Much had been accomplished, but, as more remained to be done, Bishop Henni resolved to visit Europe in order to get men and means. With this view he visited Austria, Bavaria, Wurtemberg, Switzerland, and Rome. He must have been successful in his journey, for soon after his return he purchased, with the means obtained in Europe, a site for his cathedral, seventy-seven by one hundred and seventy-seven feet, erected St. Gall's Church and that of the Holy Trinity in Milwaukee, and prepared plans for a cathedral in the Byzantine style, the corner-stone of which was laid on the 8th of July, 1848, with imposing ceremonial. Another result of his journey to Europe was the arrival in his diocese of brothers and sisters of the Order of St. Francis, and of the school sisters of Notre Dame. In a pastoral to his flock, appealing for aid to carry on his cathedral, he reminded the faithful of what had been already done: "When, six years ago, we took possession of the newly established bishopric of Milwaukee, we found nothing of note here, unless what the most urgent and immediate payments enabled us to retain. All things had to be begun; all things had to be created. We found but four priests incorporated in our diocese, laboring for this great fold of ten thousand souls. We number now over fifty priests, laboring for more than fifty thousand souls.

Churches and chapels have sprung up in unexampled numbers; schools, institutions of piety, and convents exist now not only on the Milwaukee, but on the Wisconsin and Mississippi rivers Thank God with us that he has thus blessed this diocese beyond expectation."

The Territory of Minnesota, extending northward from the Iowa line to the British boundary, westward from the St. Croix River to the Missouri, was contained in the diocese of St. Paul, erected July 19, 1850. This Territory of Minnesota had been known to the voyageur and the missionary, and their memory is perpetuated in the names now borne by many of Minnesota's lakes, cities, rivers, counties, and towns. The Rt. Rev. Joseph Cretin, chosen for the new see, was a native of Montluel, in the department of Ain, France, had come to the United States with Bishop Loras (April, 1839), and was Vicar General of Dubuque at the time of his promotion. On receiving notification of it he went to France to be consecrated in Belley, the see of his native diocese, January 26, 1851. He returned with five priests. These, with the veteran, Augustine Ravoux, were the nucleus of Bishop Cretin's clergy. He was warmly welcomed by his flock and escorted to the little log house which was to be his episcopal residence.

Outside of St. Paul there was not much to show. There was a small Canadian settlement on the Minnesota River opposite Fort Snelling, which was known then as St. Peter and is known now as Mendota. Seven miles below Fort Snelling, on the eastern bank of the Mississippi, was the city of the bishop's see, which a few years before was only a small Canadian settlement where the Rev. Lucien Galtier had raised a log chapel that he named St. Paul, in fraternal remembrance of the upper settlement, St. Peter. The title of the chapel is preserved in the name of the capital city. There were, moreover, two other small settlements, one at St. Anthony's Falls, the nucleus of Minneapolis, and the other on the St. Croix River where now stands Stillwater. The Rev. Augustine Ravoux, residing by turns in St. Peter and St. Paul, was the only priest in the whole Territory when it was erected into a diocese. Before the bishop arrived from France, Father Ravoux made purchases of real estate in the young city—a village, rather—of St. Paul that have been the source of the material prosperity of the diocese, and still constitute to-day an endowment of no mean proportions. The new diocese had ten priests and seven churches when the bishop proceeded to the Plenary Council of Baltimore.

At the request of the Seventh Provincial Council of Baltimore the territory lying between the western boundary of Arkansas, Missouri, Iowa, and Minnesota and the eastern flank of the Rockies was formed into the vicariate apostolic of the Indian Territory. The Rev. John B. Miege, S.J., named Bishop of Messenia, *in partibus infidelium*, and consecrated March 25, 1851, was put in charge of this vicariate. It comprised the present States of North and South Dakota, Nebraska, Kansas, Colorado, Wyoming, and eastern Montana. The two chief mission posts in that region were St. Mary's Pottowatomie mission and St. Francis Hieronymo's Osage mission. In the former the annual baptisms were about one hundred and seventeen, in the latter five hundred had been baptized since 1847. Not for long, however, was this vast territory to be the exclusive home of the Indians. Already white settlers were invading it at the time of the First Plenary Council of Baltimore. The vicariate was a suffragan of St. Louis.

When the treaty of Guadalupe Hidalgo (1848) added New Mexico to the United States, religion there was in a sad condition. The Mexican Bishop of Durango, Bishop Zubiria, even after the cession visited New Mexico, in October, 1850, for he had received from the holy see no notification that an ecclesiastical change had followed the civil change of that territory. However, now that it was part of the United States, the American hierarchy thought that it should be included in the body of the dioceses of the republic, and requested the holy see to provide it with a bishop. Accordingly New Mexico was erected into a vicariate apostolic, and the Rev. John B. Lamy, a native of France and a priest of the diocese of Cincinnati, was assigned to the task of reorganizing religious affairs in the vicariate. He was consecrated in Cincinnati November 24, 1850.

The vicar apostolic found crying abuses existing, and by kind and patient advice endeavored to recall the clergy to a true ecclesiastical spirit; but few would respond to his advices. Having ascertained exactly the condition of his flock, Bishop Lamy set out for the Council of Baltimore. The estimated population of New Mexico at this time was sixty thousand Mexicans and eight thousand Indians. There were twenty-five parish churches and forty scattered chapels.

The treaty of Guadalupe Hidalgo (1848) likewise brought California into the Union. The religious condition of the country was deplorable. Cut off from Mexico as it had been from Spain, no further supply of missionaries could be expected from either. When the discovery of gold was made, men poured in from all countries, who looked with utter contempt on the old inhabitants. Among the immigrants were many Catholics, not a few of them rough men and with little around them to polish their ways. Yet faith was not dead in their hearts; they soon felt the want of church and priest, of divine service, and of the sacraments at death. Big-hearted and generous men they were, ready to put up churches and support priests. Letters came to Archbishop Eccleston in Baltimore and to Bishop Hughes in New York, representing the condition of affairs, written by intelligent Americans, Catholic and Protestant. It was not in the power of these dignitaries to interfere; they could only appeal to Rome to lose no time in providing for the future of the church in a part of the country which was soon to become populous and important. News also reached Rome that an impostor, representing himself to be an apostolic nuncio empowered to arrange all ecclesiastical matters, was roaming about California. Speedy measures were necessary.

When the proceedings of the Seventh Council of Baltimore reached Rome, with the names of three clergymen proposed for a successor to Bishop Garcia Diego in the see of Monterey, matters became somewhat clear to the Roman authorities. The sovereign pontiff appointed as Bishop of Monterey Rev. Father Joseph Sadoc Alemany, a Spaniard of the Order of St. Dominic, who had been for some years on the American missions. He was in Rome at the time of his nomination, and was consecrated in the Church of San Carlo, June 13, 1850, by Cardinal Fransoni.

Oregon became, in 1810, the field of the fur-trading operations of John Jacob Astor, who made Astoria his chief post. Iroquois and Canadian Catholics came to Oregon with the expeditions of Lewis and Clark (1805) and of Hunt (1811), some of whom subsequently took service in the Northwest and Hudson Bay companies, and settled in the Willamette Valley. This was the cradle of Oregon Catholicity. The English were virtually in possession of the country, the United States doing nothing to enforce its claims. The first attempt by Americans to gain a footing in Oregon was due to Protestant missionary societies, under whom a Methodist mission was established in 1834 and a Presbyterian one in 1836. The Canadians in the Willamette Valley wrote in 1834 and the following year to Rt. Rev. Dr. Provencher, residing at the Red River, as the nearest Catholic authority, asking for a priest. He had no clergyman whom he could send to their relief, and advised them to apply to Canada.

When their application reached the Archbishop of Quebec he selected Rev. Francis Norbert Blanchet, a parish priest in his diocese, and Rev. Modeste Demers to become the spiritual guides of the Canadian settlers on the Pacific, and to establish missions among the native tribes; he moreover appointed Rev. Mr. Blanchet his vicar general for Oregon, thus assuming that it was English territory. The directors of the Hudson Bay Company, however, recognized that the Willamette Valley was certainly American territory and must ultimately be yielded to the United States. They insisted, therefore, on the establishment of the French mission at Cowlitz Portage, which they regarded as being certainly within the British limits. Very Rev. Mr. Blanchet started from Montreal in a bark canoe of the Hudson Bay Company, May 3, 1838, and was joined at Red River by Rev. Mr. Demers. A long and painful journey of more than four thousand miles brought them at last, on the 24th of November, to Fort Vancouver.

The total number of the Canadian Catholics in the different posts and settlements, with their wives and children, was estimated at about nine hundred. Many had not seen a priest, heard mass, or approached the sacraments from twenty to forty years. There was still faith, but there was great ignorance. The situation required patient instruction to be given to old and young, marriages to be validated, children to be baptized. There was labor enough here for the missionaries, but they endeavored also to instruct the Indians. Meanwhile the fathers of the Society of Jesus undertook missions among the Flathead and other Rocky Mountain tribes. These missions were founded by the famous Belgian Jesuit Father De Smet, and are to-day in a very flourishing condition.

The condition of the Oregon missions and the necessity of ecclesiastical organization for that territory were represented to the Sacred Congregation de Propaganda Fide both by the Archbishop of Baltimore and his suffragans and by the Archbishop of Quebec. The sovereign pontiff, accordingly, by his brief of December, 1843, established the vicariate apostolic of Oregon, embracing all the territory between the Mexican province of California in the south and the Russian province of Alaska in the north, and extending from the Pacific Ocean to the Rocky Mountains. The Very Rev. Francis Norbert Blanchet was appointed Bishop of Drasa, *in partibus infidelium*, and Vicar Apostolic of Oregon, May 7, 1844. Soon after receiving his bulls the bishop elect sailed for Montreal. There he was consecrated in the cathedral by the Rt. Rev. Ignatius Bourget, bishop of that city. After receiving the episcopal consecration he sailed for Europe. On reaching Rome he presented a memoir to the Sacred Congregation de Propaganda Fide on the condition of his vicariate. The result of his six years of labor was fourteen chapels and as many missions, one thousand Catholic Canadians, six thousand Indian converts, and two educational establishments. As he insisted on the necessity of dividing his vast vicariate, the sovereign pontiff (July 24, 1846) erected the archiepiscopal see of Oregon City, and the dioceses of Nesqually, Walla Walla, Fort Hall, Colville, Vancouver, Princess Charlotte's Island, and New Caledonia. But of these projected sees only Vancouver and Nesqually became realities; the others remained on paper.

Archbishop Blanchet sailed from Brest February 22, 1847, with a retinue of eleven priests and seven sisters of the Congregation of Notre Dame de Namur. After a voyage of nearly six months, their bark, "L'Étoile du Matin," anchored in the Columbia River August 13, 1847. Archbishop Blanchet set up his archiepiscopal throne in the Church of St. Paul, on the Willamette, which became his cathedral.

The diocese of Nesqually was erected May 31, 1850; but it had existed under the name of the diocese of Walla Walla since September 27, 1846, when its incumbent, the Rev. Augustine Magloire Alexander Blanchet, brother to the Archbishop of Oregon, was consecrated in Montreal. As Bishop of Nesqually he resided in Vancouver. Previous to the change of title and of territory he had resided at Fort Walla Walla, and had under his jurisdiction the districts of Colville and Fort Hall and the country between the forty-second and fiftieth degrees of latitude. After his transfer from Walla Walla to Nesqually his diocese was the present State of Washington.

We may now sum up the evolution of the hierarchy from 1829, date of the First Provincial Council of Baltimore, to 1852, date of the First Plenary Council of Baltimore. At the first council presided over by the Metropolitan of Baltimore there were present in person or by proxy his suffragans, the Bishops of Philadelphia, New York, Boston, Charleston, Bardstown, and Cincinnati. Besides these, and outside the ecclesiastical province of Baltimore, there were in the United States the Bishops of

New Orleans, St. Louis, and the Vicar Apostolic of Alabama, who did not form an ecclesiastical province, since no one of them was archbishop. Therefore the hierarchy of the United States in 1829 was made up of one archbishop and nine bishops. Since that time Baltimore, Philadelphia, New York, Boston, Bardstown, Cincinnati, New Orleans, and St. Louis branched out into other sees and dioceses. The evolution was rapid and marvelous in the North and the West, so that in 1852 the schedule stands thus: archbishoprics: Baltimore, New York, Cincinnati, St. Louis, New Orleans; suffragan bishoprics: for Baltimore: Philadelphia, Pittsburg, Richmond, Charleston, Wheeling, and Savannah; for New York: Albany, Buffalo, Boston, and Hartford; for Cincinnati: Louisville (formerly Bardstown), Vincennes, Detroit, and Cleveland; for New Orleans: Mobile, Natchez, Little Rock, and Galveston; for St. Louis: Dubuque, Nashville, Chicago, Milwaukee, St. Paul, and the vicariate of the Indian Territory; provinces, five; suffragans, twenty-four.

But this is not all. In 1846 the status and boundary of Oregon were settled by treaty with England; moreover, by the treaty of Guadalupe (1848), New Mexico and California came into the Union. Now in 1850 New Mexico was erected into a vicariate apostolic, and in California there was the diocese of Monterey. While the status of Oregon was unsettled and its boundary was in dispute, a vicariate, then a bishopric, then an archbishopric having as suffragans one American diocese, Nesqually, and one British diocese, Vancouver Island, sprang into existence apart from and independently of the hierarchy of the Eastern States. We have, then, to add to the foregoing archbishoprics the hybrid province of Oregon with its one American suffragan, and we have to add to the bishoprics those of New Mexico and California, which were not yet assigned to any province; and thus we get for the territory of the United States at the time of the First Plenary Council of Baltimore a total of six provinces and twenty-seven suffragan dioceses.

When, on Sunday, May 9, 1852, the American hierarchy, with an abbot of La Trappe, the superiors of the Augustinians, Dominicans, Benedictines, Franciscans, Jesuits, Redemptorists, Lazarists, and Sulpitians, the officials of the synod, and the theologians of the bishops, filed in solemn procession into the cathedral of Baltimore for the opening of the council, the country and the world beheld the objective lesson of a growth and extension within half a century for the like of which we must go back to the earliest days of Christianity, when in the freshness of youth and the vigor of apostolic zeal the church laid hold of the Roman empire. And when that august assembly closed its sessions it had added to the number of American bishops, for it solicited and obtained from the holy see the erection of new sees at Portland, Me., Burlington, Vt., Brooklyn, N. Y., Newark, N. J., Erie, Pa., Covington, Ky., Quincy, Ill., Santa Fé, N. Mex., Natchitoches, La., a vicariate apostolic in Upper Michigan, and an archiepiscopal see in San Francisco.

The period that now opens is the period of the Civil War that split the country in two sections, the South and the North. The hierarchy of the United States was not split; its unity stood the shock, unbroken. If, then, I head the two following chapters "The Church in the South," "The Church in the North," it is for the reason that before and during and after the great conflict the growth of the church in the South was almost null, whereas in the North it was gigantic. Growth, being the main idea that underlies this history, naturally suggests the headings which, without this explanation, might look sectional, partisan, and injurious to our religious unity. If I include in the North certain dioceses in border States more attached to the Confederacy than the Union, it is because those dioceses were suffragans of provinces that were mainly Northern. The division, while convenient for my purpose, is not absolutely perfect.

Part III. The Growth of the Church from the First Plenary to the Second Plenary Council of Baltimore (1852–66).

CHAPTER XXVI.

THE CHURCH IN THE SOUTH (1852–66).

Before proceeding with my narrative of the development of the hierarchy I must insert here the strange Bedini episode.

For several years the United States had been represented in Rome by a resident minister. Pius IX. had therefore the right to be represented, if he deemed it necessary or expedient, by a nuncio in Washington. No step, however, in this direction had as yet been taken. The Most Rev. Cajetan Bedini, Archbishop of Thebes, appointed as nuncio to the court of Brazil in 1853, was commissioned by the holy see to remain in the United States, on the way to his post, long enough to look into certain complaints made by the German trustees of churches in Philadelphia and Buffalo. He was also intrusted with a friendly letter from the Pope to the President of the United States. Arrived in Washington, Bedini had an interview with President Pierce. But when it became a question of recognizing him as a member of the diplomatic corps, the State Department raised difficulties on the ground that he was not a layman. Moreover, Gavazzi, an apostate Italian priest who was in the country at the time, aided by Italian and German revolutionists, refugees from Europe, circulated the vilest calumnies against the personal character of the nuncio. The press helped to spread them. Anti-Catholic public opinion was worked up to so high a pitch of fanaticism that his assassination was secretly plotted. Nothing daunted, Mgr. Bedini went on with the work of his mission, the examination and settlement of the complaints of the Germans of Buffalo and Philadelphia. He was not successful in this direction; but the work gave him the opportunity of visiting most of the episcopal sees of the country from Canada to New Orleans and from New York to Milwaukee. Everywhere his reception was respectful and enthusiastic from the Catholics, sullen and turbulent from the Protestants. Had not the authorities acted with energy in Cincinnati, to give but one instance, an organized attempt to hang him and burn the cathedral might have been effected. Rome had been ill advised—Know-nothingism was still rampant; the times were not propitious to a Roman envoy.

The report made by Bedini to the holy see is of the highest importance. I summarize it:

Catholicity in the United States was an organized, united, increasing body, with dioceses, churches, and institutions of every kind. Catholics were well represented in the different conditions of life; in civil, military, and naval positions. The German immigrants, largely made up of infidels and revolutionists, were active, turbulent, and by their newspapers and societies exerted a detrimental influence on their Catholic fellow-countrymen. Of the larger, and mostly Catholic, Irish immigration he noted the strong faith and attachment to the church, the result of perpetual persecution at home; but they were exposed to great losses from being led into vice, neglecting their religious duties, and in many cases from the fact that no priest or church was near to recall them. Want of Catholic schools for the education of their children was another source of possible losses.

Referring to the episcopate, Archbishop Bedini declared that an episcopal body so respected and so worthy of respect as that of the United States was a real blessing. They were all loved and venerated in the highest degree by their people and even by Protestants. Everywhere he found bishops building or encouraging the clergy to build churches and institutions, though their means were scanty. They were no longer hampered by the fatal trustee system, now confined within very narrow limits. The clergy as a body were edifying and laborious in the discharge of the complicated duties imposed upon them: compelled to collect money to build churches and schools, besides attending to the discharge of their sacred ministry. He urged, where possible, the appointment of bishops of American birth. "I myself had occasion to see that not only more deference was paid to the advice and direction of an American-born bishop, but that the bishop himself is more courageous, fearless, and steadfast in the struggles which not infrequently arise." He spoke strongly against dividing the Catholics into German and English speaking. "It is enough to reflect that no English, American, or Irish citizen learns German, and that every German seeks earnestly to acquire the English language. The rising German generation speaks and understands English so well that mothers complain they cannot understand their children when they converse together." Of the regular orders, especially of the Jesuits, Redemptorists, and Benedictines, as well as of the religious communities of women, he spoke in terms of highest praise.

The South was mainly comprised in the two provinces of Baltimore and New Orleans.

The province of Baltimore contained the following dioceses: Baltimore, Philadelphia, Pittsburg, Erie, Richmond, Wheeling, Charleston, Savannah. Taking them up in the order named, I shall review them briefly, noting the increase within them of clergy and laity, of parishes and churches, and the injuries inflicted on them by the Civil War. In the narrative of the first period I have been somewhat minute in detailing the names of priests and parishes, for the reason that the beginnings of things great, because of their smallness and remoteness, are more fascinating than is their later development. But as the field extends, as the dioceses multiply, as the clergy increase and parishes grow more numerous, the necessity of taking broader views, no less than the want of space, warns me to condense the narrative to more general considerations.

Shortly after the closing of the First Plenary Council a diocesan synod was held in Baltimore (February 22, 1853), at which were present thirty-five diocesan and seventeen religious priests. Maryland was not one of the States into which immigration flowed abundantly. Its lands were too high-priced for the agricultural newcomers; and, as it was a slave State, the immigrants who sought a livelihood by labor naturally avoided it. Consequently the growth of population was slow, and so was the multiplication of parishes and churches. In 1857 the number of Catholics in Baltimore was estimated at 80,814, for whose use there were thirteen churches. But if the younger dioceses were destined to outgrow the older in numbers, one privilege and glory was to remain to the mother see. The Pope, at the request of the Ninth Provincial Council (May 2, 1858), granted to the Archbishop of Baltimore the prerogative of place in all ecclesiastical meetings in the United States, and the right of placing his throne above even those of archbishops older by date of consecration.

The great Civil War, that assured by an appalling sacrifice of wealth and lives the faltering unity of this nation, and shattered for a time the seeming unity of many religious denominations, did but bring into clearer evidence the hierarchical unity of the Catholic Church. Its members, it is true, divided off on political grounds; it was their right and, as they supposed, their duty; but there was not any division in organization, discipline, and faith. To both sides of the conflict the church sent her heroes of charity, and oftentimes, indeed, the same heroes to both sides; detailed her priests from the parish and the college, her nuns from the orphan asylum and the schoolroom, to the camp, the hospital, the prison, and the bloody battle-field. Meanwhile her sacred edifices resounded with earnest petitions to Heaven for peace, with solemn requiems for the fallen on the field; and not infrequently they were turned into hospitals for the wounded and dying brought in from the battle raging near by.

Archbishop Kenrick survived by ten years the council over which he had presided; he was found by his household dead in his room on the morning of July 7, 1863, though the day before he had been as well as usual. His learning was of the highest order, and has not been surpassed, if equaled, by that of any other of our American prelates. Thoroughly versed in Latin, Greek, and Hebrew, he spoke French, Spanish, Italian, and German fluently. He gave to the church excellent dogmatic and moral theologies, a new English version of the Bible, with critical notes, a "Vindication of the Catholic Church," a noble book on the Primacy of the apostolic see, treatises on Baptism and Justification. His controversial works were marked with deep erudition, calmness, and charity.

Cardinal Newman, in his "Historical Sketch of St. Basil," remarks that the instruments used by God in the accomplishment of his purposes are of two kinds. The first are men of acute and ready mind, with accurate knowledge of human nature, large plans, sociable and popular, endued with boldness, instinctive tact, and zeal. Such were the intrepid Hildebrand, the majestic Ambrose, the never-wearied Athanasius; and such was, in our own history, John Hughes of New York. But there are instruments of less elaborate and splendid workmanship, less rich in political endowments, yet not less beautiful in texture nor less precious in material. Such is the retired and thoughtful student who for years has chastened his soul in secret, raising it to high thought and single-minded purpose, and then is called into active life, where he conducts himself with firmness, guilelessness, and all the sweetness of purity and integrity. Unskilled in the weaknesses of human nature, unfurnished in the resources of ready wit, negligent of men's applause, he does his work seemingly unsuccessfully, and so leaves it; but in the generation after him it lives again. Such were Basil, Peter Damien, and Anselm, and such was Archbishop Kenrick. Each class serves God according to the peculiar gifts given; and in the long run it is difficult to say which of the two classes of men served the cause of truth more effectually.

We have seen, in regard to the appointment of the Rev. John Carroll as prefect apostolic, that the federal government had refused, when consulted, to take any action in the matter. "The precedent thus established," writes the Rt. Rev. J. L. Spalding, in "The Life of the Most Rev. M. J. Spalding," "of non-interference in matters appertaining to the jurisdiction of the church has been, almost without exception, adhered to by the government of this country. But when, during the excitement of the Civil War, which seemed to threaten our national existence, the two most important sees—those of Baltimore and New York—became vacant, there seemed for a while to be a disposition to meddle with the liberty of action of the church in the choice of bishops. The urgency of the times had given to the authorities in Washington a power which they had never before exercised; and, as power often gains increase of appetite from what it feeds upon, they were inclined to stretch their jurisdiction as far as possible, without having any very nice regard for the limits assigned to it by the organic law of the land."

The Rt. Rev. M. J. Spalding, at the time Bishop of Louisville, under date of February 7, 1864, makes the following entry in his journal: "There appears to be no doubt that the government has interfered at Rome in regard to the appointments to the sees of Baltimore and New York." But, at any rate, if action was taken by the government, it does not seem to have had any result, so far as we know. The appointment of Bishop Spalding to fill the see of Baltimore, made vacant by the death of Archbishop Kenrick, met with the almost universal approval of the Catholics of the country. Many of the bishops and priests expressed their great satisfaction with the choice made by the Holy Father in terms the most complimentary. "Probably no one could have been chosen who would have been more acceptable either to the clergy or the laity of the archdiocese of Baltimore. His record as Bishop of Louisville gave assurance of his administrative ability; whilst the honorable name which he had made for himself by his writings and other labors in the cause of the church inspired the confident belief that he would be a not unworthy successor of Carroll and Kenrick. He came not among the Catholics as a stranger. They but welcomed home a not degenerate son of the pilgrims of Lord Baltimore."

The two events of public importance preceding the holding of the Second Plenary Council were the publication of the Syllabus and the assassination of President Lincoln. Both events drew from the Archbishop of Baltimore expressions that may stand for the opinions and feelings of the Catholics in the United States. The Syllabus—by no means an act of infallibility—because it was generally misunderstood, raised in this country a great outcry. "The outcry," writes the Rt. Rev. J. L. Spalding, "was that the Pope had condemned all the most sacred principles of our government." To this Archbishop Spalding replied that "to stretch the words of the pontiff, evidently intended for the standpoint of European radicals and infidels, so as to make them include the state of things established in this country by our Constitution in regard to liberty of conscience, of worship, and of the press, was manifestly unfair and unjust. Divided as we were in religious sentiment from the very origin of our government, our fathers acted most prudently and wisely in adopting, as an amendment to the Constitution, the organic article that 'Congress shall make no law respecting the establishment of religion or prohibiting the free exercise thereof.' In adopting this amendment they certainly did not intend, like the European radical disciples of Tom Paine and the French Revolution, to pronounce all religions, whether true or false, equal before God, but only to declare them equal before the law; or rather simply to lay down the sound and equitable principle that the civil government, adhering strictly to its own appropriate sphere of political duty, pledged itself not to interfere with religious matters, which it rightly viewed as entirely without the bounds of its competency.

"The founders of our government were, thank God, neither latitudinarians nor infidels; they were earnest, honest men; and however much some of them may have been personally lukewarm in the matter of religion, or may have differed in religious opinions, they still professed to believe in Christ and his revelation, and they exhibited a commendable respect for religious observances. All other matters contained in the Encyclical that accompanied the Syllabus, as well as the long catalogue of eighty propositions condemned in its Appendix or Syllabus, are to be judged by the same standard. These propositions are condemned in the sense of those who uttered and maintained them, and in no other. To be fair in our interpretation, we must never lose sight of the lofty standpoint of the pontiff, who steps forth as the champion of law and order against anarchy and revolution, and of revealed religion against more or less openly avowed infidelity. Nor should we forget the standpoint of those whose errors he condemns, who openly or covertly assail all revealed religion, and seek to sap the very foundations of all well-ordered society; who threaten to bring back the untold horrors of the French Revolution, and to make the streets and the highways run with the blood of the best and noblest citizens." Nor should we forget that the Syllabus is as technical and legal in its language as a syllabus of our courts, and therefore needs to be interpreted to the lay reader by the ecclesiastical lawyer.

The assassination of Lincoln, a man who is the more admired the better time makes him known, filled the land with dismay and indignation. An attempt was made to lay the deed to the charge of Catholics. There had undoubtedly been, some time previous to and quite unconnected with the murder, a conspiracy, which failed, however, and in which John Surratt, a Catholic, misled by his Southern sympathies, was implicated. The fact that meetings of the conspirators were held in the house of John Surratt's mother, without her knowledge of their purpose, was the insufficient ground on which that unfortunate and innocent woman was tried, condemned, and executed by a military tribunal. She was sacrificed by an alarmed administration to the country's cry for vengeance. The murderer was not a Catholic. None in the land were more shocked, none more outspoken against the dark deed, than the Catholic community. The following circular from Archbishop Spalding is but one of many that were issued in all our dioceses:

"FELLOW-CITIZENS: A deed of blood has been perpetrated which causes every heart to shudder, and which calls for the execration of every citizen. On Good Friday, the hallowed anniversary of our blessed Lord's crucifixion, when all Christendom was bowed down in penitence and sorrow at his tomb, the President of these United States was foully assassinated, and a wicked attempt was made upon the life of the Secretary of State. Words fail us in expressing detestation for a deed so atrocious, hitherto happily unparalleled in our history. Silence is perhaps the best and most appropriate expression of a sorrow too great for utterance. We are quite sure that we need not remind our brethren in this archdiocese of the duty, which we are confident they will willingly perform, of uniting with their fellow-citizens in whatever may be deemed most suitable for indicating their horror of the crime and their feelings of sympathy with the bereaved. We also invite them to join in humble supplication to God for our bereaved and afflicted country; and we enjoin that the bells of all our churches be solemnly tolled on the occasion of the late President's funeral."

In 1866 Archbishop Spalding received from Rome letters appointing him delegate apostolic to preside over the Second Plenary Council of Baltimore.

To succeed Bishop Kenrick in the see of Philadelphia Rome selected Father John Nepomucene Neumann, of the Order of Redemptorists, a native of Bohemia. He was consecrated March 28, 1852. Under his apostolic administration—for he was a saintly man—the spirit of religious devotion increased in the city that had suffered so much from schism; new parishes were formed and new churches arose throughout the diocese, not less than twenty being built in the first year of his episcopate. Conscious of his shortcomings as a financier, Bishop Neumann sought to have two more dioceses established within the territory under his jurisdiction, Pottsville and Wilmington, with the intent, it appears, to get himself transferred to one of them, leaving the more important diocese of Philadelphia to abler hands. The holy see, instead of acceding to his request for a division, named the Rev. James Frederic Wood, a native of Philadelphia, a bank clerk in his youth and a convert to the church, as coadjutor to Bishop Neumann. His consecration took place in Cincinnati April 25, 1857. In the hands of the coadjutor Bishop Neumann left entirely the onerous task of carrying on the building of the magnificent cathedral begun by his predecessor, Bishop Kenrick. The saintly Neumann did not live to see the work completed; he fell and died suddenly in Vine Street, January 5, 1860. The holy, mortified life of Bishop Neumann, his complete detachment from all earthly things, his purity and devotedness, had impressed all with a belief in his great sanctity. His intercession was sought by the afflicted in body and soul, and, it appears, not without relief in many cases. So general was the confidence and so marked the favors received that the preliminary steps for his canonization were begun. The cause was duly introduced in the Congregation of Rites in December, 1888. The episcopal process was conducted under the authority and guidance of Archbishop Ryan, and having been concluded in two years was transmitted to Rome, where it was examined and approved. This, however, is only the first step in the very long investigation that must take place before the cause is brought to completion.

On assuming charge, Bishop Wood found in the diocese one hundred and fifty churches, one hundred and forty-two priests, a flourishing theological seminary, and a Catholic population estimated at two hundred thousand. Under Bishop Wood's able financial management many churches were built throughout the diocese, and the magnificent cathedral was brought to completion and dedicated to the service of God November 20, 1864. There was another work with which his name shall be forever associated. At Overbrook, in a valuable piece of ground, he laid (December 5, 1865) the corner-stone of a new diocesan seminary which is to-day one of the grandest establishments of the kind in the land.

The diocese of Pittsburg under Bishop O'Connor had been divided, as we have seen in a former chapter, to make room for the new see of Erie. After the division it contained a Catholic population of forty thousand, seventy-five churches erected or in progress, and fifty-seven priests. Bishop O'Connor, feeling a call to the religious life, had from the very beginning refused the office of bishop, but had been compelled by positive orders from the Pope to accept it; however, he always yearned for the mode of life to which he had given his first love. In 1857, while in Rome, he tried to escape from the episcopate, but did not succeed. Again, in 1860, he laid his resignation at the feet of the Holy Father, who this time yielded to his desire. Once freed he entered a Jesuit novitiate in Europe, returned to this country a humble religious, and occupied various positions in the society until his death (October, 1872).

His successor in the see of Pittsburg was the Rev. Michael Domenec, born in Spain, but an emigrant to this country in his youth, and ordained in Missouri, where he labored many years on the missions in the West. He was consecrated in Pittsburg December 9, 1860. The statistics of the diocese at the beginning of 1862 show eighty-four churches, eighty-two priests, and an estimated Catholic population of fifty thousand.

The diocese of Erie was erected July 29, 1853. It included the counties of Mercer, Venango, Clarion, Jefferson, Clearfield, Elk, McKeon, and Potter, and as much of Pennsylvania as lay north and west of them. Here, in the last days of France's struggle to maintain her hold in North America, had been a line of military posts, and Catholic chaplains offered the holy sacrifice from Presqu Isle (Erie) to Fort Du Quesne (Pittsburg). At the time of its erection Erie had twenty-eight churches, with fourteen priests, and twelve thousand Catholics. For a short time Bishop O'Connor left Pittsburg and occupied the see of Erie; but as the candidate elected to replace him in Pittsburg refused to accept that charge, Bishop O'Connor was transferred back to his original see, and the candidate elected for Pittsburg, the Rev. J. M. Young, was sent to Erie. He was consecrated in Cincinnati April 23, 1864. Josue M. Young was a native of Shapleigh, Me., born October 29, 1808, brought up without the slightest ray of Catholic truth, and trained to the art of printing, apparently not the path to lead to a miter in the Catholic Church. A Catholic fellow-printer working by his side was often the butt of jokes, in which Young joined. But the Catholic was able to explain and defend his belief and turn the laugh. So impressed was Young that he began to read and examine, and gradually his mind cleared. In 1827, while working in Portland, he heard of the coming of Bishop Fenwick, and through his old fellow-typographer sought an interview. Bishop Fenwick at once understood his case. Young was soon convinced that the Catholic was the one true faith, and sought admission within its fold. He resolved to become a priest, and, proceeding to Cincinnati, went through the necessary studies and was ordained in 1837. Twenty-seven years afterward he became Bishop of Erie. In 1861 the diocese contained twenty-one priests, thirty-eight churches, and during the years of the war seven more were built. Bishop Young died suddenly September 18, 1866.

The diocese of Richmond under Bishop McGill had in the year 1855 ten priests; between that year and 1860 about nine churches were built. For reasons already alluded to there was no immigration to the South and consequently no great increase of Catholicity. Moreover, during the Civil War Virginia became the theater of the greatest and bloodiest battles of that memorable conflict, the tramping-ground for the armies of the South and the North. As a very large number of the soldiers on both sides were Catholics, Catholic army chaplains were frequently within the limits of the diocese, and Sisters of Charity were in attendance on the sick and wounded in camp and hospital. Wherever there were woe and misery and disease the Catholic priest and the religious woman were ready to do the works of mercy. It was only after the surrender of Lee at Appomattox that the bishop was able to visit his diocese. The condition of the church no less than of the State was heartrending. War is essentially cruel, and amid its wild ravages churches and schools had been injured and ruined; but with peace came a new era of prosperity to desolate Virginia, and the church slowly repaired her losses.

The diocese of Wheeling, when Bishop Whelan took possession, contained four churches, two priests, a few students, a convent, a boys' and girls' school, and five or six thousand Catholics. A few years later, when the Civil War broke out, there were in the diocese nine priests, and about nine more churches, mostly small chapels, had been built. Like the rest of Virginia, this western portion that formed the diocese of Wheeling was the theater of military operations, and suffered immensely. All church advance came to a standstill during the terrible conflict. But after the cessation of hostilities a new period began for the diocese. West Virginia was detached from eastern Virginia to form a new State; slavery ceased, mining and industry prospered. In 1866 the diocese, comprising the State of West Virginia, numbered twenty-three churches, sixteen priests, eight ecclesiastical students, a college, three female academies, an orphan asylum, and a Catholic population of about fifteen thousand.

After the death of Bishop Reynolds the diocese of Charleston was intrusted to the Rev. Patrick N. Lynch, a native of Ireland, but educated and ordained and laboring as a priest for many years in South Carolina. He was consecrated in Charleston March 14, 1858. No diocese suffered so much from the Civil War as that of Charleston. The cathedral, with the adjoining priests' residence, the convent, and the orphan asylum were burned; the churches throughout the State were occupied for military purposes. It was through the agency of Bishop Lynch while he was in Rome (1864) that Pius IX. addressed to Jefferson Davis, President of the Confederate States, a letter which certain persons of late have sought to interpret as an official recognition of the Confederacy. The New York "Independent" (April 4, 1895), to cite no other authority, effectually disposed of that interpretation. The document was a personal letter and carried with it no political significance. While he was in Rome Bishop Lynch made to the Propaganda the official report on the condition of his diocese: the Catholics in Charleston were 11,000, in Columbia, 2000, in Sumter, 600, in Wilmington, N. C., 1200, and smaller numbers in other places—a total of 20,000 in the two Carolinas, served by fifteen priests. After the end of the war he returned home, to find that he must begin anew, so to speak, the work of his predecessors in the building up of churches and schools, and he set about doing it with a brave heart.

In 1857 the holy see detached Florida from the see of Savannah and erected it into a vicariate apostolic. At the time Savannah was vacant by the death of Bishop Reynolds, whose successor, the Rev. John Barry, was consecrated in Baltimore August 2, 1857. He was sixty-seven years old, for thirty-two years he had been a missionary in the Southern States, and his health was seriously undermined. He died in Paris, whither he went to recuperate his shattered forces, November 21, 1859.

The vicariate of Florida, comprising the country east of the Appalachicola River, was intrusted to the Rev. Augustine Verot, a Sulpitian professor in the theological seminary of Baltimore. The number of Catholics in Florida was small and the hope of increase limited. There were only seven churches and two priests in the vicariate. From a visit to Europe in 1859 Bishop Verot brought back six more, some Christian Brothers, and sisters for the schools. After the death of the Bishop of Savannah, the Rt. Rev. John Barry, he was transferred to that see (1861), retaining, meanwhile, charge of the vicariate of Florida. Both States under his jurisdiction suffered much during the Civil War in damage done to churches and other institutions, and in the decimating by death on the battlefield and in the hospital of the Catholic Georgians and Floridians who fought for the "cause that was lost."

To resume, in one word: the condition of the province of Baltimore during this period was one of standstill in religious growth and of no small material loss from the terrible ordeal through which it passed during the memorable conflict.

The condition of the diocese of New Orleans is described as follows by Archbishop Blanc in a report made by him while in Rome (1853) to the Propaganda. It contained forty-four quasi-parishes, each with a church and one or two priests. The city had eighteen churches. The diocese had a seminary, under the priests of the mission, with an average of nine students. The Catholic population, made up of Americans, French, Irish, Germans, Spaniards, and Italians, was estimated at sixty-five thousand. Two Provincial Councils, in 1856 and 1859, were held by him, attended by his suffragans, the Bishops of Mobile, Galveston, Little Rock, and Natchitoches. Old age and its infirmities could not prevent the apostolic zeal of Archbishop Blanc from undertaking the onerous task of administering and visiting his diocese in the midst of physical weakness and pain. He succumbed to his constant labors June 20, 1860. Bishop Odin, of Galveston, became his successor. The Civil War, from which New Orleans suffered more than any other city in the Union, checked all progress in church affairs; when the time for the Second Plenary Council had come, the statistics of 1866 did not show much advance on those of 1853.

The diocese of Natchitoches was formed in 1853, taking

from New Orleans the part of the State of Louisiana between the thirty-first and the thirty-second degrees of latitude. Within that district there were twenty-five thousand Catholics, five priests, and seven churches. The bishop elected was Augustus Mary Martin. New life came with Bishop Martin; churches were built, priests from France answered his call, and the future looked bright, when the war came to stop all progress for a while.

The diocese of Little Rock, far away from the routes of immigration, progressed more slowly than any other in the Union. Add to this the woes of the war, which filled Arkansas with confusion and battles. In 1861 there were in the diocese but nine priests and eleven churches. After Bishop Byrne's death (June 10, 1862) the Rev. Edward Fitzgerald was consecrated his successor (February 3, 1867).

Bishop Van de Velde, transferred from Chicago to Natchez in July, 1853, did not long survive the transfer; he died in Natchez November 13, 1855. His successor was the Rev. William Henry Elder, consecrated in Baltimore, his native city, January 9, 1857. He found in his diocese but nine priests. The war desolated the diocese. Though the sisters and priests gave their untiring services, and not a few their lives, to the nursing of the sick and wounded from both sides in the conflict, yet insults, which we refrain from detailing, were not spared to the representatives of the church. The war over, churches, missions, and schools had to be rebuilt, repaired, and set on foot anew.

Bishop Portier's long episcopate came to an end in Mobile May 14, 1859. His successor was the Rev. John Quinlan. This was one of the oldest dioceses in the country, yet in 1861 it had but sixteen priests—slow progress compared to the giant strides made in the Northwest

States. Want of immigrants and the evils of the war account for this state of things.

The diocese of Galveston, comprising the State of Texas, was the only Southern diocese that was receiving a share of the immigration of the period. Moreover, in 1858 the legislature passed a school law that was an honorable exception in the whole country, and that had much to do in attracting Catholics. According to this law all schools giving gratuitous tuition were entitled to share in the school fund. Teachers were to be examined and were to obtain certificates of competency, and the schools were to be visited and examined by a board, to determine the proficiency of the scholars and the number to be credited to each school. As an evidence of the growth of the church under such favorable circumstances, and of the vast labors of Bishop Odin, let it be recorded that in 1858 he made a five-months' visitation of the State, traveling eighteen hundred miles and confirming 3415 persons. In 1861 he was transferred to the archiepiscopal see of New Orleans, vacated by the death of Archbishop Blanc. His successor in Galveston, the Rev. Claude Marie Dubuis, was consecrated November 23, 1862. The following year he confirmed more than five thousand persons. In 1866 there were in the diocese forty-four priests, fifty-five churches, and about fifty-five thousand Catholics.

CHAPTER XXVII.

THE CHURCH IN THE NORTH (1852–66).

THE North contained the provinces of New York, Cincinnati, St. Louis, and Oregon.

Province of New York.

In 1853 the dioceses of Brooklyn and Newark were set off from that of New York, leaving to the parent see the city of New York and the counties of Westchester, Putnam, Dutchess, Rockland, Orange, Ulster, Sullivan, and Richmond. Within that district there were about fifty churches and more than a hundred priests. The Catholics of the diocese were estimated at about two hundred and eighty thousand, more than half the churches and people being in the city of New York. As the great port of the United States, the city received nearly two thirds of all the immigrants reaching the country, and though many intended to proceed to Western homes, a considerable number lingered there for a time. They required church accommodations, priestly aid, and very often relief.

With such a man at the head of the diocese as Archbishop Hughes it is no wonder that churches and priests were multiplied with amazing rapidity. To go into details would be to carry us beyond all bounds. Between the years 1854 and 1861 he held three Provincial Councils with suffragans, the Bishops of Albany, Boston, Buffalo,

Hartford, Brooklyn, Newark, and Burlington, at which much wise legislation, needed by the conditions of time and place, was enacted. On August 15, 1858, he laid the corner-stone of St. Patrick's Cathedral, that grandest ecclesiastical monument in our country, choosing a site far beyond the inhabited quarters of the city, to the astonishment and even the merriment of men less far-sighted than himself. In 1863 he undertook the establishment of another institution, which has grown to be one of high importance and vast influence in the diocese, the Protectory of Westchester, a home and school for destitute children. And yet another institution must be put to his credit, the purchase of a former Methodist university at Troy, which was converted into the theological seminary of the province.

His administration had shown him to be a great churchman. The Civil War showed him to be a great patriot. This is proved not only by his encouragement to the Irish military organizations of New York to march to the front, by his correspondence and writings on the war and its causes, but also by his semi-official diplomatic mission to secure the neutrality of Europe during the conflict. "There arose a danger," says John Gilmary Shea, "of the recognition of the Confederate States by the governments of Europe, and after the Trent affair there came the fear that England might go even further. The United States government, which had faltered about receiving an archbishop as envoy from the Pope, now earnestly desired Archbishop Hughes to go to Europe as envoy of the United States. He absolutely declined to accept any official position, but expressed his willingness to use all his efforts to prevent the prolongation of the war and the greater effusion of human blood.

"He sailed for Europe in November, 1861, and proceeded to Paris. There he had interviews with the members of the ministry, and was honorably received by the archbishop. After some delay he obtained an interview with the emperor, Napoleon III., and placed before him in a clear light the real position of affairs in America, and showed that it was for the interest of France to adhere to her long course of amity with the government of the United States. The impression he produced was such that he went further, and urged the emperor to act, if necessary, as arbitrator between the United States and England in the difficulty which had arisen. The influence that Archbishop Hughes produced on the councils of France at this juncture is undeniable, and was fully recognized at Washington. On reaching Paris he wrote to Cardinal Barnabo to explain the nature of his mission, and after concluding his work in Paris proceeded to Rome. Though many had censured the archbishop, he found that Cardinals Antonelli and Barnabo and the Pope himself approved of his conduct."

One of his last public acts was to address his flock of New York in favor of the government at the time of the draft riots, though the forces of his life were well-nigh spent. He died January 3, 1864. Thus ended the most remarkable, the most vigorous, the most patriotic prelate the country had known since John Carroll. His figure in history will gain in grandeur as it recedes with time; it is not at this day in that perspective necessary to reveal its true proportions.

The diocese of Albany under the administration of Bishop McCloskey was constantly growing with the incoming immigration; its churches and institutions were increasing so rapidly that in 1861 it contained ninety priests, one hundred and seventeen churches, twenty-seven parochial schools, and six orphan asylums. When Bishop

McCloskey was transferred (1864) to New York to become the successor of Archbishop Hughes, the Rev. J. J. Conroy was named to the see of Albany and consecrated October 15, 1865.

The diocese of Buffalo was tormented by the last remnants of trusteeism in the land. The trustees of the St. Louis Church (German) in Buffalo had stood out against Archbishop Hughes before the erection of the see of Buffalo, and were in open rebellion against the first bishop of the see, the Rt. Rev. John Timon. The papal nuncio, Archbishop Bedini, had among other affairs the mission of settling this question. He failed to bring about a settlement; the trustees were excommunicated June 22, 1854. This was the last effective blow that ended trusteeism among us. Bishop Timon was untiring in the work of administering and building up his diocese; churches and institutions sprang up as if by magic. He passed away with a noble record, April 16, 1867.

The diocese of Brooklyn, erected by bull of July 29, 1853, comprised Long Island. At the time there were six churches in Brooklyn and two in Williamsburg; Astoria, Flatbush, Flushing, Jamaica, and Westburg had each its church. The growth of Catholicity in this new diocese since that day until the death of the first bishop, in 1891, is unparalleled in the United States. He was the Rt. Rev. John Loughlin, Vicar General of the diocese of New York. The troubles of Know-nothingism and the Civil War had no effect in checking the constant advance of the diocese of Brooklyn. Churches, schools and convents sprang into existence year by year. When the Second Plenary Council was opened (1866), thirteen years after the establishment of the diocese, there were twenty-three churches in the city of Brooklyn and twenty on the rest of the island. Evidently this phenomenal increase means that large numbers of immigrants landing in New York found homes on the island across the East River.

The see of Newark, comprising the State of New Jersey, erected in 1853, found its first bishop in a convert to the church, a scion of an old and wealthy American family, James Roosevelt Bayley. At that time Newark had three churches, the rest of the State had thirty, and in 1856 there were thirty-six priests. A few spasmodic attacks of Know-nothingism caused but little trouble to the church in New Jersey. Here the growth of Catholicity, aided by immigration, kept pace with that of the neighboring dioceses of New York and Brooklyn. In 1866 it contained about seventy-seven churches and seventy priests, more than a doubling in fourteen years.

The First Plenary Council had detached from Boston Vermont and Maine, the former forming the diocese of Burlington, the latter that of Portland. This division left to the see of Boston only Massachusetts, with sixty-three churches and sixty-one priests. No State at the time was more deeply imbued with the anti-Catholic spirit that marked the times preceding the war. Many facts might be advanced to prove this statement; let this one, as narrated by John Gilmary Shea, suffice:

"In the election of 1854 the Know-nothings elected the governor, the Senate, and every member of the House except three or four. In January, 1855, the two houses named and authorized a committee 'to visit and examine theological seminaries, boarding-schools, academies, nunneries, convents, and other institutions of a like character.' The committee visited Holy Cross College; then, adding several others to their number, they drove to the Convent of the Sisters of Notre Dame at Roxbury, and ransacked the house from top to bottom, treating the sisters with the greatest indignity, insolence, and even indecency; the rooms of the sick pupils were not respected. A convent at Lowell was next subjected to this illegal invasion of its privacy. These men pretended to go as representatives of the highest morality; yet one of them took a woman around with him, representing her falsely as his wife. The Boston 'Daily Advertiser' denounced in a scathing article the iniquity of the whole affair; and Charles Hale, one of the editors, issued 'A Review of the Proceedings of the Nunnery Committee of the Massachusetts Legislature,' which circulated widely. Caricatures of the infamous committee helped also to rouse the honest people of the State to a just indignation."

When the Civil War began, Massachusetts sent to the front two Catholic regiments, the Ninth and the Twenty-eighth, with Catholic chaplains. No sterner rebuke could be given to the anti-Catholic spirit of the day, no better proof of the loyalty of Catholics to the United States and the cause of the republic. Boston no less than the other great dioceses of the Northern States kept up a steady growth of Catholic life, urged on by the flood-tide of an immense immigration. On the eve of the Second Plenary Council Bishop Fitzpatrick, whose administration had been strong and fruitful, was carried away (February 13, 1866) by a disease that had been undermining his vigorous constitution for many years.

The Rt. Rev. Bernard O'Reilly, Bishop of Hartford, was lost at sea in the steamer "Pacific" three years after the First Plenary Council (1856). At the time of his death the diocese numbered fifty-five thousand Catholics, thirty-seven churches, and thirty-nine priests. He was succeeded (March 14, 1858) by the Rt. Rev. Francis P. McFarland. In Connecticut we meet with the anti-Catholic movement of the time, and also with a pointed rebuke given to it by the devotedness and bravery of Catholic soldiers when the call to battle came. Wherever they stood before the foe these Catholic soldiers proved that they were the worthiest of the worthy soldiers of their State. In 1866, at the opening of the Second Plenary Council, the diocese of Hartford contained fifty-six churches and forty priests for Connecticut, eighteen churches and twenty-four priests for Rhode Island.

Vermont was erected into a diocese in 1853, with the see at Burlington; and the bishop chosen was Louis de Goesbriand, a descendant from a noble family of Brittany, France, who since 1840, the date of his ordination, had labored in the diocese of Cincinnati. At the time of its erection the diocese had churches at Montpelier, St. Albans, Fairfield, Swanton, Castleton, and Burlington, with five priests. Immediately after his consecration the bishop went to France for more recruits. On his return evidences of enetgy and progress appeared on all sides. In December, 1867, the beautiful cathedral of Burlington was completed, and many churches arose throughout the State. In 1866 the diocese had nineteen priests, twenty-seven churches, and a Catholic population of twenty-eight thousand.

Portland was also an erection of 1853; it comprised Maine and New Hampshire; its first bishop was the Rev. David W. Bacon. Maine was classic ground for the church, having been a field of early Jesuit missions. Two Abenaki tribes, the Penobscots and the Passamaquoddies, the fruits of their labors, were still Christian. New Hampshire was the one State in the Union that still ostracized Catholics from the legislature and all high offices, and continued the ostracism down to our own days. Both States at this time were filled with Know-nothingism. Many acts of violence against Catholics were perpetrated; the most disgraceful of all was the railing, tarring, and feathering at Ellsworth, Me., of Father Bapst, S.J., the missionary among the Indians, in 1854. Yet the anti-Catholic opposition could not check the onward progress of the church. In 1866 there were in the diocese forty-five churches, twenty-nine priests, and forty-five thousand Catholics.

Province of Cincinnati.

The province of Cincinnati had as suffragans, as evidenced by its First Provincial Council, held May 13, 1855, Rt. Rev. Peter Lefevre, Administrator of Detroit, Rt. Rev. Amadeus Rappe, Bishop of Cleveland, Rt. Rev. Martin John Spalding, Bishop of Louisville, Rt. Rev. George Aloysius Carrell, Bishop of Covington, Rt. Rev. Frederic Baraga, Bishop of Amyzonium *in partibus infidelium*, and Vicar Apostolic of Upper Michigan, and Bishop St. Palais, of Vincennes, who was unable to attend. Here, as throughout the whole West, the progress of the church was only little less than in the great dioceses of the Atlantic coast. In 1857 the Catholic population of the diocese of Cincinnati was computed at 277,680. The Civil War, though the southern border of the State of Ohio was on the verge of its theater, did not materially retard the advance of Catholicity. In 1862 Archbishop Purcell, on whom his thirty-two years of arduous episcopate were beginning to tell, solicited and obtained as coadjutor the Rev. Sylvester H. Rosecrans, a convert to the church and brother of the well-known general of that name. In 1866 the diocese had one hundred and fifty priests and one hundred and eighty-one churches.

The diocese of Cleveland under the able administration of Bishop Rappe, and with the constant inflow of immigrants, had its share of the general religious prosperity of the period. When the diocese was formed there were in it only seventeen priests and twenty-five churches. At the end of nine years it had fifty priests and eighty churches, and in the next ten years fifty-six churches were added.

The see of Bardstown had been transferred to Louisville. A cathedral was needed there. Begun in 1849, it was completed and consecrated in October, 1852. Out of the diocese of Louisville, at the request of the Plenary Council, was formed the diocese of Covington. This division left the diocese of Louisville with that part of the State of Kentucky lying west of the Kentucky River. Here the anti-Catholic lodges of Know-nothingism were active, and resorted to acts of violence that have left a stain on the State.

"We have just passed through a reign of terror," writes Bishop Spalding, "surpassed only by the Philadelphia riots. Nearly a hundred poor Irish and Germans have been butchered or burned, and some twenty houses have been fired and burned to the ground. The city authorities, all Know-nothings, looked calmly on, and they are now endeavoring to lay the blame on the Catholics."

"It may be said," writes Bishop Spalding in "The Life of Archbishop Spalding," "of the whole anti-Catholic crusade of that day that the result was favorable to the church. A few narrow-minded bigots, whose ignorance was probably invincible, were really alarmed for the safety of the Bible and the country, and were terribly in earnest in seeking to stamp out from the American soil every trace of Catholicism. They were joined by the mob of European infidels and radicals, and by the rabble formed by the sloughing of our social sores, and this horrid mass of mental obliquity and moral turpitude called itself the American party. The American people rose up and trod it underfoot.

"They felt that Catholics had been wantonly insulted, grossly outraged; and that sympathy which the brave and the manly always have for the wronged took the place of what had been aversion, or, at least, indifference. We have been making rapid strides ever since, with renewed confidence in our fellow-countrymen, increased reverence for the institutions which God has given us, and the abiding conviction that no evil, not self-caused, will ever befall us in this free land."

Kentucky, being a border State, suffered much during the Civil War. Yet there was a compensation for all this suffering: a splendid opportunity was offered to our priests and sisters to exhibit to the country on the field of battle and in the hospital and the military prison the noble disinterestedness of charity. If material progression in church affairs was simply impossible during this period, a spiritual progression through Christian and patriotic devotedness, the very best answer to anti-Catholic prejudices, was inaugurated and still continues in its effects. God drew good out of evil. In July, 1864, after the death of Archbishop Kenrick, Bishop Spalding was transferred to the primatial see of Baltimore. He was succeeded (September, 1865) by the Rev. Peter John Lavialle, who did not long survive his consecration. He died in October, 1866, after having attended the Second Plenary Council.

The diocese of Covington, erected July, 1853, contained that portion of Kentucky lying east of the Kentucky River. The Catholic population within this district did not exceed seven thousand. George Aloysius Carrell, a member of the Society of Jesus, a native of Philadelphia, was chosen for the see and consecrated in Cincinnati November 1, 1853. The part of Kentucky in the diocese of Covington was affected by the Civil War no less than that part in the diocese of Louisville. However, the statistics at the time of Bishop Carrell's death (September 25, 1868), soon after the Second Plenary Council, show a progress remarkable for the adverse circumstances of the period: forty-two churches, thirty priests, and a Catholic population of about thirty thousand.

The diocese of Detroit had been narrowed in territory by the erection (1853) of the vicariate of Upper Michigan, placed in care of Bishop Baraga. Michigan did not attract at this time as much immigration as the other Western States, yet there was some growth of Catholic population. In 1866 there were in the diocese sixty-two priests, sixty-four churches, and a Catholic population of ninety thousand. Bishop Baraga, the Vicar Apostolic of Upper Michigan, a descendant of a noble Carniola family, had labored as a missionary since 1830 among the Indians of that territory with wonderful success. Meanwhile the mines of the Lake Superior country had attracted many whites, so that at the time of its erection the vicariate contained six churches and five priests. In 1857 the vicariate was formed into a diocese, with the see at Sault Ste. Marie. By this time the territory under Bishop Baraga's care contained twenty-three churches, sixteen priests, and sixty-five hundred Catholics. While giving to the whites the attention that their numbers demanded, the saintly bishop did not neglect his Indian children. The Honorable Commissioner for Indian Affairs, in his reports (1853-66), recognized more than once the services of this eminent missionary in Christianizing and elevating the tribes of Michigan. Bishop Baraga had from the outset of his missionary career labored to acquire a thorough and complete knowledge of the Chippeway and Ottawa languages. He published an Otchipwe grammar in 1850, a dictionary in 1853 (both reprinted in Canada in 1878), and Prayer-books in Ottawa and Chippeway in 1832, 1837,

1842, and 1846; a "Life of Christ" in Chippeway in 1837; "Bible Extracts," "Catholic Christian Meditations," and "Eternal Truths" in Chippeway in 1850; and even issued pastoral letters in Chippeway. Pilling, in his "Indian Bibliography," gives him due credit for all these works.

The diocese of Vincennes under Bishop de St. Palais was enriched with many useful institutions and gained steadily in churches and population, unhampered, most fortunately, by any violent outbreaks of the anti-Catholic movement that afflicted so deeply other sections of the country. In 1866 it had a Catholic population of seventy thousand, one hundred and ten churches, and seventy-two priests, and this after having given part of the State of Indiana to a new see.

This new see was Fort Wayne, erected in 1857, comprising the counties north of the fortieth degree of latitude. It contained, when established, twenty thousand Catholics, fourteen priests, twenty churches, and the magnificent educational establishments of the Fathers and the Sisters of the Holy Cross at Notre Dame. The Rev. John Henry Luers, a native of Westphalia, engaged in missionary work in Ohio since 1849, was consecrated for this new see January 10, 1858. The statistics of 1866 show that there had been in a few years an increase of more than one hundred percent., viz., forty thousand members, fifty-seven churches, and fifty-three priests.

Province of St. Louis.

In 1853 no city in the Union was so well provided with charitable institutions as St. Louis. It might not be amiss to make the same assertion as to its condition to-day. Between the year 1853 and the year 1866 two Provincial Councils were held by Archbishop Kenrick, at which were present his suffragans, the Bishops of Dubuque, Nashville, Milwaukee, Chicago, Santa Fé, St. Paul, and the Vicar Apostolic of the Indian Territory, which afterward was divided to form another vicariate, that of Nebraska. In 1857 the Rev. James Duggan was consecrated coadjutor to the archbishop, as a division of the diocese of St. Louis was not deemed advisable. During the Civil War Missouri was one of the theaters of the conflict. The political passions, or rather the fancied necessities, of war interfered in this State more than in any other with the religious liberty guaranteed by the Constitution.

Bishop Van de Velde at his own request was transferred by the holy see to the vacant see of Natchez in 1853. As successor to him in the see of Chicago the Rev. Anthony O'Regan was consecrated July 25, 1854. A systematic administrator and strong disciplinarian, Bishop O'Regan excited much dissatisfaction among his clergy, which was allayed only by the transfer of some of his priests, very estimable men, to other fields. These troubles and his unfitness for a work for which his early life had not trained him—for on receiving his appointment he had declined at first, declaring that he was only a bookworm—caused him to solicit relief from the episcopal charge. His resignation was accepted by the holy see, and thereafter he lived in retirement in England and Ireland. His successor (1858) was the Rt. Rev. James Duggan, the coadjutor of the Archbishop of St. Louis. In the first years of his administration the church kept pace with the phenomenal growth of Chicago; but he soon began to show signs of mental derangement in his wayward and unjust treatment of some of his best priests, so that the sad necessity imposed itself of confining him in an asylum.

In 1853 the diocese of Quincy was erected, comprising

southern Illinois. But this diocese was never fully organized; it remained annexed to Chicago until the year 1857, when the see was transferred from Quincy to Alton, and the Rev. Henry Damian Juncker was appointed its first bishop. The war made the diocese active with military movements, Cairo being a center of operations. Where so many soldiers were congregated sickness prevailed, and the wounded from battle-fields were numerous. These called for the charitable ministrations of priests and religious women; and the call was nobly answered. In 1866 the diocese had one hundred churches, seventy-five priests, and about seventy-five thousand Catholics. Two years later (October 2, 1868), Bishop Juncker died.

The Rt. Rev. Richard Pius Miles, the Bishop of Nashville, received as coadjutor (1859) the Rev. James Whelan, of the Order of St. Dominic, and died a year later (February 17, 1860). The State of Tennessee, which grew but little at that time by immigration, was, moreover, weighed down by the Civil War, some of the most decisive and bloody battles of which were fought on its soil. Here, as everywhere else, Catholic priests and religious women devoted themselves to the spiritual and temporal good of Catholics in the army, and in the hospitals the sisters showed no distinction, ministering to the sick and wounded of all creeds. Very early in his episcopate Bishop Whelan resigned and retired to one of the houses of his order. The Rev. Patrick Augustine Feehan was consecrated his successor November 1, 1865. Nashville was in a deplorable condition, morally and financially. Every mission in the diocese had the same sad story of crushing debt and scattered flocks. Bishop Feehan threw himself into the work of restoration, obtained some zealous priests, and by financial skill put many churches and institutions once more on the way to prosperity.

No Western diocese had the great and rapid growth during this period that fell to the share of Milwaukee. Its beautiful cathedral was consecrated in 1853 by the papal nuncio, Archbishop Bedini, who was impressed by the scene, and by the fact of such a cathedral in a city and State of comparatively recent origin. He understood what at Rome and Vienna had been a puzzle to him, the anxiety of our bishops to have suitable cathedrals. They were required not only to enable the episcopal functions to be becomingly performed, but they gave life and activity to the Catholic body, who looked on them with pride; and besides this they impressed those outside the fold with the permanence, solidity, and dignity of the ancient church and its services. The most notable work of Bishop Henni's administration was the building up of the magnificent ecclesiastical Seminary of St. Francis de Sales, opened in 1856. Remote from the scene of war, Wisconsin received a large immigration, German and Catholic. In 1866 it had two hundred and ninety-three churches, one hundred and fifty priests, and two hundred and fifty thousand Catholics.

Bishop Loras, of Dubuque, whose health, fast failing, caused alarm, received as coadjutor the Rev. Timothy Smyth, of the Order of La Trappe, who succeeded him in the government of the diocese after his death (February 20, 1858). A diocesan synod held in 1860 showed the progress of the diocese since Bishop Loras had taken in hand its formation; the synod was composed of forty priests, and the Catholic population was 50,156. Bishop Smyth was seized with a fatal disease and died, September 23, 1863. Under his rule of five years the diocese had so grown that at his death it had eighty churches, forty-eight priests, and ninety thousand Catholics. Those figures reveal better than anything else a vast Western immigration. His successor was the Rev. John Hennessey, the present Archbishop of Dubuque.

The wave of immigration had reached Minnesota. In 1856 the diocese of St. Paul had almost fifty thousand Catholics, with a number quite inadequate of churches and priests, so rapid had been the arrival of the newcomers. The active, energetic life of Bishop Cretin was brought to a close February 22, 1857. His successor was not consecrated until July 24, 1859. The candidate chosen was the Rev. Thomas L. Grace, of the Order of St. Dominic, still living, with the title of Archbishop of Siunia, *in partibus infidelium*, and spending his declining days in the classic shade of St. Thomas's College, St. Paul, since he resigned the diocese into the hands of his coadjutor, now Archbishop Ireland. The Civil War did not directly affect Minnesota, but an Indian uprising in 1862 desolated the frontier settlements and for a time checked the growth of the State and the diocese. Notwithstanding, in 1866 it had seventy-two churches, forty-three priests, and about seventy thousand Catholics.

The vicariate apostolic of Nebraska was erected in 1859, and comprised the Territories of Nebraska, Dakota, and Idaho. When the vicariate of the Indian Territory had been formed it was supposed to be for the Indian missions only, and that it would suffice for all religious needs as far east as the Rockies for many a year. The great immigration had not been foreseen and reckoned with. As the tide overflowed Iowa and rolled across the Missouri a new diocese loomed up as a necessity. A Trappist from the monastery near Dubuque, James Michael O'Gorman, was chosen for this new field, and consecrated May 8, 1859. He fixed his residence in Omaha. Up to 1866 the progress was slow and feeble. At that date Bishop O'Gorman had only eight priests and as many churches.

The vicariate apostolic of the Indian Territory—so called not because it was in our present Indian Territory, which was not yet formed, but because Indian missions were supposed to be, as they were at the start, the main field of the vicar apostolic—comprised, after the erection of the vicariate of Nebraska, Kansas and Colorado. The Vicar Apostolic of the Indian Territory, Bishop Miège, resided at Leavenworth, and in consequence the vicariate came to be called the vicariate of Kansas. Jesuit fathers had charge of the Indian missions in this district. But soon after the war immigration began to pour into Kansas and Colorado, and before it the Indians were driven farther West. At the close of 1860 the vicariate of Kansas had fifteen priests and sixteen churches. Even during the war, which did not spare Kansas in its ravages, Catholicity gained. By 1864 the vicariate had twenty-five churches, and a hospital and orphan asylum at Leavenworth, directed by the Sisters of Charity. The next year calced Carmelites were laboring there with Jesuit, Benedictine, and secular priests.

In 1853 the holy see erected the vicariate of New Mexico into the diocese of Santa Fé. By the Gadsden purchase of 1854 Arizona was annexed to the United States. It was added to the territory under the jurisdiction of the Bishop of Santa Fé; and in 1860 Colorado was detached from the vicariate of the Indian Territory and placed also in his care. Within this vast diocese the church made rapid progress in spite of the Civil War, which, however, affected but little this southern district lying outside the main theater of the conflict. In 1865 Bishop Lamy could report to the Propaganda that on reaching New Mexico he found twenty priests, neglectful and extortionate, and churches in ruins. He had now thirty-seven priests, and six ecclesiastics in minor orders soon to be ordained, had built forty-five churches and chapels, holding from three hundred to a thousand persons, and had repaired eighteen or twenty. He estimated the Catholics in New Mexico at one hundred thousand (nine thousand being Pueblo Indians); in Colorado, three thousand; in Arizona, five thousand.

Province of Oregon.

For years this diocese did not increase in white population; only a half-dozen priests were engaged in work among them, while the Jesuit fathers were busy with the missions of the Indians. In 1860 the western part of Idaho Territory was added to the jurisdiction of Archbishop Blanchet. Here whites were beginning to settle, and the chief efforts of the ordinary were directed to provide them with priests and churches. He could report in 1866 seventeen churches and fourteen priests. In 1864 the residence of the archbishop and the title of the see were transferred to the city of Portland.

In 1853 the diocese of Nesqually, under Bishop Blanchet, brother to the Archbishop of Portland, had a Catholic population of sixteen hundred whites and four thousand Indians, the former in charge of a few diocesan, the latter of Jesuit priests. The diocese was confined to Washington Territory after its formation in 1853. The Territory of Montana—at least the western half of it, where the Jesuits had flourishing missions—was also under the jurisdiction, for a time, of the Bishop of Nesqually. His diocese in 1866 had its cathedral at Vancouver, St. Francis Xavier's at Cowlitz, Immaculate Conception at Steilacoom, St. Patrick's at Walla Walla, a priest at Port Townsend, with Indian missions at Snohomish, Lamy, Colville, and among the Cœur d'Alènes and Pend d'Oreilles.

Province of San Francisco.

The First Plenary Council of Baltimore (1852) solicited the erection of San Francisco into an archbishopric, leaving to the see of Monterey the southern portion of the State. The immense and rapid influx of immigrants, brought into northern California by the discovery of gold a few years before, and the phenomenal rise and growth of the city at the Golden Gate indicated that the hopes of the church lay there, and not in the Spanish part farther south. The Bishop of Monterey, the Rt. Rev. S. J. Alemany, became Archbishop of San Francisco July, 1853. No diocese in the country was more cosmopolitan at the time; even Chinese Catholics had their Chinese priest, the Rev. Mr. Cian. In 1866 there were not less than fifty priests in the diocese, which number justifies us in setting down the Catholic population at not less than fifty thousand.

The see of Monterey, made vacant by the promotion of Archbishop Alemany, was filled by the Rev. Thaddeus Amat (1854). As Los Angeles was looming up as the more important city, the title of the see and the residence of the bishop were transferred to it in 1860. By 1866 the diocese of Monterey and Los Angeles had twenty-two priests, twenty-one churches, a seminary of Our Lady of Guadalupe at Santa Inez, St. Vincent's College under the Lazarists, the Franciscan College at the mission of Santa Barbara, and houses of Sisters of Charity at Los Angeles, Cieneguita, San Juan Bautista, and Santa Cruz.

The vicariate apostolic of Marysville, comprising that part of California which lies between the thirty-ninth and forty-second degrees of latitude, was formed in 1861 and put in charge of the Rt. Rev. Eugene O'Connell. Within the district he found only four priests. Five years later

(1866) he could report seventeen priests and thirty-five churches.

The Second Plenary Council.

The motives for holding a Plenary Council soon after the close of the Civil War (1866) are thus stated by Bishop Spalding in "The Life of Archbishop Spalding":

"The principal motives for holding a council, to which reference is here made, were, first, that at the close of the national crisis, which had acted as a dissolvent upon all sectarian ecclesiastical organizations, the Catholic Church might present to the country and the world a striking proof of the strong bond of unity with which her members are knit together. Secondly, that the collective wisdom of the church in this country might determine what measures should be adopted in order to meet the new phase of national life which the result of the war had just inaugurated; for, though the church is essentially the same in all times and places, her accidental relations to the world and the state are necessarily variable. Thirdly, that an earnest effort might be made to render ecclesiastical discipline, as far as possible, uniform throughout the entire extent of the United States. The fourth motive I shall give in the words of Archbishop Spalding:

"'I think,' he wrote, 'that it is our most urgent duty to discuss the future status of the negro. Four millions of these unfortunate beings are thrown on our charity, and they silently but eloquently appeal to us for help. We have a golden opportunity to reap a harvest of souls, which, neglected, may not return.'"

On the 7th of October, 1866, seven archbishops, thirty-eight bishops, three mitered abbots, and over one hundred and twenty theologians met in Baltimore to take part in the deliberations of the Second Plenary Council of the church in the United States. This was, at the time, the largest conciliary assembly since the Council of Trent, with the exception of two or three meetings of the bishops in Rome, which, however, were not councils in any proper sense of the word.

Numerous as was the American hierarchy at the time, the council deemed it necessary to enlarge it in order to answer the growing needs of the church in the country. It recommended the erection of sees at Wilmington, Del., Scranton and Harrisburg, Pa., Green Bay and La Crosse, Wis., St. Joseph, Mo., Omaha, Neb., Columbus, O., Grass Valley, Cal., and Rochester, N. Y.; and vicariates apostolic in North Carolina, Montana, Colorado, and Arizona. They also solicited the erection of Philadelphia and Milwaukee into archiepiscopal sees.

The method of selecting candidates for the episcopate had varied since the organization of the church here, as we have seen in the foregoing pages. The system adopted by the Second Plenary Council and approved by Rome is substantially the following: Every three years each bishop sends to his metropolitan and to the Congregation of Propaganda a list of the priests whom he thinks worthy of the episcopal office, accompanied by a detailed account of the qualities which distinguish them. When a see becomes vacant the bishops meet in synod, or in some other way, and discuss the merits of the candidates to be presented to fill it. Three names are then chosen by secret suffrage and are sent to Rome, together with a *procès verbal* of the proceedings. From this list the sovereign pontiff selects the person whom he thinks best suited to the office. However, in case the person to be chosen is to be an archbishop or the coadjutor of an archbishop, all the metropolitans of the United States must be consulted. This method lasted until the Third Plenary Council of Baltimore

(1884). It was then amended, and the following enactments now form the law in this country:

"1. When a diocese falls vacant, whether by the death, resignation, transfer, or removal of the bishop, and when, in consequence, three candidates are to be chosen whose names shall be proposed or recommended to the holy see for the vacant bishopric, the consulters and the irremovable rectors of the vacant diocese shall be called together, *e.g.*, thirty days after the vacancy occurs. It will be the right and duty of these consulters and rectors, thus properly assembled, to select three candidates for the vacant see. The candidates thus chosen shall be submitted to the bishops of the province, whose right it will be to approve or disapprove of them.

"2. The meeting of the consulters and irremovable rectors is called and presided over by the metropolitan of the province to which the vacant diocese belongs; or, if the metropolitan is lawfully hindered, by one of the suffragan bishops of the same province, to be deputed for this purpose by the metropolitan. Where there is question of choosing three candidates for a metropolitan see which is vacant, the meeting of the consulters and irremovable rectors of the vacant metropolitan see is called and presided over by the senior suffragan bishop, or, if he is hindered, by another bishop to be deputed by him.

"3. Before they cast their votes the aforesaid consulters and rectors shall swear that they are not induced to cast their votes for a candidate because of unworthy motives, such as that of expecting favors or rewards. They shall vote by *secret ballot*. This vote is merely consultive; i.e., it is simply equivalent to a recommendation that one of the candidates be appointed to the vacant see.

"4. The president of the meeting shall cause two authentic copies of the minutes of the meeting, containing an accurate list of the candidates chosen, to be drawn up and signed by the secretary. He shall forward one copy directly to the S. C. de Propaganda Fide, the second to the other bishops of the province. A third copy may also be drawn up and kept in the diocesan archives, as is done in England. (For the manner in which these minutes are written, see the extract from the statutes of the cathedral chapters in England, given by us below, in Appendix VII.)

"5. Thereupon, on a day fixed beforehand—*e.g.*, ten days after the above meeting of consulters and rectors—the bishops of the province shall meet and openly discuss among themselves the merits of the candidates selected by the consulters and rectors, or of others to be selected by themselves. Afterward they make up their list of three candidates to be sent to Rome. From this it will be seen that the bishops have a right to approve or disapprove of them; they are bound to give the reasons upon which they base their disapproval to the S. C. de Propaganda Fide."

It should be observed that the above presentation of candidates to the holy see, both as made, on the one hand, by the consulters and irremovable rectors, and on the other by the bishops of the province, is to be considered not as *electio*, *postulatio*, or *nominatio*, but merely as *commendatio*, which imposes upon the holy see no obligation to appoint any of the persons recommended. As a matter of fact, however, the holy see nearly always appoints one of the candidates—usually the one who is *first* on the list—recommended or presented in the manner above stated, and rarely goes outside of the list of the candidates presented or recommended to it for appointment.

It might have seemed a bold thing to make such a display as was exhibited by this grand Catholic assembly, the Second Plenary Council of 1866, before the eyes of a land which but a decade ago had been in the throes of a fierce anti-Catholic agitation. But our bishops were wise in their boldness. Says Bishop Spalding, with remarkable insight and vigor:

"The country had just come forth from a most terrible crisis, in which many ancient landmarks had been effaced and the very ship of state had been wrenched from its moorings. House had been divided against house, and brother's hand had been raised against brother. The sects had been torn asunder, and still lay in disorder and confusion, helping to widen the abyss which had threatened to ingulf the nation's life. Half the country was waste and desolate; the people crushed, bowed beneath the double weight of the memory of the past, which could no more return, and of the thought of a future which seemed hopeless. On the other side there were the weariness and exhaustion which follow a supreme effort, and the longing for peace and happiness after so much bloodshed and misery.

"All were ready to applaud any power that had been able to live through that frightful struggle unhurt and unharmed; and when the Catholic Church walked forth before the eyes of the nation, clothed in the panoply of undiminished strength and of unbroken unity, thousands who but a while ago would have witnessed this manifestation of her power with jealous concern now hailed it with delight as a harbinger of good omen. Then it must be confessed, too, that during the war men had seen more of the church, and having learned to know her better, had come to love her more. There was not a village throughout the land where some brave soldier, not a Catholic, was not found to speak the praises of her heroic daughters, who, while men fought, stood by to stanch the blood."

Part IV. From the Second Plenary Council to the Establishment of the Apostolic Delegation (1866–93).

CHAPTER XXVIII.

THE PRESENT HIERARCHY.

It behooves us to be brief in this period. Events of the highest importance crowd it—the Vatican Council, the Third Plenary Council of Baltimore, the centenary of Baltimore as an episcopal see, the inauguration of the Catholic University of America in Washington, the national or so-called Cahensly movement, the school controversy, the establishment of the apostolic delegation. The actors in these events are still alive. The events themselves are too near for history, which demands perspective and therefore a certain distance; some of them have been so burning but the other day that the embers might be fanned once more to flame by the slightest breath. I shall therefore chronicle, without appreciating, the events of this period. In fact, this chapter shall be barely statistical.

To-day (1895) we find in the United States fourteen archiepiscopal sees and provinces. At the Second Plenary Council of 1866 they were just half that number—seven, viz., Baltimore, St. Louis, Oregon, Cincinnati, San Francisco, New Orleans, New York. Boston, Milwaukee, Philadelphia, and Santa Fé were raised to the archiepiscopal dignity February, 1875; Chicago, September, 1880; St. Paul, May, 1888; Dubuque, September, 1893. This multiplication of archbishoprics either presupposed or entailed an increase of bishoprics. In 1866, at the Second Plenary Council, the dioceses were thirty-eight; in 1895 they are seventy-three, almost twice as many; so that this latter period of twenty-nine years (1866-95) has seen the hierarchy double its development of the three former periods of seventy-six years (1790–1866). The bare statement expresses a marvelous increase, a phenomenal progress. Add to this that the cardinalitial dignity has come to crown our splendid line of church prelates, first in one of New York's archbishops, and again in Baltimore's present archbishop; and, moreover, that an apostolic delegation, residing in Washington, raises the hierarchy of the United States to equality with that of any country in the world.

The sending of apostolic delegates to national churches is a prerogative that inheres in the papacy and results logically from the constitution of the Catholic Church. The church is a perfect society; that is to say, the church has from Christ, within herself, of her own right, all the elements, prerogatives, and duties that constitute a society. The Bishop of Rome, as successor of St. Peter, who was appointed by Christ his vicar and the visible head of his church, has supreme authority over the church of Christ. This authority is plenary, episcopal, ordinary, and immediate, affecting directly each and every member, without any need of reaching one class through another; so that each one, no less than the collective body, is subject to that authority. In each diocese there are two episcopal authorities, that of the universal bishop and that of the local bishop. The first is supreme, but does not absorb the other; the second, though subordinate, is nevertheless efficacious and has its proper field of action.

The Pope, therefore, has the right to be present in the church of each country through a representative, if he deem it expedient. Legates represent the person of the sovereign pontiff. They are sent to exercise his authority so far as it is communicated to them. They are not sent to seize or lessen or absorb the authority of the local bishops, no more than the papacy itself seizes or lessens or destroys the local episcopate. They are not aliens, like ambassadors to a foreign country; they are, wherever they may be, within the household of the supreme father who sent them, for they are within the church directly subject to him, they are in the ecclesiastical territory of their sovereign. To the Catholic, wherever he may be, considered from the religious point of view as a Catholic, the Pope is not a foreigner and his representative is not a foreigner.

Not only is the right to send delegates to the churches of the world inherent in the papacy, but it has been exercised by the holy see from the earliest times of Christianity, as might be abundantly proved if that question were the specific subject-matter of these pages. It is well to know that the establishment of the apostolic delegation in the United States is not due, as many suppose, to accidental and transitory causes, though such may have furnished the occasion; but that it is the natural consequence of the first principles of our church constitution, and is in perfect accord with the traditional practice of past ages. It is hardly necessary to add that the delegation to the United States is strictly ecclesiastical and not at all diplomatic. The American delegate is accredited to the church, not to the government, of the United States. Courtesy on the part of the public may recognize the rank the delegate holds within our church, as, indeed, our bishops, archbishops, and cardinal are respected and honored because of their high ecclesiastical place. Such recognition and treatment is officious, not official, and does not entail a diplomatic recognition.

I now go on to describe succinctly the present status of the American hierarchy.

Province of Baltimore.

Archbishop Spalding's life came to an end February 7, 1872. Between this latter date and the holding of the Second Plenary Council had taken place a world-wide event in which the hierarchy of the United States, and Archbishop Spalding as its leader, had no unimportant share; I mean the Vatican Council. In the beginning of that memorable assembly the question whether or not it would be opportune to define the infallibility of the Pope found Archbishop Spalding and most of his American colleagues inclined to the opinion that a formal definition would be unnecessary and possibly inexpedient. They did not deny the doctrine; they and their flocks believed it. But for that very reason there could be no necessity, they argued, for a formal definition. The better way would be, instead of proclaiming the dogma of infallibility directly, to condemn all errors opposed to it; this would be an indirect, an implicit, and not the less vigorous mode of expressing the right doctrine. Accordingly there appeared over the signature of Archbishop Spalding a *postulatum*, or schema, or, as we should say, a draft, "for the clear and logical definition of the infallibility of the Roman pontiff in accordance with the principles already received by the church." This able paper became at once one of the most remarked among the many that the great debate produced, and was the target for praise and blame. It is well known what the outcome has been, and how all

Catholicity, no part of it more loyally and enthusiastically than the United States, has accepted the defined dogma.

Bishop Bayley, of Newark, N. J., was promoted to the primatial see of Baltimore as the successor of the great Spalding, July 30, 1872. His episcopate there was a short one; he died October 3, 1877. He is known especially for his contributions to the church history of the United States—"Life of Bishop Bruté" and "History of the Catholic Church on the Island of New York." The successor of Archbishop Bayley was the Rt. Rev. James Gibbons, transferred to Baltimore from the see of Richmond October 3, 1877. Many important events mark the episcopate of the present incumbent of the primatial see—the Third Plenary Council of Baltimore (1884), his promotion to the cardinalitial dignity (June 7, 1886), the celebration of the centenary of the appointment of Baltimore's first bishop, and the inauguration of the Catholic University of America in Washington (1889), without speaking of the many civil events—centenaries, Columbian Exposition, and others of lesser note—in which he has been a prominent, if not the chief, figure. It does not befit the historian to turn panegyrist to the living. Cardinal Gibbons is among us still—and long may he remain—the pride of the church, the beloved of the nation.

Bishop Lynch, of Charleston, labored many years with a brave heart and a wonderful perseverance to restore the material condition of his diocese, ruined by the war, and died amid his labors, February 26, 1882. He was succeeded by the Rt. Rev. H. P. Northrop, transferred from the vicariate apostolic of North Carolina to the see of Charleston January 27, 1883. Richmond lost its war bishop, the Rt. Rev. John McGill, January 14, 1872, possessed for five years the Rt. Rev. James Gibbons, then passed for ten years (1878–88) under the rule of the Rt. Rev. J. J. Keane, whom it gave as first rector, indeed as founder and organizer, to the Catholic University, Washington. Of his wonderful success in this great work under adverse circumstances the future historian shall have much to say; the annalist of to-day can but record his work as phenomenal in the history of universities. Since October 20, 1889, Bishop A. van de Vyver rules the historic see of Richmond. St. Augustine lost its first incumbent, Bishop Verot, June 10, 1876, and received its present ruler, Bishop Moore, May 13, 1877. Savannah, after giving Bishop Verot to St. Augustine in 1870, obtained a successor to him (April 23, 1873) in the Rt. Rev. William H. Gross, whom it saw depart for the distant archbishopric of Portland, Ore., in 1885, to be replaced (March, 1886) by the Rt. Rev. Thomas A. Becker, transferred from the see of Wilmington. Wheeling lost its first bishop, R. V. Whelan, July, 1874. He was succeeded by J. J. Kain in May, 1875. A brilliant episcopate of eighteen years followed, to be crowned (July 6, 1893) by promotion to the archiepiscopal see of St. Louis. The incumbent of Wheeling since April 8, 1894, is the Rt. Rev. P. J. Donahoe.

Province of New York.

At the close of the Second Plenary Council the great see of New York was occupied by Archbishop McCloskey. Four important events marked his episcopate after that date: his attendance on the Vatican Council, where he occupied a prominent position on one of the committees; his promotion to the cardinalate, the first time the honor was conferred on the United States (April 7, 1875); his attendance —too late, however, to take part in the election—on the conclave of 1878 that gave to the church the present gloriously reigning Pope, Leo XIII.; and the dedication (May 25, 1879) of the magnificent cathedral of New York. The brilliant career of America's first cardinal closed October 10, 1885. Five years before he had received as coadjutor the Rt. Rev. M. A. Corrigan, transferred from the see of Newark, who succeeded him in the see of New York. When Bishop McCloskey, on the death of Archbishop Hughes, was transferred to New York from Albany, he was succeeded in that see (October, 1865) by the Rt. Rev. John J. Conroy, who resigned the position October 16, 1877, to be replaced by his coadjutor, the Rt. Rev. Francis McNeirny, who died January 2, 1894. The present incumbent of Albany is the Rt. Rev. Thomas A. Burke. Brooklyn's first bishop, the Rt. Rev. John Loughlin, died December, 1891; Bishop Charles E. McDonnell succeeded him April, 1892. On the death of Bishop Timon, of Buffalo (April, 1867), the present incumbent, the Rt. Rev. S. D. Ryan, was appointed. The transfer of Bishop Bayley from Newark to Baltimore (July, 1872) gave occasion for the appointment to the see of Newark of Rt. Rev. M. A. Corrigan (May, 1873). His transfer as coadjutor to the archiepiscopal see of New York (October, 1880) caused a new appointment for Newark—that of Bishop W. M. Wigger, who is still living. Ogdensburg was erected in 1872; its first bishop was E. P. Wadhams, who died December, 1891; its present bishop is the Rt. Rev. H. Gabriels. Rochester was established in 1868; its first bishop is the present incumbent, the Rt. Rev. B. J. McQuaid. Syracuse was established in 1886, and still possesses its first bishop, P. A. Ludden. Trenton was established in 1881, and has had two bishops—M. J. O'Farrell, who died April, 1894, and James A. McFaul, who was consecrated in October last (1894).

Province of Cincinnati.

The long and glorious career of Archbishop Purcell went down (July, 1883) in a dark cloud and a terrible sorrow—bankruptcy running into the millions. To succeed him the present incumbent, Archbishop Elder, was transferred from the see of Natchez. Bishop Rappe, of Cleveland, under the stress of calumnious accusations which were proved before his death to be false, resigned the see of Cleveland August 22, 1870. His successor, Bishop Gilmour, lived until April 13, 1891. The present incumbent is the Rt. Rev. Ignatius F. Horstmann. Columbus was established in 1868; its first bishop, S. H. Rosecrans, died October 21, 1878; since August 8, 1880, it is ruled by Bishop J. A. Watterson. The first Bishop of Covington, G. A. Carrell, died September 25, 1868; his successor, A. M. Toebbe, lived until May 2, 1884; the present occupant of the see, since January 25, 1885, is Bishop C. P. Maes. C. H. Borgess was consecrated Bishop of Detroit April 24, 1870; he resigned April 6, 1887; the present incumbent, since November 4, 1888, is Bishop John S. Foley. Fort Wayne lost its first bishop, J. H. Luers, June 29, 1871, lost its second bishop, Joseph Dwenger, January 22, 1893, and is now under the rule of Bishop Rademacher. Grand Rapids, an erection of 1882, is still under its first bishop, H. J. Richter. The present Bishop of Louisville, W. J. McCloskey, was appointed soon after the Second Plenary Council and consecrated May 24, 1868. Nashville lost to Chicago Bishop Feehan in 1880, and to Fort Wayne Bishop Rademacher in 1893; its present incumbent is Rt. Rev. Thomas S. Byrne. Bishop De St. Palais, of Vincennes, died June 28, 1877, and was succeeded (May 12, 1878) by the present incumbent, Bishop Chatard.

Province of St. Louis.

The veteran of the West, the venerable Archbishop Kenrick, who has been in the see of St. Louis since 1843, is still living, but the title of the diocese is held by the former coadjutor, Archbishop Kain. The other sees of the province, as now constituted, are of recent erection. Concordia, erected in 1887, gave its first bishop, R. Scannell, to Omaha in December, 1890; since then the see is vacant and is administered by the Bishop of Wichita, Rt Rev. J. J. Hennessey. Kansas City, Kan., though erected only in May, 1891, can trace its origin through Leavenworth (May, 1877) to the vicariate apostolic of Kansas, established June, 1871. The Rt. Rev. Louis M. Fink between 1871 and 1895 has been successively Vicar Apostolic of Kansas, Bishop of Leavenworth, and Bishop of Kansas City, Kan. Kansas City, Mo., was established September, 1880, in which year the incumbent of St. Joseph, Mo., Bishop J. J. Hogan, was transferred to Kansas City, remaining, nevertheless, Administrator of St. Joseph. This latter diocese, erected in 1868, had, therefore, for its first bishop until 1880 the Rt. Rev. J. J. Hogan, who continued to administer it until 1893, when it received as its second bishop the Rt. Rev. M. J. Burke, transferred from the see of Cheyenne. Wichita was erected in 1887, and is ruled by its first bishop, J. J. Hennessey.

Province of New Orleans.

Archbishop Odin died May 25, 1870. His successor, N. J. Perché, died December, 1883. F. X. Leray, transferred from Natchitoches to New Orleans, died September, 1887. He was succeeded by the present incumbent, F. Janssens, transferred to New Orleans from Natchez in

August, 1888. Dallas was an erection of 1890; its first incumbent, T. F. Brennan, resigned in 1892; Bishop E. J. Dunne is the incumbent since November 30, 1893. Bishop C. M. Dubuis resigned the see of Galveston in 1881, his coadjutor, P. Dufal, resigned it likewise, and the present bishop, N. A. Gallagher, was appointed April 30, 1892. Little Rock has had but the one bishop since February, 1867, the Rt. Rev. E. Fitzgerald. Mobile lost Bishop Quinlan by death in 1883 and Bishop Manucy by resignation in 1884; the present incumbent, since September, 1885, is Bishop J. O'Sullivan. From Natchez Bishop Elder was transferred to Cincinnati in 1880, and Bishop Janssens to New Orleans in 1888; the present incumbent is Bishop Thomas Heslin. Bishop Martin, of Natchitoches, died September, 1875; his successor, F. X. Leray, was transferred to New Orleans in 1883; and his successor, Bishop Durier, consecrated November, 1885, still holds the see. San Antonio was erected in 1874; its first bishop, A. D. Pellicer, died April, 1880; the second bishop, John C. Neraz, died November, 1894; just now the see is without an incumbent. Brownsville is a vicariate apostolic, established in 1874; the first occupant was Bishop Manucy until 1884; the present occupant, since November, 1890, is Rt. Rev. Peter Verdaguer. Another vicariate apostolic, established 1891, is the Indian Territory, under the Rt. Rev. Theophile Meerschaert.

Province of Oregon.

This province has not grown and extended as its sisters, though we think that there is before this northwestern section of the Union an era of wonderful prosperity. The archdiocese of Oregon or Portland lost its pioneer archbishop, the Most Rev. F. N. Blanchet, in June, 1883.

Bishop Seghers, transferred from Vancouver Island, had been since 1878 coadjutor to Archbishop Blanchet, and succeeded him only to resign in 1884 and go find a saintly but tragic death on the banks of the Yukon River in the heart of Alaska. The present incumbent is the Most Rev. W. H. Gross, transferred from Savannah in February, 1885. Boisé City, Ida., established as a vicariate in 1868, was erected into a diocese in 1893; its first occupant, Bishop Lootens, resigned in 1876; since 1885 Bishop A. J. Glorien occupies the see. Nesqually lost its pioneer bishop, M. A. Blanchet, in 1879; he was succeeded by Bishop A. Junger, who still holds the see. Alaska was made a prefecture apostolic in 1894, under Very Rev. P. Tosi, S.J.

Province of San Francisco.

The first Archbishop of San Francisco, the saintly Alemany, resigned in 1884 to go die in his native Spain; a year before his resignation he had received as coadjutor the Most Rev. P. W. Riordan, who still occupies the see. The first Bishop of Monterey, Thaddeus Amat, died in 1878; he had received in 1873 a coadjutor, Bishop Mora, who succeeded him; he in turn received, in 1894, a coadjutor, the Rt. Rev. George Montgomery. The diocese of Sacramento, established in 1886, was put in charge of Bishop Manogue, who died in 1895. Salt Lake City, from a vicariate apostolic established in 1886, was erected into a diocese in 1891; its first and present incumbent is the Rt. Rev. L. Scanlon.

Province of Boston.

Bishop Fitzpatrick died February 13, 1866. Previous to his death he received as coadjutor John Joseph Williams, who became his successor. In February, 1875, Boston was made an archbishopric, and Bishop Williams became its first archbishop. He still lives in vigorous health, having celebrated the golden jubilee of his priesthood in May, 1895. He was given an auxiliary, the Rt. Rev. John Brady, in August, 1891. The first incumbent of Burlington, Bishop De Goesbriand, still holds that see; since June, 1892, he has for coadjutor the Rt. Rev. John Michaud. Hartford lost Bishop McFarland in October, 1874. He was succeeded (March, 1876) by Thomas Galberry, who died in October, 1878. To him succeeded L. S. McMahon, who died in August, 1893. The present incumbent is the Rt. Rev. Michael Tierney. Manchester was erected in 1884 and is ruled by the Rt. Rev. Denis M. Bradley. Portland was deprived of Bishop Bacon by death, November, 1874. His successor is the Rt. Rev. James A. Healy. Providence was erected in 1872; its first bishop, Thomas F. Hendricken, died in June, 1886, and was succeeded by the present incumbent, the Rt. Rev. M. Harkins. Springfield was erected in June, 1870; its first bishop, P. T. O'Reilly, died in May, 1892; it is now ruled by the Rt. Rev. Thomas D. Beaven.

Province of Milwaukee.

Milwaukee became an archbishopric in 1875; its first archbishop, the Most Rev. John Martin Henni, died in September, 1881. One year before his death he received as coadjutor Bishop M. Heiss, transferred from La Crosse. Archbishop Heiss died in March, 1890. The present archbishop is the Most Rev. F. X. Katzer. Green Bay was erected in 1868; it had for first bishop Rt. Rev. Joseph Melcher, who died in December, 1873, and was succeeded by F. X. Krautbauer, who died in December, 1885.

Bishop Katzer succeeded him until January, 1891, when he was transferred to the see of Milwaukee. The present incumbent of Green Bay is the Rt. Rev. S. G. Messmer. La Crosse was made a diocese in 1868, and was ruled by Bishop Heiss until his transfer to Milwaukee in 1880. His successor was the Rt. Rev. K. C. Flasch, who died in August, 1891. The present bishop is the Rt. Rev. James Schwebach. The diocese of Marquette lost Bishop Baraga in 1868. He was succeeded by Ignatius Mrak, who resigned in 1878. The present incumbent is the Rt. Rev. John Vertin.

Province of Philadelphia.

The diocese of Philadelphia was made an archbishopric in June, 1875. Archbishop Wood died in June, 1883, and was succeeded by Bishop P. J. Ryan, transferred from the coadjutorship of St. Louis. Erie is ruled since 1868 by the Rt. Rev. Tobias Mullen. Harrisburg was erected in 1868; its first bishop, J. F. Shanahan, died in September, 1868; he was succeeded by the Rt. Rev. Thomas McGovern, who still holds the see. Bishop Domenec, of Pittsburg, was removed to the see of Alleghany City in 1876, and was succeeded in the see of Pittsburg by Bishop J. Twigg, who died in December, 1889. The present incumbent of the reunited sees, Pittsburg and Alleghany City, is Bishop R. Phelan. Scranton was made a diocese in 1868, and is still ruled by its first bishop, the Rt. Rev. William O'Hara.

Province of Santa Fé.

The first Bishop of Santa Fé, J. B. Lamy, died in February, 1888. His coadjutor, J. B. Salpointe, transferred in 1869 from the vicariate apostolic of Arizona, became his successor and was made archbishop in July, 1884; three years after the appointment of his own coadjutor he resigned (August, 1894), and thus the see passed into the hands of its present archbishop, the Most Rev. P. L. Chapelle. Colorado was made a vicariate apostolic in 1868, a diocese with Denver as see in 1887; the first bishop, J. P. Machebœuf, died in 1889, and was succeeded by the present incumbent, N. C. Matz, who was coadjutor since 1887. Arizona was made a vicariate apostolic in 1869; the first vicar, J. B. Salpointe, was transferred to Santa Fé in 1884. The present incumbent is the Rt. Rev. P. Bourgade, who became Bishop of Tucson in 1894 on the changing of the vicariate into a diocese.

Province of Chicago.

The Rt. Rev. Thomas Foley became Coadjutor and Administrator of the diocese of Chicago in February, 1870. During his short rule—for he died in February, 1879—he restored peace to the distracted diocese and set it on the way to that wonderful progress it has attained since. In 1880 Chicago was made an archbishopric, and Bishop Feehan, of Nashville, was transferred to the promoted see. Alton lost its first bishop, H. D. Juncker, in October, 1868. In 1870 he was succeeded by P. J. Baltes, who died in February, 1886. The present incumbent, since 1888, is Bishop James Ryan. Belleville was made a diocese in 1887, and J. J. Jansen, its present bishop, was consecrated in April, 1888. Peoria was erected in 1887 and given in charge of the Rt. Rev. J. L. Spalding, who still rules it.

Province of St. Paul.

Rt. Rev. T. L. Grace, after receiving for coadjutor in 1875 John Ireland, resigned the see of St. Paul July, 1884, and is now spending his declining years in the classic shades of St. Thomas's College near that city. St. Paul was made an archbishopric in May, 1888, and is famous throughout the world with the fame of its archbishop. St. Cloud, erected into a bishopric in 1889, was at first the vicariate apostolic of northern Minnesota. Bishop Seidenbusch, its first incumbent, resigned in 1889, and was succeeded by Otto Zardetti, who in 1894 was transferred to the archiepiscopal see of Bucharest, Roumania. In the beginning of 1895 Bishop Marty was transferred from Sioux Falls, S. Dak., to the vacant see of St. Cloud. The diocese of Duluth was established in 1889; its first bishop is the Rt. Rev. James McGolrick. Jamestown also was erected in 1889; its bishop is the Rt. Rev. John Shanley. Winona likewise was erected in 1889, and is ruled by the Rt. Rev. J. B. Cotter. In 1880 was established the vicariate apostolic of Dakota, erected into a diocese in 1889; its first bishop, the Rt. Rev. M. Marty, was transferred in 1895 to St. Cloud.

Province of Dubuque.

Dubuque was made an archbishopric in 1893, and its bishop since 1866, the Rt. Rev. John Hennessey, became archbishop. Omaha, established as the vicariate of Nebraska in 1857, was made a bishopric in 1885. Bishop O'Gorman died in July, 1874, and was succeeded in 1876 by Bishop O'Connor, who died May, 1890. The present incumbent is the Rt. Rev. R. Scannell, transferred from Concordia in 1890. The diocese of Cheyenne was erected in 1887, and remained under the rule of Bishop Burke until he was transferred to St. Joseph in 1893. Davenport was made a diocese in 1881; its first bishop was John Mullen, who died in July, 1883, and was succeeded by the present incumbent, the Rt. Rev. Henry Cosgrove. Lincoln was erected in 1887; its first incumbent, the Rt. Rev. Thomas Bonacum, still rules it.

Such is the condition of the hierarchy in the year 1895. The annexed tabular statement, taken from Hoffman's Directory, shows the number of archbishops, bishops, priests, churches, missions, seminaries and students, schools and children, orphan asylums and inmates, charitable institutions, and Catholic population. We put in a caution as to the last item, for the reason that another directory, Sadlier's, equally authorized, finds a Catholic population of over 10,000,000—a different total from Hoffman's, which is 9,077,865. In other respects we believe Hoffman's is mainly correct. Behold here the work and progress of a century! No one can deny that it is simply wonderful. It were presumptuous to indulge in foreseeings and foretellings. Yet he would be a rash man who should say that we have come to a standstill; that the church which has reached such an extension under adverse circumstances, amid the difficulties of infancy and youth, shall have no vigor to grow with still more gigantic strides in the more propitious times that are already at hand, and in the full vigor of an assured manhood.

GENERAL SUMMARY.

Archdioceses, Dioceses, Vicariates Apostolic.	[illegible]	[illegible]	Secular.	Regular.	Total.	[illegible] with [illegible]	[illegible] with [illegible]	Total Churches.	Stations and Chapels.	Universities.	Seminaries, Secular.	Students.	Seminaries, Regular.	Students.	High Schools for Boys.	High Schools for Girls.	Parochial Schools.	Children Attending.	Orphan Asylums.	Orphans.	Charitable Institutions.	Total Children in Catholic Institutions.	Catholic Population.
BALTIMORE	1		14[illegible]	[illegible]	37[illegible]	[illegible]	6[illegible]	170	1[illegible]	3	5	[illegible]	6	250	8	18	90	22 [illegible]	8	850	30	2[illegible] [illegible]	235 [illegible]
Charleston		1	14		15	11	13	24	74			5				3	[illegible]	74[illegible]	2	125	5	1 [illegible]	8 000
Richmond		1	30		30	25	24	49	33			9			3	7	21	2 401	3	150	5	3 741	72 000
St. Augustine		1	16		25	15	23	38	56			2	1	4	1	8	15	2 120	1	24	1	2 164	7 000
Savannah		1	18	[illegible]	20	17	10	27	50			5	1	42		9	14	2 103	2	142	8	2 245	20 000
Wheeling		1	31	[illegible]	35	25	45	70	56			8			1	6	9	1 458	3	125	5	2 10[illegible]	20 000
Wilmington		1	23		20	21	16	37	17			24				2	9	2 [illegible]	3	20[illegible]	3	2 30[illegible]	20 000
North Carolina		1	10		22	8	16	24	31			2	1	7	1	2	6	397	1	7	1	608	1 10[illegible]
BOSTON		1	337	[illegible]	421	136	48	[illegible]	62		1	130			3	8	100	33 410	7	767	20	35 88[illegible]	5[illegible] 000
Burlington			57		59	47	32	78	22			13	1	2	3	5	16	4 300	2	107	3	5 141	53 000
Hartford		1	195	[illegible]	214	102	76	178	40			60	1	21	1	7	48	1[illegible] 20[illegible]	3	40[illegible]	5	25 00[illegible]	[illegible]
Manchester		1	72	[illegible]	80	48	17	[illegible]	44			14			6	6	64	9 040	5	348	15	[illegible] 470	85 000
Portland		1	68		84	5[illegible]	22	72	42			12			1	4	17	5 410	2	156	[illegible]	7 30[illegible]	53 000
Providence		1	152		164	75	8	83	5[illegible]						2	8	38	17 [illegible]	4	6[illegible]	8	18 750	2[illegible] 000
Springfield		1	197	[illegible]	211	102	[illegible]	1[illegible]5	1[illegible]						1		20	15 970	3	34[illegible]	7	1[illegible] 625	2[illegible] 000
CHICAGO	[illegible]		295	[illegible]	[illegible]	1[illegible]	5[illegible]	2[illegible]	53			[illegible]5	2	30	4	17	141	4[illegible] [illegible]75	4	6[illegible]	13	51 75[illegible]	550 000
Alton		1	104		134	8[illegible]	45	133	17			25	2	26	2	2	6[illegible]	7 044		87	11	8 44[illegible]	75 000
Belleville		1	78		83	61	31	[illegible]5	1[illegible]			21			1	3	57	6 472	1	43	5	6 51	50 000
Peoria		1	1[illegible]		152	1[illegible]	[illegible]	2[illegible]	6[illegible]			15			2	9	58	7 5[illegible]	1	57	[illegible]	8 50[illegible]	110 000
CINCINNATI	1		150	[illegible]	224	141	33	174	6[illegible]		2	170	2	110	5	14	94	2[illegible] 605	4	68[illegible]	1[illegible]	25 [illegible]	[illegible]
Cleveland		1	194	[illegible]	234	165	83	248	87		1	48	1	6	2	6	138	3[illegible] 044	7	850	18	31 335	[illegible] 000
Columbus		1	73	[illegible]	8[illegible]	65	33	[illegible]8	35		1	10	1	28	1	3	3[illegible]	8 413	[illegible]	27[illegible]	7	8 [illegible]87	55 000
Covington		1	60		65	45	27	72	67			12			2	9	3[illegible]	6 687	3	145	7	7 66[illegible]	4[illegible]
Detroit		1	130	[illegible]	170	104	7[illegible]	18[illegible]	44		1	120	1	54	2	4	[illegible]4	15 5[illegible]	5	5[illegible]	13	16 7[illegible]	1[illegible] [illegible]15
Fort Wayne		1	81	[illegible]	141	[illegible]	46	1[illegible]4	55	1	1		2		1	12	75	[illegible] 8[illegible]	2	270	[illegible]	11 37[illegible]	[illegible]
Grand Rapids		1	63		77	54	67	1[illegible]	41			41				1	41	1[illegible] 3[illegible]8	2	180	8	1[illegible] [illegible]	90 000
Louisville		1	101	[illegible]	142	8[illegible]	7[illegible]	155	[illegible]				4	50	3	1[illegible]	[illegible]	[illegible] 457	3	343	15	11 875	110 000
Nashville		1	22		34	21	27	48	35			9			1	3	14	1 [illegible]	2	180	5	2 505	[illegible]3 000
Vincennes		1	123	[illegible]	16[illegible]	120	[illegible]3	1[illegible]	[illegible]		1	47	2	35	2	18	95	14 [illegible]	2	20[illegible]	10	17 325	[illegible]5 000
DUBUQUE	1		233	[illegible]	24[illegible]	2[illegible]	[illegible]	25[illegible]	11[illegible]						1	1[illegible]	10[illegible]	13 77[illegible]	1	102	8	14 535	[illegible] 000
Cheyenne			6		8	7	2	9	46			1				1	1	[illegible]0			2	29[illegible]	4 000
Davenport		1	94		10[illegible]	6[illegible]	[illegible]	155	112			23			1	7	37	4 8[illegible]			9	5 6[illegible]	56 [illegible]
Lincoln		1	51	3	54	44	45	[illegible]4	44			14				4	14	[illegible] 040			1	2 34[illegible]	[illegible] 150
Omaha		1	78	24	10[illegible]	73	73	146	71	1		23			1	5	35	3 7[illegible]	1	108	4	4 180	58 000
MILWAUKEE	1		226	41	267	17[illegible]	[illegible]	271	27		1	35	3	45	6	5	142	25 553	5	427	17	27 68[illegible]	[illegible] 000
Green Bay		1	116	[illegible]	12[illegible]	1[illegible]	67	175	1[illegible]			8				1	71	11 63[illegible]	4	200	11	11 89[illegible]	125 000
La Crosse		1	93	23	116	[illegible]	110	1[illegible]	43				1[illegible]			2	63	9 026	2	160	11	9 330	75 000
Marquette		2	52	8	60	53	18	71	6[illegible]			6				1	19	5 640	2	70	5	5 710	70 000
NEW ORLEANS	1		12[illegible]	7[illegible]	205	103	43	145	56			43	2	....	5	17	103	12 928	11	1 439	23	1[illegible] 597	325 000

Dallas		1	26	6	32	25	19	44	74			1		....	....	10	11	1 740	1	35	5	1 775	20 000
Galveston		1	32	9	41	29	21	50	38	1		10		....	1	6	20	3 000	2	100	7	3 240	34 000
Little Rock		1	29	18	38	27	29	56	37			4	1	20	....	4	30	1 550	1	10	4	1 600	10 000
Mobile		1	19	25	44	21	30	51	58			....	1	9	2	6	20	1 700	2	100	3	2 086	17 000
Natchez		1	26	....	26	24	36	60	51			17		....	2	5	24	1 872	2	145	2	2 877	16 000
Natchitoches		1	19	5	24	10	18	37	32			....	1	....	1	5	11	735		....	1	805	30 000
San Antonio			43	20	63	42	29	71	97		1	9	1	2	4	5	34	3 708	2	200	4	5 000	16 000
Brownsville		1	12	11	21	10	9	19	242					....	1	3	7	300		....	1	726	54 000
Indian Territory		1	10	13	23	17	19	36	93			7	1	14	1	1	....	1 081		....	....	1 377	12 385
NEW YORK	1	1	405	195	600	177	42	219	113		1	124	1	23	24	32	168	41 057	7	2 689	51	61 972	800 000
Albany		1	152	55	207	95	40	135	131			34	2	....	3	4	40	13 000	8	1 138	16	15 233	130 000
Brooklyn		1	251	29	280	107	15	122	27		1	80		....	3	18	110	29 412	14	4 004	27	36 714	280 000
Buffalo		1	135	78	213	113	49	162	16	1	2	130	3	63	7	17	74	20 307	5	587	20	24 042	160 000
Newark		1	163	60	223	104	21	125	93		1	32	3	30	4	16	80	28 391	6	887	22	31 790	220 000
Ogdensburg		1	80	15	95	67	49	116	25			11	1	3	8	8	20	3 800	1	61	4	4 263	72 000
Rochester		1	80	5	85	59	34	93	10		1	40		....	1	4	23	12 127	5	502	8	13 227	80 000
Syracuse		1	77	11	88	59	25	84	55			15	1	8	3	5	18	5 473	5	675	10	6 770	75 000
Trenton		1	82	16	98	67	35	102	65				1	4	....	8	32	7 240	1	61	3	7 676	60 000
OREGON	1		42	19	61	32	28	60	60		1	7	1	9	2	9	30	2 000	2	112	8	2 398	30 000
Boisé City		1	9	10	19	12	15	27	57			1	1	40	1	2	1	100		....	4	525	9 600
Helena		1	15	20	35	21	23	44	84			....		9	1	5	10	850	1	300	25	2 742	30 000
Nesqually		1	36	24	62	37	45	82	199			5	1	5	3	23	17	2 586	5	360	28	3 746	42 000
Alaska Territory			1	9	10	4	4	8	6					....	....	....	4	155		....		....	....
PHILADELPHIA	1		287	81	363	149	34	183	116		2	187	2	50	4	14	98	32 579	10	2 332	23	39 780	415 000
Erie		1	64	19	83	62	90	112	47			16	1	90	....	8	36	6 417	1	164	4	7 000	65 000
Harrisburg		1	58	3	61	45	15	60	33			11		....	....	7	32	5 550	2	....	3	5 730	40 500
Pittsburg		1	176	123	299	160	55	215	76		1	45	5	168	4	7	110	36 495	3	625	11	32 170	206 000
Scranton		1	119		119	76	40	116	33			74		....	1	10	39	11 466	1	130	2	12 200	120 000
ST. LOUIS	2		211	124	335	159	69	228	78	1	1	54	5	138	3	19	128	22 563	3	550	21	25 625	200 000
Concordia			16	7	23	17	36	53	15			2		....	....	8	12	1 477		....	....	1 600	12 000
Kansas City, Kansas		1	74	53	127	71	89	160	34			12	2	25	2	4	47	4 000	2	150	5	4 800	50 000
Kansas City, Missouri		1	35	29	64	50	45	95	84			20	1	25	2	1	37	3 900	1	92	9	5 300	47 000
St. Joseph		1	25	20	45	26	29	55	34			6	1	10	2	4	15	2 000	2	100	4	2 659	20 000
Wichita		1	17	2	19	16	31	47	11					....	....	1	9	715		....	2	735	6 500
ST. PAUL	2		165	31	196	129	67	196	40		1	68		....	1	8	70	12 500	3	225	10	13 675	210 000
Duluth		1	25	8	33	26	18	44	41			7		....	....	1	10	1 171	1	....	2	1 200	23 000
Jamestown		1	35	5	40	35	46	81	90					....	....	3	8	260		....	5	750	21 000
St. Cloud		1	37	27	64	50	34	84	38	1	1	15	1	19	1	3	46	5 100	1	86	6	5 640	40 000
Sioux Falls			48	14	62	46	79	125	110			5		....	3	4	14	1 500	2	50	7	10 000	30 000
Winona		1	50	5	55	49	47	96	18					....	....	4	17	3 005	2	20	4	3 367	38 000
SAN FRANCISCO	1		117	95	212	74	38	112	43			35	2	....	8	19	60	15 000	4	1 400	16	22 360	220 000
Monterey-Los Angeles		2	48	24	72	43	31	74	37			1	1	....	1	9	12	1 566	8	1 000	14	3 475	80 000
Sacramento		1	37	3	40	33	47	80	64			4		....	1	8			2	270	2	1 510	25 000
Salt Lake		1	9	7	16	9	8	14	23			....		....	1	2	7	555	1	36	3	891	8 000
SANTA FÉ	2		45	10	55	36	238	274	97			6		....	2	6	7	1 045	1	65	11	2 542	128 000
Denver		1	39	36	75	41	83	124	154			3			1	8	71	3 417	2	216	17	4 484	52 215
Arizona		1	17		17	14	31	45	118							6	5	1 000	1	21	5	1 100	38 000
TOTAL	17	73	7 546	2 507	10 053	5 659	3650	9309	5 194	9	28	2 120	77	1 474	182	609	3 731	775 070	230	30 867	821	918 207	9 077 8[illegible]5

CHAPTER XXIX.

CONCLUDING REMARKS.

Religious Orders.—Literature.—Losses.—Councils.

"THERE is no phase of human misery and affliction," writes Cardinal Gibbons, "for which the Catholic Church does not provide some antidote, some alleviation. She has foundling asylums to receive and shelter helpless infants that are either abandoned by unnatural mothers or bereft of their parents before they knew a mother's love. As the church provides for those yet on the threshold of life, so too does she secure retreats for those on the threshold of death." Between the cradle and the grave there is not a suffering, a privation, a degradation, there is not a shattered body or heart or reputation, for which she has not provided a home wherein the remedies and consolations of earth are combined with those of heaven to relieve the pains and repair the breakings of fallen humanity. This noble work, the most patent proof of genuine Christianity, is done by our religious orders.

The bare statistics (name, date of introduction, number of members, institutions carried on) of our religious orders of men and women fill forty-three closely printed pages in small type of Hoffman's Directory for the year 1895. Evidently space does not allow me to give even the slightest notion of their origin, introduction into this country, and their expansion. Many monographs on the subject have been written, some of which are named in the Bibliography that precedes this volume. A complete history of our religious orders would demand a special volume and would be of the highest value, for their history is the history of Catholic education and charities. Our parochial schools, colleges, academies, and charitable institutions are in their hands. The General Summary on pages 486, 487 will give the reader some notion of the great work they are doing, and of the large part they occupy in the Catholic life of the land.

Catholic literature past and present is another large field which I must pass over with the mere mention. I add the remark that the pioneer work of founding and building being now past, with our colleges, and especially our university in Washington, raising the standard and improving the methods of study, there is every hope that in the future our clergymen and educated laymen shall find more leisure and more profit in literary and scientific work than their predecessors and fathers found in the first century of our history, when the Catholics, like the rest of the community, were absorbed in the building up and the securing of the infant nation.

There has been much wild writing about the losses of the church in this country. Bishop England, whiling away his time on board ship at guessing the Catholic losses in his day, without statistics or references at hand, set down the losses in his diocese, comprising the two Carolinas and Georgia, at thirty-eight thousand. We have no statistics of that time to set against him, but history will not bear him out, for the reason that previously to his time but few Catholics settled south of the Potomac, and for the additional reason that the number of Catholics in the South Atlantic States was not the cause of the erection of the diocese of Charleston any more than it was of the dioceses of Mobile or Natchez or Little Rock or Savannah. But Bishop England was led by a further error into generalizing from his own district to the country at large. "We ought," he writes, "if there had been no loss, to have five millions of Catholics; and as we have less than one million and a quarter, there must have been a loss of three millions and a quarter within the last fifty years (1786–1836)." He assumed that in fifty years there had come into the United States eight millions of immigrants. This assumption, which is the basis of his calculation and argument, is absolutely without foundation. According to Bromwell's "History of Immigration to the United States," compiled from the best data, the total immigration into the United States from 1789 to 1835 was 514,159. Bishop England's opinion as to our losses in his time may be set aside.

A Rev. Mr. Mullen, delegate to this country from the Catholic University of Ireland in 1852, made the charge that there were two millions of apostates, mainly Irish, from the Catholic Church in 1850. To show how rash is the assertion, suffice it to say that according to the census of 1850 the foreign-born population—all nationalities—in the United States was 2,244,602.

The famous Lucerne Memorial of 1891—the same that drew from Senator Davis his no less famous anti-Cahensly speech in the senate's winter session of 1892—a memorial addressed to the holy see by Mr. Cahensly and others, states: "Calculations based on the most trustworthy statistics establish that Catholic immigrants and their descendants in the United States should number twenty-six millions; the actual number of Catholics there is hardly ten millions; therefore there has been a loss of sixteen millions."

An anonymous pamphlet, "The Question of Nationality," published in 1889, states: "In the same proportion [we pass over the computation to get at the conclusion] we would have at present about twenty million Irish-born [he means Irish and their descendants] and sixteen million German-born. Now there ought to be about eighteen million Irish Catholics and about five million German Catholics; Americans, Poles, Italians, etc., would make two millions more; total, twenty-five millions of Catholics. But according to Hoffman's Directory for the year 1889 the Catholic population was 8,157,676. Therefore there has been a loss to the church of two thirds of the Catholic body." The author of "The Question of Nationality" is an echo of the Lucerne Memorial; he deserves special honor and we owe him a special gratitude for giving us the "most trustworthy statistics" on which the memorial based its assertion of a loss of sixteen millions. How trustworthy they are—the statistics and the inferences—suffice it to say that the total foreign-born population of all nationalities and creeds according to the census of 1880 was 6,679,943.

Finally, Mr. John O'Kane Murray, in Appendix G to his "Popular History of the Catholic Church," makes out that in 1870 the total Celtic element in the population of the United States was twenty-four millions, and adds that "almost the entire Celtic element might be safely regarded as the descendants of men who were Catholics on settling in America." If that is so, and if to this Celtic element is added the Catholic contingent of the Germanic and Slavonic elements, we should have an immense Catholic population, and our losses are truly appalling.

Now the question may be solved, as far as it can be solved, partly by history and partly by statistics.

What does history say in the matter? History tells us that the loss of European Catholics—for I leave aside the Indians, having touched on their losses elsewhere—during the mission period was inconsiderable, for the reason, mainly, that there were not many to lose. The Catholics of New Mexico have been retained, and the same may be said of the smaller bodies in Texas and Florida. A few may have been lost to us in Louisiana, and for the loss there is an explanation. Louisiana was settled at a time of religious decadence in France, and by a class of French in whom the faith was not deep and firm. Moreover, the suppression of the Society of Jesus and the consequent breaking up of their mission work, the changes of government from French to Spanish, from Spanish to French, from French to American, and, above all, the long schism created by the rebellious trustees of New Orleans, were events not at all favorable to the preservation of Catholicity. And yet it may be said that the majority of Louisianian Catholics persevered, and that their descendants to-day are not the least numerous, respectable, and wealthy portion of the present Catholic population in the dioceses of Mobile and New Orleans.

We have retained the majority of the Catholics in the Illinois and Ottawa missions. Cahokia, Kaskaskia, Chicago, Prairie du Chien, Davenport, Dubuque, St. Paul, Milwaukee, Green Bay, Mackinaw, Detroit, Sandusky, Vincennes, Terre Haute, and many other places have their origins in this Canadian Catholicity of the mission period. After the cession of Canada to England there may have been some losses, for the reason, mainly, that for many years the Canadians of the West were without a sufficient number of priests; but the losses were as nothing compared with what remained. At any rate, the Canadian population of the West was inconsiderable at the time.

There remain, then, to be considered the English missions on the Atlantic coast. There are no statistics to show the exact number of Catholics who settled in Maryland. It cannot have been very great, since in a few years after the settlement the Puritans from Virginia, and some years later the Anglicans, became the majority. The statistics we have given in the history of the colonial Catholicity of Maryland show no large defections from the church, though no doubt the penal legislation of the pre-Revolutionary times and the apostasy of the House of Baltimore must have had some influence. However, we dare to say that the influence was slight and our losses inconsiderable. The Episcopalians were watchful and jealous; if they could have boasted of gaining over Catholics we should find some traces of the boasting; but it is quite the contrary: the records show constant complaints from them of the growth of the church, necessitating legislation more and more penal. Outside of Maryland in colonial times there were no Catholics to speak of, and there could not be, for the legislation of the colonies, with the exception of Pennsylvania, amounted to a strict embargo against them. A few in New York, a little more in Pennsylvania—that is all; and there is no foundation for the statement that the majority of them fell away. As to the South, neither in colonial times nor in the first quarter of this century could such a number of Catholics have settled there as to justify Bishop England in putting down the loss in his diocese at thirty-eight thousand. History furnishes no basis for the statement.

So much for the mission period. History must again be our guide for the first quarter of the century; after that we may trust ourselves to statistics. It is a fact of history that there was almost no immigration from Europe, and much less Catholic immigration, from 1800 to 1820. During that period, then, having made no great gains, we could have no great losses. In fact, I make bold to say that we had none whatever, but held our own and more.

In 1820 Archbishop Maréchal calculated the Catholic population of the United States, exclusive of Louisiana and the diocese of Cincinnati, to be 169,500; add to this the Catholics of Louisiana and the West, and we get for the year 1820, 244,500.* Remember that in 1790, the date of Carroll's consecration, there were, according to him, about 30,000 in his diocese.

After the year 1820 we have the official statistics of immigration to serve as a basis for our calculations of the Catholic population. A history of immigration would be one of the most interesting of books. We may say that a double immigration has been and is going on in this country—an internal and an external. Mr. John Bach McMasters, in his masterly "History of the People of the United States," has some highly attractive pages on both.

A few words here about immigration from Europe. The distress that followed on the ending of the Napoleonic wars in Europe sent thousands from England and Germany to the United States, to such an extent that the British press began to take alarm and demand parliamentary action to stop "the ruinous drain of the most useful part of the population of the United Kingdom." Six thousand emigrants were said to have left Ireland before the middle of 1816. A New York newspaper, the "Shamrock," contained a list of four hundred Irishmen who landed at New York from five ships between the 10th and the 17th of August. This is only one instance. Many of those emigrants were poor and totally unconscious of their future bearings. The Society of United Irishmen of Philadelphia and the Shamrock Friendly Association of New York took them in hand, procuring them work or forwarding them inland. Other societies for the same purpose sprang into existence, such as the Hibernian Society of Baltimore, the Irish Emigration Association of New York, and like societies in Philadelphia and Pittsburg. Even Congress was petitioned by these associations to give aid to and encourage emigration by a scheme—which was not enacted, however—of cheap lands and long credit.

Until the year 1842 the total number of immigrants in any one year never reached 100,000; in 1844 it fell to 78,000, in 1845 it exceeded 114,000, in 1846 it was 154,000, and in 1847 234,968. The famine in Ireland sent hundreds of thousands of that unhappy people to our shores, and in the emigration thus caused we have the source of the Catholic development and the occasion of the anti-Catholic propaganda that mark this period. In 1849 the number of immigrants had risen to 297,024; nor did the huge stream cease to flow until checked by the Civil War; and in this immigration are to be found the reasons for the issue of that conflict—the triumph and preservation of the Union. The newcomers swelled the national, not the sectional, forces of our country. They avoided the South; they crowded into the North and the Northwest, creating the population and the resources which were the decisive elements in the struggle between the free and the slave States. Immigration was the salvation of the Union; Know-nothingism, if successful, might have been its ruin, for without the emigrant and his progeny in the North the South might have triumphed.

The best Catholic authority on our church's history that we have ever had, the late Gilmary Shea, working from the official statistics of immigration since 1820, calculating as best he could the percentage of Catholic immigrants,[1] and

[1] The following study, taken from a late number of the New York "Tribune," will be of some help to any one who should seek to get at the Catholic contingent in the total immigration from Europe:

"About a third of the entire population of the United States is of foreign parentage. Thus baldly stated, the fact may strike some persons as danger-

allowing for each decade a natural increase of one third over the total figures with which the decade starts, makes out the following table:

Catholic Population.

In	1820 (according to Archbishop Maréchal's calculation)	244.500
"	1830	361.000
"	1840	1,000.000
"	1850	1.726.470
"	1860	3.000,000
"	1870	4,685.000
"	1880	7,067,000
"	1890	10.627,000

The percentage of Catholic immigration and the ratio of natural increase adopted by Gilmary Shea would make the figures in 1895 12,500,000.

Such, then, according to Gilmary Shea, should be our present Catholic population. The question arises, Have we in reality twelve millions of members to-day in the Catholic Church? Again, the question may be put to us in another form: Have you no official statistics of an un-

ous. But the proportion has increased very little within the last twenty years. It was 28.25 percent. in 1870, and although the actual immigration during these twenty years has numbered 8,058,708, the proportion has only advanced to 33.02 percent. Moreover, this includes not only the immigrants themselves, whether young or old, but all their children born in this country, and these alone number over 11,500,000; so that the persons of foreign birth number only 14.4 percent. of the entire population, or about one seventh. It is rather noteworthy that the whole number of foreign-born persons living in this country is only a million greater than the number which arrived within the twenty years preceding the census of 1890. Of the foreign-born inhabitants, too, a considerable percentage must be of children born abroad, who came hither with the enormous immigration of the last decade.

"Nevertheless, the fairest test of the proportion of foreign blood is the percentage of persons of foreign parentage to the total population, which has increased 4.75 in the two decades of largest immigration. But the figures become somewhat less impressive when it is considered how this addition from abroad is divided. The persons of foreign parentage who are of English speech, and have either come hither from portions of Great Britain or are the children of persons from Great Britain, constitute nearly a seventh of the whole population—13.63 per cent., including the English Canadian contingent.

doubted authority to go by? We are forced to answer, No. We have, it is true, two Catholic directories, equally authorized by our bishops, Sadlier's of New York and Hoffman's of Milwaukee. But, leaving aside the consideration that they do not agree, Sadlier's giving a population of 10,964,000, Hoffman's giving a population of 9,077,865; leaving aside this other consideration, that for many years the same dioceses have been returning the same numbers without diminution or increase—a very unlikely result—the directories have not and cannot have the character of an exact census, because their statistics are based not on an actual count of members, but on a computation made by the diocesan chancellors from the recorded baptisms for each year as returned from each parish.

Now such a computation is worth but little if the returns of baptisms from the parishes are not correct, and if the figure used as a multiplier is not correct and uniform in all the chanceries. Neither of these conditions is ascertained and realized. The directories' statistics, therefore, are but conjecture, mere guesswork more or less approxi-

The Irish and their children are 7.85 percent. of the entire population; from England proper came 3.07 percent., from Scotland .96 percent., and from Wales .35 percent., while 1.5 percent. came from Canada. Thus 41.6 out of every 100 persons of foreign birth or parentage are from Great Britain, and in kinship of blood and in speech are of the same great family by which the land was first occupied and then made independent. But there is also a fraction of mixed foreign parentage, not credited to either foreign country, which constitutes 1.47 percent. of the whole population, and a fair share of this must also be British on one side or the other. Thus something more than 14 percent. of the population must be credited to parentage or immigration from Great Britain, against less than 19 percent. from all other parts of the world.

"Next in importance, the German blood closely approaches one ninth of the population, the percentage being 10.94, about a third of the whole foreign contingent. The fact will not be overlooked that in a broad sense the English and German races are nearly allied, as in this country they have been ever since the Revolution. The Teutonic and the Anglo-Saxon, including the Irish, thus form 24.57 percent. of the entire population—almost a quarter—leaving 8.2 percent. for all other white immigrants and their children. Just here the relative insignificance of certain strains of immigration which

mative. The same must be said of the religious census of 1890. The church statistics of that census were not gathered by the census-takers directly from the individual inhabitants of the land, but from the diocesan chanceries. Coming, therefore, from the same sources as the statistics of the directories, the census church statistics rest on the same basis and possess the same trustworthiness. No living man knows exactly, or with any scientific nearness to the truth, what is the Catholic population of the land. Whether it could not be got at if only the bishops should adopt and impose a uniform method of census-taking is a question we do not stop to consider. The fact is as I have stated; and the fact being such, any student of our history and of our general present conditions has a right to give his guess at our population. I venture to say that we have to-day twelve millions of Catholics.

We have no doubt had some losses; not, however, so extensive as claimed by the writers named in the preceding pages. The losses are owing mainly to the following

have been largely discussed of late comes into view. In a few great centers are found crowds of Italians, Hungarians, Russians, Bohemians, or Chinese; but men are apt to forget that all of these together make up only an insignificant part of the population even when their children are included.

"Next in importance to the German is what may be termed the Scandinavian contingent, including from Sweden 1.16 percent. of the total population, from Norway .95 percent., and from Denmark .34 percent.; in all 2.45 percent. of the whole. It will surprise many to find that this element is relatively as large as that drawn from all other parts of Europe, except Germany and Great Britain. The French contingent may, indeed, be swelled by the addition of all the French Canadians and their children, but even then only reaches 1.23 percent. of the population. The Russian contingent, .41 percent., the Bohemian, .34 percent., and the Hungarian, .12 percent., cover what may be called the Slavonic element; in all only .87 percent., or less than one in a hundred of the population. The Italian, .4 percent., if reckoned with the French and the French Canadians, gives a total of only 1.63 for the Latin races. Of all other nations there are 1.78 percent. of the total population, part being from Latin and a small part from Asiatic races; but in the aggregate these elements are insignificant compared with the 67 percent. of native Americans by birth and parentage, and the 24.5 percent. of immigrants from Great Britain or Germany with their children."

causes: the persecution of the penal period; the settlement of Catholics, even before the organization of the hierarchy, in remote places where there were no means of Catholic life and training, such as Virginia, the Carolinas, and New England; the want of church organization prior to the winning of our independence; the scandals and schisms of trusteeism; the inadequate supply of priests and churches for the demands of an overwhelming immigration; the large number of orphans cast adrift and fallen into non-Catholic hands upon the death of the father or of both parents amid the hardships of a new climate, of canal-building and other public works, and amid the calamities of war; intemperance; the want of Catholic education; the social persecution of contempt for illiterate Catholics and their creed, under which weak ones apostatized or allowed their children to grow up without any or with a non-Catholic religion. Here are causes enough, and more than enough, to account for a tremendous leakage.

Happily, within the last thirty years the leaks have been repaired, and the hope is warranted that future losses will be small, especially since the church has assumed a broad attitude on the great question that concerns the masses, the relation of capital to labor. Indeed, the tide has set the other way and the church is gaining. To quote but two instances: Archbishop Spalding confirmed in five years 22,209 persons; twelve and a half percent. of them were converts. Hardly a bishop in the country to-day but could tell the same story. Hoffman's Directory for 1895 gives for some dioceses the baptisms of adults. I say some dioceses, because the statistics of each diocese are compiled at the pleasure of the bishop and his officials, there being no regulation compelling a uniformity of items or of tabular statement. Now the adult baptisms are baptisms of converts. They are reported at four thousand in twenty of the least populous and most unimportant dioceses of the country. In fact, it is only such dioceses that seem willing to give information on the score of baptisms, and yet it is from the basis of the baptisms that the Catholic population is computed.

Yes, we have had our losses. But what church in the United States has not had losses? Does the Episcopalian, does the Lutheran, hold all those who by birth or ancestry should be within these two denominations, to name no others? Many a Catholic has come to us with no faith left, with nothing but the name of a Catholic and, of course, the baptism received in infancy; and after touching our shores has ceased to consort with the church of his native country and his fathers. He went out from us not into any Protestant denomination, but into the vast crowd of no-churchmen, the largest body in the land. And as with us, so has it happened with other churches, especially the two above named. The losses do not prove that we, any more than they, are incompatible with the republican form and spirit of this government. They prove merely that man is free, may use or abuse his freedom in religion as in other matters; they prove, too, that if a man wishes to preserve his faith for himself and his children he must choose such environments of places and persons as shall be to him aids instead of hindrances.

Councils are ecumenical, plenary or national, and provincial. An assembly of all the Catholic bishops of the world, convoked by the authority of the Pope, or at least with his consent, and presided over by him or his legates, is an ecumenical council. An assembly of all the bishops of a country—say the United States—convoked by the primate or other dignitary commissioned thereto by the Pope, is a national or plenary council. An assembly of all the bishops within the territory known as a province, convoked and presided over by the metropolitan or archbishop, is a provincial council. An assembly of all the priests of a diocese, convoked and presided over by the bishop, is a diocesan synod. The acts of an ecumenical council, to be binding, must be confirmed or approved by the Pope. The acts of plenary and provincial councils must be submitted to the holy see before being promulgated; not that they must be confirmed by the holy see, for they are rarely confirmed in a formal manner, but that whatever may be too strict or inaccurate may be corrected. The acts of diocesan synods need not be submitted to revision by the holy see.

Ecumenical councils define doctrine and deal with matters of discipline concerning the church in the whole world. Plenary and provincial councils do not define, but at most only repeat the doctrine defined by the ecumenical councils; their chief purpose is to apply by explicit statutes to each country or province the universal discipline determined by the ecumenical councils and the holy see, or to initiate such discipline as the peculiar circumstances of the nation or province demand. Diocesan synods promulgate and apply more intimately to each diocese the disciplinary enactments of the holy see, the ecumenical, plenary, and provincial councils, emphasizing those enactments which the specific conditions or abuses in each diocese render most necessary.

Numerous diocesan synods have been held in the United States, and not a few provincial councils, at least in the older provinces; and three plenary councils have been held within the first century of the organized hierarchy. The collection of the acts of those various assemblies is an important source of our church history. Since provincial councils are, generally speaking, promulgations, and therefore repetitions, with such modifications as special circumstances of the province require, of the enactments of plenary councils, and since the same may be said of diocesan synods with respect to provincial councils, it follows that a fair idea of American canon law may be gained from the exclusive study of the three plenary councils. It is to be remarked, however, that the First Plenary Council has its genesis in the provincial councils of Baltimore that preceded it, and these, again, have their genesis in the First Diocesan Synod of Baltimore, held at the time when there was in the country but that one diocese. Hence the First Synod, the First, Second, Third, Fourth, Fifth, Sixth, and Seventh Provincial Councils, and the First, Second, and Third Plenary Councils of Baltimore form the absolutely necessary and the comparatively sufficient body of documents for a complete study of the ecclesiastical legislation under which live the Catholics of the United States.

The procedure and working of the American councils are not unlike those of an ordinary legislative body. Let me briefly describe the method of a plenary council. A petition is laid by the hierarchy before the holy see, or an order comes to it from Rome, for the holding of an assembly of all the bishops of the country. Papal letters appoint and commission a president with the title and powers of an apostolic delegate; he may be one sent by the Pope from abroad; so far he has been the Archbishop of Baltimore. The president delegate apostolic of the First Plenary Council was Archbishop Kenrick, of the Second Archbishop Spalding, of the Third Archbishop (only after the council Cardinal) Gibbons. Generally instructions on certain points which the holy see wants particularly to be considered and legislated on by the assembly are sent to the appointed president; or, as was the case just before the Third Plenary Council, the archbishops and other representative men are called to Rome to discuss such points with the Roman authorities.

Thus commissioned and instructed, the president issues to all who are duly entitled to sit as members of the assembly letters of convocation commanding their presence at a fixed date. Meanwhile the best theologians and canonists of the country are at work, by order and under the presidency of the delegate, outlining and drafting in preliminary form the bills, so to speak, that are to be submitted to the consideration and discussion of the bishops. These are called *schemata*, and are afterward delivered, printed, to each member in the first public session of the council. This first solemn session is usually taken up with a procession into the cathedral, pontifical high mass, the naming of the officials, the taking of the required oaths, and a sermon. Sermons are delivered throughout the holding of the council on Sundays and certain other festival days by prominent members, and, of course, may be attended by the public. The officials of a council, corresponding to the sergeants, clerks, and other minor officers of our legislative bodies, are promoter, judges of excuses and complaints, notary, secretary, chancellor, master of ceremonies, and chanter.

Before proceeding to the real business of the council, standing rules are adopted, as to the hours of meeting, the order of debate, etc., and various committees are appointed, between whom are divided the questions to be legislated on, that is to say, the already drafted bills. We may say that the council sits (1) in private committees, (2) in committee of the whole, and (3) in public conciliar sessions, when the enactments decided on by the committee of the whole and the private committees are finally and solemnly passed on. When the whole work is done and the council has closed, the minutes of the debates, called the *acta*, and the bills passed, called the *decreta*, are sent to Rome. There they are minutely considered by commissions of cardinals and theologians, who may make amendments, usually very slight and in the wording rather than in the matter. Their report is submitted to the Pope; his approval is not, however, meant to be such an act as entails papal infallibility. The decrees, after having been thus scrutinized and confirmed by the holy see, are sent back to the president of the council, are by him promulgated and communicated to all the bishops, and thenceforth become law. Provincial councils and diocesan synods make further promulgation and application of these decrees to each province and diocese; and thus priests and laymen come to the knowledge of the legislation that rules their church life.

The legislation of our councils has been universally praised, and is held up by Rome as a model to the churches of Australia and South America, which, like our own, are seeking to adapt the unchanging doctrine and the essential discipline of Christianity to the needs and aspirations of modern times, to the new environments of virgin lands and young nations. This legislation—I am speaking only of the first seven provincial and the three plenary councils of Baltimore, for the many other provincial councils and diocesan synods would make a vaster bulk—fills three octavo volumes containing twelve hundred and sixty pages, an extensive code for our first century. I cannot be expected to enter into details. One remark only. A comparison of the enactments of the Third Plenary Council with the earliest laws laid down in the provincial council that preceded it reveals that the former are a gradual development of the latter along the same lines. There has been no withdrawal from original positions, except in a very few instances and when altered circumstances in the country and the church's relations to the country demanded a revision. All the important matters so thoroughly legislated on in our last council will be found pointedly or impliedly mentioned in the first a hundred years ago.

It is a most interesting study to take up and follow, council by council, such questions as the canonical status of priests, their relations to bishops, the evolution of the metropolitan and his rights, the tenure of church property, relations between the hierarchy and the religious orders of men and women, education, seminaries, the university. Temperance, for instance, was brought under conciliar legislation, and total abstinence societies were recommended for the first time, in the Fourth Provincial Council of 1840; the whole country knows what minute and stringent legislation has been passed on this point by the Third Plenary Council, and how strictly that legislation was interpreted but the other day by the apostolic delegate, the Most Rev. Mgr. Satolli, in the famous Columbus case. Parochial schools were made matter of legislation for the first time in the First Provincial Council of 1829; since then they have been a standing subject in every council; and in these latter years further development and interpretation have been given to former legislation by the well-known decisions of the holy see in the late school controversy, and by the apostolic delegate, whose practical rulings in specific cases relating to Catholic education have been even more explicit and emphatic, if that were possible, than his famous Fourteen Propositions. In a word, if there has been, during the first century of our existence, growth in membership, clergy, and hierarchy, and if that growth has been marvelous, so also there has been no less marvelous growth in disciplinary legislation, which is to outward extension what the soul is to the body.

The preceding pages have described mostly the bodily growth of the church. Now the study of man's body and its manifestations in speech and features is the ordinary index to a knowledge of the soul, its thoughts and habits. But he will know a man best who can pierce through the outward vesture and, like the psychologist, seize in the grip of mental abstraction the spiritual principle of life. A thorough and scientific and psychological knowledge of the church in the United States would demand more than I have given—more than the consideration of its hierarchical extension; would require a minute study of its legislation and interior discipline, to which should be added an examination of those defined doctrines which are received by us here in the United States, no less than by Catholics the world over. The result of such a study, I feel confident, would be to prove that the Catholic Church is in accord with Christ's revelation, with American liberty, and is the strongest moral power for the preservation of the republic from the new social dangers that threaten the United States as well as the whole civilized world. She has not grown, she cannot grow, so weak and old that she may not maintain what she has produced—Christian civilization.

INDEX.

www.ingramcontent.com/pod-product-compliance
Lightning Source LLC
Chambersburg PA
CBHW031946290426
44108CB00011B/701
* 9 7 8 3 7 4 3 3 2 9 7 9 9 *